LOS CONQUISTADORES

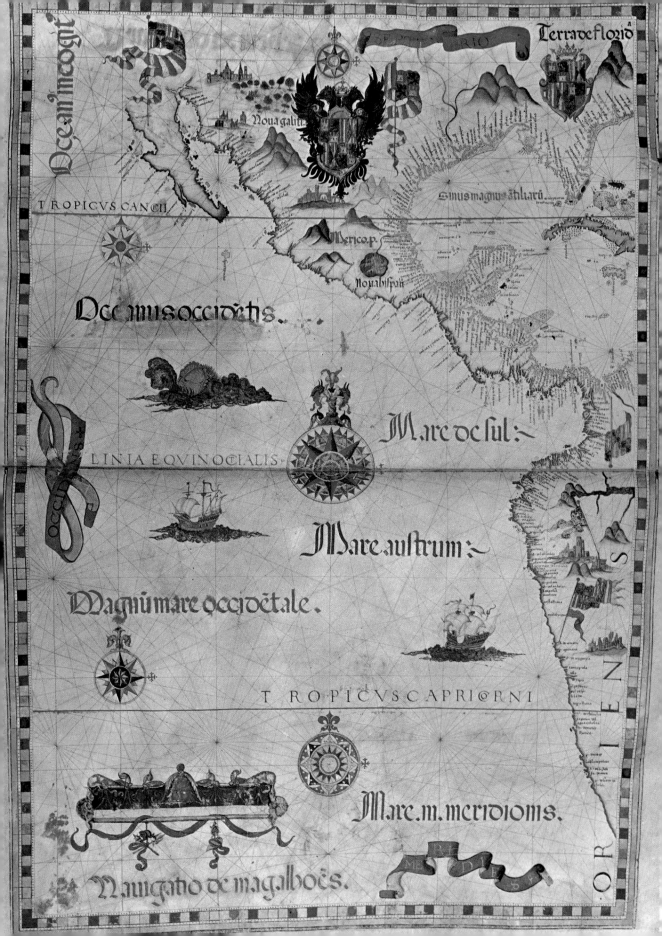

The Conquistadors

Hammond Innes

BOOK CLUB ASSOCIATES
LONDON

This edition published 1972 by
Book Club Associates
By arrangement with Wm. Collins Sons & Co. Ltd

© Hammond Innes 1969

First published in the United Kingdom in 1969 by
William Collins, Sons & Company Ltd,
14 St James's Place, London s.w.1. *and*
144 Cathedral Street, Glasgow c.4.

This book was designed and produced by
George Rainbird Ltd,
Marble Arch House, 44 Edgware Road, London w.2.
House Editor: George Speaight
Designer: Anne Petrie
Index: Wing Commander Roger F. Pemberton.
Maps: T. Stalker Miller MSIA.

Text set in Monophoto Apollo by
Jolly & Barber Ltd, Rugby, England.
Colour plates originated by Schwitter Ltd, Zurich, Switzerland,
and printed by The Westerham Press Ltd, Kent, England.
Text printed and bound by Jarrold & Sons Ltd, Norwich, England.

Dedicated to
Billy and Pierre

CONTENTS

COLOUR PLATES

FOREWORD

THE PERIOD of the great Discoverers has always appealed to me, but for a novelist to be asked to write a history is a great challenge. It was one I hesitated to accept. Three things finally decided me: First, I am essentially a story-teller, and the stories of Cortés in Mexico and Pizarro in Peru are among the greatest and most terrible in history; secondly, all my novels have grown out of the realities of the countries in which I have set them, so that respect for the truth is a built-in habit of work; finally, the physical characteristics of a country have always seemed to me the key to the nature of its people and their history.

Three years' study of contemporary records, and the much more voluminous later accounts, left me far from satisfied. So many were politically biased and posed questions that could only be resolved when I stood where Cortés and Pizarro had stood. As a result of the journeys I then undertook, I came to realise how terrain had dominated, even compelled, events. Not only terrain, but the sea as well – and here, with a sailor's eye, I hope I have been able to add something to the reader's understanding of what it is like to be the first to probe the shores of unknown lands.

My thanks are due to Dr John Street, Director of the Centre of Latin-America Studies in Cambridge University, for reading and advising on the main body of the work, and to Dr G. H. S. Bushnell, Reader in New World Archaeology at the same University, for advising on the chapters dealing with the Aztec and Inca civilizations. Also to all those who, in their official capacity, or unofficially, assisted me in my travels and researches in Spain, Mexico and Peru – in particular to Sir Robert Marett for his information about Zempoala, to Captain B. Hokansen for making me free of his chartroom and his thirty years' experience of the South American coast on the run down from Panama to Callao, to Dr J. J. Wilson of the Carta Geologica Nacional for his very detailed information about the topography of the Andes above Cajamarca, and to Señora Elejalde for introducing me to all the private collections in Lima.

I would also like to thank my friend John Hadfield for initiating the project, and George Speaight, who not only edited the book, but has contributed so much to it in maps and pictures, many of these previously unpublished. Finally my thanks are due, as always, to my wife Dorothy for her assistance with the text, and also for her work in listing items of outstanding interest in museums and private collections, and to my secretary, Nora Anderson for her untiring efforts in keeping pace with all the various drafts.

H.I.

PART ONE

Ferdinand & Isabella

Ferdinand and Isabella enter Granada in triumph after its capture from the Moors.
A sixteenth-century bas relief.

1 *The Eight-Hundred-Year Crusade*

THE CONQUISTADORS, like most human phenomena, were the product of history. They were Spaniards and they explored and conquered new worlds for the glory of God and their own profit in the early 1500s. Behind them they had centuries of constant fighting to clear their Iberian Peninsula of the Moorish invaders. They were men trained in war, crusaders in their own land who had pushed the infidel back step by step, breeding kingdoms and principalities as they advanced. The result was that their nobility were little better than armed and castled warlords. And then, in 1492, it was all over, the last Moorish stronghold taken. At the beginning of the sixteenth century Spain had newly emerged as a nation. The eight-hundred-year crusade was at an end, and her chivalry, born to the saddle and the sword, and burning with a wild religious fervour, was suddenly unemployed. The Italian wars provided an immediate outlet, but Spain's geographical position pointed inexorably west, to the new world Columbus had recently discovered.

The men who had fought their last battle against the Moors turned soldiers of fortune and followed the sailors across the sea to seek out new infidels and blaze a trail of murder and heroism that is unique in the history of European peoples. Their lust for gold was infinite, their religious fervour genuine. This strange mixture of motive, their fantastic fortitude in the face of the most frightening terrain and the most appalling odds, their ability to carve their way by guile and force through armies two hundred times their number, requires explanation. Otherwise all that is contained in this account of the conquistadors is incredible.

As always in history, geographical position and the nature of the country played a dominant role. The Iberian Peninsula is the *ultima thule* of Western Europe, its coast line part Mediterranean, part Atlantic, its southern apex facing Africa ten miles across the Gibraltar straits. It was from across these straits that the first known invaders came 4,500 years ago. Others were to follow. Placed as Spain is on the periphery of Mediterranean cultural growth, its rivers and rich valleys separated by wild mountains, the successive influences of Phoenician and Greek traders were confined to the southern and eastern coasts. So, too, was the

Carthaginian influence, which began about 540 B.C. and lasted for three centuries. More important at this time was the advance of the Celts across the Pyrenees, intermingling with the peoples of the central plateau to form the Celtiberi. Carthage never had a strong hold on the country, so that the Romans, by a policy of conciliation, gradually replaced them. At first, this infiltration followed upon the need to protect their Italian homeland from the incursions of the two great Carthaginian generals, Hamilcar and Hannibal. But by 197 B.C. the Romans were so firmly established in the Peninsula that the areas previously occupied by the Carthaginians were designated the Roman provinces of Hispania Ulterior and Hispania Citerior. Conciliation was now replaced by a more positive policy, and in the two centuries B.C. the Roman legions steadily conquered the whole Peninsula. The Celtiberi, centred around the head-waters of Duero and Tagus, had never been conquered by the Carthaginians. Like all Celts, they were a brave independent people. They held Rome at bay for half a century, were defeated by Scipio in 133 B.C. and thereafter contributed greatly to Rome's auxiliaries.

For nearly five centuries the country had peace. The influence of Rome on the development of Spanish culture was thus very great. The people became Christian, lived under Roman law, and, because of the nature of the land and the Roman method of garrisoning, the towns increased in importance at the expense of tribal organization. But at the beginning of the fifth century A.D. Spain, or Hispania as it was then called, suffered with the rest of Europe the effects of the power vacuum created by the decline of Rome. The Vandals, Alans and Sueves poured in from Europe, to be followed fifty years later by the Visigoths. The conquered Romano-Hispanic people remained Catholics, continued to live under their Roman laws, whilst the conquerors, who were Christians of the Arian sect and whose social structure was based on Germanic customs, were a Teutonic élite under their own elected kings. By the beginning of the seventh century, however, with the conversion of their king to Catholicism, and many of the clergy also conforming, the segregation of the two races ceased to be effective. Latin became the official language, Catholic bishops assumed a dominant role in politics, and about 654 a unified legal system was established. Part Roman, but basically Germanic, the *Forum Judicum* was a powerful influence that outlasted the Visigoth kingdom by many centuries to provide the basis for the local codes or *fueros* of the Spanish medieval towns. Moreover, the unification of law and religion had the effect of breaking down the barriers between conqueror and conquered. Inter-marriage, banned by Roman, not Visigothic, custom, now produced a mingling of the races, so that the Iberian Peninsula became a single unit under a king who remained elected and not hereditary. Short though this domination was, the Visigoths exercised an extraordinary influence on Spanish race and customs, an influence that was to make medieval Spain entirely different from the rest of medieval Europe.

The third great moulder of Spanish character fell upon the country in 711 in the form of Islamic hordes from across the Gibraltar straits. In seven years the Moors – mainly North African Berbers, but including Arabs and Syrians – had conquered almost the entire Visigoth kingdom of Spain and had killed the king, Roderick. They then swept across the Pyrenees into the land of the Franks. Only the north and north-western Atlantic coastal areas remained, secured by their mountain bastions, to form a nucleus for the later Christian kingdoms.

The essential weaknesses of the Moslem state were that Spain was administered as a province, subject, rather nominally, first to faraway Damascus, later to North Africa, and that its provincial *emirs* and *caliphs* were absolute and hereditary rulers. The inevitable result was that, whenever the central rule weakened, the country disintegrated into smaller provincial units. Córdoba, Seville, Granada, Valencia, Toledo, Badajoz, Saragossa were all at one time or another separate states, the unit dictated by the geography of mountain, valley, river or coast. Nevertheless, in spite of the weaknesses of the system, the Moslems were in Spain for almost eight centuries.

The basis of Moorish domination was their Arab cavalry and their single-mindedness. They were conquerors carrying the word of the Prophet at the point of the scimitar, their fast Arab horses the motive power to drive the point home. At first there was no pressure on Christians to change their religion or their laws; there was even some degree of integration. And the Moslem invasion brought to Spain the culture and knowledge of the older civilizations of the Eastern Mediterranean. The development of irrigation opened up arid lands to agriculture. Education was encouraged; the townships became literate; music, poetry, arts and science, particularly mathematics, all flourished.

But the wars went on, the free Christians, from their mountain fastnesses, pushing into the plains, in search of the crumbs of better living, hating the infidel who had raped the best of their country's land, building up within themselves a religious fervour quite as strong as that which had carried the Moors to Spain. Other European countries might embark on strange crusades to wrest the Holy Land from the Saracens; the Spaniards, locked away from the rest of Europe by the formidable barrier of the Pyrenees, had their own crusade always on their doorstep. The Cross and St James was their battle-cry. No man with any claim to breeding regarded himself as other than a fighting machine. This was his job, his life, an integral part of his faith for eight centuries. It stamped him indelibly.

This crusade against the Moors was, however, an intermittent one. True to their history, the Spanish were cursed with internecine strife. Split by racial origin and terrain into petty states based on fortified towns, or on the castled strongholds of traditional nobility, they lacked the national unity and community of interest necessary to drive the invader into the sea. Indeed, they spent more time, energy and blood squabbling amongst themselves than in fighting the Moors, and it was only the lure of the lush valleys, so well developed by the conquerors, that brought them down from their bleak mountain fastnesses. Here in the plains, they were at the mercy of the speedy Arab cavalry, and when they were successful, it was often only to exchange bleak impregnability for futile vulnerability, their labour and their crops exposed to ruthless counter-attack. Not until they had pushed the invader back over the Duero river did they have a natural barrier along which they could erect some proper form of defence work, and this was only achieved after a century and a half of sporadic fighting. Six hundred years were to pass before they reached the Tagus.

Nevertheless, disunity amongst themselves was overlaid by the unity of faith. They might resent, in their pride, the growing power of the Pope, but they were ardent soldiers of Christ, their priests assuming greater and greater power in the affairs of state and also in martial matters, even leading them into battle. Minstrels immortalised the heroic deeds of their knights. Great bardic poems like the *Poema del Cid* exercised an extraordinary moral influence, so that chivalry was raised to a peak of romantic heroism.

By the middle of the fifteenth century, the long-drawn-out crusade had pushed the Moors back into the southern stronghold of Granada, and the petty states of Christian Spain had coalesced into the three kingdoms of Portugal, Castile and León, and Aragon, with the little kingdom of Navarre still land-locked and independent within the fastnesses of the Pyrenees. We are now at the threshold of an era in which Spain was to emerge as a nation, and which was to give her, almost reluctantly, the New World and a great colonial empire.

The pioneers of this golden age of discovery were the Portuguese. The capture of the Moorish city of Ceuta in 1415 started them on their long and expensive quest for a route to the spice islands of the Moluccas. From the Tagus ship after ship sailed out into the Atlantic, probing an ocean that was believed by many to pour its waters over the lip of the world in a roaring cascade.

Their close contact with the Moors gave the seafarers not only the means of navigation, but a new type of vessel, the caravel. The descendants of this vessel can be seen in the Tagus to this day, the broad-beamed, shallow-draft wine ships known as *fragatas*. The caravel, with its lateen sails derived from the Arab dhow, was the first ocean-going vessel capable of making to windward without the use of oars. This was the key to Portuguese discovery, and the man who used it was the son of King John I of Portugal and a daughter of England's John of Gaunt – Henry the Navigator.

This extraordinary prince, who became obsessed with the desire to explore beyond the confines of existing maps and charts, set up his court at Sagres on a remote headland in the extreme south-west corner of his kingdom. This headland is the one we now know as Cape St Vincent, a low-cliffed promontory running out into the sea, the one place on the whole of that rugged coast where you look south, as well as west, across the Atlantic. It was a position from which the imagination of every seaman could easily be stirred. Anyone who has sailed his own boat past that jutting point of land, running hard under full sail before the prevailing north wind of summer – the Portuguese trades – will understand how, in the days of predominantly square-rigged ships, the sailors' attention would inevitably be rivetted to discovery southward.

Here, in what amounted to a naval operations centre, Henry gathered together cartographers, astronomers, books and charts. Here he briefed his navigators, sending them down the coast of Africa in repeated attempts to probe beyond the reefs of Cape Bojador, from which point all previous voyagers had been swept into oblivion by the combination, deadly to square-riggers, of the north-east trades and the north equatorial drift. His attempts went unrewarded for fourteen years. In 1434, however, one of his most daring navigators, Gil Eannes, sailed seaward to the tip of this fifteen-mile barrier of reefs and then beat back in his caravel, against the wind, to the flat sand coast of the Sahara. Bojador, which had been the southern limit of the Atlantic for a thousand years, was finally conquered, and after that Henry's captains probed rapidly south along the African coast. Existing maps, which dated back to the Phoenician circumnavigation of Africa almost six hundred years before Christ, all showed the continent much fore-shortened. By 1458 the Portuguese had reached the Rio Grande, reporting the coast running away to the south-east, so that at the time of Henry's death, in 1460, it seemed as though they were on the verge of success. But a year later they probed the Bight of Biafra and found the coast of Africa continuing south. It was a bitter disappointment.

Thereafter Portuguese interest in African coastal exploration declined. But a country, so dedicated and so geared to mercantile expansion, does not suddenly cease all exploration because its hopes have been dashed. Having failed in one direction, they would undoubtedly have probed in another. They had the ships, the men and the experience. The question that has fascinated students of maritime history ever since is, where did their ships go after 1461? Whereas, before, they had been prepared to publish their knowledge, now, like the Phoenician traders, their policy became one of absolute secrecy. The death penalty was introduced for revealing information about their voyages, and as late as 1503 the Basque cartographer, Juan de la Cosa, who three years earlier had drawn his *mappemunde*, was only released from arrest after he had falsified two charts for dispatch to Spain.

Portugal, by concentrating her efforts on maritime expansion, became virtually dissociated from the mainstream of events on the Iberian Peninsula. This left the two other large kingdoms of Castile and Aragon free to develop into a separate national power. These two kingdoms were very dissimilar in character. Castile, with León, ran from the Biscay coast of the Basques, south across the mountains and west-flowing rivers of central Spain, through all the land that her soldiers had won from the Moors, to the fortified stronghold of Islamic Granada. The long history of war caused all towns to be fortresses, their citizens to be trained in arms. Those who had settled newly conquered land, frontiersmen who faced the full brunt of retaliation, had been granted extraordinary privileges. Thus town and

Spain in the sixteenth century.

country were inhabited by free men living under their own democratic laws, governed by their own elected officers; this at a time when almost all the rest of Europe was feudal, the mass of the people existing in a state of serfdom. Aragon, on the other hand, became a mercantile kingdom when the union with Catalonia, and later the conquest of Valencia, gave her control of all the east-facing Mediterranean ports. Where Castile was supported by the armies of her militia and her nobility, Aragon relied on her sailors and her ships. With them she conquered the Balearic Isles, Sardinia, even Sicily.

On October 19, 1469, Ferdinand, the eighteen-year-old king of Sicily and heir to the Aragon throne, married Isabella, nineteen-year-old sister of Castile's king Henry IV. The importance of this match was evident ten years later when, with the death of Ferdinand's father, Aragon and Castile were joined in the persons of this energetic, well-matched pair. Spain was born. But not without a struggle.

With the death of the almost imbecile King Henry IV, the position of Castile was lower than it had been at any time since the collapse of the Visigoth kingdom. Portugal's King Alfonso supported the claims of Joanna, Henry's daughter. The thirteen-year-old Joanna was betrothed to prince John of Portugal and the pair proclaimed sovereigns of Castile. The War of Succession had begun.

In the low ebb of the kingdom's fortunes, Ferdinand and Isabella could barely muster 500 horse. Two months later, however, they had gathered together an army of over 40,000. But it was mainly composed of ill-disciplined militia from the towns. Defeated at Toro, Ferdinand fell back on guerilla tactics, sending light cavalry from Estremadura and Andalusia to wreak havoc in the undefended valleys of Portugal itself. Another battle at Toro resulted in a crushing defeat of Alfonso and his Portuguese. Nevertheless, the war lasted four and a half years and by the end of it Ferdinand and Isabella had taken the measure of each other's qualities, their fortitude and resilience in the face of adversity. They were ready to face their main task, the final eviction of the infidels and the unification of their country. But first it was essential to reorganize their own kingdom.

The power of the nobility had always been the most disruptive force in Castile; indeed, the kingdom's name originated from the multiplicity of their castle strongholds. In the long struggle against the Moors the higher echelons of the nobility, the *ricos hombres,* provided the bulk of the sovereign's armies from the retainers on their estates. These forces were led by the lesser nobility, the *hidalgos,* and by the *caballeros,* the knights who constituted the cavalry and were an essential counterpart of the vicious and highly successful Arab light horse. The towns and their militia were primarily defensive. Not surprisingly, considering the costs and the risks they bore, the nobility shared the spoils of war with their sovereign. As a result, their estates became ever larger, and through the years all sections of the nobility grew in power and riches. They were exempt from taxation, a privileged class living largely above the law; they could not be imprisoned for debt or subjected to torture, and could even renounce allegiance to their sovereign and serve his enemies. Thus, whenever the central authority was undermined by a weak king, the country split up into innumerable small states.

At the succession of Ferdinand and Isabella, the nobility were all-powerful, their estates larger and richer than ever before. There was one organization, however, outside their control. This was the Holy Brotherhood of the cities, the *Santa Hermandad,* a sort of police force formed for the maintenance of civil order. Its concern was the prevention of ordinary crime, but as the abuses of the nobility were such that their own or their retainers' actions often contravened the ordinary criminal code, Isabella's re-establishment and expansion of the Hermandad met with great opposition. However, she had her way, and with a new code of laws, the *Ordenanças Reales,* agreed in 1485, a court of two alcaldes in every town of thirty families to administer it, and a mounted and well-equipped police to

*Having driven the Moors from Spain, the Spaniards extended
their empire by capturing Oran in 1509. A detail from a
sixteenth-century mural.*

enforce it, the bandits and warlords that had produced such chaos throughout the country were rapidly suppressed. The Hermandad was a potent instrument in the hands of a determined sovereign. It worked because it was a disciplined, highly trained force that could be deployed in strength and immediately in any part of the kingdom.

One by one, the great families, whose long-standing feuds had fostered anarchy, were banished to their estates, the lands and castles they had annexed returned to the crown. The whole legal system was overhauled, the power of the privy council, which had been packed by the nobility and clergy, was curtailed, the position of the *alcaldes de corte,* the high court, strengthened, the supreme court of appeal permanently established at Valladolid. Merit became the path to preferment and the nobility were curbed from aping royalty and from building new castles. Moreover, the right of the crown to nominate its own nationals to vacant sees was re-established, and Isabella was able to promote men of learning and piety to positions of ecclesiastical power. Nevertheless, it was this outstandingly able woman who opened her realm to one of the greatest abuses of history.

The man who brought the Inquisition to Spain was her confessor, Tomás de Torquemada. The Jews were very numerous and they were believed to have assisted the Moorish invasion; certainly they were accepted by the Moors. Great travellers, physicians, writers, scientists, they contributed more than any other race to the culture and knowledge of the period. But they were born money-lenders, and as such they were hated. Their riches made them envied, and as the Moorish power declined, they were subjected to increasing persecution. Conversion to Christianity became ever more expedient, and consequently ever more open to the charge of apostacy. Fanatical churchmen, particularly the Dominicans, called for the introduction of the Holy Office. And since failure to satisfy such an enquiry involved confiscation of property, Ferdinand was not unagreeable. On November 1, 1478, the Pope issued a bull authorising the appointment of inquisitors.

What started in 1231 as a counter to the revival of Manichaean doctrines in parts of France and Italy, its object conversion rather than punishment, had already become a much wider and more insidious instrument. In Spain it was to reach its epitome of evil. The first edict issued by the court required all to aid, not only in the apprehension, but also in the accusation of any persons suspected of heresy. In the inflamed mood of the times, those arrested on hearsay, and such flimsy evidence as the wearing of better or cleaner clothes on the Jewish sabbath, or merely the drinking of something prepared in a special way or the eating of meat that had been slaughtered with their own hands, were so numerous that the inquisitors moved their court to the great fortress of Triana. The anonymity of accusers, even of witnesses, was so carefully preserved that only the most garbled version of the charge was ever shown to the victim. Counsel was allowed, but he could not confer with his client. Each variation in the evidence of witnesses was

Seville was the main port from which expeditions set out
for America. (See p. 32.) A detail from a sixteenth-century painting.

made the subject of a new charge. The proceedings were secret. There was no appeal. Torture was common-place. To us of the twentieth century this is all horribly familiar, but nothing we have experienced quite matches the ghastly setpiece finale of the *auto de fe*. This was the ultimate penalty – death by burning. Europe was then only just emerging from the Dark Ages. It was a period not notable for its sensibility. But the act of faith, with its priests and its elaborate ceremony, was something more than a public execution; it was the nearest the then known world had come to religious sacrifice since the Phoenicians slaughtered their first-born in worship of Baal. During the eighteen years that Torquemada was Inquisitor-General of Castile and Aragon more than ten thousand people are said to have died in this way. The effect upon an impressionable, superstitious and backward people must have been extreme. And yet, the conquistadors, most of whom must have witnessed an *auto de fe,* professed horror when confronted by another race practising human sacrifice in the name of religion.

The years 1481–1492 were largely occupied by the war against Granada, and some account of this is necessary, since the behaviour of Ferdinand and his captains set the pattern for colonial conquest.

In the early stages the war was fought by local landlords, rather than the crown, and it was the peasants in the area of hostilities who were the chief sufferers. Troops of both sides, accustomed by centuries of war to living off the land, were hardened to the destruction of crops and dwellings. Booty was their right, their only pay. But in 1484 a scorched-earth policy was adopted and thirty thousand foragers went with the troops to cut a broad swathe of desolation along the whole line of march. The Aragon fleet blockaded the Moorish ports. Deficient in artillery and other weapons, the Moors resorted to poisoning the arrows of their crossbows. At the same time Isabella's efforts to support the war were yielding results. Militia, recruited from even the most distant provinces, were trained into the semblance of a regular army. Volunteers flocked in from the rest of Europe, spurred by religious fervour and the romantic call of chivalry. One by one the frontier strongholds of Granada fell, and in 1487 Ferdinand moved on Málaga with a force of more than fifty thousand. This city, which fell after a three months' siege, was given vicious treatment as a warning to others. The whole population, assembled in the courtyard of the great fortress overlooking the sea, was informed that one-third would be sent to Africa in exchange for Christian prisoners, one-third sold into slavery to pay for the war, the rest allocated as slaves abroad in return for help received. Having announced this sentence to the entire city, Ferdinand offered them an alternative, an enormous ransom to be paid within nine months. The wretched Moors had no hope of raising such a sum, but it had the effect intended, every family revealing their hidden wealth in the hope that by so doing they could buy themselves out of slavery. It was a clever device to be repeated later in far-off Peru.

The treatment of Baza was very different. This stronghold was invested by

Ferdinand's army, now nearly a hundred thousand strong, in May 1489. It did not surrender until December 4 of that year, and then on the most generous terms, the population being given the chance of retiring into Granada with all their chattels or remaining as subjects of the Spanish crown. Cidi Yahye, the man who had directed the defence, was encouraged to enter the service of his conquerors. This again was a shrewd move. A visit to his kinsman, El Zagal, resulted in the cities of Almería and Guadix being surrendered on the terms Baza had accepted. Extreme severity, followed by the most liberal treatment of cities subsequently surrendered, had the effect of weakening Granada's will to resist when the main fortress and capital of the Moors was finally invested in April 1491. Backed by the mountain barrier of the Sierra Nevada, Granada was a formidable fortress, its bastions facing across the vega. The siege had a strangely unreal quality. There was a tournament atmosphere on the surface, the Moors sallying out, singly or in groups, to engage in knightly combat, and the whole scene made splendid through the hot summer by the luxurious state maintained by the Spanish sovereigns and their grandees. The surface, however, was deceptive. The determination of the Spaniards was made abundantly clear when they converted their camp into a solidly constructed city. Santa Fe was completed in three months, and its construction did more than any assault to undermine the resistance of the Moors. Negotiations for surrender began in October, and on January 2, 1492, the city opened its gates to the Spaniards on even more liberal terms.

Barely four months later, popular clamour and the representations of Torquemada resulted in the publication of an edict expelling all Jews. Such total proscription was harsh retribution for the failure of the Jews to integrate, but it was no more than other European countries did with less excuse, and the mood of the people probably made it inevitable. The crusading enthusiasm of the Spaniards was at its peak when Granada finally fell, and their hatred of heretics had been inflamed for several years by the proceedings of the Inquisition and the public demonstrations of the *auto de fe*. To this was added the intolerance of a new-found national unity. The Jews fled in their thousands, to Portugal, Africa, Italy, Turkey and the Levant; and Spain herself was the loser, for they represented the most cultured, industrious and knowledgeable section of the community.

2   *Birth of an Empire*

THIS THEN WAS THE WORLD into which the conquistadors were born: a world of religious and racial intolerance, of crusading knights and marching armies, of war and devastation and change. The atmosphere in which they were brought up was entirely dominated by a sense of crusading fervour and of the invincibility of Spanish arms. Santiago and the Virgin – what more did a man need to sustain him as his horse thundered into battle? The two greatest of the conquistadors both came from the same province, Estremadura; Hernán Cortés being born in 1485 in the small town of Medellín, Francisco Pizarro about ten or twelve years earlier in the city of Trujillo. There was, too, a family connection. Cortés was the son of Martín Cortés de Monroy and Doña Catalina Pizarro Altamarino. The Cortés, Monroys, Pizarros and Altamarinos were all old families of the nobility, so that his parents were *hidalgos*. Pizarro was the son of Gonzalo Pizarro, an infantry colonel, who later served with some distinction in Italy under *El Gran Capitán*, Gonsalvo de Córdoba. He was, however, a bastard, his father having had an affair with Francisca González, a woman of humble birth in Trujillo.

These two men, Cortés and Pizarro, meet once, possibly twice, during their careers. Their stature as conquerors is entirely in keeping with their backgrounds, Cortés towering head and shoulders above the other. Both had courage of no ordinary sort. Both were adventurers, soldiers of fortune, men born to lead in an age of medieval chivalry when the only proper activity for a gentleman, indeed his only *raison d'être*, was to fight. Moreover, they were from Estremadura, and it was from this high, bleak upland area that they recruited the best of their men.

If you travel the Estremadura plateau today you will find it little changed. The holm oak still covers large tracts of the country with its dark green foliage; its outsized acorns still provide fodder for pigs, horses and cattle, even a basic subsistence diet for man; the hill settlements are still little more than a scattering of hovels perched on the bare rock outcrops, the villages mainly one-storey cottages lining cobbled streets that slope to a central drainage kennel. Old castles dominate the hills and the keeps of great fortresses, like Belalcázar, still stand. At Medellín, in the town below the huge castle, there are still traces of the Cortés family home, as well as a great statue of the man himself, and the name has become a common one. At Trujillo, too, Pizarro now rides a bronze charger in the square, and inside the old walls, up twisting alleys of this still-medieval town, you come suddenly upon the church of Santa María, the only church inside the walls; climb to the belfry and you are looking down on the same grey stone buildings that Pizarro saw when he was a child.

But it is the country that makes the deepest impression. It is a hard country that has changed little, the men still of the same type that Cortés and Pizarro recruited for their expeditions: short-statured and stocky, sturdy as their holm oaks, dark features lined by the hardness of the land that is their home. This is all high pastoral country, with everywhere distant vistas, the land running away to mountains that stand like islands on the horizon. Its wide skies inspire the desire to travel and it was this, as much as the poverty of the land, that drove men to seek beyond the mountains, one vista leading to another, with more hills like islands, until at last, riding north, they reached the Tagus, which flows westward to Lisbon and the ocean. The Tagus, the Guadiana and the Guadalquivir – all these rivers brought them news from the outer world, news first of the Portuguese discoveries in Africa, later of Spanish discoveries beyond the western ocean. The combination was irresistible, and the time was right.

With the fall of Granada, there were suddenly no more infidels to slaughter, no more crusades to wage. The fighting machine of the *caballeros* had come to a halt. It was then that Christopher Columbus appeared on the scene. He was a Genoese navigator, who had left the sea at the age of about thirty and settled in Lisbon. He was married to a Portuguese woman, and a relative of hers, a well-known sea captain, left her all his papers, perhaps even his logs. With the aid of these, Columbus not only made and sold maps, but became convinced that by sailing westward a skilful navigator would pioneer a short cut to the Indies; he even cherished the idea that unknown lands lay beyond the Western Ocean.

It is hardly credible that Columbus could have dreamed this up on the basis of hearsay and some vague reference in a dead sea captain's papers. By then the Portuguese had almost a century's experience of maritime exploration. The lure throughout had been, not gold, but spices. In those days spices, particularly pepper, were in great demand for the preserving of carcases slaughtered in the

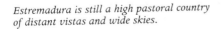

Estremadura is still a high pastoral country of distant vistas and wide skies.

autumn because of the shortage of winter feed. The spice islands of the Moluccas are situated in the East Indies and the pepper was brought to Europe via Malaya, India, Egypt, and then overland to the Mediterranean. This route, littered with pirates and potentates, was so costly in lives and tribute that a bale of pepper purchased for one ducat in the Moluccas sold for 105 ducats in Europe. This was the financial lure that had motivated the Portuguese dream of a direct ocean route south round Africa to the Indies. We know why their interest in the African shore waned shortly after the death of Henry the Navigator. What remains a mystery is why, in the treaty that ended the War of Succession in 1476, they abandoned all claim to lands beyond the Western Ocean, and why they suddenly became so secretive about their voyages of discovery.

Two years before Bartholomew Diaz succeeded in rounding the Cape of Good Hope, King John II, whose maritime enthusiasm had equalled Henry's, turned down Columbus's pleas for financial backing with the statement that he had 'information regarding the western lands more positive than the visions of the Genoese'. Had the Portuguese already explored the American coast? This seems incredible. Nevertheless, there is still much we have to learn about the early voyages. It is only in recent years that we have come to accept the idea that the Vikings were in America four centuries before Columbus. Irish monks, sailing their skin-hulled curraghs, may have been there as early as the sixth century. And what about the Phoenicians, who kept the details of their trading voyages to themselves – or the Greeks?

Who was Quetzalcoatl, the Aztec god of learning, who was tall and white-skinned, with long hair and flowing beard, and who came out of the east, out of the sunrise, and who disappeared into the sea as mysteriously as he had come? This was the god of Aztec mythology that the Mexicans were to confuse with Cortés. And the Incas, too – who was their Tici-Viracocha? The appearance recently of a new map acts as a timely reminder that, in the five centuries that have elapsed since the days of Portuguese discovery, much vital information has been lost. Indeed, the acceptance of Columbus as the discoverer of America has obscured at least one Portuguese voyage, that of João Vaz Corte-Real in 1472, who is recognised by half a dozen countries, including Portugal and Denmark, as the real discoverer of America. The sea route that the Viking longships took, and possibly also the Irish monks, was by way of Iceland and Greenland. Here the open sea passages are nowhere greater than four hundred miles and the Danes were regularly sailing the first three of these. Why not the last?

Such speculation was even more rife in the days of Columbus, and what is so frustrating is that we do not know on what information he based his belief in the possibility of reaching land beyond the Western Ocean. All we know is that he was so dedicated to the idea that, failing support for it in Lisbon, he went to Spain. The war with Granada was then at its height, nobody had any time or money to spare for such visionary exploits. He tried the nobles of the Mediterranean coast, and failed again. But interest had been aroused, and when Granada fell Ferdinand and Isabella were prepared to listen to his arguments. On April 17, 1492, at Santa Fe, they signed a capitulation appointing him admiral, viceroy and governor-general of all islands and mainlands he might discover in the Western Ocean with jurisdiction over commercial transactions and entitlement to one-tenth of the profits and a further eighth if he contributed that proportion of the costs of the voyage.

Regarded as a crank by most of the merchants and sailors of the day, he got little support from the main ports of Seville and Cadiz. It was Alonso Niño, a merchant of Moguer in the Río Tinto estuary, who finally backed him, together with the Pinzón family, who were shipbuilders. By the end of July 1492 his small and inadequate fleet of three ships – the *Santa María*, a carrack of about 80 tons, and two small caravels, the *Pinta* and the *Niña* (the feminine of Niño) – lay in the little creek port of Palos de la Frontera just over a mile from the open sea. The creek has now silted up, but in Palos itself you can still see the fontanilla, or house-well, from which his seamen filled their water casks for the last time. After a dedication service in the church at Moguer the ships dropped down-river to the bar at Saltés. The convent at La Rábida, on the low hill above the river mouth, still houses the Virgin of Milagros to whom Columbus offered up his final prayers for the success of the voyage. He sailed on August 3, his Admiral's flag flying from the *Santa María*, whilst three of the Pinzón family acted as pilots. At the mouth of the Río Tinto there is now a huge statue to Columbus facing west towards the New World; otherwise the river has changed little, a broad-flowing ribbon of water flanked by acres of mud, and below La Rábida a wide creek most suitable for anchoring the small caravels that the Pinzón family were then building. His total complement on this voyage was about a hundred sailors and adventurers.

Columbus sighted the Bahamas on October 12, visited Cuba and Haiti, where he landed men to establish the first Spanish colony in the New World. His flagship wrecked, he returned in the *Niña*, reaching Palos on March 15, 1493, after anchoring briefly in the Tagus. To the court of Ferdinand and Isabella, he brought the evidence of his discoveries – crudely made gold ornaments, specimens of plant, animal and bird life, also six of the native islanders. It was an exotic cavalcade, the first of all that wealth that was to pass out of the Indies for the support of Spanish arms and pretensions. It also symbolized the vindication of the theories that Columbus had held in the face of years of incredulity, misrepresentation and rebuff.

So great were the hopes set upon these discoveries that Juan de Fonseca, Archdeacon of Seville and a shrewd man of business, was put in charge of an office in Seville for the administration of Indian affairs, and a special customs house was allocated at Cadiz. Application was made to the Court of Rome, and the Pope issued three bulls confirming Spain in the possession of all lands discovered west of a line drawn between the two poles at a distance of one hundred leagues from the Canary and Cape Verde islands. Discoveries east of that line belonged to Portugal. But Portugal objected and by the Treaty of Tordesillas in 1494 she gained a dividing line 370 leagues west of the Cape Verdes; it was this new line which gave her a legal foothold in Brazil.

Meanwhile, on September 25, 1493, Columbus had sailed again, this time from the small creek harbour of Puerto de Santa María, which faces Cadiz across the bay. The fleet was much larger – three carracks and seventeen caravels – and he had with him fifteen hundred men. After a forty-day crossing, he found his settlement on Haiti abandoned. Haiti, now called Hispaniola, was re-colonised; but in a short time all the dissensions and conflicts of interest that were to follow each successive conquest in the New World became apparent. Though the expedition was remarkably well equipped for the times, it nevertheless carried with it the seeds of trouble. Apart from the sailors and artisans – among them, incidentally, a large number of miners, which gives a clue to the main hopes of the expedition's backers – the bulk of the adventurers were soldiers of fortune, men whose interests were personal glory and profit. There were also a dozen ecclesiastics and some of the Indians brought back on the first voyage, now converts and intended as missionaries.

Columbus, a queer mixture of mountebank, opportunist and navigational fanatic, was hardly the best man to govern effectively such high-mettled and unruly settlers. Moreover, though Spaniards might refer to him as Cristóbal Colón, he was still a foreigner. However, the main cause of the trouble was that adventurers do not make for good husbandry. It was crops, not gold, that the new colony had to offer. The Indians, outraged by the behaviour of men accustomed through war to devastating the lands they conquered and seizing whatever took their fancy, rose in rebellion. As a result, one-third of the population was killed, whilst the failure to plant crops caused a food shortage. Columbus was forced to ration supplies and issue orders for every man, whatever his rank, to work in the fields. The effect of such an order was inevitable. When Columbus returned to Spain in 1496, income from the colony had been slight, the complaints numerous. He was still well received at court, but Bishop Fonseca was less accommodating, and it was not until early in 1498 that the third expedition of six ships was ready.

Sailing from Sanlúcar de Barrameda on May 30, Columbus took a more southerly route, discovered the island of Trinidad and landed on the coast of South America itself. Arriving finally at Hispaniola, he was faced with a rebellion of the colonists themselves. This was only settled by grants of land and the allocation of Indians to work it. Thus the vicious *repartimiento* system was established. Meanwhile, complaints and accusations of his conduct came into Spain with every returning ship, and as a result, a commissioner was sent out to investigate. This over-zealous and pretentious knight, Don Francisco de Bobadilla, ordered Columbus to appear before him to answer the charges, threw him into prison and finally sent him and his brother back to Spain in irons. Columbus was released, of course, but a new governor was appointed in his place. This was Don Nicolás de Ovando of the Order of Alcántara. He sailed in February 1502 with a fleet of thirty-two ships and a complement of 2,500, among whom, as an adventurer, was the future defender of the Indians, Las Casas. The size of this expedition gives an indication of the importance Hispaniola had now assumed in the eyes of the Spanish crown.

Columbus made one last great voyage, sailing in March 1502 with orders to avoid the colony of Hispaniola. The state of his ships, however, forced him to shelter there, together with a fleet of eighteen vessels about to leave for Spain. Columbus warned the governor that a hurricane was imminent. This was the great navigator speaking from his vast experience, not the ex-governor. Foolishly Ovando ignored the warning, dispatched his ships and ordered Columbus to leave the harbour of Santo Domingo. Columbus rode out the gale in the lee of the island, but of the eighteen ships bound for Spain, only three survived. Columbus went on to explore the Caribbean sea from Honduras to Darién, searching through two long years for the passage to Asia. He died at Vallodolid in 1506, two years after his return to Spain, having been almost within sight of his goal.

In the story of Columbus we see many of the problems and trials Spain brought with her to the New World. Her interests, divided between greed and a sense of religious mission, were irreconcilable. The men who went out there as colonists were adventurers rather than settlers, and since their leaders were drawn from the lesser nobility, with a background of inter-family strife, the New World, far removed from the interference and control of the state, gave full rein to their martial and feuding instincts. With sailors grown accustomed to the long haul across the Atlantic, they were well equipped for discovery and conquest, but for little else, as the wretched Indians were to discover.

With the death of Columbus, the torch of discovery passes to Spanish nationals, to the conquistadors – in particular to Cortés and Pizarro. There is little reliable information about the latter's early life. He is supposed to have been deserted by both his parents, to have been a foundling discovered abandoned on the steps of the church of Santa María in Trujillo; there is even a story that he was suckled by a sow. There seems little doubt that, as a youth, he was occupied in herding pigs and had no education except that of a hard life. One account suggests that he served with his father in the Italian wars, even that he sailed with Columbus. But all we know for certain is that the blood of his father answered to the call of the New World, and in 1509, when he was almost forty, he took part in an expedition led by Alonso de Hojeda, was left in charge of the settlement at Urabá on the mainland, and escaped after deliberately allowing the colony to waste away until the survivors were few enough to be safely embarked in the two small vessels available.

He helped Balboa establish his colony on the Darién isthmus, was employed on several expeditions by Pedrarias after his appointment as governor, and in 1515 crossed the isthmus to trade with the natives of the Pacific. He accompanied

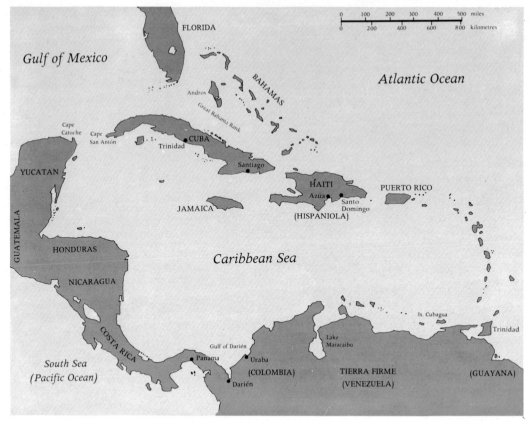

The Caribbean.

Pedrarias when he moved the seat of his government to Panama, but by the age of fifty he had little to show for his efforts, except for a tract of poor land near the capital, a *repartimiento* of Indians and his position as one of the governor's senior captains. This at a time when the much younger Cortés was marching on the Mexican capital. Yet, despite his age and his lack of resources, Pizarro was then on the threshold of three great voyages of discovery and of the extraordinary and barely credible adventures that were to make him lord of Peru and of the whole Inca empire.

Whereas Pizarro's early life is a matter for conjecture, that of Cortés is fully covered by his secretary, Francisco López de Gómara, and others. Like a number of great men, Cortés was a sickly child, 'so frail that many times he was on the point of dying'. The religious attitudes of the period inevitably attribute his recovery to heavenly intervention, in this case St Peter, picked at random by his wet nurse, according to Gómara. At the age of fourteen he was sent to study at the University of Salamanca. Accounts differ, some saying he was a Latin scholar, others that he studied law, others still that he was learning grammar and through illness, boredom and lack of money returned home after two years. The nature of the man we shall see in action later suggests that he did study law and government, as well as Latin, that he was an adept student who absorbed a great deal in a short time, and that his ambitious and active nature, thwarted by lack of funds in a student world full of the sons of men much richer than his father, induced him to use the natural excuse of illness to explain his return home.

Gómara says Cortés was 'restless, haughty, mischievous and given to quarrelling', which is a fair description of an ambitious adolescent, conscious of his latent powers and frustrated by the provincial life of a small town. At the same time he was being subjected to exaggerated stories of Spanish feats of arms in the Italian wars and of the enormous potentialities of the New World. For a high-spirited youth, who had abandoned learning for a life of action, the choice was either Italy or the Indies.

Ovando was then fitting out his fleet of thirty-two ships at Cadiz and at the same time studying at Cáceres in Estremadura. This brought him into contact with the Cortés family, who arranged that he should take their son with him when he sailed as the newly-appointed governor of Hispaniola. St Peter, however, decreed otherwise. The young Cortés was already deploying his energies in another direction, and whilst escaping from the house of a married woman, a wall collapsed, and but for the intervention of the mother Cortés would have been killed by her irate son-in-law. Injured by the fall and confined to bed by a quartan fever, Cortés lost the chance of going to the Indies with Ovando; instead he set off for Italy. But he never got there, Gómara saying that he wandered idly about for nearly a year. Since he returned to Medellín with his mind set firmly on the Indies, it is probably safe to assume that he had spent that year in the heady atmosphere of Spain's southern ports.

The year was 1503, the Italian wars coming to an end and the Indies beckoning. Already Amerigo Vespucci had completed three of his four widely publicized voyages. In the two 'letters', or descriptions, which resulted in his name being given to a continent (the first of these appeared in *Mundus Novus,* the second in *Cosmographiae introductio*), he claimed to have been south of the River Plate, almost as far as the Straits of Magellan. This was the third voyage made in 1501–02. In the second, made in 1499–1500, he is supposed to have discovered Brazil, sailing the coast from 5°S to the Gulf of Maracaibo in company with Hojeda. With him on that voyage was Juan de la Cosa, who produced the first map of the New World. One of the Niños of Palos, Pero Alonso, had reached the north coast of Colombia. Pinzón had reached the mouth of the Amazon, Lepe had also sailed the coasts of Brazil, and a lawyer, Bastidas, had explored the north coast of South America right to the Darién coast. Most of these ships came into the Atlantic ports of Spain's southern coast, into that curving bight that is called the Gulf of Cadiz.

Sanlúcar de Barrameda, just inside the estuary of the Guadalquivir, was the point of entry for Seville. The river is broad here and easy to enter, the low-cliffed headland to the south giving some protection from southerly winds, and once inside the bar, which still straddles the river, there is good shelter, with a sand shore that makes for easy landing. But it was Seville itself that would have been the chief attraction to the young Cortés, the puerto centred around the Torre del Oro, a squat circular tower that is almost all that remains to mark the nearest approach to the river of the old city walls. Here, on the dark sand beach below the walls, the boats from the Indies were hauled ashore on greased timbers. There were builders' yards smelling of wood shavings and tar, and the quays were crowded with sailors, merchants, adventurers and monks, piled with stores going out to the ships anchored off, and, much more exciting, the products of incoming vessels; the exotic scent of a new world.

Cadiz, too, was bustling with new life, not only below the fortress end of the great north-curling spit of land that protects this large natural bay, but in the creek harbour of Puerto de Santa María from which Columbus once sailed. Sanlúcar, Cadiz and Puerto de Santa María, these were all within a few miles of each other, in a group about 60 miles south of Seville; and about the same distance west of Seville, over the flat land leading into undulating hills, were the mud creeks of Moguer, Palos and La Rábida on the Tinto river. These, too, were alive with the first fantastic fruits of an empire just at the point of birth. Discovery and conquest, dreams of untold wealth, tales of shipwreck, storm and reef, of gold and Indians and strange, unknown lands – it was more than enough to excite the imagination of an ambitious youth of eighteen determined to carve out a niche for himself.

Cortés sailed the following year in a convoy of five merchant ships bound for Santo Domingo, the capital of Hispaniola. It was the year of Queen Isabella's death, and at that time a pilot's knowledge of the Indies was still very sketchy. This is hardly surprising, for the Caribbean Sea and the Gulf of Mexico are littered with a complex pattern of islands, reefs and coral cays. Swift currents sweep down along the embayed coasts of Central America and from the beginning of September to mid-October there is danger of hurricanes. At that time even the big island of Cuba was still regarded as part of the mainland.

On his arrival at Santo Domingo, Cortés lodged with Medina, a friend who was one of the governor's secretaries. He advised him to register as a citizen, which would entitle him to a *caballería*, a building plot and land for cultivation – a slow and pedestrian way to the accumulation of wealth compared with the lure of gold and the high hopes of the voyage. No doubt the governor, Ovando, offered him the same advice, for he gave him a *repartimiento* of Indians and made him notary to the town council of Azúa. During the next five or six years Cortés seems to have been content to trade and establish a position in the colony. He must have met Pizarro, for it was a tight little community and he very nearly went on the ill-fated Nicuesa-Hojeda expedition.

He was prevented, however, by what his secretary describes as an abscess behind the right knee. Others called it the buboes, a swelling of the lymphatic gland in the region of the groin caused by syphillis. His extraordinary energies had already found an outlet, and now that he was in a colony where there were few women of his own race it was almost inevitable that he should contract venereal disease, since, it was said, Indian women infected their lovers more readily than Spanish women. His recovery was probably due to a native remedy, *guayacán*, but the ultimate effects of the disease hardly explain the mystery of the remains exhumed at the Jesús Hospital Church, Mexico City, in 1947, described as those of a hunchbacked dwarf with an unnaturally narrow head, a small aquiline nose and a functional limitation of the right arm. Since this description coincides with the monster in Diego Rivera's murals, the most probable explanation is a political one, modern Mexico having done everything possible to discredit Cortés. Both the body and the murals certainly compare very strangely with the description of him given by Bernal Díaz: 'He was of good height and body and well proportioned and of strong limbs . . . had his face been longer he would have been handsomer and his eyes had a somewhat loving glance yet grave withal . . .' The only blemish was apparently a knife scar on the lower lip, got in one of his amorous brawls. This was covered by his beard, which was dark and sparse. He is also described as being lean, with a high chest, his back of good shape, but slightly bow-legged, due no doubt to constant riding.

In 1509 Don Diego Columbus arrived in Santo Domingo as Governor of the Indies, having finally established his hereditary title as son and heir of the man who had discovered the New World. Two years later, after settling the island of Puerto Rico, he sent Diego Velázquez with three hundred men to conquer Cuba, which had at last been proved an island, but was still virtually unexplored. For Cortés, who accompanied the expedition, this was the gateway to Mexico. He was twenty-six, still in a civil capacity as clerk to the treasurer, which entailed keeping account of the king's fifth. The annexation of Cuba did not take long. Velázquez was appointed lieutenant-governor and the 'able and diligent' Cortés given a *repartimiento* of Indians which he shared with Juan Juárez. Juárez owed his preferential treatment to the fact that Velázquez was in love with one of his sisters. The Juárez girls had come over from Spain with Don Diego Columbus in 1509, shopping for rich husbands, and another of them, Catalina, had thrown herself at Cortés.

A portrait of Cortés as a young man by a seventeenth-century Spanish artist right *contrasts strangely with that by the twentieth-century Mexican artist, Diego Rivera, portraying him as misshapen and avaricious* far right.

In the warm tropical atmosphere of the islands passions flared and the situation that developed would have been one of pure farce if there had been no political undercurrents. Cortés was now a very eligible bachelor: he had mines, large numbers of cattle, sheep and mares, and the first house in the new town of Santiago de Baracoa. His susceptibility to women, however, was not accompanied by any desire to marry them. Moreover, his ambitions, and his position in the new colony of Cuba, made him a natural focus for the intrigues of those who were dissatisfied at the rewards of conquest. Cortés may have been 'cunning and cautious', but he was now open to attack, and, as a result of various accusations, Velázquez had him arrested and thrown into prison.

Faced with the prospect of trial by men whom Gómara calls 'false witnesses', Cortés broke the padlock, seized the guard's sword and shield, escaped out of a window and sought sanctuary in a church. The account given by Las Casas is somewhat different. In this Cortés is chosen by a group of conspirators to plead their case before Spanish judges known to have arrived recently in Hispaniola to examine grievances, is arrested as he embarks in a canoe, and comes near to being hanged.

As he was confined to the sanctuary of a small church, a trap was laid for him, and it is even suggested that Catalina herself was used as a decoy. At any rate, he was seized, put in irons again, and this time imprisoned on board a ship. Again he managed to free himself, and having exchanged clothes with a servant boy, let himself down over the side into the ship's boat. It was night and only one other vessel was in the harbour. He cut loose its boat and rowed up-river. But, unable to make headway against the current, and fearing that his boat would be sighted if he attempted to land from it, he slipped over the side and swam ashore with apparently all the documents relating to the grievances against the governor carefully tied in a bundle on his head.

He went straight to the house of Juan Juárez, having, it seems, come to the conclusion that, despite his large following and the position he had hoped to establish for himself by arguing the case of the dissident element in the colony, it was now essential to re-establish himself with Velázquez. Since he finally married Catalina Juárez, it is obvious that he went to her brother's house to tell him he was prepared to make an honest woman of her. Velázquez was then on a punitive expedition against some rebellious natives. Juárez gave Cortés arms, and whilst he sought sanctuary in a church again, interceded for him with Velázquez. The final reconciliation took place in the governor's camp. 'They shook hands and after a long talk lay down together in the same bed where they were found next morning by Diego de Orellana who had come to tell the governor that Cortés had escaped.'

These little episodes illustrate the rough and tumble of politics in the New World, and from them Cortés appears to have realised that real power was only to be achieved through independent command and the successful conquest of unsettled lands. He was content to bide his time. He was twice elected mayor or alcalde of Santiago, and not until the latter part of 1518 did he make any move towards independent power.

By then much had happened in Spain, all of which had its repercussions overseas. The little kingdom of Navarre had fallen to Ferdinand in 1513. In January 1516 Ferdinand himself had died. He was succeeded by his sixteen-year-old grandson, Charles, who was already heir to Luxembourg, the Low Countries and the area of Burgundy then known as the Franche Comté, through his father, and through his grandfather to the Habsburg empire of Austria, and was also shortly to be elected emperor of Germany. His mother was Ferdinand's daughter Joanna, and on her father's death she became Queen of Aragon and Naples, and the great Cardinal Ximenes, Archbishop of Toledo, was appointed regent of Spain, including her possessions in Italy, Africa, France and the New World. In the two years of his regency Ximenes did a remarkable job of consolidation for the young King Charles. By encouraging the militia of the towns, he forestalled any danger provoked by the nobility smarting under the prospect of a monarch dependent on Flemish advisers; he held Navarre against the French, establishing Spain's power by the demolition of the strongest castles; and in the south, he strengthened the country's defence and held the Barbary corsairs at bay with a strong fleet. He overhauled the country's finances, neglected in the last years of Ferdinand's reign, particularly the funds of the military orders, cut out all waste in the administration, and even reduced the pensions granted by Ferdinand and Isabella. He also found time in that brief period to send a commission to Hispaniola to investigate the position of the natives, and he made a serious attempt to stop the flow of negro slaves to the new colonies. On September 17, 1517, Charles landed in Spain. Ximenes retired to his diocese and in less than two months he was dead. It was the end of an era in which Spain had become one kingdom. It was the dawn of a new era, this time beyond the seas.

Don ferdinando Cordeshirg 1529 seines
altters Jm 42 diser hat der kay
aiter karolus den funfften
haben ach hannz Jndiann
gewinnen.

PART TWO

Cortés

Hernán Cortés. Probably the most authentic portrait of the conquistador;
a drawing by Weiditz, who met him in Spain in later life.

3

Prelude to Conquest

CORTÉS SAILED for what was later to be called New Spain on February 10, 1519. He was then thirty-three and had been fifteen years, nearly half his life, in the Indies. He had served as a notary, as Velázquez' secretary-treasurer, as a civic dignitary and man of affairs in a colonial capital that was growing fast, and up to that time seems to have been content to stand on the touchline of discovery. Into Santo Domingo, the capital of Hispaniola, came news of all that was happening in the New World. The Pinzón-Solís expedition of 1508–9, which took them south by way of Yucatán and Honduras to the Brazilian coast in search of a passage to Asia, was followed, between 1509 and 1511, by the disastrous attempt of Hojeda and Nicuesa to establish themselves on the mainland coast between Venezuela and Honduras. This finally led to Balboa and Pizarro founding a colony in Darién. By then Jamaica had been subjugated and Diego Velázquez, with Cortés one of his officials, had settled Cuba. In 1513 Ponce de León, broken in health after his two-year campaign in Puerto Rico, discovered Florida, by accident and after much hardship, having lost his way in a futile quest for some incredible fountain of youth. Most exciting of all, in September of the same year Balboa discovered the Pacific.

In 1514 Pedrarias came out from Spain as governor of Darién, now the province of Tierra Firme. With him was Bernal Díaz whose extraordinary book, *Historia verdadera de la Conquista de la Nueva España,* will give us an eye-witness account of Cortés' march on Mexico. He was distantly related to Diego Velázquez and joined him in Cuba. But after 'three fruitless years' in Tierra Firme and Cuba, he was ready to try his luck again when in 1517 Hernández de Córdoba mounted the first real attempt to penetrate and settle the mainland coast of the Caribbean north of Tierra Firme.

The Córdoba expedition, with three ships and 110 men, sailed on February 8, 1517, bound for Yucatán, which is just across the sea from Cape San Antón at the western end of Cuba. But first, it would seem, they sailed northwards across the Great Bahama Bank to Andros and other islands of the Bahama group. Velázquez had ordered them to get him Indians as payment for a vessel he had let them have on credit. In view of the Spanish attitude to Caribs, the suggestion that they refused on the grounds that they were not slavers would seem open to doubt. The fact that they did not return to Cuba, but made along the north coast to San Antón, indicates that their real purpose in venturing into such dangerous and uncharted waters was pearls.

Like most expeditions sailing in search of gold and pearls and new lands, Córdoba's vessels were victualled largely with cassava bread and pigs, and carried oil and beads and cloth for barter. Bernal Díaz has given us a detailed account of their difficulties. After rounding Cape San Antón they headed west into the open sea. They were 'without any knowledge of the depths or currents, or the winds', so that they were 'in great hazard of their lives' when a storm struck. It lasted forty-eight hours and nearly wrecked them. Finally they made land at Cape Catoche, where they could see a settlement about six miles inland that was larger than any in Cuba. It had great stone pyramid-shaped structures, and because of this, they named it Great Cairo. The cacique (the Carib word for a local leader) made friendly overtures, but then led them into an ambush. Having driven off the Indians, they went up into the 'pyramids'. They were temples to the gods the Indians worshipped, and in the idol-rooms they found rudely-made gold and copper ornaments and 'many idols of baked clay, some with demons' faces, some with women's, and others equally ugly would seem to represent Indians committing sodomy with one another'. These teocallis – Bernal Díaz refers to them as *cúes* – were to dominate every city, town and village the Spaniards conquered.

Having looted what they could, they embarked and sailed on for another fifteen days to Campeche. They still thought they were exploring an island; instead, it was the organized forces of the mainland Indians that patrolled the shores. Córdoba's men were now short of water – water was always short in these small, over-crowded vessels sailing so slowly through tropical waters. They landed at several places, were driven off at one point by large numbers of Indians, dragged their anchors, and very nearly lost their ships in a northerly gale that lasted four days. By now the water casks had dried out and were leaking. They landed again, this time at Champotón, managed to collect some water, and were then attacked by a force of Indians that outnumbered them two hundred to one. They lost fifty men; Córdoba himself was hit by ten arrows; and they only just managed to escape back to their ships. Again shortage of water and a north-easterly gale with anchors dragging. Finally they sailed for Cuba by way of Florida, a round trip of somewhere between a thousand and two thousand miles with only the most elementary charts. Córdoba died of his wounds, but the expedition was important, for the gold and idols they brought back, and their accounts of large, stone-built Indian towns, turned all eyes on Yucatán.

No doubt their accounts gained in the telling, but anyone who has been to Yucatán and seen the remains of those great teocallis will appreciate the impact the country and the temples made upon Córdoba's men. Accustomed to the simple

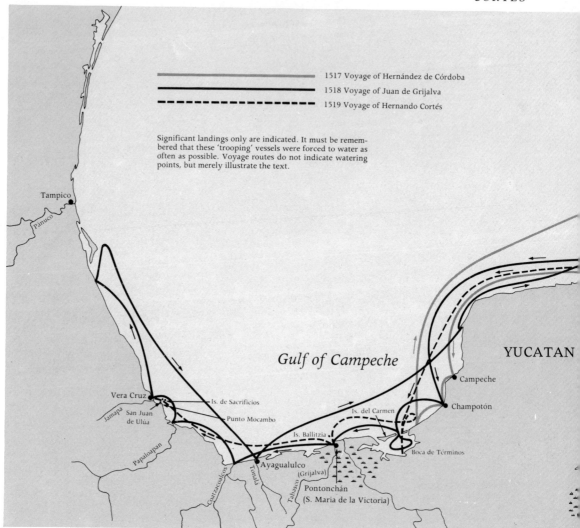

Expeditions in the Gulf of Mexico.

dwellings and primitive existence of the island Caribs, they had found a race of Indians who not only built in stone on a grand scale, but were highly skilled in all sorts of crafts, particularly gold and feather work. Moreover, they were well armed and highly organized, their warriors trained to fight under the lead of their caciques with drums sounding and banners and plumes of feathers flying. And though they were idol-worshippers and sacrificed human beings as well as birds, the ritual of their religion was very complex and their priests burned incense 'of a sort of resin which they call copal'. But however tall the stories might seem to the colonists in Cuba, accustomed to easy conquest of the island Indians, the spoils were not in doubt. Córdoba and his men had brought back enough to prove

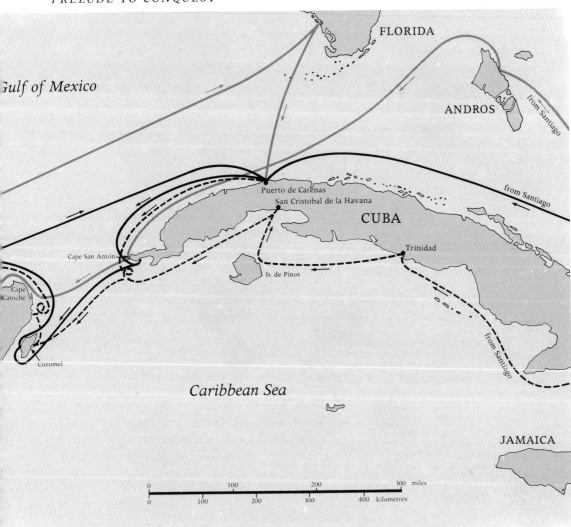

that in Yucatán lay the wealth they had dreamed of since the days of Columbus, and which they had so far failed to find.

Velázquez immediately started fitting out a new expedition with two ships of his own and two that had sailed with Córdoba. He appointed a relative of his, Juan de Grijalva, as captain-general, and the other three vessels were commanded by Alonso de Ávila, Francisco de Montejo and Pedro de Alvarado, all of whom held *encomiendas* – a grant of Indian labour given under licence by the Council of the Indies in Seville – and were thus men of substance in the colony. The expedition sailed from San Antón on May 1, 1518, and three days out discovered the island of Cozumel on the eastern side of the Yucatán peninsula. They then went north round

Cape Catoche and after eight days arrived at Champotón in the Gulf of Campeche, the place where so many men had been lost on the previous expedition.

Once again we have Bernal Díaz on board to give us an account of all that happened. The Indians, he says, were drawn up ready for battle, armed as before with bows and arrows, lances, single and double-handed 'swords', and slings and stones. These 'swords' were unusual, being made of wood in the form of a blade that was wider at the tip than at the hilt and set with razor-sharp flakes of obsidian to give a double cutting edge. It was a deadly weapon when wielded by a strong young warrior. They had shields and wore cotton armour. They also had trumpets and drums and had painted their faces black and in some cases red and white. The Spaniards, benefiting from past experience, also wore padded cotton armour, and in addition to their crossbows and muskets, they had small cannon mounted in the bows of their shore-going boats.

The Indians attacked them in fields full of locusts, which flew up in the Spaniards' faces as they advanced, so that it was difficult to distinguish between arrows and locusts, both of which were equally numerous. Spanish losses were again severe: seven killed and sixty wounded, including Grijalva himself, who received three arrow wounds and got two of his teeth broken. But this time it was the Indians who fled. The Spaniards occupied the town, stayed three days and then moved on, sailing only during the hours of daylight and anchoring at night for fear of stranding themselves on the sand-banks that extended miles off-shore.

It was slow work, and pilotage was difficult, the coast a confused waste of mangrove swamps, often lost to sight in the humid milk-haze of tropical heat. The impossibility of determining the lie of the land caused the pilot, Alaminos, to mistake the great lagoon in the south-eastern corner of what is now known as the Gulf of Campeche for an open water passage. They found good shelter behind the island of Isla del Carmen that guards the entrance, and believing now that Yucatán itself was an island, they named the place Boca de Términos. Thereafter they were sailing almost due west, the shallow sea strewn with fish traps and the Indians following their movements closely from the shore, armed and prepared to fight. At the 'Tabasco' river they were able to land again, this time on a headland covered with palm trees. It was about a mile from the large Indian settlement of Pontonchán, where the people were already erecting wooden stockades for its defence, and almost as soon as they anchored some fifty pirogues put out, full of warriors wearing cotton armour and carrying bows and arrows, lances and shields, drums and feathers. Many other canoes lay hidden in the creeks.

This time, instead of fighting, the Indians agreed to parley. But when Grijalva spoke of Spain's great emperor king, they pointed out that they already had a king of their own and also three armies of eight thousand warriors each, assembled from all the neighbouring provinces to defend their territory. They agreed finally to provide the Spaniards with provisions on a barter basis whilst their caciques and priests decided whether it should be war or peace. In the end they decided for peace, and next day some thirty of them came to the camp under the palm trees, loaded with roasted fish and fowls, sapota fruit and maize-cakes, also braziers and incense. The burning of incense was reserved for their gods, but the Spaniards did not know this and had no means of understanding why they should be subjected to this ritual. The Indians also brought gifts of golden jewels, diadems in the shape of ducks and lizards, and other small objects. When the Spaniards asked for more gold, they said they had none, and added that further to the westward there was plenty; they kept on repeating 'Culhúa, Culhúa' and 'México, México'.

Grijalva, fearing for his ships if a gale came in from the north, re-embarked his men and sailed west again. Two days later they were off the town of Ayagualulco, where warriors with turtle-shell shields, glinting like gold in the sun, paraded watchfully along the foreshore. Short of water, conscious all the time that they were breaking new ground, they passed the entrance to the Tonalá river, sailing slowly, for their ships' bottoms were becoming foul with weed, and the trade wind was now more often ahead than on the beam. The weather was bad when they reached the Coatzacoalcos river, and as they sailed into the bay in search of shelter, they saw for the first time the great mountain ranges of the Sierra Madre Occidental. If there had been any doubt before that this was the mainland, those snow-capped peaks dispelled it.

At the next big river mouth, the Papaloapan, Pedro de Alvarado, who was a reckless, daredevil of a man, took his ship in alone, against Grijalva's orders; after that the four ships kept close together until they made the Jamapa river. This is just short of the modern city of Vera Cruz and a little to the north of the river there is good shelter inside the banks under Punto Mocambo. Here the Indians actually welcomed them, and Grijalva went ashore, spoke with the caciques and traded for 16,000 pesos' worth of low-grade gold ornaments. It was here that he finally took possession of the country in the name of Velázquez for the Spanish crown.

Next they stopped at an island five miles from the shore, and on landing found two temples, both stone-built with steps leading up to altars presided over by devilish idols to whom five Indians had just been sacrificed. 'Their chests had been struck open and their arms and thighs cut off, and the walls of these buildings were covered with blood.' They named the island Isla de Sacrificios, crossed to the mainland again, and camped on the beach. The land behind them was flat and sandy – low dune country. Again the Indians came down to barter, not to fight, but as at Mocambo, they brought little gold. The fact that the weather continued fine mattered little now, as their ships were sheltered by the off-lying banks and by yet another island that crooked a low, palm-clad finger half across the bay. This, too, had a pyramid-like teocalli with a large and ugly idol called Tezcatlipoca. It was served by four priests in 'black cloaks and hoods very like those of our Dominicans'. Only that day they had cut open the chests of two boys and sacrificed their blood and hearts to the idol. When asked why they had made this sacrifice, they answered that the people of Culhúa had ordered it. The Indian acting as interpreter slurred the word, so that it sounded like Ulúa, and they named the island San Juan de Ulúa.

Bernal Díaz excuses Grijalva's failure to found a settlement on the grounds that they had not enough soldiers, thirteen of their number having died of wounds and a further four being disabled. Also their cassava bread was mouldy and full of weevils. In fact, they had had enough. They had been sailing now for about four months, much of the time exploring new ground. Encamped in the dunes, above what was later to become a great port, driven half mad by mosquitoes, it is hardly surprising that their leader decided to send Alvarado back to Cuba in the *San Sebastián*. This was their soundest vessel, and with Alvarado went most of the gold ornaments they had gained by barter. It is possible that Grijalva hoped the sight of all this loot would encourage Velázquez to send reinforcements, but it was now the hurricane season, one of their ships was leaking, and as they coasted north-westward from San Juan de Ulúa, the snow-capped mountains came closer, a visual reminder that this was no island, but a big country. The many Indian towns they had seen from sea and coast could only be regarded as outposts of more formidable cities inland. Conquest, even settlement, must have seemed utterly impracticable for such a small force, and when about twenty large canoes tried to make off with the smallest of their three vessels while the fleet lay at anchor, they held a conference and decided to return to Cuba whilst they were still in a fit state to do so.

One of the legacies of Spain's own history was that in all these voyages of discovery there was usually a democratic basis to any major decision. This was true also of the Elizabethan adventurers of Tudor England, for even the most forceful leader could not impose his will, in circumstances of danger and isolation, unless the men themselves were willing.

The Spaniards turned about, and with the prevailing northerly wind behind them, they made a quick passage back to the Coatzacoalcos. But the weather was so bad they continued on into the shelter of the Tonalá river. Here one of their ships went aground on the bar and had to be careened for repairs. Fortunately, the Indians seemed friendly and they were able to trade, obtaining, amongst other things, six hundred axes, which gleamed so brightly they thought they were made of low grade gold. One soldier raided a temple, and Díaz says he sowed some orange pips beside the pyramid. They then sailed to Cuba, this time direct, and reached Santiago after forty-five days of battling against the north-east trades.

Grijalva had opened the door to Mexico. He had sent back 20,000 pesos' worth of gold, and had achieved more in six months than almost any other expedition, without the loss of a single vessel and with only thirty men killed. Yet Velázquez regarded the venture as a failure. The governor's attitude was dictated by the political tightrope his ambitions forced him to walk. In that year, 1518, the

Indian canoes try to capture one of Grijalva's ships. An eighteenth-century engraving.

Rivera de Panuco, ô Rio de Ca

political situation was changing rapidly, both in the islands and at home in Spain. Charles V had now been king for two years. He was still only eighteen and very much under the influence of his Flemish advisers. He had little understanding of his Spanish kingdom and none of the new lands beyond the sea. He had just been elected emperor of Germany. With his Habsburg empire, this made him the most powerful monarch in Europe. He was now at Barcelona, and without a thought had already given Yucatán to his Flemish admiral. The situation in the New World was still very fluid, with Velázquez in Cuba and Francisco de Garay in Jamaica, both governors deriving their authority from Don Diego Columbus and the Council of the Indies in Seville, and Diego Columbus himself having to exert constant pressure at the young king's court to maintain his rights as viceroy and governor-general of all the lands beyond the ocean, the position given to his father and his heirs in perpetuity under the capitulation of 1492.

It is only against this background of political manoeuvring that the behaviour of Velázquez towards Grijalva becomes understandable. When the hurricane season was approaching and Grijalva had not returned, Velázquez had become concerned for the expedition's safety and had dispatched Cristóbal de Olid in a caravel to look for it. Olid struck bad weather, was nearly wrecked on the Yucatán coast, and finally returned to Cuba without having caught up with Grijalva. Meantime, Alvarado had arrived in the *San Sebastián* with the wounded and enough gold to excite the cupidity of the least greedy of governors. Velázquez immediately set about organizing another, larger expedition. At the same time, to strengthen his position in Cuba and establish his right to Yucatán, he sent his chaplain, Benito Martín, to Spain with the pick of the gold jewelry Alvarado had brought in.

In order to get himself elected emperor of Germany, Charles had had to buy the twelve Electors. He was desperately short of money, and more than willing to reward the provider of such a fortuitous and unexpected source of wealth. He and his advisers, however, were extremely vague about the geography of the New World, so that the titles tended to be conflicting. Las Casas says that Velázquez was confirmed *adelantado* of Cuba only, whereas Oviedo, who was in Barcelona at the time, says that he was also made governor of all the lands he had discovered. This meant Yucatán; and, to confuse the issue, Garay seems to have been made governor of it also on the grounds that he had sent an expedition there from

*Diego Velázquez, governor of Cuba left;
Santiago, the chief port and capital
of the island right.*

Jamaica. Moreover, there was another claimant – the Flemish admiral to whom Charles had previously granted the territory. He sent over five ships with peasant settlers to found a colony, but by then Diego Columbus had at last been able to re-establish his hereditary rights. He refused to let them proceed.

This was the situation when Grijalva finally came into Santiago. There was nothing more he could add to the extraordinary and fascinating story Alvarado had already told. The welcome that should have been his had already been given to his lieutenant. Even the six hundred 'gold' axes turned out to be made of copper. What Velázquez needed, and needed desperately, to support his claim to the governorship of the mainland, was colonization; and that was the one thing Grijalva had failed to achieve. He was, therefore, of no further use to his kinsman, whose energies were already urgently directed to preparations for the new expedition. He had the ships and the men; all he lacked was the right person to lead it, a man who, even if he had no authority to conquer and settle the country – and the wretched Grijalva had certainly not had that – would, in fact, do so.

From his central position as alcalde, or mayor, of the Cuban capital, Cortés had watched the situation develop with more than usual interest. He had bided his time now for fourteen years, and this was a political mélange which a man of his legal training and latent powers of leadership could turn to advantage. Velázquez, though still politically astute, had grown fat; he was too physically lazy to lead the expedition himself. His strength had always lain in his ability to use other people, and he had never been one to risk his own money if he could persuade others to do it for him. Cortés, too, had been careful, nursing his farms and his mines. He was now thirty-three and quite a rich man. Moreover, by mingling with the leaders and soldiers of each expedition, he had at his disposal a great fund of knowledge and experience, all gained at the expense of others. His hour of destiny had struck.

According to Bernal Díaz, he only held command of the expedition by entering into a secret profit-sharing agreement with Velázquez' secretary, Andrés de Duero, and the king's accountant, Amador de Lares. Whatever the truth of this, his ability as a leader and as a horseman, his shrewdness, above all his wealth, made him a natural choice for the ambitious and thrifty governor. On his appointment as captain-general he was able to mortgage his *encomienda* for 4,000 gold pesos plus a like sum in kind, all borrowed from the merchants of Santiago. By gambling his estate on the success of the venture he not only relieved Velázquez of almost the entire cost of fitting out the fleet, but made it clear that he would press forward with colonization regardless of whether he had legal sanction to do so from the crown. As for his loyalty, this was guaranteed by the fact that he was connected to the governor by marriage through his wife, Catalina; Velázquez was godfather to their daughter.

However, the choice of Cortés, or any other man for that matter, was bound to cause jealousy and split such a small, isolated community into factions. There were at least three of Velázquez' own family who thought they had a claim to the post. Many of those who had served in the last expedition wanted Grijalva as their leader, and Vasco Porcallo also had considerable support. The governor was said to be 'afraid that Porcallo might raise the fleet against him, for he was a daring man'. So, too, was Cortés, a fact which Velázquez was to remember too late.

The agreement between Cortés and Velázquez was signed on October 23, 1518, before Grijalva, or even Olid, had returned from Yucatán. Despite Velázquez' interest in conquest and the establishment of a new colony, no instructions to this effect are specifically given in the document. Exploration and discovery, the conversion of the natives to the Christian faith and their acceptance of Spanish sovereignty – these are the stated objects of the voyage. No carnal intercourse was to be permitted between Spanish soldiers and any woman outside of the Catholic faith. The utmost solemnity was to be observed in taking possession of those parts of the 'island' they discovered. And there was a useful little escape clause that gave Cortés power to take any decision that was in the best interests of God and the king. The Spaniards, particularly the Spanish colonists, were adept at serving their king whilst at the same time looking after their own interests, and because of their strange history it was accepted that, when a man's decisions ran counter to the crown's instructions, he could still claim with the utmost sincerity that it was all done according to the king's will and in his name. As Bernal Díaz puts it, 'the document was drawn in the very best ink'.

That Cortés himself regarded the document as licence to promote his own designs is evident from his subsequent actions. He had two standards and banners 'worked in gold with the royal coat of arms and a cross on each side and a legend that read: ''Brothers and Comrades, let us follow the sign of the Holy Cross in true faith, for under this sign we shall conquer.''' His proclamation, trumpeted throughout Cuba in the name of the Emperor Charles, and also of Velázquez and himself, announced that those who accompanied him to the newly-discovered land 'to conquer and settle' would receive a share of all the gold and silver and other plunder, and also an *encomienda* of Indians once the country was pacified. The glittering stories Alvarado had told brought men flocking to the dangle of this lure. Rich settlers sold their farms to buy arms and horses. The whole of Cuba was in a ferment.

Cortés had purchased a brigantine and two caravels, one of which was the vessel in which Alvarado had returned. Velázquez had provided another brigantine and supplies to the value of 1,000 gold pesos borrowed from the estate of Pánfilo de Narváez, who was absent in Spain. It was Cortés, therefore, not the governor, who was seen to be spending boldly on arms and ammunition, provisions and articles for barter. Having watched so many expeditions sail in high hopes, only to return battered and exhausted, he was determined that this time nothing should be overlooked, least of all the governor. He was constantly in attendance on him, knowing that the Velázquez faction were doing everything possible to undermine his position. They even employed the governor's fool, who interrupted the Sunday church parade to cry, 'Take care, Diego, or he may run off with your fleet.'

In the end this was exactly what Cortés did, for Velázquez, always jealous of his own power and position, began to be alarmed at the thoroughness of his captain-general's preparations and the way all in the island flocked to his standard. Accounts differ, but it seems fairly certain that the rift between them occurred shortly after the signing of the agreement. Cortés, who had a well-developed sense of the dramatic, took pains to dress the part he had been called upon to play, 'wearing a plume of feathers with a medallion and a chain of gold and a velvet cloak trimmed with gold', and going about all the time with a large armed following. In less than a month he had six ships in Santiago harbour, and a complement of some three hundred men. Since Velázquez had ventured little of his own money and only one ship, the anti-Cortés faction had no difficulty in playing upon the governor's fears, particularly as he had alienated Grijalva, who had retired with his own four vessels to Trinidad, a port on the south coast of Cuba.

Cortés, well aware from long experience of the way the Governor's mind worked, rushed his final preparations. Abrupt departure was the only course if he were not to have his appointment revoked before he sailed. On the night of November 17, 1518, he ordered his force to embark, and the following morning he weighed anchor, having stripped the town's slaughter house of all its meat and said goodbye to Velázquez from an armed boat full of his most trusted men.

Though he had left Santiago, Cortés did not yet regard the expedition as complete. He sailed first to Trinidad, where he lodged with Grijalva, and by liberal promises and ten days' frantic efforts, enlisted about two hundred of the soldiers who had so recently returned from Yucatán. He also gathered to his standard some of his greatest captains – Montejo, Sandoval, four of the Alvarado brothers, including the dashing Pedro, Juan Velázquez de León, and Alonso Hernández Puertocarrero, who was to become his closest confidant. He even persuaded Grijalva to let him have his own four ships, and Ordaz 'captured' another one for him loaded with provisions and belonging to a rich merchant, Juan Núñez Sedeño, who was prevailed upon to join the expedition.

Meanwhile Velázquez, now thoroughly alarmed, had sent two messengers to Ordaz, who was one of his own following, with orders for Verdugo, the alcalde of Trinidad, to arrest Cortés. Ordaz himself seems to have persuaded Verdugo to ignore the order, and Cortés even enlisted one of the messengers into his service, while sending the other back with the customary assurance that all would be done according to the king's wishes. The stranding of Cortés' own ship gave Velázquez one more opportunity to stop him. His captain-general marched overland to San Cristóbal de la Havana in search of provisions, but all the governor's lieutenant in that town could do was report that he 'dared not arrest Cortés because he was very strong with soldiers'. Attempts to foster disaffection in the fleet and have

Ordaz take command also failed, Cortés resorting to the simple expedient of dispatching Ordaz on a foraging expedition. The result of all this was a deep rift between the governor and his captain-general, a rift that inevitably had repercussions later.

When Cortés finally sailed on February 10, 1519, he had eleven ships of seventy to a hundred tons, five hundred and eight soldiers and about a hundred sailors, also two hundred Cubans, several negroes, some Indian women and, most important of all, sixteen horses and mares. He took no chances, ordering all the ships to rendezvous off Cape San Antón and proceed in company to the island of Cozumel. Why he should have chosen to sail to Cozumel, which meant he would later have to round Cape Catoche in the teeth of the prevailing northerlies, is nowhere stated, but this was the route Grijalva had followed, and no doubt he wanted to test the mood of the mainland Indians at the point where he had an island base to fall back on. In any case, to sail direct to San Juan de Ulúa would have meant taking his still undisciplined force on a much longer voyage, one which would give him the mangrove swamps of Yucatán as a dangerous lee shore.

From the outset Cortés' behaviour was quite different from that of any other expedition leader. Almost his first action on arriving at Cozumel was to clap Camacho, the pilot of Pedro de Alvarado's vessel, in irons for disobeying orders and going on ahead without waiting for the rest of the fleet. And he ordered Alvarado's men, who had plundered an Indian village, to hand back their loot. The villagers were given a present of beads and instructed to request the cacique of the neighbouring town to visit the camp. An inspection was held, guns, muskets, and crossbows overhauled, the men given target practice, the horses exercised.

The fleet did not sail again until March 4. By then Cortés had welded his men into the beginnings of a disciplined force. He had traded and talked with the natives, and since Cozumel was a place of pilgrimage and caciques came from many of the towns of Yucatán to worship its idols, by the time he sailed he had learned a great deal at first hand about the country. The fact that he had overthrown the idols and set up a cross in their place would, he knew, be reported and commented on. His was a cold-war policy, designed to soften up the opposition, and he allowed plenty of time for it to work upon the minds of the natives.

Whilst at Cozumel, he recruited a Spaniard named Aguilar, who had been wrecked with fifteen others eight years before on a voyage from Darién to Santo Domingo. Aguilar was a useful acquisition for he had been a slave to the Indians and spoke the Tabascan tongue, and it was to Aguilar that Cortés was supposed to have made a particularly revealing comment: the ex-slave had offered to lead him to a place where there was some gold, but Cortés said he was not after such small gain – he was there to serve God and the king. By which, of course, he meant that he was only interested in conquest.

Keeping a fleet of eleven ships together on a low coast littered with uncharted shallows, where the north wind could suddenly blow gale force, must have been a nightmare. Even rounding Catoche, Cortés twice had to put back with his whole fleet to pick up a stray. And all the time he probed the inlets, checking on Grijalva's discoveries, breaking new ground of his own. Boca de Términos seemed a possible port for a settlement, and Escobar, the captain of a fast, shallow draft vessel, was sent ahead to explore. He found the country fertile and full of game. He also found a greyhound bitch left by Grijalva's men, or possibly Córdoba's. She was sleek and fat and came down to the shore wagging her tail at the sight of the ship. But when Cortés and the rest of the fleet arrived off the entrance there was no sign of Escobar. A strong southerly wind had carried his vessel far out to sea, and by the time they had caught up with him, they had been blown back up the coast to a point almost opposite Champotón, where both Córdoba and Grijalva had suffered such heavy casualties.

Bernal Díaz is probably right in saying that Cortés wanted to put in here and teach these warlike Indians a lesson. Such an action would have been good policy, but navigationally the place was dangerous; the river was too shallow for the ships to enter, and they would have to lie anything up to six miles off-shore on account of the Champotón Banks where the prevailing wind builds up a very big tide. In any case, the wind was fair now for continuing along the coast, and the safer anchorage off the Grijalva river was only three days' sailing away.

They reached it on March 12, the larger ships anchoring off at sea as before, the smaller vessels, filled with soldiers, moving into the shelter of what is now called Isla Ballitzia. Here, in calmer water, they transferred to the boats and rowed up-river to land on the same headland covered with palm trees where Grijalva's expedition had gone ashore. They were then about a mile from the Indian town of Potonchán, later called Tabasco after the cacique of that region. But the Tabascans, who had been friendly to Grijalva and had given him gold, were now hostile. The river bank and the mangrove swamps were crowded with armed warriors, many in their canoes, and there were some twelve thousand more assembled in the town of Tabasco itself. Cortés sent Aguilar in to try and persuade the Indians to let his men land for water and to trade for food, but they had been so taunted by the people of Champotón for their failure to fight off Grijalva's men that they were determined to prevent a landing.

So we come to the first of the many battles Cortés' small force was to fight. On the morning of March 13 mass was said and the men embarked in the boats. Ávila was sent with a hundred men to attack the town, whilst Cortés and the rest forced the estuary. The canoes came out to meet them, and again Cortés stopped to parley, appealing through Aguilar to be allowed to trade peacefully, speaking of God and the king he served, and making certain that Diego de Godoy, the Royal Notary, recorded his peaceful overtures. But it was no good, and when they tried to land, they were met by showers of fire-hardened arrows. The battle cry of Santiago was answered by Indian war cries of *Al calachioni*, which was an incitement to kill Cortés himself. But the fire power and sword play of the Spaniards gradually prevailed, and with the town finally taken, Cortés halted his men in a great courtyard where there were large halls and three idol-houses. Here, with his soldiers and the Royal Notary to witness the act, he took formal possession of the land in the king's name.

Fourteen Spanish soldiers had been wounded in this little skirmish, but throughout the campaign that was now just beginning the conquistadors seem to have regarded wounds as little more than a temporary inconvenience. Only the dead were casualties. The rest marched and fought, and if they didn't die their wounds healed.

It was here at Tabasco that Melchior, an Indian interpreter, defected. Encouraged by him, the Indians launched a large-scale attack on the Spanish beach-head. But by now Cortés had got his horses ashore. They were stiff and almost scared to move after being confined on board ship for so long. Nevertheless, they were fitted with their steel breastplates all jangling with bells, and the knights put on their steel armour and equipped themselves with lances. This small cavalry force was the most potent weapon Cortés possessed, the sixteenth-century equivalent of an armoured squadron, since the trained horse was unknown to the Indians. The Spaniards were outnumbered three hundred to one, arrows and sling-stones fell like hail, and when Mesa, the artillery man, fired his guns, the Indians threw dirt and straw into the air to hide the havoc they wreaked. 'In this battle there were so many Indians to every one of us that the dust they made would have blinded us, had not God of his unfailing mercy come to our aid.' There is nothing sententious about this. The Spaniards were still fighting a crusade, believing implicitly that they were soldiers of Christ and that God was on their side.

Five Indians were captured, including two of their war chiefs. These Cortés released and sent back into the town with gifts to explain to their caciques that he came in peace. He knew by now that the mainland Indians were far too numerous to be conquered by force. Each Spaniard who died, each horse that fell, was an absolute and total loss that he could not replace. Diplomacy – the mailed fist in the velvet glove – was the only key to conquest; he was the first commander of an expedition in the Indies to appreciate this, and his nature and training were such that he was able to carry it through. Guile was something the Indians understood; it was a part of their nature, also. They sent some slaves in ragged cloaks and blackened faces and a small gift of food, but Aguilar already understood the way his leader's mind worked, and he sent them back with a demand that the caciques themselves come with a proper gift. They came the following morning with fowls, fish, fruit and maize-cakes, and the request that they be allowed to bury their dead before the hot sun made them smell or the jaguars ate them. They had lost some eight hundred killed. Cortés took the opportunity to stage a demonstration.

There were thirty caciques in all, and he received them at midday outside his tent. It was very still and hot, the air heavy with the smell of the copal the Indians

*On landing in Mexico, Cortés set about building the settlement of Vera Cruz.
(See p. 68.) A seventeenth-century Spanish painting.*

6
Hacese la Villa
Rica, Por manda-
do de Cortes á que
aiudan los Yndi-
os Totonaques.

had burned when incensing the assembled Spaniards. A mare that had just foaled was hidden away behind the place where the caciques stood, and after Cortés had upbraided them with a great show of anger and informed them they were vassals of the mighty Emperor Charles, he gave the signal and the largest cannon was fired close beside them. The randiest stallion in the fleet was brought up and, catching the scent of the mare, stood pawing the ground and neighing, his eyes rolling wildly as he stared straight at the Indians.

It was all very childish, very theatrical; but it was nevertheless a most effective demonstration of power, with his men all about him, rank on rank and armed, and the ships riding off the land. The caciques were terrified. The result was peace and a plentiful supply of food. But Cortés was not thinking of the local gain. He knew they had a system of picture-writing and that all he did and said on the coast was being reported by this means; in pictures the scene he had set would be most effective. Cold war propaganda, in fact, and in the circumstances then ruling – about which he had no inkling at the time – it was to prove quite deadly.

It was typical of Cortés' colonizing methods that his first order to the caciques was to bring all the people back into the town as a sign of peace. This gesture, and the atmosphere of normality it produced, was essential to his purpose. He ordered them also to abandon their idols. This again was policy as much as proselytizing, since the destruction of these symbols of their inherited faith struck at the roots of their confidence. He showed them a picture of the Virgin and Child, and in absolute submission they asked for it to be given them to keep. As always, he stage-managed the business so that the request came from them, and he then had an altar erected and a great cross set up. Examining them and learning the reasons for their hostility, that they had been pushed into battle by the cacique of the Champotóns, he demanded that the man be brought before him. Their reply was startling: he had already been sacrificed for giving them such bad advice! Next day the town was renamed Santa María de la Victoria, the cross set up and Fray Bartolomé de Olmedo, the expedition's chaplain, said mass before all the important people of the town and then baptized them.

Cortés had not neglected the financial side of the expedition. But each time he demanded a gift of gold and jewels he was answered by the words 'Culhúa' and 'México'. They meant nothing to him then. He was, however, given a present of twenty women, and bearing in mind the instructions about his men not cohabiting with heathens, he had them all baptized and distributed them among his captains. He did not realize it at the time, but this gift of women was of far greater value to him than gold, for it included one who was 'a great lady and a cacique over towns and vassals since her childhood'. She was christened Marina, and because of her high birth, she is always referred to as Doña Marina. Since she was good-looking and a princess, Cortés gave her to his friend Alonso Hernández Puerto-carrero. Throughout the campaign Cortés strictly adhered to the letter of his instructions regarding cohabitation with native women. They must first be

Incidents in the early stages of Cortés' march. (A) *The Spaniards sink their ships;* (B) *they set out;* (C) *sandstorms;* (D) *Indian priests and their idols;* (E) *a skirmish with Indians;* (F) *who make peace with the Spaniards;* (G) *and serve them a meal;* (H) *some Indians are baptized;* (I) *but spies have their hands cut off;* (J) *the Spaniards are reduced to eating dog flesh. A seventeenth-century Spanish painting.*

baptized and they then acquired the status of *barragana*, a peculiarly Spanish institution that amounted to legal concubinage. Thus Doña Marina became Puertocarrero's wife in the eyes of all but the Church. This energetic and intelligent woman, who quickly learned Spanish, was to have a remarkable influence on the Conquest, for she spoke Náhuatl, which was the language of the Aztecs of both Culhúa and Mexico. Aguilar only spoke Tabascan, so that as the expedition marched inland, she soon replaced him as the 'tongue' of Cortés.

The fleet sailed on the Monday before Easter, and four days later it arrived at San Juan de Ulúa, where Alaminos anchored the ships close under the island safe from northerly gales. Two pirogues put out from the shore and made straight for the flagship. To the Indians the scene must have been utterly fantastic: the great high-sterned carracks riding in the quiet waters that, except for Grijalva's visit, had remained empty down the centuries, and, in the centre, Cortés' ship with the royal standard and pennants streaming in the sunlight.

From these Indians Cortés heard for the first time the dread name of Moctezuma.* Their lord, they said, was a servant of this great king and he had sent them to discover the purpose of their visit and to supply whatever they needed. Unlike the Tabascans they came in peace, which augured well, though Cortés must have been aware that this embassy was concerned less with establishing friendly relations than with probing the strength of the invading force.

By Good Friday the Spaniards were all ashore with their horses and guns. Having set up an altar, mass was said in the blistering heat of the sand dunes, and after that they set to work cutting wood and establishing a hutted camp. On the Saturday, they had the assistance of large numbers of Indians, who came into the camp with a gift of provisions – fowls, maize-cakes, plums which were then in season – and also some gold jewels. They had been sent by Cuitlalpitoc, who governed the province for Moctezuma and was the same man who had visited Grijalva the year before. He and Teudilli, another of Moctezuma's officials, came into the camp on Easter Sunday with more gifts of food, including this time vegetables. In those days scurvy was regarded as an infectious disease, rather like the plague or leprosy. Thousands of sailors were to die in agony during the next

*See author's note, page 321.

two hundred and fifty years because of a vitamin C deficiency in their diet, but in Mexico fruit and vegetables were always available, so this was one hazard with which Cortés and his men did not have to contend.

Since it was Easter Sunday, Fray Bartolomé, assisted by the padre, Juan Díaz, chanted mass whilst the Indians looked on in amazement. Afterwards Cuitlalpitoc and Teudilli dined with Cortés and his captains. Since they were Mexicans, and Aguilar did not then understand the Náhuatl language, Doña Marina was brought in to act as interpreter. It was a clumsy arrangement, Aguilar interpreting into Tabascan and Doña Marina from Tabascan to Náhuatl. But by the end of the meal Cortés had learned that Moctezuma was not only lord of the great city of Mexico-Tenochtitlan, but also supreme overlord of Culhúa, a confederacy of city-states that lay several days' march beyond the mountains, and that his power stretched right down the coast, his warriors having within recent years conquered the area of San Juan de Ulúa.

This information, almost certainly supported by some indication of the enormous number of warriors that could be mobilized against him, confirmed Cortés' earlier estimate of the situation – that he could only dominate the interior with the co-operation of Moctezuma. In other words, he would have to rely on a cold-war battle of wits rather than force of arms. He started to work on the minds of the two Mexicans immediately, trying to explain Christianity and talking to them of the greatness of the emperor he served. His object was to impress upon them the desirability of an early meeting between himself and Moctezuma. The reply was evasive, but as evidence of goodwill Teudilli produced a chest full of golden objects and also ten bales of cloth worked with brilliant feathers. These were gifts from Moctezuma himself. Large quantities of food were also produced – fowls, fruit and baked fish. It meant peace, for the time being at any rate.

It was better than fighting, but it didn't satisfy Cortés, since the object of the expedition was not advanced. However, the two governors had brought with them a number of picture-writers, who were busy all the time drawing on cloth the ships, the cannon, the details of the religious ceremony, even portraits of Cortés and his captains. It was a further opportunity for an effective demonstration of power. Cortés had the cannon loaded with extra heavy charges and fired them under the noses of the Mexicans; all the horses were paraded with bells on their

The Indians sight the Spanish ships. From a sixteenth-century drawing by a Mexican artist far left. On coming ashore Doña Marina acted as interpreter for Cortés left. Overleaf The Spaniards impressed the Indians by firing their cannon and galloping their horses on the beach. A seventeenth-century Spanish painting.

VERA(

breastplates, and Alvarado galloped his small cavalry force furiously along the hard sand at the sea's edge. The painter-scribes recorded it all.

Then an odd thing happened. Teudilli noticed one of the soldiers wearing a gilded and rather rusty helmet, asked to see it, and, having examined it, said he would like to show it to his master, the great Moctezuma. Cortés hinted that his emperor would be pleased to accept the helmet back filled with nuggets or grains of gold; his object in making this request was to check on the quality of their gold and the way in which they obtained it.

He got the helmet back seven days later, filled to the brim with mined gold, small grains of high quality worth 3,000 pesos. Teudilli brought it himself, having in the space of a week made the journey to Mexico-Tenochtitlan, reported to his master, and then journeyed back to the coast accompanied by a Mexican prince named Quintalbor and a hundred Indians carrying yet more gifts. This was the biggest haul of the voyage, and Quintalbor, who had been specially chosen by Moctezuma's priests because he resembled Cortés in appearance, presented the gift to him after all the Indians had first kissed the ground and their priests had perfumed the Spaniards with incense.

Here for the first time the word *teules* was used. *Teules* means gods. The earthen braziers pouring forth incense were a part of the ceremony of worship used at the teocalli. So, too, was the prostration and kissing of the earth. But Cortés, though he was learning fast, was more interested in hearing about Moctezuma's power and military dispositions than his superstitious beliefs. Had he, or his Indian 'tongue', Doña Marina, appreciated the significance of the helmet and the behaviour of Moctezuma's embassy, he would have been at pains to act the role to which the Mexican prince had assigned him.

At that moment, however, his main interest was in the unusual value of the gifts now spread out before him on *petates*, or mats, covered with cotton cloth. Two items immediately held the eyes of every Spaniard. A golden disc, shaped like the sun, 'as big as a cartwheel . . . a marvellous thing engraved with many sorts of figures' and another similar disc of engraved silver representing the moon. The sun and the moon, both about ten hand-spans in diameter, and the helmet full of gold were probably worth more than 20,000 gold pesos, but there was much else besides – twenty golden ducks, ornaments in the shape of dogs, others like pumas or jaguars and monkeys, ten necklaces, pendants, twelve arrows and a strung bow, and two rods 'like staffs of justice 20 inches long'. All these were finely worked in gold. There were crests of silver and gold with plumes of green feathers, fans, models of deer, and thirty loads of the finest cotton cloth patterned and decorated with many-coloured feathers. It was, in fact, a farewell present, for when Cortés asked again about a meeting between himself and Moctezuma, he was told it was out of the question.

By then he knew enough about the power of Mexico and its allies to realize that he had no hope of advancing into Culhúan territory by force. He had sensed that

Moctezuma was afraid of something; the behaviour of the Indians and the value of the gifts made that clear. But he probably thought it was due to the ships, the cannon and the horses; at any rate he persisted in his request for a meeting, since it was only through diplomacy, through flattery and guile and the threat of a power unknown, that he could see any hope of gaining a permanent foothold on the mainland. The governors were emphatic that his request was pointless since Moctezuma had already refused to see him, but in the end they agreed to return to their master for further instructions. They left with various gifts for their king, including a Florentine glass cup 'engraved with trees and hunting scenes and finely gilded'.

It was whilst the Spaniards were waiting for the result of this further embassy that Cortés sent Francisco de Montejo with two ships to reconnoitre the coast to the north. Montejo got as far as the area of the Pánuco river, where the modern oil port of Tampico now stands, about fifty miles further north than Grijalva had reached. Here he was halted by the strength of the adverse current. The only important information Montejo brought back was news of a town called Quiahuitztlan, thirty-six miles up the coast from San Juan de Ulúa. He described it as a fortified port, and since the harbour, which Alaminos, the pilot, thought might give shelter from the northerly winds, was the mouth of the San Juan river, it must have been about where the dusty little timber and thatch village of La Antigua now stands in its clearing amongst the trees.

The voyage had taken a fortnight, possibly more. Meantime, the main Spanish force, camped in the sultry heat of the sand dunes, plagued with mosquitoes, was getting short of food. The Indians coming to barter became fewer and more fearful. The cassava bread they had brought with them was sour and rotten with weevils. By the time Teudilli returned from Mexico they were reduced to eating the shellfish off the shore. He brought more presents, including a further 3,000 pesos' worth of gold, but that was all. Moctezuma flatly refused to see Cortés.

There now followed one of those religious interludes that makes the history of the conquistadors so bizarre. The bell was sounding through the camp for Ave Maria, and once again the Indian governors saw the whole Spanish force go down on their knees to pray before the cross they had erected on top of one of the dunes. To men accustomed to the bloody rites of human sacrifice and ritual cannibalism, this pacific, even humble behaviour must have presented an extraordinary spectacle. Afterwards, in answer to their questions, Cortés again spoke to them of Christ and his teachings, and then informed them that the great emperor he served had sent him to destroy their idols and abolish their sacrificial customs. A theological discussion through an interpreter is never very satisfactory, and it is probable that they went away more confused than ever as to the exact nature of the Spaniards and their intentions, particularly as almost immediately afterwards the soldiers began bartering for small objects of gold.

After that the Indians ceased coming to the camp altogether. Moctezuma had

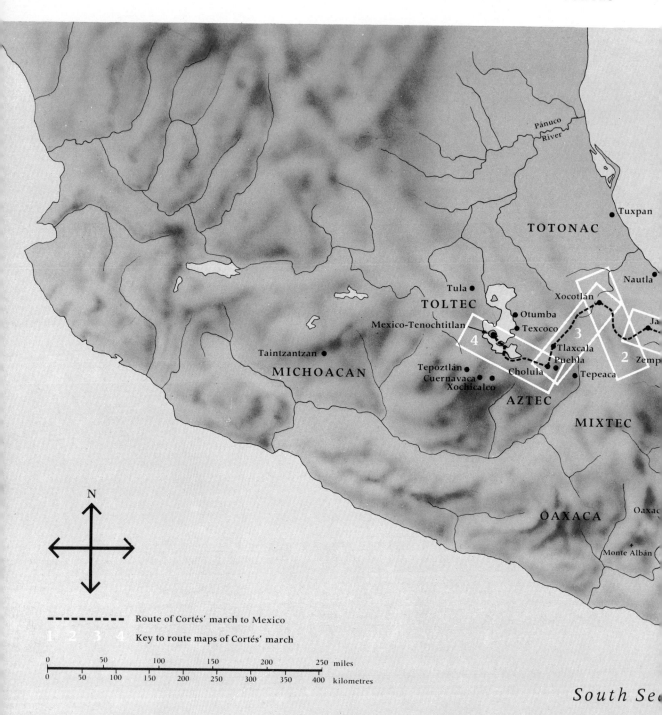

Pánuco
River

TOTONAC

Tuxpan

Nautla

Tula

TOLTEC

Xocotlán

Mexico-Tenochtitlan

Otumba

Texcoco

Ja

Taintzantzan

4

3

MICHOACAN

Tepoztlán
Cuernavaca
Xochicalco

Tlaxcala
Puebla

2

Zemp

Cholula

Tepeaca

AZTEC

MIXTEC

OAXACA

Oaxac

Monte Albán

N

- - - - - - - - Route of Cortés' march to Mexico

1 2 3 4   Key to route maps of Cortés' march

0   50   100   150   200   250 miles
0   50   100   150   200   250   300   350   400 kilometres

South Se

Mexico at the time of the Conquest, showing the areas of earlier civilizations.

Gulf of Mexico

Chichén Itzá ●

MAYA

Quiahuitzlan
Vera Cruz
San Juan de Ulúa
Is. de Sacrificios

OLMEC

TABASCAN

ZAPOTEC

Tehuantepec ●

(Pacific Ocean)

also decided on a war of nerves. The Spaniards waited in the sand dunes, uncertain, nervous and short of food, conscious of a growing atmosphere of hostility. The heat and the sense of insecurity inevitably fostered the dissension that had never been wholly suppressed. They had a small fortune in gold and other gifts, more than any other previous expedition had got; and those with farms and wives back in Cuba were increasingly clamorous to take what they had and get back home.

It was at this point that they were visited by five Indians of the Totonac tribe. They came from the town of Zempoala and had great holes in their lower lips and in their ears, in which were round stone discs and sheets of gold. They said they had not dared to enter the camp whilst the people of Culhúa were there, but now that they were gone, they wished to see for themselves the men who had defeated the people of Tabasco and Champotón. They were, in fact, spies endeavouring to assess the potentialities of the Spaniards as allies against the Mexicans. It was the first intimation Cortés had that the recently conquered tribes of the coast were restless under Moctezuma's rule. He gave them presents and sent them off with a message to their cacique that he would shortly pay him a visit.

On this expedition he took with him most of his force, for he knew very well that inactivity was at the root of a lot of the trouble in the camp. A brief march of three leagues* took them out of the dune country, away from the mosquito-ridden swamps, and into rich maize country, a sort of savannah that stretched inland for miles, almost flat, but steadily rising towards the distant mountains. Beyond the San Juan river they came to a storehouse of adobe and timber with many rooms filled with honey and maize, also cotton garments decorated with feathers and gold. There were other houses, a dusty huddle of adobe and thatch, and Cortés had his crier make it known that any man found looting would be summarily executed. He was anxious to demonstrate his peaceful intentions to these Indians who might provide him with the support he desperately needed.

There was a temple here, described by Gómara as resembling a house with a low but massive tower topped by a sort of chapel containing several large idols. Access to this chapel was by twenty steps, and here they found many pieces of paper soaked in blood and a block on which human victims were stretched. There were also flint knives with which the breasts of sacrificial victims were sliced open to get at their hearts. The whole place was spattered with blood. They visited several other villages, none of them bigger than two hundred houses, all abandoned, 'but full of provisions and blood like the first'.

Since accounts vary slightly at this point, it is probable that Cortés himself was undecided what best to do. He had hoped to recruit Indian irregulars, but all he had found was abandoned villages. It was as bitter a disappointment as Moctezuma's refusal to meet him. He returned to the camp, determined to move north to

---

*A Spanish league is in theory 1/25th of a degree of latitude – i.e. about 2·6 miles. Seven leagues was generally regarded as a day's march on horseback.

Quiahuitztlan and moor his ships in the curve of the San Juan river's mud banks, where the thick tree growth would give absolute shelter from any gales. His camp, too, would be sheltered and clear of the swarms of mosquitoes that bred in the swamps beyond the dunes.

But the Velázquez faction was now open in its opposition, backed by all those who already had a stake in Cuba. Only the have-nots, the true soldiers of fortune, were prepared to go on and face the unknown. Most of these had been amongst the four hundred who had reconnoitred northwards with him. Through his most loyal captains – men like Puertocarrero, the Alvarados, Olid, Lugo, Ávila and Escalante – he appears to have indoctrinated the rank and file with all his own arguments for not abandoning the beach-head they had gained, and also with the idea of founding a settlement, complete with its *alcaldes* and *regidores*, or aldermen – a complete town council, in fact, which, once constituted, would have the right to elect its own *Capitán* and *Justicia Mayor*. Thus Cortés manoeuvred himself into the position of bowing to the wishes of his men. The settlement – the first in New Spain – was named Villa Rica de la Vera Cruz (the Rich Town of the True Cross), because of the richness of the interior and the fact that they had landed on that particular stretch of the coast on Good Friday.

By this simple expedient Cortés immeasurably strengthened his own position. It was rather like forming a private company, for once it was properly constituted, by the desire and will of all the people present, the settlement assumed an entity of its own, with all the legal rights of a Spanish town – the right to elect men to govern, to issue orders, draft laws, and, most important of all, to deal direct with the Spanish crown. In short, it assumed at once an existence quite separate from the expedition sent out by Diego Velázquez, governor of Cuba. And Cortés, as its elected Captain and Chief Justice, was vested with the powers that stemmed from the town itself and not from his appointment to the command of an expedition. It was a shrewd move that only a man trained in law and civic affairs would have thought of. Henceforth he was perfectly entitled to by-pass Velázquez and deal direct with Spain. In addition, his men gave him a 20 per cent share of all gold obtained after deduction of the king's fifth. This he had insisted upon, for power without the means to support it is like a building without foundations.

The change in Cortés' position is characteristically and immediately reflected in action. As alcaldes, he appointed Puertocarrero and Velázquez' friend, Montejo. Those others of the Velázquez faction he could not win over he seized and clapped in irons. Later he released them, of course, since men in irons were of no use to him. Meantime, the disaffected rank and file, about a hundred in all, he sent inland on a foraging expedition under the command of Pedro de Alvarado. All they found were deserted villages and teocalli where the bodies of recently sacrificed men and boys still lay with their arms and legs torn off. Walls and altars were splashed with their blood, and their hearts lay before the idols. Alvarado brought back provisions, chiefly maize; but the fact that every village had been abandoned on the day of his arrival left little doubt in Cortés' mind that the Indians were now hostile. He decided, therefore, to move his camp to Quiahuitztlan, where he hoped the Totonac Indians would be more friendly. It was an important decision, for it not only set the actual location for the original settlement of Vera Cruz, but at the Totonac town of Zempoala, which was on his line of march up the coast, he found the key that was to unlock for him the gates of Mexico.

Zempoala was vastly different from the sand dunes in which they had been living for weeks, 'all gardens and greenery and well-watered orchards'. It was the largest Indian habitation they had seen during the whole voyage: a city, in fact, its streets packed with people come to see them march in; and the courtyard where they were lodged had walls newly lime-washed and burnished white as silver.

Zempoala is now only a village, its streets dusty tracks, its houses little more than shacks, but the ruins of the great square can still be seen. The polished plaster that gleamed like silver has long since crumbled to dust, but the water-worn stones taken from the river beds still remain as facings to the main buildings. The pyramids, platforms and walls have been excavated and partly reconditioned so that, standing on top of the great pyramid looking out over the flat country that runs east to the coast, west to the snow-capped bulk of Orizaba and the hazy line of the mountains, one can understand how Cortés and all his Spaniards must have felt. Beyond those mountains lay the greater Aztec cities, and here in Zempoala they were being given a foretaste of the power and grandeur of Aztec architecture. Even today, though half overgrown with grass, it is immensely impressive. To the north stands the great pyramid, the tiers of its bulk rising like terraces, the steps to the top like a great stone ladder; to the east a temple of unusual design with pillars – they now look like a series of chimneys – that once supported a roof, presumably of palm-thatch; and further to the east, outside the area of the courtyard, another temple with jutting faces of stone and the walls inside adorned with frescoes. Some distance away, in the town itself, is an older, probably pre-Aztec temple, the steps in front broken by side-facing steps and the rear of it a blank half-circle wall of stones, so that from that angle it looks something like a Pictish *broch*. This place was dedicated to the worship of Quetzalcoatl.

The cacique of Zempoala met Cortés and his captains in their lodgings. All around them was the life and bustle of a big Indian city, the whole place with its trees and gardens dominated by the shining magnificence of its public and ceremonial buildings, the gypsum plaster facings bright and glittering in the sultry sunlight, the air sleepy with the humidity of the coast. The cacique himself was a very friendly, very fat man, and he had with him a retinue of Indian chiefs, all with large gold lip rings and rich cloaks, and offering bouquets of roses.

After the Spaniards had been given food, the fat cacique brought a small present of gold jewelry, called Cortés 'lord of great lords', and began a long and bitter diatribe against Moctezuma, describing his great power and how every year their sons were taken for sacrifice, the pick of their wives and daughters raped by

Mexican tax-gatherers, all their golden jewelry requisitioned. This was sweet music to Cortés' ear. He did his best to fan the flames of latent revolt by describing the great power of the emperor king beyond the sea, and explaining how he had come to overthrow their idols and stop the senseless sacrifice of their people.

Next day the Spaniards marched back down the river with its lush growth of maize and fruit, crossed the flat savannah land of dry gravel and sand to the next river, the Santa María, and, after fifteen miles, a good day's march, came to its junction with the San Juan. They took the Indian fortress of Quiahuitztlan without a fight. The inhabitants had fled, and when the Spaniards got to the top of the fortress, 'to the square on which their temples and their great idol-houses stood', they were met by nothing more daunting than fifteen priests who welcomed them with incense and explained that the people had been frightened by their appearance and that of the horses. Cortés had barely established himself when the cacique arrived from Zempoala in a litter. A further conference followed, the cacique obviously toying with the idea of rebellion, but needing constant reassurance of Spanish power. Suddenly messengers burst in with the news that five of Moctezuma's tax-gatherers had arrived. The effect of this upon the guilty consciences of the Totonacs was one of sheer panic.

Bernal Díaz' graphic description of the entrance of the tax-gatherers into the main square illustrates the haughty confidence of Moctezuma's representatives. Faced with the full power of the Spanish invaders, whom they had never seen before, they nevertheless passed by Cortés and the rest without a word, each one smelling at the roses he carried. They were dressed in loin-cloths with richly-embroidered cloaks, their hair shining and tied close to their heads. They behaved with 'cocksure pride', but it was nevertheless an impressive performance. They were taken to lodgings that had been hastily decorated with flowers, and after a meal that included chocolate to drink, they sent for the fat cacique and the rest of the Totonac chiefs and upbraided them for entertaining the Spaniards.

The situation was one of unparalleled opportunity, and Cortés was quick to seize it. Chance had put into his hands the means of re-opening his duologue with Moctezuma. The Totonac chiefs were by now thoroughly frightened. Cortés offered them a way out: arrest the tax-gatherers and cease paying tribute to Moctezuma. The physical presence of the Spaniards was undoubtedly the decisive

The ruins of Zempoala today.

factor, and Cortés' advice was acted upon immediately, the tax-gatherers being secured with long poles fitted with collars. The intention was to silence them for ever by sacrificing them; but Cortés had other plans. His object now was to involve the coastal Indians so deeply that they would never dare to break faith with him. Already he had instructed the cacique to send messengers through all the towns of the district, including those of Zempoala's allies, to spread the news of what had happened and to announce that they no longer owed obedience to Moctezuma. He insisted that the prisoners be kept alive. That night he managed to arrange for two of them to escape. They were brought to him, and after giving them food and saying how much he deplored the treatment they had received at the hands of the Totonacs, he sent them on their way with orders that they should tell Moctezuma how he had befriended them, and that he only wanted to be of service to their master, whom he was most anxious to meet.

It was trickery of the most cold-blooded kind. In the morning Cortés pretended to be furious at the prisoners' escape. He had the three remaining Mexicans bound in chains and taken for greater security on board one of his ships, which were now anchored in the river. Here he promptly released them. Meantime, he told the caciques that they and all their people must obey his orders and join forces with him against Moctezuma. The poor devils were now so committed that there was no turning back, and in the presence of the Royal Notary they took the oath of allegiance and became legal vassals of the Spanish crown.

Cortés now had the whole district, which amounted to some twenty towns, with him to a man. To consolidate his position he started work immediately on the construction of his settlement. The site he chose was on the flat land beside the river about a mile and a half from Quiahuitztlan. He worked at carrying earth and stone and the digging of the foundations himself; and, following his example, his captains worked alongside the soldiers. Vera Cruz was planned with a church, a plaza, arsenals, watch towers, barbicans – it was, in fact, a typical Spanish fortress town, and with the aid of the Indians the major part of it was completed in a very short time.

It was whilst they were still building Vera Cruz that an embassy arrived from Mexico with presents of gold and cloth. It was an important embassy, including two nephews of Moctezuma, and to Cortés it was the first indication that his policy of driving a wedge between the Mexicans and the people they had conquered was having the desired effect. To the accusation that the Spaniards had fostered rebellion, Cortés loftily replied that the Totonacs were now vassals of the Emperor Charles and could not be expected to serve two masters. He added that he and his captains were now on their way to visit Moctezuma and place themselves at his service. As evidence of good faith he then produced the three tax-gatherers, well dressed and well fed, and after Alvarado had given a display of Spanish horsemanship, the ambassadors left for Mexico with the released prisoners and a gift of coloured beads.

Though Cortés had said he was on his way to visit Moctezuma, he was still far from ready for such a dangerous expedition. He needed allies. He needed also the support and authority of his king for what he was doing. In addition, there was the persistent problem of dissension in his own ranks; seven soldiers had already tried to desert in a stolen boat.

When he heard that the Culhúans were attacking the town of Cingapacinga twenty-five miles away, Cortés marched at once with his entire force, supported by two thousand Totonac warriors. But the Zempoalans had lied. There was a feud between Zempoala and Cingapacinga, and they were simply using the Spaniards as a front for looting. Cortés was furious. He made them hand back all they had stolen, and having thus ingratiated himself with the Cingapacingans, he lectured them on the true faith and had them swear allegiance to the Spanish crown.

On the way back one of his own soldiers was caught looting. He had him strung up as a lesson to the others, for if his men looted he knew he would lose the support of the Indians, and that would mean ultimate disaster. But he could ill afford even the loss of a single Spanish soldier and he was probably relieved when Alvarado, of his own accord, cut the fool down just before he choked to death.

Cortés' anger at the behaviour of the Zempoalans seems to have seriously alarmed them, for on his return to the city he was presented with eight girls, each with a golden collar round her neck and gold ear-rings. They were the daughters of chiefs, and they were offered in the usual Indian fashion to cement the alliance by bearing his captains children. The time had come for Cortés to destroy their last link with Mexico. He said that if they accepted the girls they would become the Indians' blood-brothers, and this they could not do unless the girls became Christians and the Indians ceased sacrificing human beings and gave up sodomy. At that time they were regularly sacrificing anything up to five humans a day, offering up their hearts to the idols and eating the arms and legs. They also had boy prostitutes dressed as girls.

The Indians at once became extremely menacing, prepared to defend their idols and their beliefs. But when Cortés threatened to abandon them to the wrath of Moctezuma, official opposition suddenly collapsed and most of the people stood apathetically by whilst some fifty Spanish soldiers threw the idols down the steps of the temples. But at the sight of this desecration some of the warriors would have attacked if Cortés had not seized the cacique and half a dozen of the priests, threatening them with death if a single arrow was loosed. Finally, on the instructions of the cacique, the priests in charge of the temples took the broken idols away and burned them. The description of these priests is quite horrific: 'They wore black cloaks like those of canons, and other smaller hoods like Dominicans. They wore their hair very long, down to their waists, and some even down to their feet, and it was all so clotted and matted with blood that it could not be pulled apart. Their ears were cut to pieces as a sacrifice and they smelt of sulphur. But they also smelt of something worse – of decaying flesh.' These priests were unmarried, but practised sodomy.

Next day, when the whole place had been cleaned and the walls white-washed, an altar was set up and four of the priests, their hair washed and cut and with clean white robes, were put in charge of it. They were shown how to make candles from a local wax and ordered to keep them burning before the image of the Virgin and the Holy Cross. It was religious showmanship, but its effect was powerful, particularly when mass was said and the Indian girls were baptized. Moctezuma, two hundred miles away and getting accounts of it by spies, perhaps at second or third hand, must have found it very confusing. These *teules* with their cannon, their horses and their ships, armed for battle and demanding gold, yet kneeling humbly in the dust before a piece of wood and a picture of a woman with a child . . . it cannot have made much sense to a man whose gods devoured human hearts by the thousand.

On their departure for Vera Cruz the Spaniards took the eight girls with them. The most beautiful had been christened Francisca, and once again Cortés had given her to his friend Puertocarrero. He himself had been presented with the fat cacique's niece, who was extremely ugly; and possibly as a rude joke she had been baptized Catalina. For a man who had been a notorious womaniser Cortés showed himself singularly uninterested in Indian girls. Certainly at this moment he had other things on his mind. A ship had come in from Cuba with Francisco de Saucedo and ten soldiers. More important, they had a horse and a mare on board. They also brought news that Velázquez had been confirmed as *adelantado* of Cuba and had been empowered to trade and found settlements.

Cortés and his men had now been more than three months on the coast. It was time to move inland. But first a ship must be sent to Spain with a glowing account of the country and all they had achieved, and enough gold to support their own claims. Then all the rest of the fleet must be destroyed, so that thereafter every man would be committed, with no prospect of saving his skin unless they succeeded. Only by this drastic and irrevocable action could the threat of desertion, even mutiny, be finally extinguished.

As usual Cortés had prepared the ground so carefully that he appeared to be yielding to popular pressure, rather than giving orders. The soldiers themselves prepared a letter to the Emperor Charles summarising all their achievements. This was to be accompanied by all the gold they had so far gained, every man finally agreeing to forego his share so that the total might be as impressive as possible. They also sent four Indians they had rescued from the cages at Zempoala, where they were being fattened for sacrifice. Puertocarrero and Montejo were chosen as envoys. The best ship in the fleet was got ready, fifteen sailors were picked and two pilots allocated, including Alaminos, who knew the Bahamas and so could steer direct for Spain. The soldiers' letter attacked Velázquez, accused the president of the Council of the Indies, Bishop Fonesca, of having been bribed, and

A landscape typical of the country through which Cortés marched.

it petitioned that Cortés be confirmed in his office as captain-general in New Spain. Cortés sent his own letter, the first of the five long dispatches he wrote to his king, and the envoys sailed on July 26, 1519, with orders to avoid Cuba.

The need to destroy his ships before marching into Mexico was impressed on Cortés by yet another attempt to seize a vessel and escape in her to Cuba. This time he sentenced the two leaders to be hanged, the pilot to have his feet amputated, and the men, who all seem to have been from Gibraltar since they are referred to as Men of the Rock, to two hundred lashes. He then left immediately for Zempoala to finalize plans with his Indian allies, and in his absence it is probable that the executions were not carried out. At Zempoala the soldiers themselves seem to have pressed for the destruction of the ships, chiefly on the grounds that by releasing sailors it would reinforce their numbers by almost a hundred. At any rate, the order was finally given and Juan de Escalante, who had been appointed chief constable, was sent to Vera Cruz to see it carried out.

The plan was to get all the stores and gear ashore, bore holes in the ships' bottoms and then beach them. It was to be done on the grounds that their hulls were rotten, a fairly reasonable excuse since everyone knew that teredo worm was active in the warm waters of the Gulf. However, sailors are not the most willing collaborators in this sort of work. The job was botched, only five ships being beached as arranged, and Cortés was forced to abandon his subterfuge and order the remaining vessels to be sunk. By then, of course, there was considerable opposition. But once it was done the outcry quickly subsided, for nobody thereafter had any alternative but to support their leader and the will of the majority.

Cortés took the opportunity to make one of his periodic speeches. He was very good at haranguing his troops, and by the end of it they were with him almost to a man, and those that were not now had no means of escaping their destiny, which was to fight and go on fighting until they either died or conquered.

With the destruction of the ships, Vera Cruz assumed greater military importance as the base on which they could fall back if necessary, and also as a port through which they might ultimately receive reinforcements from Spain. A question that must have occupied Cortés' mind as he pressed on with his plans for the advance into the interior was the proportion of his force needed to secure his base. It would have the support of the surrounding country, a total of fifty towns and villages capable of putting something like fifty thousand warriors in the field, and it is probable that his first intention was to leave only a token force. But before he began his march from Zempoala, Juan de Escalante, whom he had left in command at Vera Cruz, sent word that a ship had been sighted off the coast.

Leaving Pedro de Alvarado in command of his army, Cortés took Sandoval and three other horsemen and galloped the fifteen miles back to Vera Cruz. One of his greatest qualities as a leader was his ability to meet trouble head-on, and in person. His haste, and the fact that he ordered fifty of his soldiers to follow him as fast as they could, indicates his concern that Diego Velázquez might be

The volcano of Popocatépetl towered over the route that the Spaniards followed.

Cortés sank his ships; an eighteenth-century Spanish engraving above; *and set out on his march into the interior; a sixteenth-century Mexican codex* below. Opposite *Cortés' route map 1.*

attempting a landing from Cuba. In fact, the ship turned out to be one of a fleet of three sent out by Francisco de Garay, Diego Columbus's governor of Jamaica. This they learned from three Spaniards they captured on the foreshore. Garay had obtained a commission from Fonseca giving him the governorship of any lands he might discover north of the San Pablo river, and his captain, Alonso Álvarez de Pinedo, with a force of two hundred and seventy men, was already establishing a settlement two hundred miles to the north on the Pánuco river. Cortés made an unsuccessful attempt to seize the vessel, but all he got was two of her sailors who had jumped ashore from a boat.

Cortés must have been very conscious now of the pressure of events building up behind him. It was not only Velázquez he had to fear, but Garay as well. To secure his base would require a larger force than he had originally intended. All told, including sick and wounded and the older soldiers, he left about a hundred and fifty men for the defence of Vera Cruz. The cream of his army he took with him, a total of about four hundred men, and on August 16, 1519, he marched out of Zempoala. He was accompanied by between forty and a hundred fighting chiefs of the Totonacs, and two hundred *tamemes,* who carried the artillery and stores, each Indian capable of fifteen miles a day with a fifty-pound pack on his back. He had fifteen horses and six guns. His soldiers wore cotton armour and hemp shoes and they carried shields. A few had arquebuses, muskets or crossbows, but in the main they were armed with lances and swords. Only the captains and horsemen wore steel armour. By the route they took it was almost two hundred and fifty miles to Moctezuma's capital. There were three great mountain ranges in their path, the first two overshadowed by volcanic peaks of more than 14,000 feet, the third by Popocatépetl and Iztaccihuatl, both over 17,000 feet high, and it was all unknown territory, much of it probably hostile. Few men before them had ever embarked upon such a hazardous march with the odds so heavily weighted against success. Whatever their motives, whatever their behaviour, they were brave men; and Cortés himself, a man who never faltered, never despaired even when the outlook was utterly hopeless, must rank as one of the greatest military leaders in history.

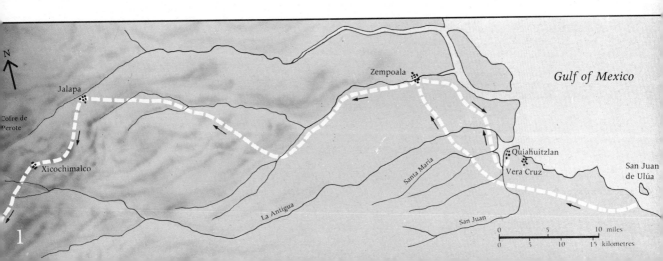

4 *The March to Mexico*

FOR THE FIRST THREE DAYS of Cortés' march on Mexico-Tenochtitlan his army was advancing through friendly territory, but they still had scouts out ahead and a picked company marched in advance of the main army. The going was easy, generally flat, with the plain tilted from the coast towards the mountains fifty miles inland. Food was plentiful, for wherever there was water, crops grew without regard to season, and at that time, both on the plains and in the mountains, there were a great number of deer. It was mid-summer and the *tierra caliente* of the coastal belt was hot and very humid. Directly ahead of them they could see the rounded bulk of Cofre de Perote topped by a bare rock mass, square like a fortress, and though the mountains, blurred with haze, represented the first great barrier on their line of march, at least they offered the prospect of some relief from the burning heat. The country was fairly thickly populated, the villages oases of cultivation in the dry plain. But as they approached the foothills, where the cooler atmosphere of increasing altitude draws rain from the moisture-laden north wind, the savannah country gradually merged into a thick jungle growth full of tropical flowers, bright-plumaged birds and large butterflies.

By the end of the second day, marching finally through rain and mud, they reached Jalapa, a fairly large town sprawled on the slope of a hill. They were into the *tierra templada* at last, at a height of over 4,500 feet, the air relatively cool. But ahead of them now lay the first of the great mountain ranges, and they were at the furthest limit of friendly Totonac territory. Neither Cortés nor Bernal Díaz makes any reference at this stage to the support of Indian auxiliaries, but the chiefs who accompanied them certainly would not have done so alone, and, since Cortés' policy on the coast had been one of consolidation, it may be presumed that the little army was augmented by local forces. How many of these Indian warriors advanced beyond Jalapa to brave the heights, and the dangers of potentially hostile territory, we do not know.

It was on the fourth day that they began their march into the mountains, climbing steeply to a fortified town which Bernal Díaz calls Socochima and Gómara refers to as Xicochimalco. This place was approached by two paths cut like

Opposite Cortés' route map 2.

staircases in the rock and could easily have been defended. However, the cacique had orders from Moctezuma to let them pass. At this high altitude the fields of golden maize were smaller, the corn short-stalked, and in the gardens the passion fruit was grown on trellises. Far below them valleys glimmered green, hazy vistas of grass and tropical vegetation dotted with farms and villages; above them was nothing but the sombre dark of pine and cedar.

They were now climbing the slopes of Cofre de Perote itself, with the whole *massif* of the Sierra Madre running away to the south to end in the snow peak of Orizaba. Details of the march at this stage are somewhat conflicting, both as regards the names of Indian towns and the distances between them, even the order of events. Cortés in his Second Letter, dated October 30, 1520, and therefore written within a year of the events, says they bivouacked the night in a pass 'so rocky and at such an altitude that there is not one in Spain more difficult to pass'. They were then at about 10,000 feet in grim country where the soil is the lava spill of old eruptions from the now extinct volcano. Descending from the pass, which they called Puerto de Nombre de Dios, they came upon a number of farms scattered round a fortified hill town, the name of which, according to Gómara, was Ixhuacan. The dwellings in this sad land have probably changed little down the centuries; grey, dismal hovels – grey adobe, grey wood palings, roofs of grey cedar shingles, all merging with the soil to give a sense of extreme bleakness. Thereafter, for three days they marched 'through a desert land uninhabitable on account of its barrenness, lack of water and great cold'. Gómara says it was desert country 'uninhabited and saline', the water salt. To the west of Cofre de Perote there is a forty-mile stretch of desert, at the southern end of which are salt marshes and brackish lakes. For an army already short of food and water this would have presented a serious obstacle. Even today it is uninhabited, a flat sand area with patches of short-stalked maize and a hill like a pyramid sticking up out of the middle of it. There would have been no maize when they saw it, the sandy top surface of the clay soil baked as dry and powdery as it is today and the wind raising sand devils. They had a choice then, either to cross it or to turn north, back into the hills, to the very edge of the escarpment with its deep gorges that lead to distant glimpses of the coastal plain. Gómara not only refers to the salinity of the water, but also to sandstorms. The inference is that Cortés took the desert route, a not unreasonable decision since to go north to

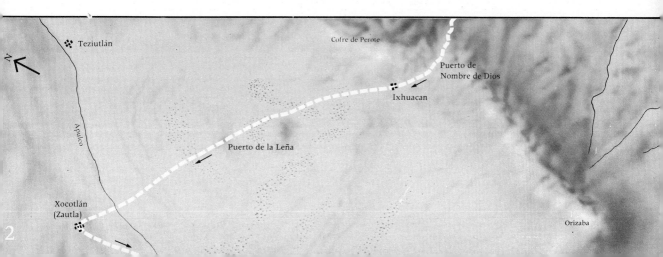

Teziutlán meant a wide detour in hilly country, whereas ahead of him it was flat, easy going, and he would have just been able to see the line of tree-clad hills on the far side. Even here, in this desert, they were at an altitude of around 8,000, and the nights were cold. The contrast after the heat of the coast was very violent.

Coming down from the pass they had been caught by one of those violent storms caused by the build-up of the torrid, humid atmosphere of the coast against the cool barrier of the mountains. Cortés describes it as a 'whirlwind of hailstones and rain'. The Spaniards lay shivering through the night with no protection against the bitter cold but their cotton armour. 'I thought many were like to die', Cortés continues, 'and certain Indians from Cuba who were scantily clothed did indeed thus perish.'

Beyond the desert they reached the line of low hills towards which they had been marching all day. Here, in a pass, they found a small idol-tower 'like a roadside chapel' piled round with cord-wood, all neatly stacked – 'a thousand cartloads' Cortés says and called it Puerto de la Leña. Some two leagues beyond the pass 'the land again became poor and sterile'. Cortés describes the people, too, as very poor. But they were approaching the Apulco river and shortly afterwards they reached a large town where the houses, stone-built and lime-washed, gleamed so white in the sunlight that it reminded them of southern Spain. Bernal Díaz says that they called it Castilblanco and that its Indian name was Xocotlán. It is now called Zautla, and Fray Bartolomé, who had done his best to spread the faith in the towns and villages of the Totonac Indians, would not even allow a cross to be erected, discouraged by the evidence of sacrifices on a large scale. There were thirteen teocalli, each with its attendant pile of skulls, and Bernal Díaz estimated their number at more than one hundred thousand.

When Cortés spoke of the emperor he served, Olintetl, the chief cacique, expressed astonishment: 'Is there anyone who is not a slave or vassal of Moctezuma?' He was talkative, and from him Cortés learnt a great deal about Mexico-Tenochtitlan: the Aztec capital was built on the waters of a great lake, its houses constructed so that they could be converted into fortresses, all roads into the city were guarded by drawbridges, and Moctezuma, lord of the world, sacrificed twenty thousand men a year and had thirty vassal chieftains each capable of putting a hundred thousand warriors into the field. Even allowing for exaggera-

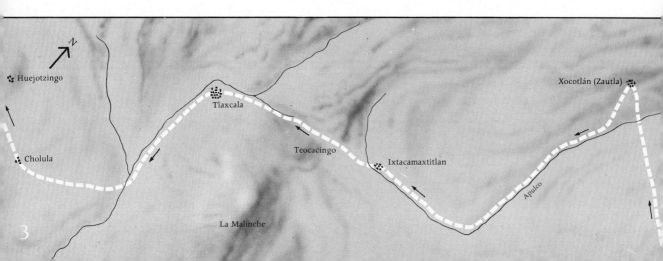

tion, it was a terrifying prospect. The only encouraging news was that there was a great store of gold and silver in the capital.

What Cortés needed now was allies, and since the Zempoalans assured him that the Tlaxcalans, whose territory lay ahead, were friends of theirs and enemies of Moctezuma, he sent four of them in advance as envoys. At this point Bernal Díaz appears to confuse Jalacingo, a town twenty miles back in the hills to the east, with Ixtacamaxtitlan. The only explanation would seem to be that Cortés was safeguarding himself against treachery, and at the same time providing his men with better quarters, by billeting some of them in the neighbouring towns – Olintetl alone is reported to have had twenty thousand vassals, which suggests that the population in this district was considerable. Cortés himself stayed four or five days at Xocotlán and then moved upstream to Ixtacamaxtitlan. The cacique here had been one of two who had already visited him with gifts – 'a few golden collars of little weight or value and seven or eight slaves'. He discreetly refrains from telling his Emperor that the slaves were, in fact, girls.

The main fortress area of Ixtacamaxtitlan was 'perched on a lofty ridge' with houses for five thousand people surrounded by 'a wall, barbican and ditch'. There were also a large number of dependent settlements strung out for three or four leagues along the valley; so close, in fact, that it was a sort of riverside ribbon development. Here he paused another three days, waiting for the return of his envoys from Tlaxcala. The question he had to decide now was which route to take. There were two. The easiest route followed the edge of the desert country they had already crossed, past the swamps and lakes they had seen from the hills behind them, making a long southward curve that led to the religious city of Cholula. The cacique, acting presumably on orders from Moctezuma, offered to guide the Spaniards by it. The Zempoalans, however, insisted that it was a trap and that it would lead inevitably to the Spaniards, and themselves, being killed and eaten, for Cholula was at least twenty miles south of Tlaxcala, and they would be marching all the time through Culhúan territory.

It was a difficult choice. Cortés was a long way from his base. He did not trust the Indians, and he certainly did not trust Moctezuma. He had still received no word from Tlaxcala, but since they were in a perpetual state of war with Culhúa it seemed the lesser of two evils; so he ignored the easier route and marched up the

Cortés' route map 3 left. He sends envoys to the Tlaxcalans. From a sixteenth-century Mexican codex right.

valley into the hills. At the exit to the valley was a wall marking the Tlaxcalan border. Cortés describes it as being 'of rough stone about one and a half times the height of a man, crossing the whole valley from one ridge to the other, about twenty foot broad and with a parapet about a foot and a half broad running its entire length, from which one could fight. The entrance, moreover, was ten paces wide and ran for about thirty yards in the form of a double arc like a ravelin, in such a fashion that the entrance turned on itself instead of proceeding straight-forwardly.' Once again his hosts and his Zempoalan allies began arguing about the advantages and disadvantages of their advancing into the territory of Moctezuma's enemies. The matter was finally settled by the army passing through the wall and marching to the top of the defile. Four leagues beyond this point the two horsemen acting as scouts ran into a party of fifteen warriors, wearing badges and feathered head-dresses. These Indians were lookouts and immediately retreated.

Cortés, with three horsemen, galloped after them, hoping to take them prisoner, for he needed information and men to send to Tlaxcala with messages of peace. But the Indians, who considered that, if taken alive in battle, they could only expect to be sacrificed, turned and fought with such desperation that two of the horses were killed – some accounts suggest that their necks were cut clean through, reins and all, by the two-handed obsidian-edged swords! Two more horses were injured, as well as three of the horsemen; all the Indians were killed. It was a clear warning against the use of horses in a confined space for, including four more horsemen who had joined in the mêlée, eleven of the cavalry had been required to kill fifteen Indians. By now some three to five thousand warriors, who had been waiting in ambush, were advancing into the open. Cortés sent one of the horsemen back to hasten the arrival of the main body of the army, and when the Indians saw the infantry advancing, they retired, pursued by the cavalry, who, on open ground, were able to slaughter some fifty or sixty of them with impunity. This skirmish marked the start of the Tlaxcalan campaign.

That night the Spaniards slept by a dried-up river bed. Here messengers arrived from Tlaxcala, together with two of the four Zempoalans, claiming that Tlaxcala was a federation of Indian towns and that the attack had been made on the orders of the local chief. They had, in fact, been Otomí Indians from one of the towns of the federation whose responsibility it was to defend that particular section of the border. Cortés accepted both the explanation and their invitation to visit the city of Tlaxcala, ignored their offer of recompense for the dead horses, both carcases having been hurriedly buried, and sent them back to their chief, Xicotencatl, with expressions of goodwill. Meantime, his men were short of food. They were camped in open country surrounded by fields of maize, hedged with maguey cactus, but the settlements were all deserted and empty of provisions. Bernal Díaz says that they 'supped very well on some small dogs, which the Indians breed for food'. And since they had no oil, they dressed their wounds with fat rendered down from an Indian corpse.

Guards were posted throughout the night and the army marched again at dawn. The sun rose as they reached a village and here they were met by the other two Zempoalans sent to Tlaxcala. They said they had been bound ready for sacrifice but had escaped in the turmoil produced by the Spanish invasion of Tlaxcalan territory. At this point Bernal Díaz says that 'two armies of warriors, about six thousand strong, came to meet us with loud shouts and the noise of drums and trumpets, shooting their arrows, hurling their darts, and acting with the utmost bravery'. Cortés gives the number as a thousand. Few Indian battles seem to have begun without a period of confrontation, rather similar to the display technique of animals, and Cortés had time to make signs of peace and even to talk to them through his interpreter. But in the end they attacked, and it was Cortés himself who raised the old battle cry of 'Santiago'. Many Indians, including three of their chiefs, were killed in this first charge. They then retired towards some woods where the Tlaxcalan war chief, Xicotencatl, was waiting in ambush with forty thousand warriors 'all wearing the red-and-white devices that were his badge and livery'. The ground was too broken for the effective use of cavalry, but when the Spaniards had forced the Indians out into more open country, the position changed and Cortés was able to bring his half dozen cannon into action. Even so, the battle lasted until sunset, and though Cortés' claim that the Indians numbered a hundred thousand is probably an exaggeration, there can be no doubt that the Spaniards and their allies were heavily outnumbered, for Xicotencatl is reported to have had five captains under him, each commanding ten thousand warriors.

Gómara says his total force numbered a hundred and fifty thousand warriors, and he gives this description of them as they advanced into battle:

> The men were splendidly armed in their fashion and their faces were painted with red bixa, which gave them the look of devils. They carried plumes and manoeuvred marvellously well. Their weapons were slings, pikes, lances, and swords; bows and arrows; helmets; arm and leg armour of wood, gilded or covered with feathers or leather. Their breastplates were of cotton; their shields and bucklers, very handsome and not at all weak, were of tough wood and leather, with brass and feather ornaments; their swords of wood with flint set into them, which cut well and made a nasty wound. Their troops were arranged in squadrons, each with many trumpets, conches, and drums, all of which was a sight to see.

They advanced with the Tlaxcalan banner of a golden crane with outstretched wings in the rear, which was its place in battle.

Bernal Díaz gives the date of this first encounter with the main Tlaxcalan force as September 2, 1519, and says that at one stage of the battle the Tlaxcalans made a determined attempt to capture one of the horses ridden by Pedro de Morán. 'Some of them seized his lance so that he could not use it, and others slashed at his mare, cutting her head at the neck so that it only hung by the skin. And he adds that when they retired, they took the dead mare with them and 'cut her in pieces to show in all the towns of Tlaxcala'. Also that 'they made an offering to their idols of her shoes, the red Flemish hat and the two letters we had sent them asking for peace'. In this, and in subsequent battles, any estimate of the number of Tlaxcalans killed would seem to be pure guesswork, since they invariably removed their dead from the field, but it was learned later that eight of their war chiefs had been killed.

Both before and after the battle Cortés released prisoners with messages of goodwill. He wanted peace, not war. The country itself was terrifying enough. They were now turning the flank of the volcano they named La Malinche. It lay to the left of their line of march, looming right over them, and behind they could still just see the peaks of Orizaba and Cofre de Perote. But what must have appalled Cortés was his first sight of the greatest obstacle of all, the twin peaks of Iztacci-huatl and Popocatépetl, fifty miles to the west. Five volcanoes in all, and the last two sprawled right across his route, only the white of their snow-capped summits as yet visible above the horizon. At whatever cost he had to subdue the Tlaxcalans and secure his line of march before he could attempt to cross that final mountain barrier.

That night the Spaniards made themselves secure in one of the temples of Teocacingo. For the next three days Cortés maintained an aggressive initiative, probing first in one direction, then in another, leaving the bulk of his army to defend the camp. These raids were made by the cavalry and about a hundred foot soldiers, supported by four hundred Zempoalans and three hundred warriors who had accompanied him from Ixtacamaxtitlan. His army had now moved into the more open country surrounding Tlaxcala, fields of maize hedged with maguey and many villages. These they burned, taking a large number of prisoners.

It was on September 5, according to Bernal Díaz, that the next major battle was fought. 'We left the camp with our banner unfurled and four of our company guarding its bearer, and before we had gone half a mile we saw the fields crowded with warriors, with their tall plumes and badges, and heard the blare of horns and trumpets.' Cortés claims that the Tlaxcalans numbered 139,000. The battle was fought on a plain about six miles long so that both cavalry and cannon were at their most deadly. The Tlaxcalans, badly led, attacked en masse. The artillery mowed them down in swathes, and the Spanish soldiers, now battle trained, moved into the packed enemy with the tight discipline of Roman legionaries. The cavalry was a powerful armoured weapon, particularly destructive in pursuit, but there were now only a dozen horses left, and it was Spanish steel, the cutting edge of the foot soldiers' sword, that won Cortés his battles. And on this occasion there was dissension among the Tlaxcalans, two of Xicotencatl's captains refusing to join him. The result, after four hours' fighting, was a rout. But by then all the horses were injured.

'We gave thanks to God', Bernal Díaz says. And well they might, for they had lost one man, though sixty had been wounded; but the Spaniards never seemed concerned about wounds. The Tlaxcalans, too, were learning fast. Thereafter, they attacked in smaller groups, each company vying with the next for the honour of capturing a Spaniard alive. But by then the nearby chiefs were beginning to come into the camp to make their own peace. Two days after the battle, fifty Indians appeared in the camp, mingling with the soldiers and offering them gifts of food, mainly flat pancakes of maize flour, turkeys and cherries. Warned that they were spies, and seeing that they were over-interested in the army's defences and dispositions, Cortés had them arrested. Under interrogation they admitted that they had come to spy in preparation for a night attack. He sent them back to Tlaxcala, all fifty of them with their hands cut off, and then he set to work to prepare his camp for attack. This night attack was carried out by about ten thousand warriors, who began moving down from the neighbouring hills at sunset. Xicotencatl had been assured by his priests that the valour of the Spaniards deserted them at night. Unfortunately for him, this was not the case; Cortés moved his army out into the open maize fields and met the Indians there. By then the moon had risen and the Tlaxcalans, unaccustomed to night fighting, were quickly routed.

After three days of sporadic fighting, Cortés made a night attack on two towns, which he did not burn for fear of arousing the whole neighbourhood. At dawn he attacked a larger town 'so suddenly that all rushed unarmed, the women and children naked, into the streets'. Xicotencatl came the following day with fifty other chiefs to sue for peace. The Tlaxcalan war chief is described as being about thirty-five, a tall, broad-shouldered man with a long pock-marked face, who carried himself with great dignity. This was the end of the Tlaxcalan campaign, for he not only made protestations of lasting friendship, urgently inviting the Spaniards to enter his city, but he also complained bitterly of Moctezuma's constant demands.

Nothing could have suited Cortés better, for he already had in his camp a further embassy from Moctezuma – six chiefs with a retinue of two hundred, who had come bearing presents of gold for Cortés, congratulations on his victory and, what was more important, the news that Moctezuma was not only prepared to become a vassal of the Spanish emperor, but also to pay a yearly tribute – so long as the Spaniards did not enter Mexico. It was both a bribe and an offer of Danegeld. Thus Cortés was able to embark on an elaborate game of political poker. He did

The Tlaxcalans sue for peace.

not yet trust the Tlaxcalans and he admits that he 'continued to treat with both one and the other, thanking each in secret for the advice he gave me, and professing to regard each with greater friendship than the other'.

Warily he waited six or seven days in his camp, a pause that gave his men a chance to rest and enabled him to send dispatches back to Vera Cruz and to receive news that all was well with the settlement. It also allowed the details of his victories to percolate through the surrounding country, and doubtless grow in the telling. He was only six leagues from Tlaxcala and, in the end, the threat of what he might do to the city brought all the chiefs once more to his camp, touching the ground with their hands, kissing the earth and, whilst the priests burned copal, pleading with him to enter the city as a sign of friendship. The next day, September 23, he broke camp, and as the army, all in proper formation, neared the city, it was met by a great procession of chiefs, with all the priests straight from sacrifice, 'the blood clotted in their long hair and oozing from their ears'.

In entering Tlaxcala Cortés was not only gaining a city of about thirty thousand inhabitants, according to his estimate, but a whole state measuring 'some ninety leagues in circumference', for this was the capital of what politically might be termed a republic. The city itself, which Cortés says was 'larger than Granada and much better fortified', lay in a hollow amongst the hills with some of its temples on the high ground surrounding it. It was packed with people from all the country round come to see the *teules*. Their leaders offered hostages as security for friendship. They also offered five virgins, each the daughter of a chief, to cement it. But they would not throw down their idols or abandon their sacrifices.

During his stay in Tlaxcala Cortés gathered a great deal of information about the Mexican capital, and about the Mexicans themselves. The Tlaxcalans could tell him the number of drawbridges on the causeways and even the depth of the water in the lake. Moreover, they put the strength of Moctezuma's Mexican armies alone at a hundred and fifty thousand men, and they had reason to know, for they had been at war with the Culhúan confederacy for over á hundred years. The normal assembly point for these attacks was the neighbouring city of Cholula, and when they heard that Moctezuma's chiefs were advising Cortés to move there, they warned him that the people were treacherous, that Moctezuma had a large force of his warriors camped about two leagues from the city, that the royal

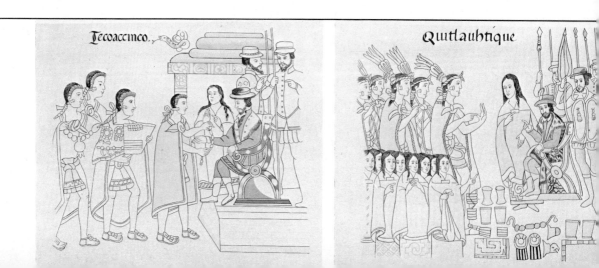

road leading into it had been blocked and a new one constructed with pits and sharpened stakes to trap the horses, and that the streets themselves were barricaded, the flat roofs of the houses piled with stones ready for use as missiles. In the circumstances it is hardly surprising that Cortés stayed nearly three weeks in Tlaxcala.

During that time he consolidated his position. Once the Tlaxcalans were convinced that the Spaniards represented their only hope of finally breaking the power of Mexico, he had the support of the whole republic, a really powerful ally who for years had maintained a remarkable independence. Behind him, as far back as his base on the coast, all the territory was friendly.

His men were well aware of this. But they, too, had been listening to the tales of Moctezuma's might. They had seen the cages and the blood-soaked priests; they knew their fate if they were surprised and captured, and now that they had fought with the Indians, they were under no illusions as to what would happen if the Tlaxcalans proved treacherous or they were deserted by their other allies. Every account of the battles so far attributes victory to God and the power of Spanish arms. This is natural; but it is clear from the attitude of the men who had fought and bluffed their way up from the coast that they would have been destroyed without the support of their Zempoalan allies. Many of the Spaniards had had enough and wanted only to return to Vera Cruz, where a ship could be built and sent to Cuba for reinforcements. They argued, very reasonably, that they were too few for the task of facing the full force of Moctezuma's armies.

How Cortés felt about this, what doubts he had himself, we do not know, since he was careful never to reveal his own feelings. And we only have a garbled version of the arguments by which he persuaded his men to soldier on with him into Mexico. These speeches give an impression of absolute confidence, and it is interesting to note that here, and subsequently, he always kept his men in the picture and never took a major step that might involve fighting without their willing support. This leadership by consent, which had its roots in Spanish history, and also in the voyages and frontier atmosphere of the New World, is one of his most outstanding qualities. Fortunately for him, he had the advantage of a very persuasive tongue.

Having shamed his men once again into following him, he was now faced with

quitlaqualmacaque .

The Tlaxcalan envoys bring gifts to Cortés far left; and offer him hostages and virgins left; they advise him about the approach to Tenochtitlan right.

a further choice of routes. Mexico lay due west. Should he take the direct route, or should he go by way of Cholula, as Moctezuma's ambassadors advised? The Tlaxcalans gloomily warned him that Cholula was a trap, that Moctezuma was not to be trusted and that his forces would be waiting there in ambush to destroy the Spaniards. Whilst Cortés was still considering the matter, he received yet another embassy from Moctezuma – four chiefs with presents of gold jewels, worth about 2,000 pesos, and warnings that the Tlaxcalans were only waiting an opportunity to kill and rob the Spaniards. It was such an obvious attempt to drive a wedge between him and his new allies that Cortés ignored it.

At this point he decided to send an embassy of his own to Moctezuma, and Pedro de Alvarado and Bernardino Vázquez de Tapia had actually set out for the capital, the four chiefs being held as hostages for their safe return, before he had second thoughts and recalled them. Messengers he had dispatched to Cholula now returned with four minor chiefs, who said their caciques could not come to swear allegiance in person, as the caciques of other towns round about had done, because they were ill. This excuse was a very transparent one and Cortés had now got himself into the same position as he had previously with the Tlaxcalans. He dared not lose face, and so he sent four of his Zempoalans with an ultimatum – if the caciques did not come within three days, he would regard the Cholulans as rebels. The reply he received was that they dared not come since the Tlaxcalans were their enemies, but that if Cortés would leave Tlaxcala and come to them, he would be well received. This excuse was not an unreasonable one, and though he marched on Cholula with the support of about a hundred thousand Tlaxcalans (this is Cortés' figure, Tapia gives forty thousand), he managed, with some difficulty, to persuade most of them to return to their city. He was then about five miles from Cholula, and as it was now late in the day, he camped the night in a dry river bed.

The country here is very flat, a somewhat arid plain, the very flatness of which emphasises the staggering abruptness of the twin volcanoes of Iztaccihuatl and Popocatépetl. Iztaccihuatl, 'the sleeping lady', is a sprawling, feminine mountain; seen in silhouette against the setting sun it looks like the body of a woman laid out for burial, the head, the breasts, the feet, all visible in outline against the flaring sky. Popocatépetl, 'the warrior', is entirely masculine, a sharp, pointed peak brilliantly capped with snow. The height of these twin peaks above the plain is over 9,000 feet, for the plain itself is almost 8,000 feet above sea level. From his camp Cortés could see quite plainly the pass between them – the pass that is known to this day as the Paso de Cortés, though modern Mexico has now expunged almost any other reference to the Spanish conquistadors. 'From the higher of the two', Cortés writes, 'both by day and night a great volume of smoke often comes forth and rises up into the clouds as straight as a staff, with such force that although a very violent wind continuously blows over the mountain range yet it cannot change the direction of the column.' Halfway between Cholula and the volcano two small hills stand like miniature replicas of the twin peaks, the only relief in the flatness of the plain. Though arid-looking and dusty, the plain is well supplied with water from the melted snows. Wherever irrigation was practical there were settlements. The country was, therefore, thickly populated, and looking south that evening Cholula itself must have presented an extra-ordinary spectacle, for it was not only a large city – Cortés says that it had twenty thousand houses, and, including the outlying villages, the total population probably numbered about a hundred thousand – but it was also a great religious centre with more than three hundred and sixty temples.

On the far side, dominating the whole flat sprawl of adobe dwellings, was the great pyramid-pile of the temple of Quetzalcoatl. This temple is composed of seven distinct layers, each layer completely encasing the previous temple and representing a thank-offering at the completion of a 52-year cycle. The most important temples throughout the Aztec world were treated in this way, so that they grew steadily in size each half century. And, since the last 52-year cycle had ended only a dozen years before the Spaniards arrived, the great temple at Cholula would have looked not only enormous, but also gleamingly new.

Early next morning the Spaniards were on the march, accompanied now by their 'faithful' Zempoalans and only about five or six thousand Tlaxcalans. They were met on the road by the chiefs of Cholula 'with great noise of trumpets and drums, and many of their so-called priests dressed in the vestments they wear in the temples and singing in the same fashion'. After their twenty days in Tlaxcala, the Spaniards were well rested. Nevertheless, apart from their allies, they were a small force of only four hundred determined men about to enter a city that was allied to an Indian prince of almost fabulous power. They were moving towards his territory uninvited, and behind them they had left a trail of revolt that no man, however great his power, could afford to ignore. It was a desperate gamble; and Cortés must have wondered why he had been allowed to get so far, always being offered gifts and fair words. What was Moctezuma afraid of? Or was he just biding his time, cruelly waiting for the kill, intent upon sacrificing the Spaniards to his filthy gods?

To understand the situation, it is necessary to view the Spanish invasion from Moctezuma's point of view, against the background of Mexican history and the social, cultural and religious structure of the Aztec civilization.

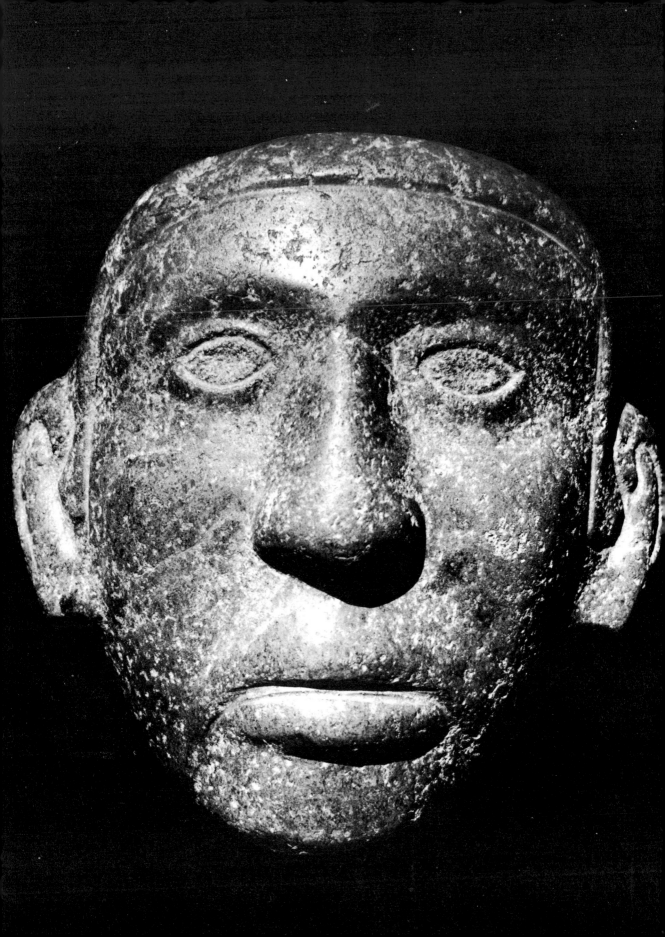

5   *The Aztecs*

THE AMERICAN INDIAN is now generally believed to have stemmed from a Mongoloid-red movement from Asia across the area of the Bering Straits more than 20,000 years ago. However, the earliest radio carbon-dated sites of unquestioned human association are about 11,500 years old. Discoveries at Iztapan and Tepexpan in Mexico indicate that primitive man may have established himself in the lake area of Middle America by around 9000 B.C. By 5000 B.C. hunting and fishing was being supplemented by cultivation of beans, later of maize; and by the middle of the third millenium B.C. some form of cultural life was beginning to emerge among the nomadic tribes of this area. There is evidence of pottery handcraft in established village centres during the next 500 years and it was some time after this that the first advanced culture, that of the Olmecs, began to develop in the lowlands of the Gulf Coast.

The belief that this was a theocracy is supported by evidence of ritual development; in Mexico this was marked first by the construction of platforms and altars, later by the building of pyramid-like structures. Initially, these were probably of earth and oval in shape – the 80-foot cone-shaped pyramid of Cuicuilco, which was later buried by lava, is a development of these. Burials, which had previously been in pits, became more elaborate, and many temples were built, chiefly to the god of fire or sun – ultimately the god of war.

In the first millenium B.C. the Maya civilization emerged in the southern forests. It lasted more than a millenium and spread north as far as Yucatán, where the ruins of the great city of Chichén Itzá testify to its advanced cultural development. In Mexico the even larger city of Teotihuacán began to rise on the north-east shores of Lake Texcoco in the first two centuries A.D. It represents the first urban civilization in Middle America and eventually covered seven square miles – a great ceremonial and commercial centre that constantly adapted itself, being altered and rebuilt several times. It influenced most of Middle America for five hundred years and though its destruction by fire in the seventh century A.D. presaged a collapse of what is called the Classic period, its temple structures provided the architectural models upon which most subsequent religious edifices were based.

This Classic period is almost bewildering in the profusion of culture revealed

A stone sculpture of an Aztec head – the race that imposed its rule upon all the peoples of Mexico.

by archaeological excavation and renovation. From Chichén Itzá in the east, right across the crumpled mountain face of Mexico, to Monte Albán in the west, the whole country is littered with cultural remains of extreme complexity, being both individual in their local development, yet interwoven with the main stream of Middle American Indian development. Teotihuacán was almost certainly a great religious centre, and, since it was from this city that most of the elaborate ceremonial of later cultures stemmed, it has inevitably attracted the greatest archaeological attention. Not only have the colossal pyramids of the Sun and the Moon – the former is some two hundred feet high and in volume larger than the Great Pyramid in Egypt – been repaired, but the two-mile long Street of the Dead, the buildings of which had become mounds overgrown with maguey, the great Square of the Moon, the remarkable Temple of Quetzalcoatl, later covered to form the Ciudadela, have all been cleared of the wind-blown earth and undergrowth that buried them.

It is astonishing now to contemplate the gigantic architecture of these people as revealed in the sites of their city-states, the high level of their arts and crafts, the intricacy of their metalwork, and to realize how little of all this imaginative ability was put to practical use. They knew about the wheel, yet they did not use it, except for toys, and even when the conquistadors entered Mexico-Tenochtitlan in 1519 the Indian method of transport was still confined to the human back or to their lake boats. They did not even use sleds, for they had not domesticated any animals other than dogs, which they bred for food.

Their metalwork was confined largely to the jewellers' art – some of the best examples are from the Mixtec culture, hundreds of necklaces, pendants and ear-rings found in Tomb 7 at Monte Albán. Their jewellers' technique was so advanced that they could cast by cire-perdue and even solder, the ornamental work so fine that it is hard to believe that it was executed without the use of a magnifying glass. Yet their skill in handling metal was mainly confined to the working of gold and copper. They had no knowledge of steel or even of the most primitive form of iron, and for the cutting edge of their 'swords' and the ritual cardiectomy of their victims they were back in the Stone Age, using 'flint' blades and knives of volcanic obsidian.

The earliest levels of Monte Albán, the religious centre of Oaxaca, two hundred miles south-east of Mexico, pre-date Teotihuacán; and with its hundred tombs of the priests, its huge complex of temples – a whole hill cut in terraces, it finally almost rivalled it in size. But the influence of Teotihuacán was much more widespread, though this did not apparently lead to any sense of military unity, so that its ultimate destruction was inevitable. Throughout pre-history there had not only been nomadic migration back and forth across Middle America itself – a movement that resulted in the cross-fertilizing of the developing Indian culture – but there had also been constant infiltration by hardy nomadic tribes from North America itself, drawn south by the warmer climate and to the lake area of the central Valley

A giant Olmec head above left; a crouching female form from western Mexico above right; the pyramid of the sun at Teotihuacán below.

in particular by the richness of its volcanic soil and the cool clear brightness of its climate. It may have been one of these southward migrations that finally destroyed the city.

But, though Teotihuacán itself was destroyed, the worship of one of its gods, Quetzalcoatl, was not, and this has some bearing on the Spanish conquest half a millenium later. At about the beginning of the tenth century yet another nomadic tribe infiltrated into the Valley. These were the Toltecs, a tough, warlike people, whose god was Tezcatlipoca, god of the sky with a taste for human sacrifice. They were armed with club-shaped wooden 'swords' set with obsidian blades, spoke the Náhuatl tongue, and they absorbed the culture they found in the Valley and its gods. It was they who gave Teotihuacán its present name, taking the people who had built those fantastic structures to be giants. Teotihuacán means the place of the gods, by which they meant the ancient gods, and they gave Quetzal-coatl, god of learning and of the wind, the name by which he has always since been known – *Quetzal* is the Náhuatl name for the brightly plumaged trogon birds still found in the rain forests of Guatemala and Costa Rica, *Coatl* means serpent; i.e. Feathered Serpent. Led by their chief, Mixcoatl, these people founded a military state that included most of what is now the province of Mexico.

It was at this stage that the story of Quetzalcoatl the god becomes confused with that of Quetzalcoatl the man. The latter was the son of Mixcoatl by a woman he took during the campaign in the Morelos district. The woman died in childbirth. The father was assassinated by his brother, Ihuitimal. The son was taken to Tepoztlán, a little town nestled in a magnificent gorge with temples built high up on the rock face to the north. Here, and at Xochicalco, not far away, he was brought up by the priests of Quetzalcoatl. He was called Topiltzin, and when he was grown up, he avenged his father's death, killing the uncle who had usurped the throne and burying Mixcoatl's bones on the Hill of the Star. The Toltec capital was Culhuacán, but after he became king he built a new capital at Tula, where he erected a temple to Quetzalcoatl and became its high priest, assuming the name of the god and thereafter having all the virtues of Quetzalcoatl attributed to him.

Since he represented a more enlightened religion, he was opposed by the old priesthood, who were devoted to war and insisted on human sacrifice in the name

A Zapotec head left; a Toltec 'chac-mool' near right; Quetzalcoatl, the Aztec feathered serpent middle right; the arch at Labná, a late Maya city in Yucatán far right.

of Tezcatlipoca. Inevitably, the old guard won, for he was a man in advance of his time. His defeat is charmingly attributed to a technicality – Tezcatlipoca introduced him to *pulque* (a form of beer produced from the fermented juice of the maguey cactus), which he had never touched before, and when he was drunk had him seduced by a woman. He abdicated and fled to the Gulf Coast, where he took a boat to Yucatán.

Quetzalcoatl's arrival in Yucatán may well have given rise to the Maya stories of the appearance of a culture hero called Kukulkán, which in Maya means Feathered Serpent. In Chichén Itzá itself the most conspicuous buildings date from the Toltec period – late tenth to thirteenth centuries – and since the beginning of this phase coincides with the date of Topiltzin-Quetzalcoatl's expulsion from Tula, the Maya legend may explain the uncanny resemblance of the buildings to those at Tula. On the other hand, it may have been solely due to the spread of Toltec influence, for besides being a warrior race, they were great builders, constructing temples, palaces, even their houses of stone. They used mortar, also stucco and plaster, and had a form of steam bath which they called *temascal*. The Greco-Roman analogy is thus a reasonable one, and with the replacement of the Classic period by the post-classical Toltecs, we are now at the dawn of Mexican history, the names and dates of their kings, their customs, even their mythology reasonably known.

This mythology is more basic than most. An example quoted by Dr Bernal symbolizes the conflict between the Toltecs and new warrior tribes driven by a period of drought to the rich irrigated land around Tula. It occurred during the reign of Huemac, last king of Tula, about the middle of the twelfth century. Tohueyo, a lusty young warrior who was the physical embodiment of the rising foreign element in Tula, was sent into the market place disguised as a seller of chile peppers. He took up a position opposite the royal palace, sitting naked like all the warriors of his tribe. Huemac's daughter, who had turned up her nose at all the eligible Toltec chiefs, doubtless because they were too effeminate for her liking,

looked towards the market place and saw Tohueyo naked, and his genital organ, and after having seen it went back into the palace and took a sudden fanciful desire for the

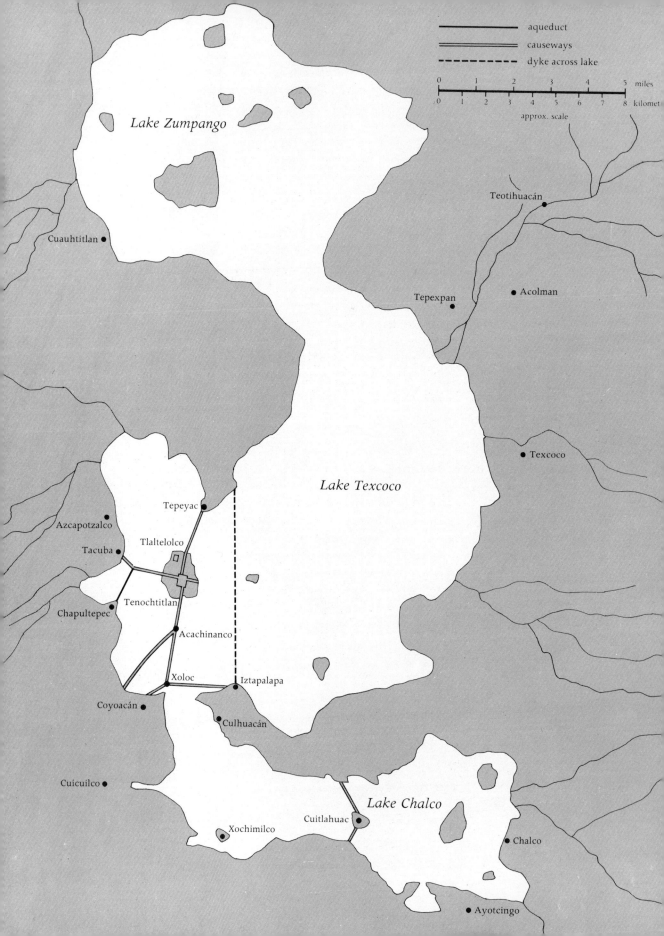

aqueduct

causeways

dyke across lake

0   1   2   3   4   5 miles
0   1   2   3   4   5   6   7   8 kilomet

approx. scale

Lake Zumpango

Teotihuacán

Cuauhtitlan

Tepexpan   Acolman

Texcoco

Lake Texcoco

Tepeyac

Azcapotzalco

Tlaltelolco

Tacuba

Tenochtitlan

Chapultepec

Acachinanco

Xoloc   Iztapalapa

Coyoacán

Culhuacán

Cuicuilco

Lake Chalco

Cuitlahuac

Xochimilco   Chalco

Ayotcingo

organ of the young Tohueyo and then became very sick because of the love for that which she had seen; all her body was swollen and Lord Huemac learned that she was very ill and asked the women who guarded his daughter: 'What illness does my daughter have?' And the women replied to him: 'Lord, the cause of this sickness was the Indian Tohueyo and she is sick with love for him.' The king ordered his men to search for the seller of chile who had disappeared. At last they found him and brought him before the king. The latter ordered him to cure his daughter. Tohueyo refused. But the servants took him, washed him, painted his body, dressed him sumptuously, and brought him to the bedroom of the young girl who 'then was cured and regained her health'.

It was, in reality, a marriage of convenience, an attempted political merger of the Toltecs and the new warrior races. It was unsuccessful. The Toltecs rebelled, Huemac fled, and early in the thirteenth century Tula ceased to be a power.

This pre-Mexican period saw the growth of five cities in this central area – Culhuacán, Texcoco, Azcapotzalco, Cholula, and Tenochtitlan – and the merging of the Toltecs with yet another immigrant branch of the Chichimecs. The city-state of Culhuacán virtually bridges the gap between the decline of the Toltec capital of Tula and the rise of the Tenochcas, the Aztec power centred on Mexico-Tenochtitlan.

The Tenochcas first appear on the Central American scene as a primitive people who are thought to have emerged from a lake island in the western part of the country early in the twelfth century. They worshipped Huitzilopochtli (Humming-bird Wizard), an idol that they are supposed to have found in a cave; they carried it with them everywhere and through it their priest-leaders directed all their wanderings. The migratory period lasted almost a hundred years. During this time they were a simple, nomadic farming folk, moving from site to site, sowing and harvesting crops on a year-to-year basis. They came into the Valley by way of Zumpango, the northernmost lake, still desperately poor, and there they existed on the sufferance of the great cities. Adversity taught them eventually to be warlike, cruel and perfidious. About 1248 they settled at Chapultepec, a rocky fortress of a hill standing high above the waters of the main lake; it is now a castle and the centre of a great park to the south-west of Mexico City. Here, during the

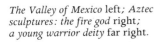
The Valley of Mexico left; Aztec sculptures: the fire god right; a young warrior deity far right.

next half century, they developed a cultural life, but the ambitions of their priests and their increasingly warlike behaviour so provoked the Tepanecs of Azcapotzalco and the Culhuacáns that these two cities formed an alliance against them. The Tenochcas were defeated, their chief sacrificed in Culhuacán and the majority of the people carried off as slaves. The few that escaped fled into the reed marshes of the lake itself.

A more unpleasant version of the flight is that Achitometl, king of Culhuacán, allowed them to settle in Tizapán, a snake-infested area in what is now the district of Mexico City known as San Ángel. He also gave them his daughter, no doubt seeking an alliance with them against rival cities. Instead of marrying her to their chief, however, they killed and skinned her, and when, at their invitation, Achitometl visited them, he was taken into a dark idol-room to burn incense to their god, lit the flame and was faced in the sudden flare, not by Huitzilopochtli, but by a priest dressed in the skin of his daughter. If this is true, and even if it were done with the intention of driving the Tenochcas into the safety of the reed marches, it presents a revolting picture of priests whose minds were twisted and evil.

The reed territory, indicated by Huitzilopochtli's instructions to settle where they saw an eagle feeding, was a clever choice, for the rock islands gave security and the water a means of transport. Moreover it was the meeting point of three city-kingdom boundaries, so that thereafter the Tenochcas were subject to no particular king and could ally themselves first with one and then with another. It was on these advantages that the ultimate greatness of Mexico-Tenochtitlan was based. But it took time; the first rude settlement was built in the water about 1325 and it was not until the beginning of the fifteenth century that the city began to emerge as a military power. It then rapidly extended its domain and influence until it rivalled the old-established city of Texcoco.

From this brief summary of the origins and background of the Aztecs it will be seen that – extraordinary though their race was – they were not the creators of the advanced civilization that the conquistadors found at Tenochtitlan. They inherited it, and there is no evidence that they contributed very much to that inheritance. Nevertheless, the city they built out into the waters of Texcoco Lake was one of the wonders of the world. The map on p. 136 shows its Venetian construction, the enormous extent of it, its complex yet precise military design, the great focal centre of its temples, palaces and market place. As with the city itself, the culture they inherited and adapted for their own needs is best shown in illustration. We shall concern ourselves here primarily with the psycho-religious reasons for their disintegration and defeat in the face of a small and determined force of Spanish adventurers.

The Tenochcas had come out of the wilderness with one god, Huitzilopochtli – god of the sun and god of war also. They now had others to worship; in particular, Tezcatlipoca, the sky god, Tlaloc, the rain god, and Quetzalcoatl, god of learning or Feathered Serpent. But their paramount god remained Huitzilopochtli, and the

demands of this terrible idol, combined with the revised version of the old Toltec god, Tezcatlipoca, became such that, in the end, their military power, though extending throughout most of Middle America, was aimed less at empire than at providing captive sacrifices. Indeed, a warrior's prowess was assessed, not by the men he killed, but by the number of captives he brought in to join the endless stream climbing the steps of the temples to end their lives on the sacrificial stones. This subordination of the warrior to a limited objective undoubtedly had a bearing on the low ratio of killed to wounded in the Spanish ranks.

The Aztec belief that the natural forces to which their geographical situation exposed them could be explained in human terms, and that by representing those forces in idolic form they could influence them by propitiation, is a part of almost every pagan religion. The introduction of human sacrifice was sparing at first, the ultimate offering to propitiate the gods at the time of supreme disaster. Even at its height, when captive humans stood in queues waiting to have their hearts torn out, the Aztecs seem to have shunned those refinements of human cruelty – the flaying alive, the plucking out of nerve threads – practised by their North American cousins. Their cannibalism was initially a ritual affair, the truncated limbs going to the family of the warrior who had made the capture. It grew, however, to be such a habit that one of the conquistadors, writing anonymously, was driven to state categorically that they 'value it more highly than any other food in the world; so much so, that they often go off to war and risk their lives just to kill people to eat'.

Nevertheless, the revolting nature of their religious rites should not blind us to the fact that the Aztecs were the culmination of a remarkable cultural development and that they were in many respects as advanced as the Spaniards. In manners, dress, design and architecture they rivalled medieval Europe; the largest of their temples were almost as grand as the pyramids of Egypt, their gardens as beautiful as Babylon; their stonework matched the structures of ancient Greece; their plastered and lime-washed palaces were as fine as those of Moorish Spain.

From the European point of view, however, it was a civilization full of the strangest anomalies. Picture-writing was highly developed. By this means records could be accurately kept, events and scenes faithfully portrayed. But it was largely useless for the conveying of ideas and impossible to adapt in the Chinese manner to a written language. They had considerable knowledge of astronomy. Indeed, their religion was a peculiar mixture of astrology and what may reasonably be described as necromancy, the priesthood the interpreters, not only of the word of their gods, but of the stars. The book of fate – the *tonalamatl* – was consulted at the birth of a child, and at marriage. Every action – whether personal or political – stemmed from the priesthood, who were as powerful an influence as they were in the Egypt of the Pharaohs.

Circumstances, chiefly climatic and geographical, produce the variety of racial characteristics and the politico-religious organization of individual civilizations.

The pyramid at El Taijn, in the Vera Cruz area, has 365 niches.

Aztec religion was based upon human sacrifice: a scene from a Mexican codex above. Information was conveyed by picture-writing right; in this codex a tribe is submitting to a Zapotec ruler; the formalised footprints indicate the journey they have made; the year and the date are shown by calendar symbols (the year is indicated by the symbol resembling a capital A, the other symbols indicate day names).

So it was with the Aztecs. The Valley of Mexico – they called it Anahuac, which means beside the waters – positioned only 18 degrees north of the equator, has one of the most perfect climates in the world. Where the coast swelters in great heat, here in the *tierra templada*, more than seven thousand feet up, the climate is temperate, the soil rich. But the land which Cortés described by crumpling a sheet of parchment in his fist and saying 'There is your map of Mexico', is thick with old volcanoes, and though names like Popocatépetl and Iztaccihuatl may make strange music to our ears, to the Aztecs these were mountains of dread, capable of belching forth fire and smoke and burning ash. It was these towering volcanic vents, always there, always a part of their visual horizon, that dominated their lives, so that they felt themselves to be a part of the natural forces of their universe, and sought always to propitiate and to be in tune with the rhythm of those forces. Life, and the land in which they lived, was as capricious as the gods they served. The idol representations of these gods were grotesque, and, like much of their design in pottery, stone and precious metals, reveal a certain affinity with the poorer cultures of the North American Indians. In the case of the Aztecs, however, the grotesqueness of their idols was highly symbolic, the significance of each item of grotesquery and adornment matching the complexity of their beliefs and religious rituals.

Their administrative system, however, was not much inferior to that of sixteenth-century Europe. All power stemmed from the monarchy. But their kings were not hereditary. They were chosen from the ruling house by a small number of electors, who subsequently constituted a sort of privy council and became the crown's principal advisers. Thus, there was continuity of stable government with their kings trained from birth to the position they might attain by election. As might be expected in a martial race, the successful candidate must have distinguished himself as a warrior in battle, though by the time Moctezuma the Second came to the throne, the priesthood had reached such a dominant position of power that the choice of the electors was greatly influenced by his position in the priesthood. His enthronement involved complicated rites at the great temple built by his uncles: he first of all pierced his ears, arms and legs with sharp slivers of bone and then, streaming with blood, he took two quails, cut off their heads and sprinkled the blood on the altar flame. Mounting to the top of the teocalli, he entered the great idol-room of Huitzilopochtli, kissed the earth, pierced his body again, sprinkled the blood of more quails around the room, and finally he incensed the four corners of it. It was the king of Texcoco who crowned him, placing on his head a mitre-shaped covering of the most superb featherwork ornamented with gold and jewels.

His palace was designed and constructed as the administrative centre of the Aztec world. It included council chambers and courts of justice, and besides providing accommodation for himself, his wives and his personal attendants, it also housed his bodyguard, which was much like a court, since it included the chief nobles of the state. It was thus a huge rambling place, the seat of government for all the vassal cities and provinces of the Aztec empire, the centre of power. What that power amounted to is at least indicated by one Spanish writer's claim that thirty of the greatest caciques, who resided part of the year in Mexico, could each count a hundred thousand vassals on their estates. And since these great estates, and others much smaller, were built up through grants of land made as a reward for military service and entailed obligations in the event of war, the whole system was essentially feudal.

The business of war was highly organized. As in the Roman Empire, all vassal states had to supply their quota of warriors. There were also military orders, similar to those in Spain, which provided the élite of the army. They had their own distinctive liveries, their own insignia, which was sometimes reproduced in carving on their wooden helmets, and they were granted special privileges. The maturer warriors were distinguished by their dress, the richness of which was in proportion to their prowess, and the war chiefs carried frameworks on their backs brilliantly peacocked with feathers. The military unit, the equivalent of the legion, or regiment, was about eight thousand warriors, sub-divided into some twenty companies, each under its junior commander. Every unit and every tribe had its own brilliant standard of featherwork, so that the cumulative effect of a large Mexican force was one of fantastic colour.

Disobedience to command was punishable by death. But that was not the spur to valour that was to shock even the battle-hardened Spanish men-at-arms. To the Mexicans war was a religious rite, the human equivalent of the perpetual struggle of the elemental forces of nature. To be in battle was to be in tune with the terrible rhythms of the universe. From early youth they toned up their muscles in the ball court, hips and elbows thrusting like lightning at the solid rubber ball as they endeavoured to drive it through the rings set along the side wall. This highly energetic game goes back to the Formative period in the first millenium B.C. and may well have been what anthropologists would now describe as a 'displacement activity' designed to divert aggressive instincts and so reduce the dangers of war. The Aztecs, however, used it simply as a means of exercise. When there were no campaigns to fight, their warriors engaged in formalized, gladiatorial combats known as the War of Flowers. This was something akin to the jousting tournaments of European chivalry; warriors slain were cremated with full honours, for their spirits were translated to the Aztec Valhalla, and captured warriors went glorying to their deaths on the sacrificial stone. War was the sublimation of earth's cataclysmic struggles. But there was a softer side to it. There were hospitals for warriors wounded in battle, even for the sick and permanently disabled, and the diplomatic immunity of envoys was strictly observed, provided they kept to the main tracks.

Communication between Mexico and the outlying provinces was by runners specially trained from youth. With posthouses every two leagues, which is every

Moctezuma's palace also served as a law court, here seen in session *above left*. Warriors were graded according to the number of prisoners they had captured *above right*. Young men exercised themselves in the ball courts, shown here at Chichén Itzá *below*.

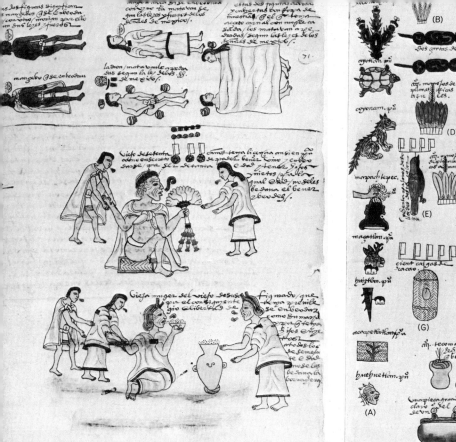

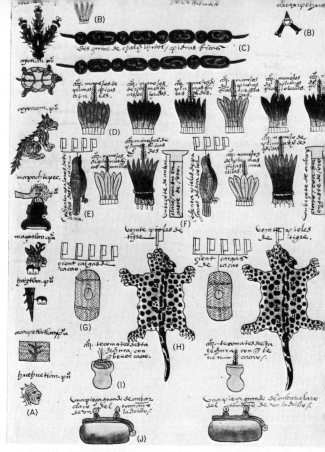

Punishments were severe in Aztec society *above left*: those guilty of drunkenness, stealing and adultery were put to death by stoning (as shown in the upper part), but old people were permitted to get drunk (as shown in the lower part).

A tribute roll from a tropical region *above right*; the glyphs down the left (A) stand for the towns paying tribute; the glyphs (B) indicate the bi-annual dates on which the tribute was due; the other symbols indicate the tribute to be paid: (C) strings of jadeite beads; (D) handfuls of feathers; (E) skins of birds; (F) lip ornaments of amber with gold setting; (G) loads of cacao; (H) ocelot skins; (I) cups for drinking cacao; (J) pieces of amber.

An Aztec calendar stone *right*, in the form of a model of the Temple of the Sun at Tenochtitlan, for which it served as a dedication stone.

5·2 miles, information could be relayed very swiftly indeed. The royal table in Mexico is believed to have been served regularly with fish within twenty-four hours of its having been caught in the Gulf sea over two hundred miles away, an average courier speed of almost ten miles an hour over the mountains.

The revenues of the state were derived partly from tribute and partly from taxes. These were levied primarily on the produce of the land. But there were, nevertheless, taxes on manufactured goods. The crown itself possessed vast estates which contributed direct to the exchequer. Tribute from conquered cities and tribes was levied by tax-gatherers who could call on local garrisons to enforce their demands. And since any defaulter could be arrested and sold into slavery, the system was open to abuse. In the absence of coinage, tribute was in the form of produce and goods, which was paid into the granaries and warehouses provided in each town centre, and then transported to Mexico on the backs of the *tamemes*, or carriers. The following detailed list gives some idea of the tribute exacted and the sort of products that the conquered territories yielded:

20 chests of ground chocolate; 40 pieces of armour, of a particular device; 2,400 loads of large mantles, or woven cloth; 800 loads of small mantles, of rich wearing apparel; 5 pieces of armour, of rich feathers; 60 pieces of armour, of common feathers; a chest of beans; a chest of chian; a chest of maize; 8,000 reams of paper; likewise 2,000 loaves of very white salt, refined in the shape of a mould, for the consumption only of the lords of Mexico; 8,000 lumps of unrefined copal; 400 small baskets of white refined copal; 100 copper axes; 80 loads of red chocolate; 800 xícaras, out of which they drank chocolate; a little vessel of small turquoise stones; 4 wooden chests full of maize; 4,000 loads of lime; tiles of gold, of the size of an oyster, and as thick as the finger; 40 bags of cochineal; 20 bags of gold-dust, of the finest quality; a diadem of gold, of a specified pattern; 20 lip-jewels of clear amber, ornamented with gold; 200 loads of chocolate; 100 pots or jars of liquid-amber; 8,000 handfuls of rich scarlet feathers; 40 'tiger'-skins; 1,600 bundles of cotton.

The legal system was quite highly developed. Every city had its supreme judge appointed by the crown. Below him was a magistrate's court of three. In the country districts there were local magistrates chosen by the people themselves, and at the family community level the responsibility for law and order was assigned to what amounted to a village constable. Corruption in officialdom was punishable by death. Inured to the cruelty of their religious rites, capital offences were many – for murder, of course, even for the murder of a slave, for thieving, for altering land boundaries, giving short measure, prodigality, even drunkenness. Lesser crimes were punished by slavery. No man or woman could be born into slavery, but parents could sell their children. Slavery, however, was itself governed by very exact laws so that the cruelty of the system was not apparent in Mexico until after the Conquest.

As in the Dark Ages of medieval Europe, it was religion that raised the crafts to the level of fine art, particularly the stonemasons' craft. One of the best examples of this is the intricate motif-sculpture of the great Calendar Stone. The central part is a representation of the four eras of the world's destruction and re-birth, the mythology of earlier Indian cultures having been incorporated by the Aztec priests into their own theological teaching. The rest of the stone is extremely practical, a clear statement of the way the astronomer-priests operated their solar calendar. The division of the year into 18 months of 20 days each, left a short month of 5 days, all of which were considered unlucky and required propitiation rites. A god or goddess ruled over each 20-day month, rather like our signs of the zodiac. The days were designated by a number and a month name as in our own calendar (i.e. 15 Tozoztontli). There was also a 260-day divinatory cycle based on 13 numbers and 20 signs repeated in series (i.e. 5 Calli or House). Each day could thus be designated by reference to either system. It was very complex, the divinatory cycle being set down in picture-writing in the *tonalamatl*, a long folded strip of amate, or figbark paper, with usually two 'pages' for each week of the year. This was the priests' handbook of ritual, a sacerdotal almanac that was used for casting horoscopes and dominated the lives of all.

Each year was designated by the name of the day in the 260-day cycle on which it began and mathematically this was restricted to 4 out of the 20 (i.e. Rabbit, Reed, House or Flint Knife), each with its appropriate number. The number 1 attached to one of these four only came up on the first day of the year every 13 years. As with cards, these 13-year 'suits' resulted in 'packs', or sheafs, of 52 years. In this way the two systems came together, for the dual designation of two numbers and two names meant that, again mathematically, the four of them could only be repeated in each 52-year cycle, 52×365 days being the lowest common multiple of 365 and 260. Thus the year of completion of the Calendar Stone would be recorded as 13-Cane of the 7th sheaf. The change from one cycle to another was as important to the Aztecs as the centuries are to us, the death of one sheaf and the birth of the next being marked by the New Fire Ceremony.

Moctezuma came to the Aztec throne in 1503. He had been chosen out of a number of candidates by twelve electors who included Nezahualpilli, king of the powerful and allied city-state of Texcoco, just across the lake from Tenochtitlan. Moctezuma was then about twenty-three years old, and because the end of each cycle or sheaf of years could be the end of an era, he was chosen more for his close observance of the ritual ceremonies of their religious beliefs than for his ability as a warrior. Thus the electors paved the way for Cortés' entry into Mexico and their own destruction.

Moctezuma's father, Axayacatl, had died in 1481, the year 2-House of the 7th sheaf. He had been succeeded by his brother Tizoc, who had been war chief and who had begun the reconstruction of the huge joint temple to the gods of war and

The feathered serpent, the chief god in Aztec mythology. One of the stone carvings on the palace of Quetzalcoatl at Teotihuacán.

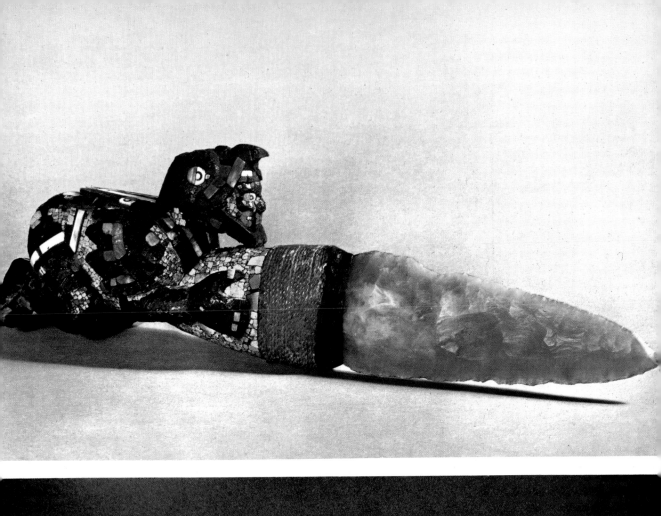

rain – Huitzilopochtli and Tlaloc. He was responsible also for the carving of the greatest of the sacrificial stones, and when he died, supposedly poisoned by his own captains, he was succeeded by his brother, Ahuitzotl. This was in 1486, the year 7-Rabbit, and it was Ahuitzotl who completed the great temple and for its dedication amassed the staggering total of twenty thousand human sacrifices.

The survival of Aztec man depended on the strength of his gods, and since a human being was the most precious offering they could make, they presumed a diet of human hearts provided the best nutriment. War, being the prime business of the state, the hearts of captives were regarded as superior – the more virile and combative the warrior captive the more beneficial the offering of his heart to the god. But when so many were required, it was the tributary tribes who had inevitably borne the brunt of the demand for human victims. The effect of this blood-bath was wide-spread revolt, particularly in the Puebla region, where the war-like Tlaxcalans and Cholulans resisted strongly. All of which Ahuitzotl probably enjoyed. He was a ferocious and blood-thirsty man, whose military prowess greatly extended the Aztec empire. As a result, Mexico-Tenochtitlan expanded to such an extent that he had to construct a new aqueduct. He died of a head injury while supervising the reconstruction of the dykes after a disastrous flood in 1503.

This then was the position when his nephew, Moctezuma, succeeded him – the cult of human sacrifice at an absolute peak and the Tlaxcalans, the Cholulans and other tribes only kept in submission by the force of Aztec arms; and the end of the 52-year cycle only four years off. What sort of a man Moctezuma was it is difficult to say at this distance of time. He was not lacking in military ability, for he kept a tight hold on the conquered tribes, and in one campaign against the rebellious Oaxacans was able to sacrifice some twelve thousand captives to Huitzilopochtli. And he was certainly not lacking in cunning, for he lured his Texcocan allies into an ambush as a reprisal for the death of his sister, and when their king, Nezahualpilli, died in 1516, he appointed a successor of his own against the wishes of the Texcocan electors. Politically, this high-handed action was ill-advised, for it very nearly broke the alliance. This underlines the out-standing weakness of the Aztec empire. Military successes were never consolidated into an administrative unit. The word 'empire' is, therefore, misleading. The Aztecs, like every Middle American Indian power before them, exacted tribute from the tribes they conquered, but left them organizationally independent. This was the Achilles' heel upon which Cortés was able to play with such effect.

Aguilar, writing like Bernal Díaz at the end of a long life, when he had been more than forty years a member of the Dominican order, describes Moctezuma as being 'of medium height and slender build, with a large head and somewhat flat nostrils. He was very astute, discerning and prudent, learned and capable, but also harsh and irascible and very firm in his speech.' The description given by Bernal Díaz is similar, but more detailed: 'The great Moctezuma was about forty

Mixtec culture: a sacrificial obsidian knife with mosaic handle above; *a two-headed mosaic serpent* below. *These objects are believed to have been among the treasure presented to Cortés by Moctezuma.*

years old, well-proportioned, spare and slight, and not very dark, though of the usual Indian complexion. He did not wear his hair long, but just over his ears, and he had a short black beard, well-shaped and thin. His face was rather long and cheerful, he had fine eyes, and in his appearance and manner could express geniality or, when necessary, a serious composure.' And he goes on to say that Moctezuma was very neat and clean, and took a bath every afternoon, and that he had many women as his mistresses; these were daughters of chieftains, but two of them were legitimate wives and were caciques in their own right. He says that Moctezuma did not practise sodomy, but that when he had intercourse with any of his wives it was so secret that only a few of his servants knew about it.

Moctezuma had apparently a guard of some two hundred chieftains lodged in rooms beside his own, only some of whom were permitted to speak to him; and when they entered his presence they were compelled to take off their rich cloaks and put on others of little value. They had to be clean and walk barefoot, with their eyes downcast, for they were not allowed to look him in the face. The same applied to all the great chieftains who came to visit him from the distant lands of tributary tribes.

His meals were served to him by two handsome Indian women, and if the weather was cold, a large fire was made of the bark of a sweet smelling tree, and round him was placed a screen with the figures of gods worked in gold. Before he ate, four beautiful girls brought water for him to wash his hands. When he had been handed maize-cakes, very white, made with eggs and served on plates covered with clean napkins, the women retired and his only companions during the meal were his four closest advisers, all old men, relatives and chieftains. 'He talked with them every now and then and asked them questions, and as a great favour he would sometimes offer one of them a dish of whatever tasted best . . . and if he gave them anything to eat they ate it standing, with deep reverence and without looking in his face.' He was served with a great variety of dishes, all cooked in the native style, and they were put over small earthenware braziers to keep warm. Díaz talks of more than thirty dishes and over three hundred plates of food, including fowls, turkeys, pheasants, local partridges, quail, tame and wild duck, venison, wild boar, marsh birds, pigeons, hares and rabbits. The food was served on red and black Cholula ware, and whilst he was dining the guards in the adjoining rooms were not allowed to speak above a whisper. With his food Moctezuma drank chocolate, sometimes out of cups of pure gold. And he was attended by jesters and clowns, and even stilt-walkers, all drawn from a quarter of the town reserved for entertainers. 'They also placed on the table three tubes, much painted and gilded, in which they put liquid-amber mixed with some herbs which are called tobacco. When Moctezuma had finished his dinner, and the singing and dancing were over and the cloths had been removed, he would inhale the smoke from one of these tubes. He took very little of it, and then fell asleep.' After that it was the turn of the guards and the household servants to feed, and 'more than a thousand plates of food must have been brought in for them, and more than two thousand jugs of chocolate frothed up in the Mexican style, and infinite quantities of fruit'.

For his amusement Moctezuma had an aviary full of every type of Mexican bird, from the gay-feathered species of the coastal swamps to the eagles of the high mountains. There was also a zoo, where, besides every kind of beast from his dominions, Tapia says Moctezuma 'kept men and women monsters, some crippled, others dwarfed or hunchbacked'. He also describes another house in which he kept water fowl in such numbers that six hundred men were employed in taking care of them. There was an ornithological sick bay for birds that were ill, and in this house the king also kept human albinos. All these houses and cages were in the gardens, which 'were a wonderful sight and required many gardeners to take care of them. Everything was built of stone and plaster; baths and walks and closets and rooms like summerhouses where they danced and sang.'

Moctezuma came to the throne at a bad time, the shadow of the 52-year cycle's end already looming. The sheaf was always tied in a 2-Cane year, and 2-Cane was only four years away. Since he was at that time already the head of the priesthood, he knew only too well how bad the omens were. Even at the time of his accession, the astrologers were beginning to prophesy that the end of the 7th sheaf would mark the end of the world, the end of the 4th era, the era of Fire Sun. After what Ahuitzotl had done, the sacrifice of twelve thousand Oaxacan captives was perhaps not too much to propitiate the gods against such a dread prospect and to satisfy his people that everything possible was being done to ward off the threat of doom that faced them. Moreover, word had been brought by far-travelled traders of strange men with white skins and beards and ships like castles. The story of Columbus and those who had followed him had doubtless grown in the telling, and in the picture-writing the ships would probably have seemed like fortified islands emerging from the waves.

The Dark Ages were a world-wide phenomenon in man's cultural development. It was an age of superstition, and just as the Spaniards, clad in the chivalric armour of the Christian faith, ascribed every victory or escape from death to the intervention of Divine Providence and rode to victory with the names of saints as their battle cry, so the Aztecs, like children, twisted natural, even imagined events, to prophetic purpose. Sahagún gives no less than seven omens of doom beginning in the year 12-House (1517) with a comet 'like a flaming ear of corn', and continuing through to the last year of the cycle: the temple of Huitzilopochtli burst into flames; another 'was struck by a blow from the sun' – a lightning bolt; another comet, showering sparks, streaked across the sky in full sunlight; the great lake of Tenochtitlan boiled on a windless day, rising for no apparent reason and washing away many houses; a woman was heard weeping, night after night, and crying, 'My children, we must flee away from this city!'; and fishermen caught a crane in their nets that was the colour of ashes and had a mirror in its head in which Moctezuma is supposed to have seen the Spanish cavaliers riding into battle against his people.

The cumulative effect of these portents was that Mexico and all the rest of the Aztec world waited in growing terror as the last days of the 7th sheaf drew to a close. Throughout those last days, the five unlucky ones, they fasted and prayed. On the fifth day all fires were extinguished according to custom, even the sacred flames on the temple altars; and all household furniture, utensils, ornaments, all the little family gods, were thrown into the lake, the empty houses swept clean, the pregnant women locked up for fear they might be changed into wild beasts, the children forcibly kept awake to save them from being turned into rats.

As the sun finally set, Moctezuma, with the priests and all the chieftains and civic dignitaries of the city, climbed to the top of the old crater of Huixachtecatl, the Hill of the Star, to the temple on its summit that looks out over all the Valley of Mexico. The end of the world, or the birth of a new sheaf of fifty-two years – which was it to be? The suspense was appalling. Fear ran naked through the night and the massed multitude of Aztecs stood silent and awed, their eyes on the little group of astrologers on the temple summit of the old volcano.

Moctezuma had prepared against this moment, instructing his warriors to produce from the year's fighting a captive suitable for the occasion. The man chosen was a chieftain of the tribe of Huejotzingo. His name was Xiuhtlamin, and now this wretched man stood waiting in the idol-room with the priest whose duty it was to kindle the new fire. The priests had all put on the masks of the deities they served, and on the platform at the top of the teocalli the astrologers watched for the moment when certain stars would pass the meridian. The dark night wore on. No conflagration destroyed the earth. The world did not end.

Suddenly there was a movement among the astrologers. Word was passed to the idol-room; five priests seized Xiuhtlamin and flung him across the sacrificial stone. An obsidian blade slashed open his chest, the heart was plucked out, and in the gaping wound the new fire was kindled by the oldest of methods, a wooden spindle. It was a moment of wild rejoicing. Runners lit their torches from the solitary flame and ran through the starlit night, from village to village, relighting the altar fires of the temples. Long before dawn bonfires blazed the length of the Valley, and every hearth in every home burned with the new-born fire. The next cycle had begun – the cycle of the 8th sheaf – with the promise of fifty-two years before fear of the world's ending again threatened them.

This event undoubtedly made a deep impression on Moctezuma. The strain of it had been very great, for the shadow of it had lain over him ever since he had come to the throne. But for him it did not end with the birth of the 8th sheaf. The function of the priesthood in a religiously primitive and therefore superstitious community is leadership through intelligent anticipation of events and the interpretation of supernatural omens in such a way that the people are prepared and the events themselves controlled, or at least influenced. Trained to the leadership of the priesthood, Moctezuma understood these functions very well, but at the same time he was himself deeply involved in the mythology of the past, so that his statesmanlike qualities were clouded by his religious beliefs, his martial instincts sapped.

In the years that followed, vague reports of the activities of men of another race were constantly coming in – from traders, from captives, from people of the coastal districts in touch with the Caribs. They were so persistent that they could not be ignored; and because of his training he was inclined to interpret every peasant's highly-coloured, emotional account of some unusual happening as a sign of ill-omen. Feeling himself threatened from the east, he became haunted by the old prophesy of Quetzalcoatl, that the prophet-king would return, pale-skinned and bearded, from out of the east where the morning star rose. And there were unusual happenings – a comet trailing sparks, lightning striking at the thatched roof of a small temple, a strange pillar of white smoke rising in the east. For a superstitious mind already filled with foreboding, these phenomena were far from reassuring.

Then, in the year 12-House, the fourteenth of his reign, came messengers from the coast with more definite news of the bearded white men. They had come out of the sea, from fortified islands that moved on the water; they had weapons that thundered flame and smoke and killed at a distance; and they were mounted on strange beasts like deer. An Indian description gives some idea of the impact of the horse on Moctezuma's warriors:

> The 'stags' came forward, carrying the soldiers on their backs. The soldiers were wearing cotton armour. They bore their leather shields and their iron spears in their hands, but their swords hung down from the necks of the 'stags'. These animals wear little bells, they are adorned with many little bells. When the 'stags' gallop, the bells make a loud clamour, ringing and reverberating. These 'stags', these 'horses', snort and bellow. They sweat a very great deal, the sweat pours from their bodies in streams. The foam from their muzzles drips onto the ground. It spills out in fat drops, like a lather of *amole* [plants from which soap was made]. They make a loud noise when they run; they make a great din, as if stones were raining on the earth. Then the ground is pitted and scarred where they set down their hooves. It opens wherever their hooves touch it.

Moreover the strangers were demanding gold. Grijalva had landed on the coast of Yucatán.

6   *The Enigma of Moctezuma*

WHEN CORTÉS LANDED in the year 1-Cane – this was the sign that ruled Quetzalcoatl and therefore the year of his prophesied return – Moctezuma, watching upon events in his distant capital, seems to have been strangely inhibited from direct action. He appears to have decided to discourage his war chiefs from leading their warriors into battle. Instead, he gave his sorcerer priests full rein. Some of the gifts sent to the Spaniards, possibly some of the food as well, had been doctored with the witchcraft of these necromancers. Quintalbor, the Mexican who resembled Cortés, was probably the equivalent of an effigy stuck with a needle. When the sorcerers had done their worst by incantation and sacrifice and all the devilish arts of the Aztec religion, without any effect whatsoever, no priest could accuse Moctezuma of having failed in his religious duties. It left him free to act as he thought best.

A crucial factor was Teudilli's arrival with the helmet and Cortés' request that it be filled with gold. The helmet was apparently somewhat similar to those worn by their ancestors, the people of Quetzalcoatl. It was just one of the many things that reinforced the growing belief that the Spaniards might be the followers of the great prophet-king their forefathers had spurned. Moreover, the pictographs sent back from San Juan de Ulúa were sufficiently clear in their portrayal of ships and guns and horses for Moctezuma's war chiefs to realize they would be faced with weapons that were quite new to them. In fact, in their portrayal of the Spaniards, they reinforced the godlike image already created by rumour. Pictographs, however, could not convey the intentions of the Spanish captain nor indicate whom he said he served. All Moctezuma knew for certain was that Cortés was stirring up trouble in the provinces, that he wished to visit him and was demanding gold.

Buying time is an old diplomatic move, but this explanation of Moctezuma's generous stream of gifts is an over-simplification. His reactions were undoubtedly more complex, for his mind was torn between belief in the superstitions of his religion and the practical problems of his dual position as religious and temporal leader of his people. He must have known he had the power to destroy the invaders, but he was already convinced that behind these invaders would come others, a whole host rising out of the sea, and in any case he half believed they were gods, and as gods they should be propitiated. Thus, instead of armies, he sent them gold and presents and priests with copal to sprinkle them with incense as they did the gods. Anything, so long as he did not have to meet them face-to-face. And so, by prevarication, he lost even the will to resist.

At this stage, however, he had not finally decided on capitulation to what he felt was inevitable. The diplomat, the priest and the warrior in him were still at odds, so that his actions appear capricious and uncertain, his policy line difficult to understand. Thus, when Cortés has defeated the Tlaxcalans, Moctezuma expresses his willingness to become a vassal of the Emperor Charles, whilst at the same time instructing his emissaries to make every effort to dissuade Cortés from entering into an alliance with Tlaxcala. He is still hoping to put off the evil day. But the weakness resulting from the failure of the Mexicans to absorb the tribes they had conquered now became apparent. With Tlaxcala, and all the tribes back to the coast, in open revolt, the defection of Cholula was inevitable unless positive action were taken immediately. He had twenty thousand warriors – Cortés says fifty thousand – in the neighbourhood of Cholula. If the Spaniards could be lulled into a false sense of security, and by guile and treachery ambushed, then they would never again trust the Cholulans, or any other tribe, as allies.

On the day that Cortés entered Cholula Moctezuma sent an envoy to the caciques to arrange the ambush, with a present of jewels and cloth and a golden drum. The Cholulan chiefs agreed to the plan and at once ceased to have any contact with the Spaniards. On the third day, in accordance with Moctezuma's instructions, they ceased to supply them with food, and when Cortés thereupon decided to resume his march, he was informed that it was out of the question as there was no food available in Mexico to supply his army. The Cholulans, meanwhile, had agreed to provide him with an escort of two thousand warriors, much as the Tlaxcalans had done for the march to Cholula. They undertook to send them into the camp the following morning. The Mexican force was now split; half moved into the city itself and the other half concealed itself in what would now be termed a *barranca*, a dry river-bed. The trap was set, and throughout the night and all next day Moctezuma waited anxiously for news, going through the daily routine of sacrifice and prayer.

When at length his ambassadors returned, hot-foot and dusty, and scared half out of their wits, it was with a story of total disaster. Cortés, they said, had known about the plot the previous evening. He had told them so to their faces, accusing Moctezuma of treachery. Then he had put them under a strong guard and at dawn the whole Spanish army had stood to, prepared for attack. As the sun rose far more than the two thousand Cholulan warriors promised as escort crowded into the great square where the Spaniards were encamped. Cortés had immediately informed their chiefs that he knew what they intended and that he proposed to repay their treachery in kind. He locked them up and ordered an arquebus to be fired; at the signal the guns had opened up and the bright blades of Spanish steel had flashed in the sunlight. Without their chiefs to lead them, the Cholulans lacked direction. The slaughter had been dreadful. In two hours, the ambush that was to have been the end of the Spanish invaders had been itself destroyed. Moreover, those attacking from without the camp had been mowed down as they charged up the broad avenues by guns carefully sited in the gateways. By then Cortés' Tlaxcalans and Zempoalans were fighting their way into the city from the fields outside, and with the horsemen and foot soldiers advancing, the Cholulan and Mexican warriors had been caught between the hammer and the anvil of a double attack. At the end of five hours some six thousand of them were dead and some of the priests, who had climbed up to the top of the largest idol-tower, had been burned there, lamenting all the time that their idol had forsaken them.

This news, which was quickly followed by the return of the Mexican forces that had waited in ambush outside Cholula, seems to have completely unnerved Moctezuma. His reaction was to sacrifice several prisoners to the god of war, then shut himself up with ten of his chief priests and devote himself to prayer and further sacrifices. Ultimately he sent another embassy to Cortés, with yet more gifts, to plead his innocence and disclaim any responsibility for what had happened. He may even have been relieved to hear that Cortés affected to believe these protestations, for by then the Spanish general had Cholula in absolute submission and had even persuaded the chief cacique, whom he had appointed governor in place of his brother, who had been slain, to make peace with their old enemies, the Tlaxcalans. With these two tribes as allies, and all the country round supporting him, Cortés could now put into the field a confederate army of such power that the Mexican war chiefs themselves were probably by then advising caution.

Dazed, apparently, by the magnitude of the disaster, Moctezuma let more than a fortnight slip by without making any decisive move, thus allowing the Spaniards to consolidate their position in Cholula. In the end, it was Cortés who forced the issue, sending emissaries with a final request for permission to enter Mexico-Tenochtitlan. As remembered long afterwards by Bernal Díaz, the message Cortés sent to Moctezuma was a typical example of the sort of double talk at which his lawyer-trained mind excelled, making him more than a match for Indian cunning. The gist of it was that in order to fulfil the purpose for which their lord the king had sent them, the Spaniards had crossed many seas and distant lands, and all this for the sole purpose of visiting Moctezuma and telling him certain things which would be very profitable to him when he understood them. Furthermore, that on their way to his city his ambassadors had guided them to Cholula, which they said was tributary to him, and that for the first two days they spent there the inhabitants had treated them well, but that on the third day they had treacherously plotted to kill them. But since the Spaniards were men against whom no trickery or double-

dealing or wickedness could be plotted without their immediately discovering it, they had punished some of the Cholulans who had hatched the plot; but knowing that they were the subjects of Moctezuma, they had, out of respect for his person and because of their great friendship for him, refrained from destroying and killing all those who had shared in the planning of this treachery.

Cortés' ambassadors had then made the point that both the priests and the caciques of Cholula had declared that the ambush had been arranged on his, Moctezuma's, advice and at his command. Having made this point quite clear, they then went on to say that Cortés had refused to believe that so great a prince would give such commands, especially as he had declared himself the friend of the Spaniards; and that they had inferred from his character that if his idols had put such an evil thought into his head as to make war on them, he would do it in the open field. 'However, we do not care whether we are attacked in the open country or in the town, by day or by night, for we will kill anyone who ventures to do so.' And the emissaries added that as Cortés felt quite certain Moctezuma was his great friend, and wished to see and speak with him, he would set out for Mexico immediately to give him a very complete account of what his king, the Emperor Charles, commanded the Spaniards to do.

The implacable determination of Cortés, his ruthless singleness of purpose, was something new to the Indian mind. It was surely the behaviour of a god, and, with this final message, Moctezuma seems to have decided he could no longer avoid the confrontation he dreaded. Special sacrifices and prayers produced the answer that undoubtedly matched the thoughts of his political and military advisers. A city built on water, where every causeway was protected against surprise by a series of drawbridges, constituted the ideal trap. If the Spaniards could be induced to enter the city with only the relatively small force of Tlaxcalans they had with them in Cholula, the drawbridges could be raised behind them and they could be dealt with at leisure, their hearts fed to the gods. This, at any rate, was what the Spanish soldiers believed; and, since it is not borne out by the reported behaviour and speeches of Moctezuma, we can only presume that there was already a conflict of policy between the king and his chief military advisers. He himself appears to have decided that no further attempt should be made to obstruct the Spanish advance, for he dispatched six of his chiefs with a present of gold and jewels and a speech of welcome: 'Our lord the great Moctezuma sends this present, and begs you to accept it with the great love he has for you and all your brothers. He says that the wrong which the people of Cholula did you grieves him greatly and that he wishes to visit further punishment upon them, for they are a wicked and lying people, in that they tried to lay the blame on him and his ambassadors for the crime they attempted to commit.' And the message went on to say that Cortés could come to the city whenever he wished.

So the final stages of the march into Mexico began.

A jade mosaic mask of Maya workmanship.

On a field of his own choosing, and supported by large numbers of his Indian allies, Cortés had a reasonable chance of defeating the Mexicans in battle. But many of his Zempoalans were convinced that the Spaniards would be marching into a trap, that not one of them would escape from Mexico alive – they would either be killed or sacrificed to the Aztec gods. And since they requested leave to return to their homes, Cortés loaded them with presents and let them go. Nevertheless, when he finally began this last stage of his march, he claims that he had with him 'four thousand Indians from Tlaxcala, Huejotzingo, Cholula and Zempoala'. The number was almost certainly very much larger, but what is interesting about this statement is that the Cholulans were now marching with the army. Not only had they mounted a treacherous attack on the Spaniards, but, according to Tapia, the Spaniards, or more probably their Indian allies, had retaliated by doing everything possible to destroy the holy city; Cortés had not put a stop to the destruction for two whole days. It only goes to prove that here, as in many parts of the world today, the ruthless use of force induced respect, even admiration, rather than hatred.

It is not clear how long Cortés had stayed in Cholula, but it was long enough for him to receive the embassy from Moctezuma and also for him to send a detachment of ten soldiers to reconnoitre the pass between the two volcanoes. In fact, they very nearly reached the top of Popocatépetl itself, a remarkable achievement since the mountain was then in the throes of a minor eruption. Their report confirmed that there was a good track through the pass, and since it was the most direct route Cortés decided to take it, even though it meant climbing to over 11,000 feet.

The approach march, which passed near Huejotzingo, an Indian town allied to Tlaxcala, was south of the route advised by Moctezuma's chiefs. This would have taken them across the north flank of Iztaccihuatl, roughly the line of the present motor road. The altitude would have been lower, but the track passed through Culhúan territory to Chalco, a Mexican-held city, and Cortés was not to be deflected from his purpose even by the assurance of a plentiful supply of food. He may have feared a trap, but there is no doubt that the main attraction of the Huejotzingo route was the desire to add to his force of Indian auxiliaries. This would explain why the army made only so few miles on the first day.

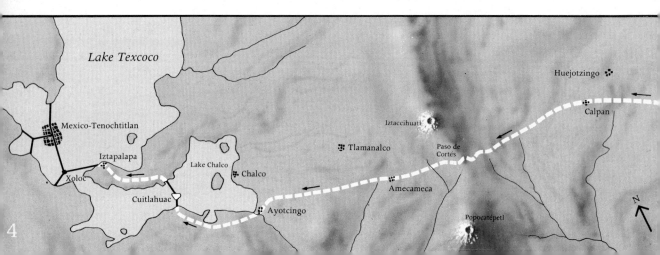

Cortés route map 4 left. *The massacre at Cholula* above. *An imaginative seventeenth-century engraving depicting the Spaniards' ascent of Popocatépetl* below.

They stopped the night at Calpan, just short of the twin hills that are so similar in outline to the huge range they were about to climb. This settlement was very close to Huejotzingo and the chiefs and priests of the town came out to meet them with food and small gifts of gold. Bernal Díaz says they warned Cortés that when he reached the top of the pass he would find two tracks; one had been blocked by felled trees so that it was impassable for horses, the other had been cleared. If the Spaniards took the cleared track, they would suddenly find it blocked by earth and here the Mexicans would be waiting for them in ambush behind ditches and barricades. More to the point, they offered him 'plenty of men' to help the Tlaxcalans clear the trees on the blocked path. The army must have marched again at first light, for Bernal Díaz says they reached the pass a little before mid-day. There is no suggestion that they bivouacked a night at the foot of the mountains – Cortés merely states that 'two days after leaving Cholula we climbed the pass'. If they did not pause on the way, then the army covered about fifteen miles and climbed four thousand feet in under six hours, a quite incredible achievement since, in the latter stages of what is a pretty steep climb, they would be suffering from the effects of the altitude and also from the cold – the snow line of Popocatépetl reaches down almost into the pass. A probable explanation is that Bernal Díaz was in an advance party sent on ahead to secure the pass. As they reached the top, marked now by the only monument to Cortés in the whole of Mexico, it began to snow.

The information about the two routes down from the pass proved correct. The right hand path, which led to Tlamanalco, a settlement very close to Chalco, had been cleared for them; the other, leading down to Amecameca and following roughly the line of the present road, had been blocked by trees. When Cortés demanded an explanation from the Mexican chiefs, they said it had been done to ensure that the Spaniards went by way of Chalco where they would be fully provided for. It must have struck him as an odd way of signposting the route. At any rate, he took the Amecameca path. By the time the Tlaxcalans and their allies had manhandled the fir trees out of the way dusk was closing in, and with the snow still falling and lying thick on the ground, the army had a cold night of it in the shelter of some shacks. However, Cortés says they did not lack for timber to make fires; probably only the sentinels and patrols suffered from the cold.

One of the paths leading down from the pass had been blocked.

It was all downhill after that, and in the flat country around Amecameca, where they camped the night, food was plentiful again. They were now into the curious geographical phenomenon that had attracted so many waves of Indian settlement – the great upland valley of Mexico, which lies at a height of 7,250 feet and is more than half-encircled by mountains, the source of water for a whole complex of large, shallow lakes. These have now almost all been drained, but at that time extensive irrigation combined with the sunshine and the clarity of the air at that altitude to make it a land of quite unbelievable plenty. Like much of the country the Spaniards had already marched through, it had something of the quality of the Estremadura – the sense of space, the wide skies, the hot sun, and always the mountain vista in the distance. Here, however, the hills that rose up out of the plain were not old rock hills, but bare, bleak slag heaps, the lava pustules of recent volcanic action.

At Amecameca they were still outside the ring of lakeside city-states that constituted the Culhúan confederacy. Indians poured into the camp from all the neighbouring towns, including Chalco, full of curiosity to see the *teules*. They brought presents of gold and cloaks and women, and their chiefs made the usual complaints about Moctezuma, accusing his tax-gatherers of robbing them of all they possessed, of violating their wives and daughters in front of them and recruiting their men for forced labour. Asked about the swept route, they said that all traces of the ambush had been removed and that the war god had now advised Moctezuma that the Spaniards were to be destroyed in Mexico itself. By then, Cortés was fairly accurately informed about the city. He knew that its canals and drawbridges constituted a potential trap from which he had little hope of escape. Yet he did not falter in his resolve, or even hesitate.

He marched again in the morning, and almost immediately he was met by a fresh embassy from Moctezuma with more gold and more richly designed cloaks, and this message:

Malinche, this present is sent to you by our lord the great Moctezuma, who says that he is sorry you have endured so many hardships in travelling from far distant lands to see him, and that he has already sent to tell you that he will give you much gold and silver and many *chalchihuites* [the jade plaques that the Mexicans prized above everything for their colour and rarity] as a tribute for your Emperor and yourself and the *teules* of your company, provided you do not come to Mexico. Now he begs you once more kindly not to advance any further, but to return whence you came, and he will send to the port a great quantity of gold and silver and precious stones for your king, and to you he will give four loads of gold, and to each of your brothers one load. Your entry into Mexico, however, is forbidden. All his vassals are in arms to prevent it. What is more, there is only the narrowest of roads, and no food there for you to eat.

Cortés' reply to this was polite, but firm: If the Mexicans had not enough food to supply his men, then it did not matter, they were all of them hardy and could exist on very little. He was now on the final stage of his march to Mexico and he expected Moctezuma to welcome him to his city. This was the last of the ambassadorial exchanges. In all of them Cortés had had the benefit of Doña Marina as his interpreter. She had been at his side ever since he had entered Náhuatl-speaking territory. She was much more than a captive Indian princess acting as interpreter. She was a part of the expedition. She rode with Cortés, accompanied him everywhere, in the dual role of his mouthpiece and his adviser on Indian affairs, interpreting not only their speeches, but also their intentions.

This remarkable woman had, in fact, so identified herself with Cortés that she had become in effect his *alter ego*. It was she who, through an Indian woman, had uncovered the plot at Cholula, and her interpretation of his speeches to the Indians so matched the force and determination of the Spanish original that it is probably true to say that she did more to further his aims on the march to Mexico than the bravest of his captains. Indeed, the Indians themselves, in giving him the title Malinche in every formal speech, testify to the impact of her personality. Unable, like the Chinese, to sound the letter 'r', they called her Malina, and in the duality of their manner and behaviour, Cortés, as her lord, was called Malinche. She was almost certainly in love with him – at any rate, she gave herself to him and eventually bore him a son. But whatever the nature of their personal relations, the fact is that, without the proud and dominant character of this Indian princess to convey his thoughts, it is doubtful whether Cortés would ever have reached Mexico other than as a captive. There is much more to interpretation than mere accuracy of translation, and the paralysing effect of Cortés' personality on Moctezuma – a virtual hypnotizing of the Mexican king, from a distance, into a state of fearful inactivity – was very largely her doing.

The Spaniards spent the night at Ayotcingo on the edge of Chalco Lake, where for the first time they saw Indian houses built half out into the water. Early the next morning, just as they were starting out to cross by the causeway that passed through Cuitlahuac, four nobles arrived, with a large crowd of Mexicans, to announce the approach of Cacama. For Cortés this was the equivalent of a major victory. Cacama was a nephew of Moctezuma, lord of Texcoco, twin city of the Culhúan alliance. 'He came borne on a litter, most richly worked in green feathers with much silver decoration and precious stones set in tree designs that were worked in the finest gold.' On being set down, he made a deep bow and said: 'Malinche, we have come here, I and these chieftains, to place ourselves at your service, and to see that you receive everything you require for yourself and your companions and to instal you in your home, which is our city. For so we have been commanded by our lord the great Moctezuma, who asks you to pardon him for not coming with us himself. It is on account of ill-health and not from lack of very good will towards you that he has not done so.'

Still no meeting with Moctezuma, but it was clear from Cacama's speech that

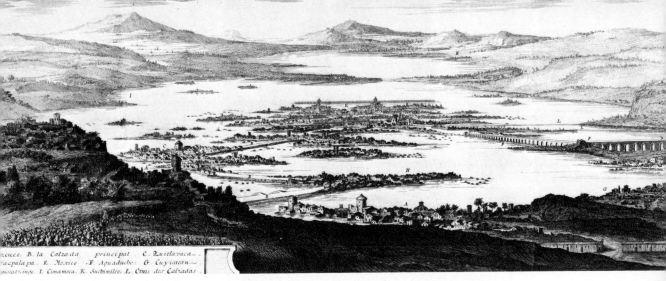

Tenochtitlan lay in the middle of a great lake and was connected to the shore by causeways. This early eighteenth-century engraving, made before the area had been drained, shows the town as rebuilt by the Spaniards but still surrounded by water.

the opposition to his entry into Mexico was crumbling. Or was it merely the mouth of the trap opening? If he felt that, Cortés does not admit it. Nevertheless, the position was extremely dangerous. He had had sentries posted throughout the night against surprise attack and they had killed more than a dozen Indian spies who had come in by canoe. His Tlaxcalan irregulars were undoubtedly nervous and even his four hundred Spaniards must have been very conscious of the fact that they were now nearing the end of the long road up from the coast, about to enter a forbidden city whose warriors had terrorized all the country through which they had marched. Yet Bernal Díaz' manuscript gives no indication of this. Instead, his photographic mind concentrates on recording the impact of that first view of the Valley as they approached the city of Iztapalapa. They had crossed the Cuitlahuac causeway and as they skirted the north shore of the lake, the fantastic view across the main Texcoco lake opened up before them:

> And when we saw all those cities and villages built in the water, and other great towns on dry land, and that straight and level causeway leading to Mexico, we were astounded. These great towns and cúes and buildings rising from the water, all made of stone, seemed like an enchanted vision . . . It was all so wonderful . . . this first glimpse of things never heard of, seen or dreamed of before.

At Iztapalapa they were met by more nobles, lodged in palaces built of stone and cedar wood and other sweet smelling trees, the stucco walls shining in the sun and the rooms and courts shaded by cotton awnings. There were gardens, too, full of roses and fruit trees, and the canoes came right into the gardens from the lake.

Next day, November 8, 1519, was the day of their entry into Mexico. The causeway ran due west at first, and then, after almost four miles, turned north, running eight yards wide and straight as a die to Tenochtitlan, the southern part of the city they could now see mirrored white in the still, sunlit surface of the huge Texcoco Lake. They marched, as always, in battle formation, alert and ready against any eventuality. But, with an escort of some of the greatest nobles in the land, the nervous tension had already been dispelled. The guns and steel were still there, reflected in the waters of the lake, glistening in the sunshine, but the whole Spanish force was infected by the holiday atmosphere, for the crowds of Indian sightseers were so thick on the causeway that the troops had difficulty in forcing a passage. The lake swarmed with canoes, and at every drawbridge the defence towers were jammed with spectators. All Mexico was en fête to see the *teules*, and particularly the men on horseback, about whom they had heard such strange and fabulous stories.

The entry into Mexico is described in great detail by Cortés himself. The causeway, along which they were advancing, was more than five miles long and about two lances wide, so that eight horsemen could ride abreast. In those five miles they passed three cities of between three thousand and six thousand houses, all the people there being involved in the lake salt trade. At Xoloc, where the causeway turns north and is joined by another from the mainland, he was met by about a thousand of the chief citizens of Mexico, all dressed in the liveries of the different military orders. Xoloc was a strongpoint with two small towers or shrines built out over the water, walls twelve feet high and only two gateways. Cortés was held up here for about an hour whilst each of the caciques put his hand to the ground and kissed it and bade him welcome in the name of Moctezuma. It was the final embassy, and they marched on till they came to the outskirts of Tenochtitlan. Here there was a wooden bridge, ten paces broad, the beams of which could be removed. They crossed it, and from that moment they were inside the trap. But the extraordinary thing is that there was no trap.

Moctezuma himself, with two hundred of his chiefs, all barefoot and dressed in rich liveries, now came to meet him. The chiefs approached in two processions, hugging the walls of the street, which was 'very broad, and straight, and beautiful and very uniform from one end to the other'. Moctezuma came down the middle of the street, supported below his arms by his brother, Cuitlahuac, who was king of Iztapalapa, on one side, and Cacama, king of Texcoco, on the other, with a canopy over him made entirely of green feathers and bordered by gold and silver, pearls and *chalchihuites*. Moctezuma was the only one who wore sandals. The soles were of gold, the uppers decorated with precious stones, and as he advanced, some of his chiefs swept the street in front of him and others laid rich cloaks for him to walk on. All kept their eyes averted from his face.

'I descended from my horse', Cortés writes, 'and was about to embrace him, but the two lords in attendance prevented me, with their hands, that I might not touch him, and they, and he also, made the ceremony of kissing the ground.' He was at last face-to-face with the Mexican king.

Cortés enters Tenochtitlan. A seventeenth-century Spanish painting.

18

Entrada de
Cortés En Me
xico, Por la Cal
sada de S. Anto
nio Abad.

18

Miguel Gonz.ᶻ fecit añ. 1698.

19

Recivimiento de
Motecuhzuma à Don
Fer. de los Mexicanos
en Canoas por la
Laguna.

20

19

Moctezuma made him a speech of welcome and Cortés took off a necklace of pearls and glass diamonds he was wearing and put it round Moctezuma's neck. Cuitlahuac now took him by the arm and, thus supported, Cortés followed Moctezuma into the city. This mark of esteem was a public demonstration before all the people of Mexico that the Spaniards were the honoured guests of their king. After walking through several streets, one of Moctezuma's servants arrived with 'two collars, wrapped in a cloth, which were made of coloured shells . . . and from each of the collars hung eight golden shrimps executed with great perfection and about a span long'. The collars were placed round Cortés' neck by Moctezuma himself. The gesture was a revealing one, for these were the insignia of Quetzal-coatl himself.

Aztec sources give this account of that first meeting: After the necklaces had been given, Cortés asked the giver if he were really Moctezuma.

And the king said: 'Yes, I am Motecuhzoma.' Then he stood up to welcome Cortés; he came forward, bowed his head low and addressed him in these words: 'Our lord, you are weary. The journey has tired you, but now you have arrived on the earth. You have come to your city, Mexico. You have come here to sit on your throne, to sit under its canopy.

'The kings who have gone before, your representatives, guarded it and preserved it for your coming. The kings Itzcoatl, Motecuhzoma the Elder, Axayacatl, Tizoc and Ahuitzol ruled for you in the City of Mexico. The people were protected by their swords and sheltered by their shields.

'Do the kings know the destiny of those they left behind, their posterity? If only they are watching. If only they can see what I see!

'No, it is not a dream. I am not walking in my sleep. I am not seeing you in my dreams . . . I have seen you at last! I have met you face to face! I was in agony for five days, for ten days, with my eyes fixed on the Region of the Mystery. And now you have come out of the clouds and mists to sit on your throne again.

'This was foretold by the kings who governed your city, and now it has taken place. You have come back to us; you have come down from the sky. Rest now, and take possession of your royal houses. Welcome to your land, my lords!'

The palace of Axayacatl, Moctezuma's father, had been allocated as the Spaniards' quarters. It backed on to the great teocalli and was only separated from Mocte-zuma's own palace by the aviary and the temple of Tezcatlipoca. It was a huge, rambling place, part treasury, part temple, that had been used as a convent for priestesses, with many halls, one of which was big enough to house a hundred and fifty men. In fact, there were rooms enough to accommodate the whole army, and in every room there were braziers burning and beds of matting had been prepared, each with an awning of its own. Here Moctezuma took Cortés by the hand, led him to a room that looked out over the main courtyard and sat him on a dais, on a rich throne-like seat decorated with gold and precious stones. After

Moctezuma goes to welcome Cortés. A seventeenth-century Spanish painting.

leaving him there for a while, he returned and presented him with gifts of gold and silver and six thousand pieces of 'rich cotton stuffs, woven and embroidered in divers ways'. Moctezuma then sat himself on another dais and Cortés records this extraordinary speech:

> We have known for a long time, from the chronicles of our forefathers, that neither I, nor those who inhabit this country, are descendants from the aborigines of it, but from strangers who came to it from very distant parts; and we also hold, that our race was brought to these parts by a lord, whose vassals they all were, and who returned to his native country. After a long time he came back, but it was so long, that those who remained here were married to native women of the country, and had many descendants, and had built towns where they were living; when, therefore, he wished to take them away with him, they would not go, nor still less received him as their ruler, so he departed. And we have always held that those who descended from him would come to subjugate this country and us, as his vassals; and according to the direction from which you say you come, which is where the sun rises, and from what you tell us of your great lord, or king, who has sent you here, we believe, and hold for certain, that he is our rightful sovereign, especially as you tell us that since many days he has had news of us. Hence you may be sure that we shall obey you, and hold you as the representative of this great lord of whom you speak, and that in this there will be no lack or deception, and throughout the whole country you may command at your will, because you will be obeyed, and recognized, and all we possess is at your disposal.

Moctezuma's two speeches of welcome are of great significance. Both are similar, except that in the Indian version Moctezuma invests Cortés himself with the mantle of Quetzalcoatl. It does not really matter whether it is Cortés or the Emperor Charles; the point is that, publicly at any rate, Moctezuma was prepared to attribute the Spanish invasion to divine intervention. This makes his attitude one of deliberate policy.

To accuse Moctezuma of pusillanimity, even of personal cowardice, is to fail in an understanding of the appalling calamity with which the Mexican king was faced. As an intelligent ruler, he saw further than his advisers. He knew that this was not an isolated force, that his people were threatened by a power they could not in the end repulse. He had thought at first that he could buy them off. They wanted gold, which his own people did not prize, except when it was transformed into the intricate beauty of jewelry. When that failed, he had tried to frighten them; as a last resort, and probably against his own judgment, he had agreed to the attempted ambush at Cholula. He had even offered to become a vassal of their emperor. He had, in fact, tried every diplomatic trick to keep them out of Mexico. When nothing had stopped them, he had fallen back on the myth of Quetzalcoatl, thus resigning himself to the inevitable.

Whether Moctezuma actually believed in the myth, or whether he was using it as a means of saving his own face and at the same time leading his people in

Tenochtitlan.

The meeting of Moctezuma and Cortés, as represented in a Mexican codex above *and a Spanish painting* below.

BOLCAN DE MEXICO
N°3

the direction in which he felt they must go, is not clear. By instinct and religious training he was a fatalist. By accepting Cortés as the emissary of Quetzalcoatl he absolved himself from the need to resist; and this self-deception was supported by the logic of his mind, which warned him that there was no future for his people in resistance. Cortés, like a volcanic eruption, and all the other portents that bedevilled the Mexican world and provided the foundation for their religious beliefs, must have appeared to him as a part of the rhythm of the universe. Fatalism dictated that he should believe the Spaniards to be a natural continuation of the mythological story of his people.

There is another factor that may, just possibly, have carried even more weight. Quetzalcoatl was worshipped as the god of learning. Moctezuma was the high priest of a debased religion. Was he, like all deeply religious men, in search of the ultimate god? Did he recognize in the meek action of these hard-bitten soldiers, kneeling humbly before their cross and their images of the Virgin and Child, a higher form of religion than the worship of a whole host of idols feeding on the heart's blood of innumerable victims? The mind of Moctezuma is an enigma that will always fascinate, the motives of his actions concealed by Indian impassivity and the lonely isolation of his position as an absolute ruler. Only one thing is certain, that he recognized in Cortés the qualities of a great leader, and thought, therefore, that he could treat with him as an equal, that by agreeing little by little

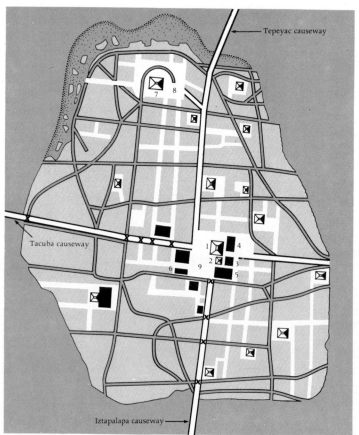

The island city of Mexico-Tenochtitlan.

1 *Great teocalli of Tenochtitlan*
2 *Teocalli of Tezcatlipoca*
3 *Aviary*
4 *Palace of Axayacatl*
5 *Palace of Moctezuma*
6 *House of the Dancers*
7 *Great teocalli of Tlaltelolco*
8 *Market place of Tlaltelolco*
9 *Market place of Tenochtitlan*

to all his demands he could buy a secure future for his people. His is the pathetic optimism of so many leaders whose countries have been overtaken by events

'I know very well', Moctezuma continued, 'that the people of Zempoala, and Tlaxcala, have told you many evil things respecting me. Do not believe more than you see with your own eyes . . .' And he emphasized that they had lied when they told Cortés that his houses had walls of gold and that he made himself out to be a god. 'The houses you have seen are of lime and stone and earth.' And then, Cortés states: 'He held up his robes, showing me his body, and said, ''Look at me, and see that I am flesh and bone, the same as you, and everybody, and that I am mortal, and tangible.'' And touching his arms and body with his hands, ''Look how they have lied to you! It is true indeed that I have some things of gold, which have been left me by my forefathers. All that I possess, you may have whenever you wish!'' '

This surely is the speech of a man accepting Cortés as the representative of a more powerful ruler, a declaration of good faith and an appeal for restraint and understanding. And then, finally, there is this assurance of peaceful intent: 'You will be provided here with everything necessary for you and your people, and you shall suffer no annoyance, for you are in your own house and country.'

Even if Cortés did know about Quetzalcoatl and understood the confusion in Moctezuma's mind, he could not accept such complete and absolute submission

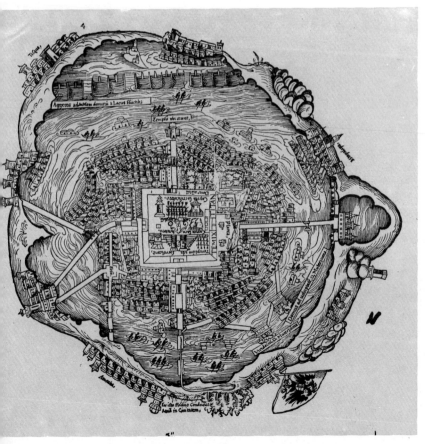

A sixteenth-century plan of the city, believed to have been drawn for Cortés. (The plan is orientated with the east at the top).

at its face value. The phrase 'your own house' is still the welcome in Spain of any good host offering hospitality. It was so then, and Cortés must at this stage have been very wary and in a mood of extreme nervous tension. He was now at last in the seat of Mexican power and the only certainty he had of holding the city was the force of his army. As soon as Moctezuma left him, he set about positioning his artillery, organizing the defence of the army's quarters, warning his troops to remember Cholula and be watchful, alert, and always ready for battle.

In his second letter to the Emperor, Cortés gives no indication of his feelings, hopes or plans. He simply says: 'Thus I passed six days well provided with everything necessary, and visited by many of the lords.' And both Gómara and Bernal Díaz are no more communicative. Yet the diplomatic exchanges during that week must have set the pattern for future events. Cortés was meeting Moctezuma daily and the ascendancy that he had achieved over the Mexican king at a distance seems to have been reinforced by his personality and bearing. There was much, too, that he and his men had to see and try to understand, a whole new way of life.

Camped as they were in a palace that backed on to the great teocalli of Huitzilo-pochtli, the whole ebb and flow of Mexican life surging round them, the Spanish soldiers were in the position of privileged spectators. Nevertheless, they went armed at all times, and it says much for the discipline instilled into them by their leader that there is no record of any serious incident between them and the inhabitants of this city of more than sixty thousand houses. The proximity of the great temple and that of Tezcatlipoca acted as a constant and sanguinary warning. The description of the idols themselves, best given by Tapia, is startling enough:

At the top were two rooms, higher than a pike and a half, and here was the principal god of all the land. He was made from all kinds of seeds, which had been ground and kneaded with the blood of virgin boys and girls. These they killed by cutting open their breasts and taking out the heart, and from there they took the blood and kneaded it with the seeds into a mass thicker than a man and as high. At the time of their feasts they adorned the figure with the kind of gold jewelry they wore when they dressed for great festivals. They wrapped the figure in very thin mantles, making a bundle, then with many ceremonies they made a beverage and put it with this figure inside the room at the top of the tower. They say they also gave some of this beverage to the one they elected captain-general when there was a war or something of great importance. They put these things between the outer wall of the tower and another inner wall, leaving no opening so that it seemed there was nothing there.

Outside the hollow wall were two idols on large stone bases the height of a measuring rod. The idols were nearly the height of three measuring rods, and the girth of an ox. They were of polished granite covered with mother-of-pearl, which is the shell that the pearl grows in. Over this they used a glue in the form of a paste to incrust gold ornamentation, and designs of men, serpents, birds, and other figures made of large and small turquoises, emeralds [jade], and amethysts, so that all of the mother-of-pearl was covered except in some places where they left it to make a design with the stones. These idols wore thick gold serpents, and for necklaces some ten or twelve human hearts made of gold. For faces they had gold masks with mirror eyes, and at the nape of the neck hung another face like a human head without flesh.

There were more than five thousand men in the service of this idol, some of them superior to the rest in rank as well as dress. They had their high priest whom they devoutly obeyed, and whom Moctezuma as well as all the other lords held in great veneration. They arose promptly at midnight for their sacrifice, which was the letting of blood from the tongue and the arms and thighs – sometimes from one place and sometimes from another – and wetting straws in the blood and offering them before an enormous oakwood fire. Then they went out to the idol-tower to offer incense.

Bernal Díaz makes the point that the precious stones depicting birds, snakes, animals, fish and flowers, the thick snakes of gold twined round their waist, and the necklaces of golden humming birds, the golden masks with mirrorlike eyes, and the dead man's face at the back of each idol's head, all had their meaning and symbolism. However, it was the sight of the skull rack, about a stone's throw from the main gate of the great temple, that must have had a deadly fascination for the Spaniards. It was in the form of a theatre with skulls set row upon row between the stones, teeth outward. At the end of the theatre were two towers, built entirely of mortar and skulls, and on the upper part were over seventy tall poles bristling with pegs. 'These pegs stood out like studs, and each of them had five skulls impaled on it through the temples.' A total of 136,000 skulls were counted, not including the uncountable number forming the two towers.

More attractive were the markets. These were held every five days, each community having its own market square. In the two main districts of Tenochtitlan and Tlatelolco, the markets were continuous; the former, surrounded by an arcade, was large enough to hold about a hundred thousand people. As in an Arabian *suk*, each trade, each type of merchandise, had its own place, the bulkier commodities – building materials such as stone, adobe, lime and lumber made up into boards, cradles, beams, blocks and benches – spreading out into the main thoroughfares, which were continuations of the three great causeways. The profusion of goods in the market proper reflected the high standard of living

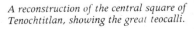
A reconstruction of the central square of Tenochtitlan, showing the great teocalli.

of the Mexicans and the great climatic range of their dominions, which extended to more than sixty great cities and their provinces. Though the potter's wheel was unknown to them, the variety of their earthenware was very extensive in size, colour and glaze. Charcoal was used for cooking, and wood was, of course, plentiful. Flint knives were in great demand, for they were used by masons for shaping stone, as well as by woodworkers, housewives, hunters and warriors, and there were axes of bronze, copper and tin. As always in a hot climate at high altitude, salt was important and valuable. Cotton was the main material. It was sold in mantles of various sizes, shapes and colours, in the form of cloaks, shirts, head-dresses, tablecloths, napkins, bed-coverings, even handkerchiefs. There were also mantles of maguey and palm fibre and the skins of animals, particularly deer, which were very plentiful throughout the whole country. Deer-skin, both tanned and raw, and coloured with vegetable dyes, was sold for sandals, shields, jackets, and for combining with wood to form protective armour.

The most colourful section was the bird and plumage market. The birds were sold live, and they included all the tropical varieties from the mangrove swamps and dense forests of the Gulf coast. The feather market was even more brilliant, and since they used the plumage of birds for their ceremonial dances, as well as for personal adornment and general decoration, the featherwork of Indian craftsmen was quite exceptional. 'They will make a butterfly, an animal, a tree, a rose, flowers, herbs and rocks, all done with feathers, and with such fidelity that they seem alive or natural. So absorbed are they in placing, moving and adjusting the feathers, scrutinizing them from one side or the other, in the sun, in the shade, or in the half light, that sometimes they will not eat all day long. In a word, they will not let the work out of their hands until it is absolutely perfect.'

The same concentration and perfectionism was to be seen in the silver market. 'They can cast a parrot that moves its tongue, head and wings; a monkey that moves its feet and head and holds a distaff in its hand so naturally that it seems to be spinning, or an apple that it appears to be eating.' The work of their silver-smiths and goldsmiths is described as of a higher standard than that of Spanish craftsmen, but they were not so expert with precious stones, which were rather rough cut, and work in copper, lead or bronze was not much prized.

The food markets were big and varied, since they would 'eat almost anything that lives: snakes without head or tail; little barkless dogs, castrated and fattened; moles, dormice, mice, worms, lice'. Deer, with wild sheep, hares, rabbits, musk-rat, fowl and birds provided the meat. There was fish from the lakes and rivers, grain, beans, herbs, and fruit and vegetables in great variety. They also used algae for food, a sort of blanket weed netted from the lake, dried and sold in cakes that looked like bricks and tasted like cheese, and canoe-loads of human excrement were brought up the creeks bordering the market for sale to the manufacturers of salt and the curers of skin. All sorts of vegetable dyes were on sale, also herbs for curing almost any ailment, and there were doctors, as well as barbers in attendance

Opposite *A feather shield of Aztec workmanship.* Overleaf *The final Spanish attack on Tenochtitlan. (See p. 184.) A seventeeth-century Spanish painting.*

in the market place; judges, too, and law officers to ensure that the sellers' measures were correct. There was oil for cooking, pitch-pine for torches, paper made from bark and called *amal*, tobacco, honey-paste and sweets like nougat, syrups made from wheat and even trees and plants, *pulque*, which was alcoholic and used in religious ritual as well as for entertainment, and wines of various kinds. All purchases were on a barter basis, the only forms of money being cacao beans and goose-quills that acted as purses for raw-mined gold. There were eating places, too, where meat and fish were served, either baked or fried in batter or made into pies, and omelettes made from the eggs of a great variety of birds.

In those first six days, whilst the off-duty soldiers were able to tour the sights, Cortés and his captains were exchanging formal visits with Moctezuma and his nobles. As a result of these exchanges, it is reasonable to assume that the fears, which had made Moctezuma so reluctant to face Cortés, were more than confirmed and that he began to appreciate the full extent of the power the Spanish captain represented and the demands that would be made upon himself and his people. Cortés was also in a difficult position. Accustomed to command events, he was very conscious of the danger of doing nothing. He had achieved his goal. He was in Mexico, his force intact. They were being treated like conquerors. But it was a victory without substance. They were there on sufferance, entertained as honoured guests, yet still dependent, as they had been throughout the march, on the goodwill of the Indians, even for their food. Their Tlaxcalan allies were also provided for and the horses were fed on *alcacer*, a grass that grows all the year round, on flour and grain, and were bedded down in a litter of roses and other flowers as though they, too, were gods.

Throughout the week Moctezuma's behaviour as host was impeccable. He loaded Cortés with gifts, treating him as a brother and almost his equal in rank. But since he was an autocratic and absolute ruler, Cortés knew only too well that a change of mind, the pressure of his advisers, his own fears, or a single incident, any little thing could spring the trap shut. They were in his hands entirely. And to Cortés, an autocrat himself, this was intolerable.

His plan to build four brigantines, with which he could dominate the lake and protect his flanks in case he had to fight his way out down one of the causeways, was a sensible one, and it met to some extent the fears being expressed by his captains. But Cortés was not thinking in terms of evacuation, and building the ships would take time. It was whilst he was considering what best to do to regain the initiative that his attention was drawn to the wall of one of the rooms in Axayacatl's palace.

They had been looking for the best place to construct a church with a permanent altar for worship. All the way up from the coast they had been conscientiously proselytizing the Christian faith. In the smaller towns and villages they had been

A Mixtec gold mask of Xipe Totec, the god of spring.

able to convert the Indians and destroy their idols. But in the big cities, like Tlaxcala and Cholula, the best they had been able to do was to erect crosses. Since coming to Mexico, Cortés had done his best to expound to Moctezuma the tenets of his faith, but with little result. Gómara claims that the total of the gods worshipped by the Mexicans was in excess of two thousand. This is an exaggeration, but they were certainly very numerous, and the inclusion of one more seemed to the Spaniards a small matter. To Moctezuma, however, even the setting up of one simple cross within the precincts of the great temple was blasphemy and bound to bring down upon his people the wrath of their gods. More practically, he probably saw it as the thin end of the wedge, intended to destroy the ritual-social community strength of his people. He had, however, agreed to the Spaniards building a church within the confines of their own quarters and had given instructions for them to be supplied with stonemasons and all the necessary materials. In one of the rooms, which they had been considering as a possible location, the shape of a bricked-up door showed through the plaster and lime-wash. Cortés had it torn down by one of his carpenters, more out of curiosity and the boredom of inaction, one imagines, than the hope of finding the treasure of Axayacatl, about which they had all heard rumours.

The result was beyond the dreams of the most avaricious Spaniard. The cavity led into several rooms, all of them heaped with the wealth accumulated by Moctezuma's father during the twelve years of his reign – idols, featherwork, jewels, precious stones, silver, and a great deal of gold. Cortés let his men enter and view it. Bernal Díaz says: 'The sight of all that wealth dumbfounded us. Being only a youth at the time and never having seen such riches before, I felt certain that there could not be a store like it in the whole world.' In this he was wrong; there was to be a bigger store for the gold seekers in Peru.

Cortés knew very well that there was nothing like the prospect of fabulous loot for putting heart into the Spanish soldier. He let them feast their eyes on it, and then had the cavity bricked up again and plastered over. Next morning two Tlaxcalans came secretly with news of trouble on the coast. Cualpopoca, Moctezuma's governor in the province of Nautla, had killed two Spaniards sent as emissaries to demand his allegiance to the Emperor. Nautla was in the Pánuco river area claimed by Francisco de Garay, governor of Jamaica. The constable of Vera Cruz, Juan de Escalante, had immediately set out on a punitive expedition with fifty Spanish soldiers and ten thousand Zempoalan irregulars. In the battle that followed both Escalante and his horse had been killed, and also six Spanish soldiers. Now all the Indians of the coastal area, Totonacs as well as Mexicans, were out of control.

Cortés' reaction to the news was immediate and positive. Taking with him five of his captains, including Juan Velázquez de León, and his two interpreters, Doña Marina and Aguilar – altogether about thirty of his most trusted followers – he went at once to Moctezuma. There is no doubt that he had already been toying with the idea of seizing the person of the king and holding him as hostage for the submissive behaviour of his war chiefs and warriors. The trouble on the coast, and the report that Cualpopoca had been acting on the direct orders of Moctezuma, now provided him with the excuse he needed. Gómara says they entered Moctezuma's apartments with their arms concealed. Díaz claims there was no attempt at concealment, since the Spaniards always went armed, merely doffing their helmets in Moctezuma's presence; also that they sent word to the king that they were coming, so that he was already apprehensive, having himself been informed of what had happened on the coast.

In a mood of conciliation, Moctezuma is said to have given Cortés more jewels and to have offered him one of his daughters. Cortés was coldly formal. 'Lord Moctezuma', Díaz quotes him as saying, 'I am greatly astonished that you, a valiant prince who have declared yourself our friend, should have ordered your captains stationed on the coast near Tuxpan to take up arms against my Spaniards. I am astonished also at their boldness in robbing towns which are in the keeping and under the protection of our King and master, and demanding of them Indian men and women for sacrifice, also that they should have killed a Spaniard [Escalante], who was my brother, and a horse.' He referred again to the attempted ambush at Cholula, accused Moctezuma of encouraging his war chiefs and vassals to kill the Spaniards, and then abruptly demanded that Moctezuma accompany him to the Spaniards' quarters.

Faced with that little group of harsh-visaged, bearded men, all of them armed, Moctezuma not only offered to summon Cualpopoca and his officials from Nautla, investigate the truth of the affair, and, if necessary, have them punished, but he actually dispatched several of his chiefs with the war god's seal, a small stone figure he wore on his arm, to enforce the order. Still Cortés insisted, politely but firmly, that Moctezuma accompany him. 'I earnestly prayed him', Cortés writes, 'not to feel pained at this, because he would not be kept a prisoner, but would have entire liberty; that I would place no impediment to his service and authority in his dominions, and that he might choose any room he pleased in the palace where I was, where he should remain at his pleasure, well assured that he should suffer no annoyance or unpleasantness, but rather that, in addition to his own attendants, my companions would also obey his commands.'

In demanding the person of the king, Cortés was walking a tightrope. Moctezuma had only to call out and his guards would rush in; the whole city would rise in arms, and not a Spaniard would escape. After an hour of wrangling, with Moctezuma still refusing to leave his palace, Juan Velázquez became impatient. 'What is the use of all these words? Either we take him or we kill him.' Doña Marina did not translate this, but instead advised Moctezuma to do as they wished. 'I know they will treat you honourably as the great prince you are. But if you stay here you will be a dead man.'

Moctezuma went. But not before he had made one final attempt to avert this personal degradation by offering his legitimate children, one son and two daughters, as hostages. He had been king for nearly eighteen years, absolute lord over all the men of his world, and in all that time no-one had dared look him in the face in public. He was both dictator and religious leader. The absolute power of such an exalted position must inevitably produce a reaction when the man himself is suddenly exposed to the threat of physical violence. Already his will to resist had been slowly whittled away. The inexorable progress of these *teules* from across the sea had been a part of the necromantic nightmare of his superstitious beliefs.

Still, one cannot help feeling that, if he had been faced with any man but Cortés, he would not have yielded his person. The sheer magnetism and determination of the man dominated him, as it had dominated his own men and all the Indian chiefs of the cities through which he had marched. Moctezuma's policy was one of appeasement, but now he must have begun to realize that the road of appeasement is a long one that leads finally to degradation. Once he had moved his quarters voluntarily to the Spanish camp, doubtless justifying himself on the grounds that it was to save his people from ultimate destruction, there was for him no turning back. By that single act, he made himself the willing tool of the invaders.

On Cortés' instructions, he was treated with the utmost deference, and every endeavour was made to ensure that, to all outward appearances, he was no more a captive than he had been in his own palace. But it is impossible to hide the capture of a ruler in the midst of his own city. In the quarters set aside for him, he was still the great lord. But when he went outside the camp, to carry out the ritual worship of his gods or to hunt, he was now accompanied by an armed escort of Spaniards.

Some twenty days later Cualpopoca arrived in Mexico with his son and some fifteen nobles. Incredibly, since he must have known what had happened to his lord and master, he had answered the summons of the emissaries bearing the seal of Huitzilopochtli. He entered the city borne on a richly-decorated litter carried on the shoulders of his servants and vassals. Moctezuma saw him and then handed him over, with his son and his nobles, to Cortés for judgment. Nobody records how Cortés was able to persuade him to such a base abdication of his own jurisdiction. Nor are we now able to judge whether Cualpopoca had been acting on Moctezuma's orders or not in repulsing the Spanish advance into the province of Tuxpan. What we do know is that this abject betrayal of his subordinate, who had come like a dog to his master's call, was a dangerous misuse of his dictatorial powers. It is possible, of course, that he still did not realize the ruthlessness of the man with whom he was dealing. For the whole month Cortés had been in Mexico he had kept a tight rein on himself. On the surface, at any rate, he had maintained good relations with Moctezuma, always friendly, often jocular, courteous, even sympathetic. This was the lawyer in him tempering expediency with diplomacy. Now, Moctezuma's eyes were suddenly opened to the other side of the man.

Cualpopoca, his son and nobles, were at once subjected to interrogation.

Gómara states quite categorically that, after Cortés had seen them, 'they were more severely questioned'. And since this further questioning extracted from them a confession that they had acted on the express orders of Moctezuma, it is reasonable to assume that Cortés borrowed his methods from those of the Inquisition and that they were tortured. Certainly his harsh sentence stems from the Holy Office. He ordered them to be burned alive at the stake, publicly in the great square. Then he told Moctezuma that he was implicated, and had him put in chains. To add to this indignity, and to drive the lesson home, Cortés had the stakes and faggots set up outside Moctezuma's own quarters.

For such a novel form of execution the whole city would have turned out. The fires were lit, the sentence carried out, and Gómara says the people 'looked on in complete silence'. Life was cheap in Mexico, cheaper even than in the Spain of those days, but though they were inured to death by sacrifice, to the scattering of blood on the altars of their gods and the ritual consumption of human flesh, this novel, and to them barbarous, form of killing came as a great shock. After the event, the news of it ran like wildfire through the Valley and over the mountain passes to the most distant provinces. Not only the Mexicans, but the whole Indian world was paralysed with shock. Worse, the involvement of their king, his apparent acquiescence, struck at the very roots of their submission to the chosen leader.

Cortés had calculated what that effect would be. He now had the fetters struck from Moctezuma's wrists and ankles, spoke to him kindly, even affectionately, promising him that he would make him lord of an even greater empire that would include all the Indian people that the Mexicans had not yet been able to conquer. Finally, he offered him his freedom. He could go back now to his own palace, if he wished . . . *if he dared* would have been a better way of putting it.

Moctezuma, with tears in his eyes, declined. He did not dare, for it would look as though he had purchased his own liberty at the price of Cualpopoca's terrible death. He was afraid, he said, that if he went back to his palace the Spaniards would take the opportunity to set up a puppet king in his place, and this would lead to civil war, which he wished to avoid at all costs. In any case, the war god had instructed him to remain their prisoner. With these specious arguments he did his best to save his face and to cover up the shame he must have felt at being so abominably used. The man he had once respected, he now feared. His world was crumbling. The Fire Sun era had now revealed itself as more likely to end in the flames of war than in volcanic eruption. But the door of appeasement, once opened, is not easily shut. His only hope was to buy time and wait upon events.

Now begins the second interlude. The Spaniards are no longer just privileged visitors; they are puppet-masters manipulating the strings of power.

There is a sort of deadly unreality about the whole situation. Cortés and Moctezuma play *totoloque*, a Mexican game involving the throwing of pellets and plaques of gold, the stakes being gifts to the soldiers of the one and the favourites of the other. Moctezuma is attended everywhere by the Spanish page, Orteguilla, to whom he has taken a fancy. There is an air of forced gaiety, with much joking together between the two leaders. The old soldier, Bernal Díaz, finds time in his accounts to give a couple of amusing sidelights on guard duties. One of the guards set over Moctezuma relieves himself noisily in the king's presence. True to form, Moctezuma tries to persuade the man to improve his manners by the gift of a gold jewel worth 5 pesos. The next time the man is on duty, he deliberately pisses again, in the hopes of a further 'reward' for his endeavours. Instead he is replaced by the captain of the guard and severely reprimanded. Another guard, a big crossbowman, says in Moctezuma's presence: 'To hell with the dog. I'm sick to death of guarding him.' He is flogged, and thereafter Cortés orders that the guards carry out their duties 'silently, with good manners'. There is also the problem of communion wine, 'for as Cortés and some other captains and a friar had been ill during the Tlaxcalan campaign, there had been a run on the wine that we kept for Mass'. The atmosphere is peculiarly relaxed, and even when two sloops have been built they are used, not for guard duty, but to take Moctezuma and his nobles hunting on a rocky island in the middle of the lake, the picnic party rounded off by a demonstration from the cannon mounted in the bows.

Only those who have travelled amongst primitive peoples will fully understand the strange behaviour of Moctezuma during this interlude, the living for the day, the fatalism, the almost animal willingness to be led; or that of his people – their subservience to despotism, their acceptance of cruelty as an integral part of life, their admiration of cunning as one of the finest qualities of leadership. Thus, Cacama, who, as lord of Texcoco, was the natural focal point of insurrection, was destroyed without the Spaniards having to fire a shot. Politics were involved, for it was reported to Moctezuma that Cacama intended to seize power for himself. Cacama was the young man who had first welcomed Cortés on the Cuitlahuac causeway. He was Moctezuma's nephew, and he had the support of the lords of Tacuba and Coyoacán, and also of Moctezuma's brother, Cuitlahuac, lord of Iztapalapa. With Texcoco, these cities were four of the most important of the Culhúan confederacy. It was a dangerous situation for Cortés, and his immediate reaction was to attack the insurrection at its centre. But when he asked for an auxiliary force of Mexican warriors for an assault on Texcoco, Moctezuma pointed out that the city would be difficult to take. It was strongly fortified and surrounded by water; also, it would be supported by the vassal cities of Culhuacán and Otumba, both of them built like fortresses. Cortés then tried to bluff Cacama into submission. Emissaries went back and forth, Moctezuma himself summoned Cacama to his capital to make friends with the Spaniards. Instead of replying, Cacama announced publicly that he would kill every Spaniard within four days, and accused his uncle of being a coward.

Time passed in these exchanges, and time was not on Cacama's side. The inability of the Indians to combine together, except at the command of an absolute ruler, is clearly revealed in the council of war convened in Texcoco. The assembled nobles were eager enough to fight, but first Moctezuma must be informed of their intention, and if he agreed, then, and only then, would they attack. Cacama was young and headstrong. He had three of the nobles arrested and sent a message to Moctezuma saying that 'he ought to be ashamed of himself for commanding him to make friends with men who had done him so much harm and dishonour as to keep him a prisoner'. He asserted that the Spaniards had robbed him of his great strength and courage by witchcraft or because their gods, particularly the 'great woman of Castile' (by which he meant the Virgin), had given them strength, and that, whatever his uncle said, he intended to attack them.

It amounted to civil war, the very thing Moctezuma was determined to avoid. He summoned six of his most trusted war chiefs, and once again the seal of Huitzilopochtli was used to maintain Spanish domination. They left for Texcoco immediately. Unfortunately for Cacama, his high-handed behaviour had made him enemies amongst his own nobles. The seal was shown to several disaffected chiefs, who seized him in his own palace, with five of his captains, bundled him into a pirogue and brought him in state to Mexico. Moctezuma dealt with him as he had done with Cualpopoca, handing him over to Cortés, who imprisoned him, but set his captains free. Cortés then made Moctezuma arrange for the arrest of Cacama's fellow-conspirators, the kings of Tacuba, Coyoacán and Iztapalapa. All three of them were put in chains. Finally, he arranged for the appointment of Cacama's brother as lord of Texcoco. He was a pleasant and ineffectual youth, who had fled to Mexico. Later he was baptized and took the name of Don Carlos.

Peace having been re-established, Cortés now gave his attention to the consolidation of his position. If he were to be confirmed as governor-general of Mexico, it was necessary that the Indians became vassals of the Emperor Charles and paid tribute. At his insistence Moctezuma called a council of his Indian chiefs. The wretched king was now so deeply involved with the Spaniards that he was apparently willing to buy peace at any price.

In his speech to his lords in council he repeated the history of Quetzalcoatl, telling them that the Emperor Charles was the king they had been expecting. 'I hold it to be certain, and you must hold it so.' And he went on, 'Since our predecessors did not act justly towards their sovereign lord, let us do so, and let us give thanks to our gods, because that which they looked for has come to pass in our times. I heartily pray you, inasmuch as all this is well known to you, that, as you have obeyed me as your sovereign, henceforward you will regard and obey this great king, because he is your rightful sovereign, and, in his place, you must hold this, his Captain; also that all the tributes and services, which until now you have paid to me, you do give to him, because I also shall pay tribute, and serve in all that he may command me. In so doing, you will do your duty as you are obliged to do, and you will, moreover, in doing this, give me great pleasure.'

Despite his imprisonment, despite the burning of Cualpopoca and the incarceration of Cacama and three other kings, including his own brother, Moctezuma's word was still law. The habit of absolute obedience dies hard. Cortés, describing the scene, says, 'All this he told them, weeping the greatest tears, and the greatest sighs a man can give vent to; and all those lords who had heard him were likewise weeping so much, that, during a considerable time, they were unable to answer. And I assure Your Sacred Majesty, that there was not one among the Spaniards who heard this discourse who did not feel great compassion.'

Thus, publicly, before the Royal Notary and witnesses, Moctezuma became a vassal of the Emperor Charles, and all his lords and the people of Mexico followed his example. The matter of tribute was then dealt with. Expeditions were dispatched into all the gold-mining provinces, and to the gold dust and nuggets brought in, and the tribute collected, Moctezuma added the contents of the treasure rooms of his father, saying, 'When you send it to him [the Emperor], tell him in your letter that it is sent by his loyal vassal, Moctezuma.' And he added that he would send some very precious stones: 'They are *chalchihuites* and must not be given to anyone but your great prince, for each one of them is worth two loads of gold.' He also gave Cortés twelve blowpipes 'decorated with very excellent paintings of perfect hues, in which there were figures of many different kinds of birds, animals, flowers, and divers other objects, and the mouthpieces and extremities were bordered with gold, a span deep, as was also the middle, all beautifully worked'. Included with the blowpipes was a gold network pouch to hold the balls, and Moctezuma promised that the balls themselves, which he would send later, would be of solid gold. Rather pathetically, he added that he would have wished to give the Emperor more of his own possessions, but these would only be small, 'for all the gold and jewels I had, I have given you at one time or another'.

The treasure rooms in Axayacatl's palace were then opened up again, and the division of the spoils began. It took three days, and, as with any share-out, there was dissatisfaction. Bernal Díaz claims that Cortés filched a third of the great treasure pile before even the king's fifth was subtracted, and that some of his captains, particularly Juan Velázquez de León, were having large gold chains and

Gold ornaments were collected from all over the country as tribute for the Spaniards.

table ware of gold made up that was far in excess of their share. For this purpose goldsmiths had been brought in from the neighbouring city of Azcapotzalco, and from them Cortés himself ordered jewels and a great dinner service. The soldiers, too, had got their hands on the stuff, and there was a great deal of gambling with home-made cards.

The rumbles of dissatisfaction were so great that Cortés felt it necessary to make one of his diplomatic speeches, even undertaking to forego the fifth his men had agreed to give him when they elected him captain-general. In the end, the fabulously beautiful silver and gold work from the treasure store was melted down into ingots. Weights were made, the king's fifth subtracted and the gold bars stamped with a home-made die. Cortés got the fifth he had been promised; he also got the expenses of mounting and fitting out the expedition, the value of the ships destroyed, even the cost of the embassy sent to Spain. Fray Bartolomé de Olmedo and the priest got double shares, as did the captains, the arquebusiers and musketeers, the crossbowmen, and those who had brought horses with them. The seventy men in Vera Cruz were not forgotten, and the horses that had been lost were paid for. In the end, Bernal Díaz says, very little was left, 'so little indeed that many of us soldiers did not want to touch it'. He claims that Cortés gave some of them gifts as a kind of favour, and by big promises and smooth words got them to accept the situation.

This vast treasure was the visible, material symbol of the expedition's success. However Bernal Díaz may grumble, it increased the morale of the army enormously. As for himself, Cortés knew that it would buy him recognition at home and establish his position beyond all question. But he was much too statesmanlike a leader to regard gold as the sole purpose of conquest. Writing to his emperor, he emphasizes that throughout the six months since his arrival in the city on November 8, 1519, his forces had been actively employed in 'pacifying and winning over many provinces, thickly-peopled countries, very great cities, towns and forts; and in discovering mines, and learning and enquiring into many of the secrets of Moctezuma's dominions . . . so many and marvellous that they are almost incredible'. All, as he points out, with the willing assistance of Moctezuma and the Indians. He had even developed ninety acres as a sort of agricultural research farm, experimenting in the growing of maize, beans and cocoa, the breeding of hens, and also ducks for the production of feathers. And in the search for new and better anchorages on the coast he had arranged with Moctezuma for the pictographic mapping of the Gulf shore, and as a result had sent Ordaz with ten men to explore the possibilities of the Coatzacoalco river. All these activities, together with guard duties and the need to be constantly on the alert against insurrection, kept his men fully occupied.

To what extent their off-duty hours were relieved by fraternization with the natives is nowhere stated, not even by Bernal Díaz. Cortés and his captains certainly had Indian 'wives', but how he catered for the sexual appetites of his men we do not know. Discipline was very tight and there is no doubt that he adhered rigidly to his instructions forbidding cohabitation with non-Christian women. The probability is that a far greater number of the Indian women were 'converted' than is actually recorded.

   Knowing the power of the Church at home, conversion of the Mexicans to the Christian faith, the overthrow of their idols and the prevention of human sacrifice must always have been uppermost in his mind. This was not just a matter of expediency. He and his captains — many of his men, too — believed implicitly that they were engaged on a crusade. Gómara claims that shortly after Moctezuma's arrest, Cortés felt himself strong enough to begin the work of destroying the idols. When Moctezuma persuaded him to desist, since the Mexicans would undoubtedly resist such sacrilege, Gómara quotes a long speech in which Cortés says all the things that the Holy Office at home would expect him to say, and adds that he had crosses and images of the Virgin Mary and other saints set up amongst the idols in the altar room of the great teocalli. 'This Christian deed won more honour and glory for Cortés than if he had vanquished them in battle.' This is clearly a political record designed for home consumption. Cortés could not possibly have attempted such an attack upon the establishment of the priesthood until the threat of Cacama's insurrection had been dealt with and the Mexicans had sworn allegiance to the Emperor.

   In fact, it was now, when for the first time he really felt himself master of the situation, that he was finally free to let his rage at the devilish activities of the priests get the upper hand. Whether the desperate act of desecration he committed was premeditated, or whether it was a natural and spontaneous outburst of revulsion, nobody will ever know for certain. But since its effect was to undo the work of months, we must presume the latter.

   Bernal Díaz simply says that Cortés delivered an ultimatum to Moctezuma: he was to order his priests to stop the sacrifice of human beings, remove the idols of their gods, and replace them with the cross of the true faith and a statue of the Virgin. If they would not do it, then Cortés' men would do it for them. 'After a good deal of discussion our altar was set up some distance from their accursed idols, with great reverence and thanks to God from all of us.' This seems insufficient grounds for the sudden and violent change in the attitude of the Mexicans that followed. Cortés himself says, 'The principal idols . . . I overturned from their seats and rolled down the stairs, and I had those chapels, where they kept them, cleansed, for they were full of blood from the sacrifices; and I set up images of Our Lady, and other Saints in them, which grieved Moctezuma and the natives not a little.'

   In the discussion that followed, Moctezuma is described as agreeing that the Mexicans probably erred in their religious beliefs, because of the great length of time that had elapsed since they had left the country of their origin, whereas Cortés had just arrived from that country. This acquiescence — and Cortés says

Moctezuma and his caciques were present throughout the destruction of the idols – does not suggest that the act led inevitably to the expulsion of the Spaniards. But there is one account that does fit the pattern of subsequent events. Andrés de Tapia claims that he was with Cortés in the great teocalli when he attacked the idols, and he makes it clear that it was a personal attack. He also confirms that it followed the final submission of Moctezuma. He says that the Spanish forces in the city at the time were small because most of the soldiers were away in the provinces collecting tribute for the Emperor. Cortés and Tapia went up to the tower of the great teocalli with less than a dozen soldiers, pushed aside a hemp curtain festooned with bells, using their swords, and entered a very dark chamber. Here the walls were lined with stone images 'and in their mouths and over parts of their bodies were quantities of blood two or three fingers thick'. Tapia tells the story in detail:

> When the marqués [Cortés] had seen the stone carvings and looked about at what was to be seen, he was saddened. He sighed, saying so that we all heard him: 'Oh God! Why do You permit such great honour paid the Devil in this land? Oh Lord, it is good that we are here to serve you.'
>
> He called the interpreters, because some of the priests of those idols had come at the sound of the bells, and he said: 'God Who made heaven and earth made you and made us and all men. He grows what sustains us. And if we have been good He will take us to heaven, but if not we shall go to hell, as I shall tell you at greater length when we understand one another better. Here where you have these idols I wish to have the images of the Lord and his Blessed Mother. Also bring water to wash these walls, and we will take all this away.'
>
> They laughed as though it were not possible to do such a thing, and they said: 'Not only this city but all the land holds these as gods. This is the house of Huitzilopochtli, whom we serve, and in comparison with him the people hold for nothing their fathers and mothers and children, and will choose to die. So take heed, for on seeing you come up here they have all risen in arms and are ready to die for their gods.'
>
> The marqués told a Spaniard to go and see that Moctezuma was well guarded, and to send thirty or forty men to the tower. Then he said to the priests: 'It will give me great pleasure to fight for my God against your gods, who are a mere nothing.' And before the men he had sent for arrived, angered by some words he had heard, he took up an iron bar that was there and began to smash the stone idols. On my faith as a gentleman I swear by God that, as I recall it now, the marqués grew supernaturally tall, and rushed to attack, gripping the bar in the middle, striking as high as the idol's eyes and thus tore down the gold masks, saying: 'Something must we venture for the Lord.'

Cortés always had a great sense of the dramatic. In giving vent to his feelings in such an act of desecration, with the priests standing there as witnesses, it is clear that, though the timing may have been fortuitous, the decision that prompted the act had been taken in cold blood. He had achieved complete domination of the Indians through the person of their king, but to break them finally to his will it was essential to destroy their religion and superimpose his own. The desecration must, therefore, be regarded as an act of policy. But the way in which he chose to implement that policy was a mistake. No doubt he had become frustrated by the constant opposition of the priests. No doubt also, as a result of Moctezuma's acquiescence in everything else, he had become too confident. The realization that he had over-reached himself is implicit in the way his action is covered up, both in his own dispatches, and in Gómara's accounts. And it is obvious that he also concealed it from his soldiers, since Bernal Díaz makes so little of it.

Moctezuma was horrified. He warned Cortés that the city would rise, that he could not control his people in the face of such an affront to their gods. And Cortés, from demanding the instant abandonment of all devil worship, retreated into a face-saving compromise. With Moctezuma's agreement, a space was made available in the temple for an altar. A cross was set up with a statue of the Virgin, and all the Spanish garrison then in the capital attended a sung mass.

Though this was done with Moctezuma's reluctant support, the priests were not so amenable. They saw it as a threat to their traditional position of power. They announced that Huitzilopochtli and Tezcatlipoca had spoken to them; both gods would abandon Mexico unless the alien Spanish god was removed from the temple. To this threat of disaster they later added an incitement to rebellion: the gods would only stay if the Spaniards were destroyed. During the night, and throughout much of the following day, Moctezuma was in conference, not only with the priests, but with his war chiefs as well. The page, Orteguilla, who acted as Cortés' spy at court, said the king was very agitated. The position had suddenly become explosive. So explosive, in fact, that Moctezuma finally summoned Cortés into his presence and told him that he must leave Mexico at once. If he did not, he and all his men would be killed. The gods had spoken. The word was war.

Cortés temporized, playing for time. He said he could not leave because his ships had been destroyed. And when he did leave, Moctezuma would have to accompany him, to pay court to the Emperor, since he was now his vassal. The end of it was that Moctezuma agreed to provide wood for the construction of ships to replace those that had been destroyed. Meantime, he would persuade his priests not to foment trouble and, in propitiating the gods, to avoid human sacrifice. Cortés, on his part, undertook to proceed with the construction of the ships as fast as possible and leave Mexico when they were completed. What he had in mind, of course, was to use the ships to procure reinforcements. Without more men, arms and horses, he now realized he could not hope to have physical control over such a large and turbulent country. Núñez, and López, the ship's carpenter, were instructed to design and build three vessels, the wood to be cut by the Indian woodsmen provided by Moctezuma. The necessary gear was in store at Vera Cruz.

The situation, however, remained distinctly ugly. Doña Marina warned Cortés repeatedly that an attack was imminent. The Tlaxcalan irregulars he had brought into Mexico with him confirmed it. So did the page, Orteguilla, who was now 'always in tears'. The men slept in their armour. The horses stood saddled and bridled throughout the day. From being the power behind the throne, the maker and breaker of kings, the captain-general who had brought a whole new country into the vassalage of his emperor, Cortés was now in a state of siege. All because he had meddled with their religion. Yet he knew that without the destruction of their gods he could not hold them, for, as in any country, particularly of that period, their religion was their strength, giving them the moral fibre to resist.

Then disaster struck. The first indication was a change in Moctezuma's manner when Cortés made his usual daily call. The king's health, which had been deteriorating under the strain, was suddenly much improved. He seemed almost light-hearted. He did not attempt to hide the reason, but told Cortés, with unconcealed pleasure, that a fleet of ships had arrived off the coast. He showed him the pictograph his messengers had brought him. There were nineteen vessels painted on the cloth, and the pictures also showed a large number of men and horses disembarking in the neighbourhood of Vera Cruz. 'Now you will not need to build ships', Moctezuma said. What he did not say was that he was already in touch with the commander of this expedition, had sent him gifts, and knew that he had come to destroy Cortés.

When Cortés returned to his quarters, he found the news had already leaked to his men. The excitement was intense, horsemen galloping around, shots being fired. They assumed that the arrival of the fleet constituted the reinforcements they so urgently needed. Cortés at once called a conference of his captains and disillusioned them. A fleet of that size would not have been sent from Spain. It could only have come from Jamaica or Cuba, and that meant that they were to be robbed by their own people of all they had worked and fought for during the course of the past year. He did not waste time bewailing the injustice of it. Nor did he try to colour his judgment with wishful thinking. He knew too much about Spanish power politics.

His reaction, as usual, was positive. He paraded his men, took them into his confidence, and bluntly told them the worst. They had one great advantage; they were seasoned troops, who knew the country and the Indians. The new arrivals were raw and untrained men. Moreover, here in this fleet were the arms and horses they needed. As always, his speech was effective. They were with him to a man.

The fleet was, in fact, an expedition fitted out from Cuba by Diego Velázquez. What had happened was that, contrary to instructions, the ship that had been dispatched from Vera Cruz with emissaries to Spain almost a year ago had put into a port in Cuba. As a result, somebody, probably Montejo, had sent the governor of Cuba full details of what Cortés had done – the founding of Vera Cruz, his election as the settlement's captain-general, his direct approach to the Emperor and his intention to march on Mexico and conquer the entire country. Velázquez had immediately dispatched two caravels to intercept the vessel, but instead of going on to Havana, as had been suggested, the ship had headed direct for the Bahamas strait. The caravels never even sighted their quarry. Velázquez had then sent letters of complaint to the Vice-regal Court at Santo Domingo. This court, however, was composed of the three Jeronomite priests who had given Cortés his commission, and when he got no satisfaction from them, Velázquez had poured out all his carefully hoarded wealth in the fitting out of a fleet. The size of that fleet makes it clear that he was now fully conscious of the great prize that was slipping from his grasp. The man he put in charge of it was Pánfilo de Narváez; Velázquez was under some obligation to him for having borrowed money from his estate whilst he was absent in Spain, and no doubt he felt that the resulting community of interest was a guarantee of Narváez's reliability.

Narváez was greeted off the Gulf coast by a singular stroke of luck. One of the expeditions Cortés had sent out from Mexico to report on the gold mines in the provinces had been commanded by a relative of his, a twenty-five-year-old captain called Pizarro. He had been sent north into the country of the Chinantecs with an escort of five soldiers. He had returned with only one. The others he had left to organize cocoa, maize and cotton plantations, the land being very fertile. Cortés had reprimanded him for wasting men he could ill afford on such a task and had sent orders for them to return. They had not done so, and now three of them joined up with the newly arrived fleet. Narváez thus had first-hand information about the political situation in Mexico and the position of Cortés and his men.

Why Narváez did not attack Vera Cruz at once is incomprehensible. All he did was to send three envoys to demand its surrender. This gave Sandoval, who had been appointed constable after the death of Escalante, time to dig in. Young, tough and reliable, he not only prepared for a siege, but arrested the three envoys and sent them under escort to Mexico. It was a most rewarding move. From them, Cortés learned the strength of the fleet. Narváez had eighty horsemen and the same number of arquebusiers, a hundred and thirty crossbowmen and six hundred foot, a total of more than eight hundred men. It was a formidable force, almost double his own. He did not hold on to the envoys, however, but sent them back loaded with presents and dazzled by the splendours and opportunities of Mexico. The result was as he had hoped. Deserters began to straggle into Vera Cruz, and Narváez, becoming alarmed, moved inland to Zempoala. There was an exchange of letters, which did not help Narváez's cause, since he called Cortés' men traitors and bandits, and threatened them with death and the confiscation of the treasure they had won; all of which Cortés read out to them.

The time for action had now arrived. Cortés set out for the coast with two hundred and fifty picked men, leaving Pedro de Alvarado in command of the remainder, with instructions to be on his guard and keep a close watch on

Moctezuma. He went by way of Cholula and Tlaxcala, but there is no evidence that he enlisted Indian auxiliaries. He had no desire to see Spaniards slaughtered; he was in too great a need of reinforcements. Somewhere between Tlaxcala and Zempoala he was met by Duero, a friend of Cuban days who had lent him money when he was fitting out his fleet. Duero tried to persuade him to accept the authority of Narváez and surrender his forces. If he did not, he would be regarded as a rebel. A notary, who was with him, tried to serve Cortés with a writ. The upshot of it was that Cortés said he would fight unless Narváez could show that his instructions came direct from the Emperor. Since he knew very well they did not, he sent Duero back, accompanied by Fray Bartolomé and Juan Velázquez de León and other envoys, with a further letter to Narváez, requesting him not to stir up unnecessary trouble in a country that was not fully pacified. The real object, of course, was to confirm his opponent's strength, to discover his dispositions, and above all to suborn his men.

Narváez appears to have made some sort of an effort to wrest the initiative from Cortés, but after marching several leagues along the Tlaxcala road without encountering him, he retired again to Zempoala. As Gómara says: 'The one was as tepid and careless in his actions as the other was careful and cunning.' Narváez had no real chance against a leader of Cortés' experience and ability.

Dazzled by all the talk of Mexican gold, many of Narváez' men fought halfheartedly when the attack was delivered, suddenly, in the night. It was damp; the touch-holes of the guns (they had between thirteen and nineteen) were filled with wax to keep out the rain; and fireflies flickered, adding to the confusion by looking like the matches of arquebusiers. The teocalli, where they were lodged and which might have been successfully defended, were quickly surrounded, and Narváez himself was wounded by a pike thrust in the eye. It was all over inside of an hour with very little loss of life.

Narváez was sent in irons to Vera Cruz, where he was held prisoner for several years. His men, 'with greater or lesser willingness', went over to Cortés. He knew most of them anyway, and the fabulous accounts of the prospects in Mexico, with which they had been so sedulously fed, would have made them eager to serve under such a successful commander. Nevertheless, the incorporation into his force of such a large number of raw troops presented Cortés with a

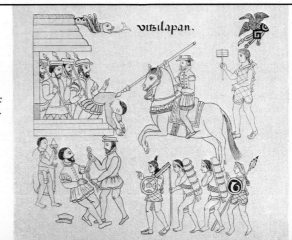

Narváez was defeated in a surprise attack and made prisoner.

problem. Some he allocated to the garrison at Vera Cruz, others were included in a detachment of two hundred to be sent to the Pánuco river under Juan Velázquez de León to found the settlement that Cualpopoca had blocked. The rest were to go with him on the return march to Mexico.

News of the victory had been sent at once to Alvarado in Mexico, but it arrived too late. Just before the battle, Narváez had sent another embassy to Moctezuma. Alvarado was aware of this: aware, too, that the Mexican war chiefs had been mustering their men – one account gives a figure of a hundred thousand warriors waiting ready to attack. Hot-headed, impatient, a man who believed in steel rather than words, Alvarado had indulged in an unprovoked blood-bath. As a result he had precipitated the crisis that Cortés had been at such pains to avoid. Twelve days after the defeat of Narváez two Tlaxcalans arrived in Cortés' camp with a message from Alvarado urgently requesting aid. He had already lost seven men killed and many wounded, the palace of Axayacatl had been set on fire in two places, and the Mexicans were besieging it.

Cortés proceeded at once by forced marches, leaving only the wounded in Vera Cruz, and abandoning once again his attempt to found a settlement on the Pánuco river. Moctezuma had already been informed of Cortés' victory over Narváez, and four of his chiefs now arrived with the Mexican version of what had happened in the city. Some of their people had obtained Alvarado's permission to perform the *macehualixtli* dance, which is a sort of harvest festival, in the great temple. Alvarado and his soldiers had then set upon them. Many Mexicans, including some caciques, had lost their lives, and in defending themselves, they had killed six Spaniards.

At Tlaxcala there was more news. Alvarado's men were short of food and water and near the point of exhaustion. The Mexicans, however, had ceased their attacks. Cortés pushed on fast to Texcoco. Nobody came out to welcome him, not even the youth he had made king. The place was deserted, the houses empty. But at Mexico he was greeted by Moctezuma, who congratulated him on his victory. Cortés was barely civil. He went straight on to his own quarters, where he was met by Alvarado.

Why Cortés had chosen Alvarado to command in his absence is nowhere clearly stated. He knew the man was impetuous. But it has to be remembered that Cortés' position at the time was desperate – Narváez and his fleet at Vera Cruz and anything up to a hundred thousand Mexicans ready to attack. Alvarado was one of the bravest of his captains, a born leader, whom the men trusted. With him in command, they would fight to the bitter end. That he might provoke an attack was something Cortés had been forced to risk.

In justification of his action Alvarado said he had positive information that, when the *macehualixtli* dance was over and the Mexicans had sacrificed to their gods, then the attack would begin. It was night, and the uproar they were making –

Pedro de Alvarado was left in command of the Spanish force in Tenochtitlan. An early seventeenth-century portrait.

drums thumping, conches blaring, trumpets and bone pipes sounding – convinced him that this was the frenzied prelude to the attack. When he had arrived at the temple, with some fifty of his men, he had found as many as a thousand Indians dancing naked, except that their bodies were covered with jewels and pearls and precious stones, plumes of brilliant feathers nodding from their heads. He had blocked the entrances and slaughtered nearly all of them. Indian chroniclers give this picture of the massacre:

> They ran in among the dancers, forcing their way to the place where the drums were played. They attacked the man who was drumming and cut off his arms. Then they cut off his head, and it rolled across the floor. They attacked all the celebrants, stabbing them, spearing them, striking them with their swords. They attacked some of them from behind, and these fell instantly to the ground with their entrails hanging out. Others they beheaded; they cut off their heads, or split their heads to pieces. They struck others in the shoulders, and their arms were torn from their bodies. They wounded some in the thigh and some in the calf. They slashed others in the abdomen, and their entrails all spilled to the ground. Some attempted to run away, but their intestines dragged as they ran; they seemed to tangle their feet in their own entrails. No matter how they tried to save themselves, they could find no escape.

Was this reckless act really justified as an attempt to cow the Mexicans by a cruel show of force? Did Alvarado panic, faced with that macabre scene and under pressure from the nervousness of his men? Or was it greed at the sight of all that wealth of jewels glinting on the naked bodies in the smoking light of the pitch-pine torches?

Cortés, though he upbraided Alvarado angrily for his stupid provocation, accepted the excuse that he had done it in an attempt to forestall an attack. He had no alternative, for he needed Alvarado now, needed all his seasoned troops. The situation in Mexico was as bad as it had been at Texcoco. No caciques had come to meet him, no markets were being held. The city was dead, its silence oppressive, menacing. The smell of revolt was in the air. He had come up from the coast with the better part of eleven hundred men. More than eight hundred of these were new arrivals, soured now with disappointment after all the inducements, the wonderful rewards, they had been promised. He did not trust them.

The Spaniards attack the Mexican dancers.

For the first time Cortés' normal sang-froid seems to have deserted him. The arrival of two chiefs, requesting him to visit Moctezuma, sent him into a towering rage. 'Visit him?' he is quoted as saying. 'The dog doesn't even keep open market for us . . . Why should I be civil to a dog who was holding secret negotiations with Narváez, and now doesn't even give us any food?'

This outburst, which is not mentioned in his dispatches to the Emperor, is so unlike his normal diplomatic behaviour that it is probably correctly reported. Cortés had gone through a period of great strain. For more than six months he had supported himself and his men in Mexico by his wits, only to have his authority and position threatened by a fleet from Cuba. He had marched nearly 250 miles along the blistering tracks and back over the bitter cold of the Sierra Madre Occidental, defeated a force four times his own in number, and had then had to hurry back, again by forced marches. All this he had done inside a month. And now that he was back in Mexico he found the work of a whole year in ruins. Both physically and mentally he must have been near breaking point.

He sent Moctezuma's ambassadors packing, with orders to have the people back in their houses and the markets functioning normally, or he would not be responsible for what his men would do to them. This ultimatum was to prove utterly disastrous. It was conveyed to Moctezuma, who replied that as he was a prisoner he could do nothing, but that if Cortés would release his brother, Cuitlahuac, all would be done according to his wishes. This Cortés did, though Cuitlahuac, lord of Iztapalapa, was one of those who had supported Cacama's insurrection.

Cortés appears to have failed to understand what was in Moctezuma's mind. Though there is no reason why he should have been conversant with the constitutional arrangements in Mexico, he knew very well the sort of man Cuitlahuac was and his dominant position in the Mexican hierarchy as Moctezuma's kinsman. Instead of re-establishing the markets, Cuitlahuac at once summoned the elective council of the Indian state, the *tlatlocan*. This was composed mainly of war chiefs, who from the beginning had wanted to throw the invaders back into the sea. They immediately deposed Moctezuma and elected Cuitlahuac in his place.

Cortés knew nothing of this. But, tired though he was, he spent the night reorganizing the defences. In the morning a badly wounded soldier arrived from Tacuba with the news that the causeway was crowded with armed warriors, and one of the bridges was already destroyed. Cortés states that the man was a messenger he had dispatched to Vera Cruz, but Bernal Díaz describes him differently, as 'escorting some Indian women who belonged to Cortés, among them a daughter of Moctezuma', who had been left in the care of the king of Tacuba during his absence.

Cortés at once ordered Ordaz, with four hundred men, to reconnoitre the Tacuba causeway; but the force was heavily engaged before it had even got out of the city. The Mexican attack was delivered head-on in the streets, supported by heavy arrow-fire from the roof-tops on either side. In the first assault Ordaz lost eight men killed and another as he retreated back to the temple square. By then hordes of Mexican warriors were attacking the palace of Axayacatl itself. Arrows, javelins, sling-stones poured in upon the Spaniards. Forty-six of them were wounded in this one onslaught. The din was so great that orders could not be heard, the pressure of the attack so heavy that the sword-play of the Spanish soldiers seemed to have no effect.

In the end, it was the guns that cleared a way for Ordaz' force to enter. But by then it had been badly mauled and there was scarcely a man unhurt; fourteen were dead and Ordaz himself had been wounded three times. They were followed by a great horde of howling warriors. The attack was pressed, breaches were made in the palace walls, and only the fire of the falconets, crossbows and arquebuses kept the Spaniards from being overwhelmed. Even so, the Mexicans penetrated into the quarters and fired the palace. With no water, the only way to put the flames out was to pull the walls down on top of them. The battle raged all day and the Spaniards got little rest during the night, for they had to repair their defences and put out the fires. There was not much food, and the only water they had was from holes dug in the ground. There were over eighty seriously wounded, and Cortés himself was in great pain from an injury to his left hand.

Anybody who has seen the canals in Amsterdam will appreciate the tactical difficulties facing the Spaniards. Cortés, in describing Mexico to his Emperor, says: 'Its streets are very broad and straight, some of these, and all the others, are one half land, and the other half water on which they go about in canoes. All the streets have openings at regular intervals, to let the water flow from one to the other, and at all of these openings, some of which are very broad, there are bridges, very large, strong and well-constructed, so that, over many, ten horsemen can ride abreast. . . . They might', he adds, 'by raising the bridges at the exits and entrances, starve us out without our being able to reach land.'

Nevertheless, at dawn the following day he mounted a counter-attack, two forces of two hundred men each, led by himself and one of his captains. But the bridges were already down and they were unable to charge. They got caught up amongst the houses and had to retire under the weight of stones and weapons being thrown down upon them. They were pursued by the Mexicans, yelling and whistling, blowing conches and trumpets, beating drums. Men who had fought against the Moors declared afterwards that they had never faced such a fierce and determined enemy, and veterans of the Italian wars said that even the French king's artillery was easier to face than these Indians, who charged and charged again in massed attacks that were no sooner broken than they reformed. Thirty or forty were killed at each charge, but it made no difference. Periodically they would lure the Spaniards out from the protection of their defences by feigning flight, and by combining cunning with incredible bravery they slowly reduced the numbers of the defenders.

That day the Spaniards lost another dozen killed and there was hardly a man left unwounded. Since they could not go on like that indefinitely Cortés decided to construct a number of mobile engines of war, wooden towers, each capable of holding some twenty men, from which his arquebusiers and crossbowmen could dominate the rooftops of the houses and so enable the cavalry to clear the streets. They were completed the following day in conditions of great difficulty, the Mexicans keeping up their attacks, so that as often as the breaches were bricked up, they broke in again. All the time their war chiefs urged them on, shouting that the Spaniards would have their hearts torn out and offered to the gods, and that the Tlaxcalans, who were with them, would be fattened in cages for sacrifice. The yelling and whistling went on through the night, stones and arrows pouring in upon the defenders.

At dawn, when the Spaniards sallied out with their towers, the Mexicans seemed more numerous than ever. The horses were useless, for they were stopped by newly erected street barricades, and though armoured, they faced such a deadly hail of missiles that their charges faltered before they could break the Mexican ranks. Even on the few occasions when they did, the Mexicans saved themselves by diving into the water, where other warriors stood waist-deep, stabbing up at the horses' bellies with long lances. The Spaniards tried to fire the houses, but it was a slow business, for they took a long time to burn, and as they were intersected by numerous canals, there was no hope of starting a general conflagration. In the end, the towers were badly damaged and the Spaniards forced to fall back on their quarters again.

It was another bad night, the quarters half hospital, half building camp, as the Spaniards dressed their wounds and rebuilt their walls, plagued all the time by the Indians outside. It could not go on like this. Narváez's men had reached the point of open mutiny. Withdrawal from Mexico was the only course left.

In the morning Cortés tried once again to play the only card he had ever really had – Moctezuma. But when he sent to the king, requesting him to tell his warriors to cease their attacks as the Spaniards had decided to leave the city, Moctezuma is reported to have declared sadly: 'Fate has brought me to such a pass because of him that I do not wish to live or hear his voice again.' Fray Bartolomé and Olid then went to reason with him, but all he said was that he did not believe he could

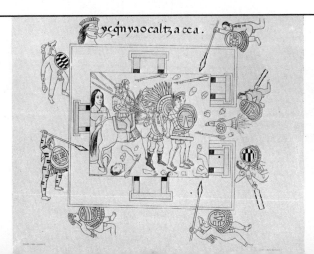

The Spaniards were besieged in the palace of Axayacatl left.
Overleaf Moctezuma addresses the Mexicans from the rooftop of the palace.

do anything to end the war. The Mexicans had chosen Cuitlahuac as king in his place. And he added: 'I believe, therefore, that all of you will be killed.'

Nevertheless, Moctezuma did attempt to speak to his people. Whether of his own volition or not is another matter. He is described as being 'lifted' to one of the battlements of the roof with a guard of Spanish soldiers to protect him. He was apparently seen and recognized by his war chiefs, who at once ordered the attacks to cease, and four of them came forward to talk with him. The tenor of their speech appears to have been extraordinarily conciliatory, considering the disasters he had brought upon them. But there were others present who were not prepared to wait submissively whilst the ex-king once again sapped their warriors' will to fight. Cuitlahuac was one of them. Another was Cuauhtemoc, a youth born to be king, and trained to violence and war.

Whether any order was given, and if so who gave it, we do not know, but the parley ended with a sudden shower of stones and arrows. In face of this barrage the soldiers were unable to give Moctezuma full protection and he was hit in three places – on the leg, the arm and the head. Gómara says he lived for three days in great pain and then died. Bernal Díaz, who must have been one of those who actually saw him brought down from the battlement, said he refused to have his wounds dressed or to eat any food; 'then quite unexpectedly we were told that he was dead.' And he adds: 'Cortés and all of us captains and soldiers wept for him.'

Neither source gives details of the actual death. Nor does Cortés, who simply writes in his dispatches that a stone struck Moctezuma on the head with such force that 'within three days he died'. And he adds: 'I then had him taken out, dead as he was, by two of the Indian prisoners, who bore him away to his people; but I do not know what they did with him, except that the war did not cease . . .' Others, who were not there at the time, have described how he was found dead with chains on his feet and five dagger wounds in his breast, how the Spaniards plunged a sword into his fundament, and also, how many of the other prisoners were murdered – Cacama with forty-five stab wounds. But these are no more than political afterthoughts aimed at Cortés, for though the dispatch of prisoners, who have become an embarrassment to an army in retreat, is fairly common, and Cortés now had every reason to distrust Moctezuma, he certainly had no intention of making him a martyr. In any case, why wait three days? It is much more probable that Moctezuma had reached the point where death was preferable to life. An Indian, deeply involved in a primitive, superstitious religion, he was quite capable of dying through lack of the will to live, and, even though he had been privy to the election of a new and more militaristic king, he cannot have viewed the future with much enthusiasm. In any case, what had the Spaniards to gain by his death? True, the sight of his body being carried out of the camp produced shrieks and lamentations, but it did not result in any slackening of the attacks. Indeed, it had the opposite effect, for the death of the man who had ruled them for more than seventeen years was bound to excite the Mexicans to vengeance.

The Noche Triste. The Spaniards fight their way out of Tenochtitlan, while the Indians acclaim Cuitlahuac as their new king. (See pp. 172-3.) A seventeenth-century Spanish painting.

34 Retirada de
los Españoles la no=
che triste 35 Aclaman
á Quauhtemoc por Rey
36 Guerra entablada, y
queman los Españoles
las Cassas.

42. Hacen
prisionero á Cor=
tés los Indios, y lle=
vandolo á Sacrificar,
le libra Christoval de Oléa
con quatr. Esp.s y
Tlaxcaltecas

7 *Defeat and Conquest*

AT THE TIME OF HIS DEATH Moctezuma had been a 'voluntary' prisoner of the Spaniards for more than six months. Now, suddenly, their tenuous hold over the realm was gone. Henceforth, they must rely on the strength of their arms alone. The position was untenable, for, as Cortés says, if twenty-five thousand Indians perished for every Spaniard, his men would still be destroyed. But to get his force out of the city, he had to have control of the short Tacuba causeway. The day after Moctezuma died he tried again, attacking westward with his mobile towers, four guns and over three thousand Tlaxcalans. But after fighting all morning, he was forced to retreat, harried right to the gates of the camp.

It was at this point that the Mexicans occupied the great temple – Cortés says with about five hundred 'notable persons'; Bernal Díaz claims 'more than four thousand warriors ascended it'. Whichever figure is correct, its terraces and its single stairway of 114 steps made it a natural fortress. Moreover, as can be seen from the plan of the city, it dominated the Spanish quarters. That the Mexicans had not occupied it before was probably due to religious scruples. Now, however, they were commanded by a man who was trained, not to the priesthood, but to war. Cuitlahuac may also have been motivated by the fact that his election as king had not yet been solemnized, a ceremony that involved sacrificial rites at the war god's temple.

Cortés reacted immediately, for 'besides doing us much injury from it, they also gained fresh courage to attack us'. And when his troops failed to conquer it, he sallied forth himself, surrounded the base of the temple and mounted a frontal attack up the stairway. It was a bitter struggle. The cavalry was ineffective in the courtyard below, the horses slithering on the smooth surface of the flagstones, and though the guns mowed the Indians down in batches of ten or fifteen at a time, the enemy was so numerous that the ranks closed immediately. It was Spanish steel that finally prevailed. Fighting hand-to-hand, and advancing a step at a time, they reached the top, 'all streaming with blood', and then hunted out the wretched defenders, pitching them down from the terraces the way their priests discarded the corpses of their sacrificial victims. Aided by the Tlaxcalans, they burned the

When the Spaniards returned again to besiege Tenochtitlan, Cortés was nearly captured by the Indians. (See p. 186.) A seventeenth-century Spanish painting.

towers, the idol-rooms, the idols themselves. It was the first real victory since Alvarado had so senselessly massacred the defenceless dancers. 'Some of their pride was taken out of them', as Cortés laconically puts it.

But, at the parley that followed, it was clear that the Mexicans were now determined to destroy the Spaniards utterly. They had broken down all the bridges, and if they couldn't kill the Spaniards, then they would starve them out. That night Cortés made a surprise attack, captured a street, burned some three hundred houses, and then returned by another street, burning more, and also some terraces that overlooked the quarters. He was out again at daybreak, fighting through to the Tacuba causeway, where there were eight 'very large deep bridges', by now simply gaps in the road, all protected by barricades of adobe and clay. He captured four of these bridge-sites, filled the gaps with the debris of the barricades and burned the houses and terraces overlooking them. By nightfall he was sufficiently in command of the situation to mount guards on the rubble-filled gaps. The next day he was out again, breaking right through to the mainland, where news reached him that the Mexicans were suing for peace. With several horsemen, he galloped back to the quarters.

The Mexican chiefs were indeed offering peace. The details were arranged by a high priest the Spaniards had captured, and he went with them, at their request, to see that the truce was carried out. As when Moctezuma requested the release of Cuitlahuac, Cortés does not seem to have understood the Indian mind, and Doña Marina failed to advise him of their real intention. Religious ceremony was the basis of their society, and the presence of this high priest was necessary for the installation of Cuitlahuac as king.

Cortés had just sat down to a much-needed meal when news arrived that, far from ceasing their attacks, the Mexicans had re-taken all the bridges on the Tacuba causeway. According to his own version, he recaptured the lot in one swift assault at the head of a small group of cavalry, reached the mainland, and found himself cut off. The Mexicans had closed in behind him, pulling the rubble from the gaps, swarming over the causeway, and had massed in canoes on the lake. Cortés fought his way back, jumping the six-foot gap where the last bridge had been, only his armour saving him and his horse from being killed. By the time he had fought his way back to the quarters it was being rumoured that he was dead.

Four bridges were now held by the Mexicans, four by the Spaniards. It was time to get out of the city, regardless of loss of face or loss of men, for even if the Mexicans sued for peace again, he dared not trust them.

Now begins what the Spaniards have named the Noche Triste. A mobile bridging unit was constructed and Cortés detailed a hundred and fifty soldiers with four hundred Tlaxcalans to carry it, place it in position and guard it whilst the army crossed. The artillery was to be carried by two hundred Tlaxcalans, supported by fifty soldiers. Sandoval and Ordaz were to lead the army, whilst two companies of fifty men each, under Saucedo and Lugo, were to spearhead counter-attacks wherever the march was opposed. Alvarado and Juan Velázquez were to bring up the rear, and three hundred Tlaxcalans, with thirty soldiers, were to guard the prisoners. The evacuation would be made that night, when there was a chance that the Mexicans would be taken by surprise and offer little opposition.

It was a sensible plan. What was not so sensible was that, instead of travelling light, they marched out encumbered with gold. Not unnaturally, Cortés was determined that the king's fifth at least should be saved; and no doubt he wanted his own treasure saved as well, for he knew he would have need of it if he were to return to complete the conquest of Mexico. There was by now the colossal total of 700,000 pesos' worth of the stuff (at present values around £3,000,000) weighing anything up to eight tons. Alonso de Ávila and Gonzalo Mejía, the two Treasury officials, took charge of the royal share, and to transport it Cortés gave them seven wounded horses, a mare of his own, and over eighty Tlaxcalans. But once the treasure hall was open, there was no stopping the soldiery. It was every man for himself. Those whose eyes were bigger than their experience – the Narváez men, in particular – loaded themselves down with gold. Old campaigners, like Bernal Díaz, were content to pocket a few of the *chalchihuites,* taking the beautifully-cut pieces of jade from the small boxes in which they had been packed.

Thus encumbered, they marched out of their quarters shortly before midnight on June 30, 1520,* having been camped in the palace of Axayacatl almost eight months. It was a dark night with a mist hanging over Texcoco lake and a light drizzle falling. Sandoval and Ordaz reached the start of the Tacuba causeway

*Gómara's date. Bernal Díaz gives July 10.

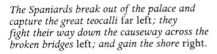

The Spaniards break out of the palace and capture the great teocalli far left; *they fight their way down the causeway across the broken bridges* left; *and gain the shore* right.

without opposition, and the prefabricated bridge was placed in position over the first of the eight gaps. Cortés states that it was the sentries posted at the causeway-end who gave the alarm. More likely they simply gave the signal for the attack to begin, for before the Spaniards had reached the second bridge-gap they were set upon by an 'infinite multitude'. The movement of such a large body of troops and horses, with bridging equipment, cannon, baggage and treasure, could not possibly have been concealed. Clearly, the Mexicans were waiting for them at the point where Cuitlahuac thought they would be most vulnerable. The lake on either side of the causeway was thick with canoes and the Indians stood in the water and in the gaps stabbing with their long spears.

Cortés crossed the second bridge and, with five horsemen and five hundred soldiers, forced a passage down the causeway, swimming the gaps, until he reached the mainland. He then went back for the rest, acting as a rearguard, with three or four horse and about twenty foot, until all the survivors had reached the mainland.

Like any general in his dispatches Cortés makes it all sound very orderly, even though he admits that many men and horses were lost and all the artillery, treasure and baggage. In fact, he had been neatly ambushed and the whole retreat turned into a shambles. The musketeers and crossbowmen had abandoned their weapons at the second bridge. It was hack, hack, hack, with steel cutting flesh and bone, as the soldiers fought their way through band after band of Mexicans, the water on one side, the flat roofs on the other and the lake full of canoes. Horsemen were pulled from their mounts, men trampled underfoot, dragged down into the water, drowned in the gaps. The rear of the column bore the brunt of it. Juan Velázquez was killed. Alvarado was wounded in the foot, his famous sorrel mare killed under him, but he still fought on, lance in hand. Eighty of his men were dead. The wooden bridge unit had been destroyed and the approaches to the gap were littered with dead men, dead horses and boxes from the baggage train. Alvarado had finally crossed by leaping the gap, pole-vaulting it with his lance; this is the bridge that was afterwards called Alvarado's Leap, and a section of the Tacuba route out of Mexico City is still called Puente Alvarado. He finally broke through to Cortés with four soldiers and eight Tlaxcalans, 'all of them pouring blood from many wounds'. A massive old ahuehuete tree on the Calzada Mexico-Tacuba is

Cortés and his troops find shelter in a hill-top temple.

supposed to mark the spot where Cortés stood in tears at the wreckage of his hopes – but whether they were tears of rage or sadness is not recorded.

When at last they reached Tacuba they re-grouped on the high ground overlooking the lake, at a teocalli where the church of Los Remedios now stands – throughout Mexico almost every temple site is marked by a church. But even here the Indians continued to harry them. Early next morning they took stock and found they had lost more than six hundred of their men, mainly the Narváez contingent, who had died at Alvarado's Leap, weighed down by gold and drowned. But it was the Tlaxcalans who had suffered the heaviest losses – over two thousand killed, by Cortés' reckoning. This does not necessarily indicate that they had borne the brunt of the fighting; simply that they met the Mexicans on equal terms, which the Spaniards did not. The cavalry were certainly in the thick of it, for, armoured though they were, no less than forty-five horses were killed, only twenty-three surviving.

None of the prisoners survived, not even the son and daughters of Moctezuma, whom the king is supposed to have committed to Cortés' care on his deathbed. They died at Alvarado's Leap, as did Cacama, according to Bernal Díaz. But that determined and indomitable Indian Princess, Doña Marina, came through it all alive, together with María de Estrada, the only Spanish woman in Mexico, and Doña Luisa, Xicotencatl's daughter. They had been saved by a group of Tlaxcalan warriors. All the other women had been abandoned to their fate.

Cortés and the remnants of his army were besieged in the temple all that day, and at midnight they left, heading north towards Cuauhtitlan and the north end of Texcoco lake. Watchmen, hearing them go, raised all the neighbouring towns, and they had a bitter day of it in bad country. They spent the night in another hill-top temple, hardly a man unwounded, and with very little food. They were on the march again an hour after daybreak, in thickly populated country and under constant attack as they skirted north round Zumpango and two other lakes. A small town they captured gave them a twenty-four-hour break, and then on again, still short of food, and constantly losing the track that was supposed to lead to Tlaxcala. That night they camped in some hovels on the edge of a plain. When they started out in the morning there were Indians posted on a hill to the right of their march. Cortés took five horsemen and a dozen soldiers and reconnoitred

They sleep on the march.

round the base of it. On the other side he found the great city of Otumba. Indians swarmed out of it and he was himself wounded in the head by two sling-stones. The Spaniards made little progress that day and camped the night in the open, supplementing their meagre diet of maize and herbs with the flesh of a horse killed in the day's fighting.

The Mexicans now made a tactical blunder that was to deprive them of their advantage and indeed pave the way for the final subjugation of their country. Instead of persisting with their harrying tactics they decided on a pitched battle. For this final blow Cuitlahuac had massed a great army of his warriors in the open maize fields outside Otumba. He had never seen Spanish cavalry in action on level ground; nor had any of his war chiefs. Accounts that had filtered through from the coast, and from Tlaxcala and Cholula, had almost certainly been regarded as exaggeration, since they were quite contrary to their experience of horsemen in the city confines of Mexico. They had no idea of the thundering weight and deadly thrust of armoured horses at full gallop.

Cortés, realizing that he now faced the final test, ordered the badly wounded, who had been carried on horseback, to march as best they could. The horses – all twenty-two of them – were prepared for battle. They were to charge and return, charge and return, their riders aiming always at the enemies' faces. The foot soldiers were to drive their swords always into the Mexicans' bellies.

The battle of Otumba was fought on July 7, 1520. 'It was a destructive battle and a fearful sight to behold', says Bernal Díaz, who, like Cortés, gives God the credit for victory. 'We seemed all to be given double strength.' The cavalry broke the massed ranks of the Mexicans. 'And then, commending ourselves most heartily to God and the Blessed Mary, and calling on the name of our patron St James, we charged them, altogether. . . . We moved through the midst of them at the closest quarters, slashing and thrusting at them with our swords, and the dogs fought back furiously, dealing us wounds and death with their lances and their two-handed swords. And, the field being level, our horsemen speared them at pleasure, charging and retiring and charging again.'

No estimate is given of the Mexican strength, but it is significant that the battle raged throughout most of the day. Bernal Díaz claims that there had never been seen throughout the Indies so many warriors assembled for battle. 'All the flower of Mexico, of Texcoco, of all the towns around the lake, and of many others in the neighbourhood, was present.' The size of the Mexican force is confirmed by Cortés himself – 'so great a multitude of Indians came out to encounter me, that all about us we could not see the ground, so completely was it covered by them. They attacked us on all sides so violently that we could not distinguish each other, for being so pressed and entangled with them. Certainly we believed that to be our last day. . . .' And he adds, 'They were so many that they hindered one another, and were unable to fight or fly.' There is no doubt about the courage and ferocity of the Mexican warriors, but autocracy was their weakness in battle, as it was

The Spanish cavalry defeated the Mexican foot soldiers at the battle of Otumba.

in politics. Their war chiefs wore feathered head-dresses, great golden plumes that waved in the sunlight above the struggling mass of their fighting men. On Cortés' orders the Spanish cavalry made a dead set at them, and as one by one their leaders fell, the warriors lost heart and their ranks began to break. 'Then', Bernal Díaz says, 'all our horsemen followed them, and we felt neither hunger nor thirst. It was as if we had suffered no disaster and undergone no hardships; we followed up our victory, dealing death and wounds, and our allies the Tlaxcalans became like very lions.'

The Spanish force was now reduced once again to little more than four hundred men. But though the Mexicans followed in the wake of their march, they no longer attempted to attack them, and next day, when they reached the Tlaxcalan border, which was marked by ancient defence works, the Mexicans vanished. The Spaniards were among friends again, with the caciques of Tlaxcala coming out to meet them, commiserating over their misfortunes, offering them food and shelter.

One of the most extraordinary things about this whole campaign is the loyalty of the Tlaxcalans. They have their counterpart in all mountain country – the Scots, the Montenegrans, the Berbers. Fiercely independent, they saw in the Spaniards their only hope of survival, and despite their frightful losses, they were still prepared to support them. It was, in fact, the Tlaxcalan alliance that enabled Cortés to fight back and recover all the ground he had lost.

Cortés himself never seems to have wavered in his intentions. He sent at once to Vera Cruz for powder, crossbows and the crews of two of Narváez's ships that had gone aground, harangued his men, told them bluntly that the war would be prosecuted until the whole country was subject to Spanish rule, and with the backing of his old guard, shamed the remnants of Narváez's men, who wanted nothing but to get back to Cuba, into staying with him. He had, of course, no field hospital of any sort, but Tlaxcala's proximity to the high mountains made it a healthy place. Wounds healed. Many of his men, however, were maimed for life – he himself had lost two fingers of his left hand – and all the reinforcements he got from Vera Cruz were seven sickly sailors. Nevertheless, after three weeks' rest, he ordered his men to march against the Mexican-garrisoned town of Tepeaca, to the south and slightly east of the old volcano called La Malinche. Primarily it was a punitive expedition. Sixteen Spanish soldiers had been killed there. But it was also a training march, designed to instil some discipline into the Narváez men and to test the loyalty of his Tlaxcalan allies. They provided two thousand warriors, and when they joined him, it must have put new heart into his own men, for they were a brave sight, marching into the camp in ranks twenty abreast, all dressed in white and in perfect order, drums beating, trumpets blowing, bright plumes nodding and the banners of their republic gleaming in the sunlight. This colourful scene was completed by the ritual sacrifice of some Mexican spies and the induction of a chief's son to full warriorhood by blooding him five times across the face with a still-palpitating heart.

However, by Indian standards it was a small enough force, and when he reached Tepeaca the inhabitants decided to defy him. Cortés seized on this opportunity to draw up a decree before the Notary Royal condemning them to slavery as renegade Spanish vassals. This decree embraced all allies of Mexico who had revolted after swearing allegiance to the Spanish crown; it should be borne in mind that this was perfectly in accordance with contemporary thought and practice. Cortés probably did it because his war chest was almost empty. He needed funds to

support the campaign he was already planning, and slaves were the equivalent of gold. However, in his second dispatch to the Emperor he finds it necessary to produce reasons to justify his action – 'For in addition to having murdered the Spaniards and rebelled against your Majesty's service they eat human flesh . . .' His third reason is perhaps the most convincing – that he had done it as an example to all the other Mexican tribes. An attempt, in fact, to terrorize them into obedience.

The defenders of Tepeaca now repeated the mistake the Mexicans had made at Otumba; they came out and fought the Spaniards on the level ground of the maize-fields, where the cavalry cut them to pieces. Most of the wretched inhabitants of the town were branded with a special brand and sold into slavery.

This ruthlessness was almost certainly inspired by the campaigns of Philip against the Moors, and its effect was similar. Towns hastened to renew their allegiance, whilst his captains and his Tlaxcalan allies ranged far and wide, destroying Mexican garrisons and bringing in slaves and loot. His luck, too, had turned, favouring, as luck always does, the man of single purpose and determination. Two ships from Cuba put into Vera Cruz, loaded with arms, powder and stores for Narváez' ill-fated expedition, and Garay sent a force from Jamaica to settle the Pánuco river, backed by a further shipload of reinforcements, all of which fell into Cortés' hands. Thus, his hostile rivals for conquest, the governors of Cuba and Jamaica, unwittingly contributed a hundred and fifty men, twenty horses, cannon, arms and powder, all of which he desperately needed.

In addition, he had an unseen ally – smallpox. This deadly disease had been brought into the country by a negro, who was a slave in the Narváez expedition: a fair return, Bernal Díaz comments, for the buboes, or syphilis, which the Spaniards had got from the Indians. Starting from Zempoala, where the negro had died, smallpox had now spread through the country, and Cortés was much in demand as the arbitrator of land disputes and the appointer of caciques to replace those who had died. The disease had penetrated to Mexico itself. Cuitlahuac had died of it and had been succeeded by Cuauhtemoc, who was the husband of one of Moctezuma's daughters.

Another ship arrived, this time from Spain, and the arms and powder and stores on board were purchased with gold. Cortés was now able to send a vessel to

On arrival in Tlaxcalan territory the Spaniards re-provisioned from their base at Vera Cruz far left; they sent a punitive expedition to Tepeaca left; and set about building brigantines for the recapture of Tenochtitlan right.

Jamaica to buy horses secretly from the settlers there, and another to Spain, via Santo Domingo, with Ordaz and Ávila, to put his case against the representations of Diego Velázquez. At the same time, he began the construction of thirteen sloops to operate on Texcoco lake.

All this took time, and it was not until Christmas 1520 that he was ready to march. The first objective was Texcoco, which he found as deserted as it had been when he had marched to the relief of Alvarado. By April 1521 his forces were moving round the lake, subduing town after town in spite of the Mexicans, who constantly harried them and operated from the lake in great numbers of canoes. Battle followed battle. At Xochimilco, now the only place where you can see the beauty of the lake as it once was, Cortés nearly lost his life. He was riding a fat, pampered chestnut called El Romo, which means Mule – throughout all the campaigns horses were so important that their names are recorded as punctiliously as those of the captains who rode them. The animal faltered in the midst of the fray and Cortés was dragged from its back. Immediately the Mexicans closed in, hoping to achieve fame by capturing him alive for sacrifice. A group of his old guard fought their way through to him and, though he was wounded in the head, he was able to remount in the brief space they cleared for him.

The battle for Xochimilco was the toughest of this particular campaign. After its capture, they climbed to the temple tower and from there they could see all the cities of the lake, and Mexico itself shining white in the sunlight. They also saw some two thousand canoes heading towards them and more warriors advancing overland – ten thousand of them. It was time to retire, and they marched north in good order, though many were wounded. Coyoacán was deserted. They pushed on to Tacuba. It was raining heavily now. They looked at the causeway, where they had lost so much gold and so many comrades in the retreat of the Noche Triste, but decided against any attempt to force it. North again, marching in deep mud to Azcapotzalco, which was also deserted. Continuing north, they completed the circumnavigation of the lake, returning to Texcoco.

Here a mutinous element, composed mainly of Narváez' men and led by Antonio Villafaña, hatched a plot to murder Cortés. Villafaña was one of the Velázquez faction, which had caused so much trouble at the start of the expedition more than eighteen months before. A ship had just arrived from Spain and the plan was for several of the conspirators to bring a sealed letter to Cortés whilst he was dining with his captains. They were to say the letter was from his father, Martín Cortés, and stab him and his captains as he sat reading it. Like all conspirators, however, they could not keep it to themselves. They even sounded out and elected a new captain-general and all the various officials to replace those already appointed. Inevitably a soldier blabbed. The plotters were surprised in Villafaña's quarters, and after a brief trial, in which Villafaña confessed, he was hanged from his own window. The others, who had been arrested with him, were released. Cortés needed all the men he had, and the hanging of their leader seems to have acted as a sufficient warning, since he had no more trouble with them after that.

The ship from Spain had brought more arms, and also some hidalgos with their own horses, young soldiers of fortune who had come out to join the expedition for what they could get out of it. Even better, it brought the news that Fonseca was out of favour at court and the Emperor was now shifting his support from Diego Velázquez to Cortés. The fame of Cortés was spreading, his star in the ascendant. The Church itself was lending him support, sending a Franciscan with bulls from a new Pope offering, doubtless at a price in gold, absolution from any and every type of sin that the soldiers might have committed during the struggle. With the new arrivals, Cortés now had a cavalry force of 86 horsemen, 118 cross-bowmen and musketeers, and more than 700 foot soldiers, as well as three heavy iron guns, fifteen small bronze field pieces and half a ton of powder. Moreover, the thirteen sloops, or brigantines, were finished.

After mass on Sunday, April 28, 1521, the boats were launched, with their flags flying. Then Cortés reviewed his army and gave them his customary pep-talk. He was ready to march, and the following day he sent messengers throughout the provinces of Tlaxcala, Cholula and Huejotzingo summoning their warriors to gather for the attack on Mexico within ten days. In less than a week the ever-loyal and fiercely eager Tlaxcalans arrived, marching into Texcoco in a well-disciplined column fifty thousand strong, all well armed and in closed ranks, their feathered head-dresses nodding to shouts of 'Castile, Castile', and 'Tlaxcala, Tlaxcala'. They took three hours to enter the city, their banners flying and the white crane standard, with its wings outstretched, carried high.

By the feast day of the Holy Ghost Cortés had more than seventy-five thousand Indian warriors assembled in Texcoco. Two days later he paraded his army and issued his battle orders. His force would advance in three divisions. Alvarado, with 30 horse, 18 crossbowmen, 150 foot and 25,000 Tlaxcalans, and Olid, with 33 horse, a further 18 crossbowmen and 160 foot, together with 20,000 Indian warriors, were to march north round the lake: Alvarado to occupy Tacuba, Olid to take up his station at Coyoacán. Sandoval, with 24 horse, 4 musketeers, 13 crossbowmen, 150 foot and another 30,000 Indians, was to strike south at Iztapalapa, destroy the city and advance along the causeway by which they had first entered Mexico. Cortés himself would command the brigantines, to each of which were allocated nineteen Spaniards – a captain, six archers or musketeers, and the rest at the oars.

The Indians moved out ahead of the Spaniards, probably because their numbers were so great that they had consumed all the food they had brought with them. The whole plan of campaign was nearly wrecked at the outset by the defection of the Tlaxcalan war chief, Xicotencatl the Younger. Cortés, who was utterly dependent on the Tlaxcalans to fight his way through the Mexican hordes, acted swiftly. He notified the Tlaxcalan war chiefs, including Xicotencatl's father, that in the Spanish army desertion in the face of the enemy was punishable by death.

The Spanish brigantines are engaged by Mexican canoes in the lake above; meanwhile Cortés' forces and those of his allies converged upon Tenochtitlan from different directions below.

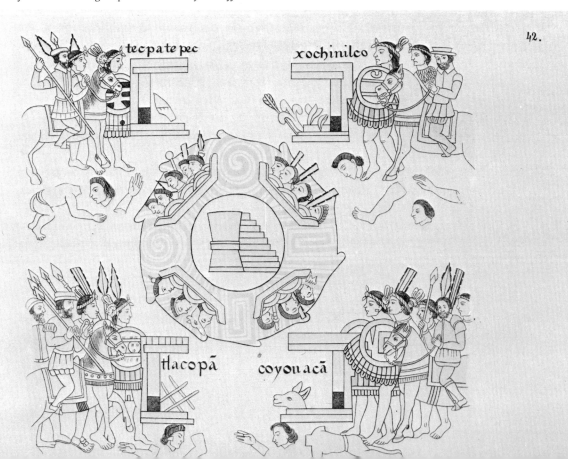

42.

tecpatepec

xochinilco

tlacopã

coyouacã

Xicotencatl was executed, and since the Tlaxcalan code also punished desertion with death, even his father accepted it. All this took time.

The volatility of his own men now proved almost as dangerous as Indian politics. On arriving at Acolman, Alvarado and Olid nearly came to blows in a stupid dispute over quarters. Again Cortés had to intervene, but thereafter the two captains were barely on speaking terms, so that when they reached Tacuba and Alvarado wanted to keep the two forces together, Olid insisted on sticking to the letter of his instructions and moved his men on to Coyoacán. This was after Alvarado's men had fought most of the day to carry out their orders and destroy the wooden pipes of the main aqueduct supplying water to Mexico.

Sandoval, meanwhile, was having great difficulty in taking Iztapalapa. In the midst of the battle, smoke signals were seen rising from a nearby hill. This call for reinforcements was answered by smoke signals from the lake towns, and Cortés, who was then attacking a rocky island close to Mexico itself, found himself faced with more than a thousand canoes. There was no wind at the time, but by rowing hard his men managed to keep clear until the breeze came in with the sun and filled their sails. Immediately, Cortés turned his brigantines about and headed into the Mexican fleet. 'We destroyed an infinite number of canoes and killed and drowned many of the enemy – the greatest sight to see in the world'. Thus, gloating at his success, which gave him virtual command of the lake, Cortés went on to capture the little causeway fortress of Xoloc. Then began the campaign against Mexico. It was to last two months and involve the Spaniards in the most bitter fighting.

The defence of Mexico by the Aztecs, though little known, must rank as one of the epics of military history. Under their young commander, Cuauhtemoc, they fought with an utter disregard of death, with the bravery of men whose business was war – first on the causeways, and then, when the bridge-gaps were all filled in and the watchtowers taken, in the streets of the city itself, defending it house by house, canal by canal, rebuilding during the night the barricades that the Spaniards had torn down during the day, re-opening the canal gaps that had been filled. It was an incredible display of energy and determination by men who, in the later stages of the siege, were suffering from hunger, thirst and the stinking accumulation of unburned corpses. They were ingenious, too, driving in stakes to keep the brigantines from giving close support to the Spaniards fighting their way up the causeways, digging underwater pits to trap soldiers and horsemen attempting to wade the gaps, using captured swords tied to long poles to halt the charges of the Spanish cavalry. At first, they were able to bring food and water in from the lake country at night by canoe; but as the blockade tightened the supplies dwindled, and with the defection of the lakeside towns, they ceased altogether. The Mexicans existed then on brackish water sieved from mudholes in the city, on roots and plants and the bodies of men killed, or those captured and sacrificed.

The Spanish attack on Mexico was mounted from the south and west using three causeways. Cortés, with Olid's force, attempted to break in by the main causeway from Xoloc; Sandoval by the small subsidiary causeway that joined it at Acachinanco; whilst, from the west, Alvarado advanced by the Tacuba causeway. He was supported by four of the brigantines, and two more were sent to aid Sandoval on the smaller causeway. Without the brigantines to hold off the canoes the Spaniards would have had little hope of destroying the water defences of the city. The causeways were so encumbered with houses and fortresses, so interrupted by bridges and impeded by barricades thrown up by the Mexicans, that every yard gained was a major battle. Moreover, because of the obstructions and the mud and slime, the horses, which were the main advantage the Spaniards possessed on land, were of little use. And each night the gaps they had so labor-iously filled were torn open again. Nevertheless, within a few days Cortés had penetrated into Tenochtitlan, the southern part of the city, had reached a square and captured a temple that was a hundred steps to the top, almost as high as the great teocalli itself. Now that Cortés was actually in the city proper, the young lord of Texcoco brought up the warriors of his province, so that the Spaniards were now advancing daily up the three causeways supported by no less than a hundred thousand warriors. The end seemed almost in sight. But the city itself was criss-crossed by innumerable canals, and with the bridges over them destroyed and the Mexicans defending each gap with extraordinary ferocity and pouring sling-stones and arrows down from the surrounding roof-tops, progress could only be made by filling each canal gap and destroying all the buildings that overlooked it. So began the house-by-house destruction of one of the world's most beautiful cities.

It was at this point that Alvarado's impetuosity nearly proved disastrous once more. Cortés had been trying to link up the two prongs of his attack by forcing a passage through some streets that connected with the Tacuba causeway. He was faced, however, with half a dozen canal gaps, and, after capturing three and filling them in, he retired for the night. His objective seems to have been the market square. Alvarado had the same objective, but his men were under such pressure that they were forced to retreat back down the causeway each night to their quarters in Tacuba, posting guards on the gaps that had been filled. A sort of rivalry seems now to have developed between Alvarado and Cortés, each wanting to be the first to reach the square, which, being a large open space surrounded by arcades and dominated by a number of temples, was ideal as an advance base. The Tacuba causeway led straight into it, and Alvarado, flushed with success after capturing several of the intervening bridges and barricades, made a dash for it, lured on by the fact that the Mexicans appeared to have broken and were in full flight. It was, however, a trap. Behind him he left a shallow water gap, sixty feet wide, through which he had plunged with his horses and men. Fifty soldiers had just begun the work of filling it in when the

teçiquauhtitlã

The Spaniards and Tlaxcalans fight their way down the causeway, supported by boats in the lake *above, and break into the city* below.

ycquinualtocaquecaltzalan.

Mexicans turned abruptly and attacked with great ferocity. Canoes, waiting in ambush, closed in on the gap. The brigantines, impeded by a carefully prepared stake barricade, could not come to their aid. Alvarado fought his way through to another street and forced a passage across a much deeper gap where pits had been dug under water. It was a near thing, and he was lucky to save his life and escape with the loss of only one horse. But, apart from killed and wounded, five Spaniards had been taken alive.

Cortés was justifiably annoyed at this reverse, for he had repeatedly warned both his own men and Alvarado not to advance beyond an unfilled gap. Then, a few days later, he was himself caught in exactly the same trap. He was again making a determined effort to fight his way through to the market square. He had just captured a somewhat deep water opening across which the Mexicans had purposely left a very narrow causeway with several gaps in it. As he moved to occupy it they retreated as though they had now lost courage, luring him on step by step until suddenly they broke and fled. Cortés and his men followed hard on their heels, leaving the gap behind them unfilled, though Cortés later claimed that he gave orders for it to be filled. Bands of Mexican warriors under their bravest captains had been concealed in the houses, canoes were ready to attack the gap, and stakes had been driven into the mud to keep the brigantines off. The trap was sprung in an instant, and Cortés and his men were caught in a great rush of warriors. He himself was badly wounded in the leg, was dragged from his horse, and was down in the water and mud of the gap when Olea, one of his old guard, who had saved his life once before at Xochimilco, hacked off the arm of the Mexican chief who was dragging him towards one of the canoes. Once again he was saved from death solely by the desire of the Mexicans to take him alive so that he could be sacrificed. Other soldiers rushed to his rescue, but by then Olea was dead. Altogether, Cortés lost some forty men in the ambush, most of them captured alive, and a thousand of his Indians had been killed. It was the worst defeat the Spaniards had suffered since the start of the siege.

Flushed with their victory, the Mexicans renewed their attack on Alvarado's men. 'Uttering loud yells', Bernal Díaz says, 'they threw in front of us five heads, streaming with blood, which they had just cut off the men of Cortés' company.' They were yelling that they had killed Cortés and Sandoval and would kill them, too. Worse, as the Spaniards retreated on to the Tacuba causeway, they heard the sound of trumpets from the great temple six miles away in Mexico, and the beating of the snake-skin drum, 'a very sad sound' – sad, because the Mexicans were then sacrificing ten of the Spaniards' comrades.

On the other side of the city the war of nerves was carried into Cortés' camp. The Mexicans, who had pursued him there and were attacking in force, threw four more severed and flayed heads amongst his men, screaming that they included the heads of Alvarado and Sandoval, whom they had killed. Fearing the worst, Cortés sent Andrés de Tapia, with an escort of three horse, round by land to

The Indians decapitate their Spanish prisoners, and cast their heads at the feet of Cortés.
A seventeenth-century Spanish painting.

43 Comen
los Indios Carne
de Españoles, y
tienen assadas Com á
vico cavezas de Esp=
añolo los Indios
Ha menuado Haur á
lonis pocos los
demas.

43

44

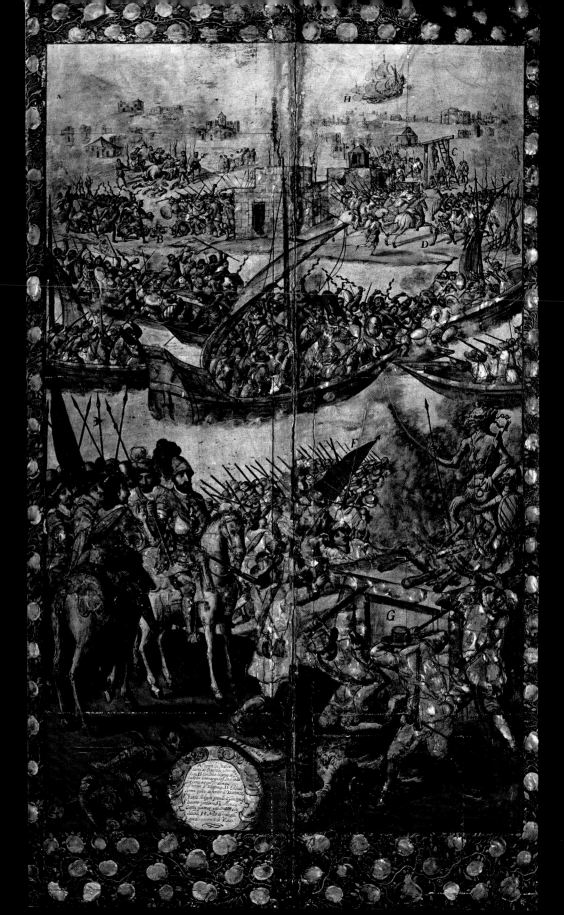

Tacuba to get news of the situation there. Meanwhile, Sandoval, who had been advancing steadily in his own quarter of the city, was faced with such a press of warriors that he had to fall back after he had lost six men killed and had himself been wounded in the head, the thigh and left arm. The Mexicans displayed six more heads. Again they were all men that Cortés had lost, but they claimed that one was the head of Cortés himself and another Alvarado's.

Wounded as he was, Sandoval immediately galloped off to Cortés' camp. Finding his captain safe, but alarmed at the absence of news from Alvarado, he rode on to Tacuba. He was just in time to prevent one of the brigantines, which had run aground, being captured, and got a sling-stone in the face for his trouble. He was wounded yet again in an endeavour to clear the causeway of the hordes of Mexicans attacking down it, leading the cavalry in charge after charge, despite the slippery surface, with the crossbowmen and musketeers shooting whilst others loaded for them, the soldiers hacking and stabbing. Even cannon fire seemed to make no impression on the Mexicans, who attacked in a frenzy, drunk with victory. There was no let-up in the fighting until the Spaniards had retreated almost to the Tacuba end of the causeway and had put a broad gap of water between themselves and their attackers.

Now the great snake-skin drum* sounded its dismal note again, to the accompaniment of conches, horns and trumpets. When the Spaniards looked towards the great temple, which stood out high above the city, they saw more of their comrades, who had been captured in Cortés' imprudent charge, being dragged up the steps to a small platform where the priests stood waiting.

> We saw them put plumes on the heads of many of them, and then they made them dance with a sort of fan in front of Huitzilopochtli. Then, after they had danced, the priests laid them on their backs on some narrow stones of sacrifice and, cutting open their chests, drew out their palpitating hearts which they offered to the idols before them. Then they kicked the bodies down the steps, and the Indian butchers who were waiting below cut off their arms and legs and flayed their faces, which they afterwards prepared like glove leather, with their beards on, and kept for their drunken festivals. Then they ate their flesh with a sauce of peppers and tomatoes.

There is another account of the Mexicans attacking and throwing roasted arms and legs into the midst of the Spaniards, screaming, 'Eat the flesh of these *teules* and your brothers, for we are glutted with it – stuff yourselves on our leavings.'

To us today these accounts are horrifying, but the Mexicans were fighting for their lives, for the state they had made the greatest state in the Indian world, for their beautiful city, and for the glory of their own true faith. From their point of view, what they did to their invaders was no more than their normal practice, and

---

*Bernal Díaz – the customary drums for sacrifice were wooden.

Victory. (A) *The Indians eat the flesh of their prisoners;* (B) *and throw their heads before the Spaniards;* (C *and* D) *Xicotencatl the Younger, the disloyal Tlaxcalan, is captured and hanged;* (E) *Cuauhtemoc is captured;* (F) *Tenochtitlan is stormed;* (G) *and the Indian idols are destroyed;* (H) *a Spanish ship off Vera Cruz. A seventeenth-century Spanish painting.*

to taunt the Spaniards with the remains of their captured victims was merely grim psychological warfare. Undoubtedly it had an effect on the Spanish soldiery, inducing in each man the thought that there but for the Grace of God . . . Indeed, Bernal Díaz says frankly that the fear of being captured alive was always with him before a battle, so that 'a sort of horror and gloom would seize my heart, and I would make water once or twice and commend myself to God and His blessed Mother'. As soon as he was in action, the fear left him, but as battles were daily occurrences this fear of being captured, which all of them must have experienced, undoubtedly constituted a terrific nervous strain, though it probably added to their value as fighting machines.

This form of psychological warfare seems to have had its effect also on their Indian allies; or perhaps they were getting bored by the protracted nature of the campaign. Indian campaigns were normally short-lived affairs since they refrained from living off the country, always carrying their own supplies of food with them. Whichever it was, they began to drift away. Bernal Díaz claims that the Spaniards on the Tacuba causeway were entirely deserted and worked for four days on a rota system, one company acting as labour corps, whilst two others did the fighting, until all the gaps that had been torn open again were filled in. This is not borne out by Cortés, who records that Chichimecatl, the Tlaxcalan war chief, mounted an independent and highly successful attack of his own whilst Alvarado's Spaniards were resting in their camp.

Cortés had, in fact, given orders for the Spaniards to rest, only sending small companies into the city to give an appearance of aggressive activity. June to August is the rainy season in Mexico and his men had been fighting constantly for more than a month in wet conditions and with poor food. They needed time to recover, to refurbish their weapons and to bring up more powder from Vera Cruz, where a ship belonging to Ponce de León's ill-fated expedition to Florida had providentially sought refuge. Moreover, there was trouble brewing in the surrounding country. After their victory the Mexicans sent the hands and feet of Spaniards they had sacrificed, and the heads of horses they had killed, through all the towns of their defecting allies. To stop the rot Cortés sent Tapia to Cuernavaca and Sandoval to Otomí, each with a considerable force ostensibly to 'protect' these allies. Sandoval had the support of sixty thousand Indians, which probably explains why the Spaniards on the Tacuba causeway felt themselves deserted. With this large force to aid him, Sandoval inflicted a crushing defeat on the Culhúan insurgents. All this took about ten days, but it had the desired effect, so that when Cortés resumed full-scale operations against Mexico, he was supported by the staggering total of 150,000 Indian auxiliaries. He opened his new offensive by following the example of the Mexicans and staging carefully prepared ambushes. The most successful of these occurred after nearly a week of hard fighting when he had gained the market square. Some five hundred 'of all the bravest and most valiant of their principal men' were killed, and he adds without

In a final assault the Spaniards and their Indian allies massacred the remaining defenders of Tenochtitlan.

comment or show of feeling, 'our allies supped well because they cut up all those whom they had killed and captured to eat'. Next day he killed and wounded a further eight hundred, and the day following he linked up with Alvarado's force. Since the resumption of the offensive, his orders not to advance beyond a gap before it had been filled in had been strictly obeyed, and using his Indians as demolition squads he was systematically destroying every building, levelling whole streets.

He claims that he repeatedly tried to induce the Mexicans to surrender and that he did his best to restrain his Indian allies from looting and senseless slaughter. The offensive was now degenerating into a massacre. In one engagement the Mexicans lost 12,000 killed, in another 40,000. Seven-eighths of the city was in the hands of the invaders, 'which left them not even a place to stand, save upon the bodies of their own dead', and 'our allies handled the enemy most cruelly, for they would in no wise spare any life'. The other side of the picture was that in every quarter the Spaniards took they found the houses and stockades full of heads and corpses. 'We could not walk', Bernal Díaz says, 'without treading on the bodies and heads of dead Indians.'

The Mexicans appear to have made two overtures of peace, but either they were only to gain time to prepare their defences or else on each occasion they were overruled by the stubbornness of their priests. Cortés, impressed by their suffering, also made offers, which were rejected. The end came suddenly on August 13, 1521, when Cortés mounted a final all-out attack on the small area of the city in which

Cuauhtemoc was captured as he tried to escape above, and the Tlaxcalans returned home laden with booty right.

ycyaquiatēpan. qlpito
albaez.

the Mexican survivors had been penned. More than fifteen thousand of them died that day. In the end, Cuauhtemoc and the remnants took to their canoes. Owing to its state trappings, the one occupied by Cuauhtemoc was easily recognized, and he was captured by a brigantine.

So ended the epic defence of Mexico. For two whole months the Aztecs had fought upwards of 150,000 of their own race, had faced without flinching the new instruments of war imported by alien invaders – cannons, ships, muskets, steel and the terrible power of armoured cavalry. They had also faced hunger, thirst and pestilence. Bernal Díaz gives a horrifying description of conditions in the quarter of the city which was the last to be over-run:

> We found the houses full of corpses, and some poor Mexicans still in them who could not move away. Their excretions were the sort of filth that thin swine pass which have been fed on nothing but grass. The city looked as if it had been ploughed up. The roots of any edible greenery had been dug out, boiled, and eaten, and they had even cooked the bark of some of the trees . . . there had been no live birth for a long time, because they had suffered so much from hunger and thirst and continual fighting.

Yet, though they ate the flesh of those they killed or captured, they did not eat their own dead. Conditions were so desperate that Cuauhtemoc requested permission to evacuate all his people to the mainland. 'Three whole days and nights they never ceased streaming out, and all three causeways were crowded with men, women and children so thin, sallow, dirty and stinking it was pitiful to see them.'

After ninety-three days of constant fighting and the noise of war, an unnatural silence had now fallen on the city. Cortés ordered his forces back to their quarters, away from the cloying smell of rotting flesh and the danger of pestilence. That same night the old gods seemed to take flight. It rained heavily and the pitch-black sodden darkness was rent with lightning, the stillness by great rolls of thunder as though the war-gods' drum, magnified a thousandfold, was being beaten for the last time. Cortés and his captains were then celebrating their victory.

In the morning the work of cleansing the city began. Fires burned night and day, particularly in the northern quarter of Tlatelolco where the corpses lay in heaps. Cortés now had no further need of his Indian allies. They were paraded, speeches were made, gifts exchanged, and they marched away, loaded with loot and captive slaves. By then they numbered about 200,000 warriors. He then paraded his army for a service of thanksgiving. Led by Fray Bartolomé, the statue of the Virgin backed by the torn banners of Castile that they had carried with them through so many bloody battles, they marched quietly and in peace to receive the sacrament.

Uppermost, however, in the minds of almost all of them was the desire to know what had happened to all the gold they had lost on the night of the Noche Triste and the much greater quantity they had abandoned in the halls of Axayacatl's palace. No trace of it had been found in the city, though plundering the dead had produced many bucklers of gold, plumes and fine featherwork. Counting what they got out of the houses, the total was valued at 130,000 pesos – a very small amount compared with what they had abandoned. Cuauhtemoc was repeatedly questioned, also his chieftains. Their explanation was that it had gradually filtered away by canoe to the lakeside cities and the surrounding country. Their greed unsatisfied, the army began accusing Cortés of having sequestered it for his own use. The accusation was even scrawled on the lime-washed walls of his headquarters in Coyoacán. Pressed by his men, and also by the treasurer, Alderete, he finally allowed Cuauhtemoc and the cacique of Tacuba to be tortured and their feet were 'put to the fire'. All they got out of the Mexican king was that most of the gold had been thrown into the lake. Persistent diving produced a few items, and in a pond in the gardens of his palace they found a large golden calendar-wheel.

The king's fifth, together with carefully selected examples of the finest jewelry work, was sent to Spain by three caravels, which finally left Vera Cruz in December 1522. Fonseca had planned to seize the treasure on arrival in Spain. Instead, the ships were attacked by a French privateer, who delivered their contents to his own king, Francis I. It was one of those extraordinary twists of fate, for the treasure assumed much greater importance in the French king's hands than it would have done otherwise, and helped considerably in furthering Cortés' affairs at the court of the Emperor Charles.

Cortés was now the absolute ruler of a great slice of central America, extending from Vera Cruz west across the mountains to the rich volcanic uplands of the central lake area. It was doubled in size almost immediately by an alliance with the king of Michoacan. The territories of this Indian king stretched to the western coast, and his submission gave Cortés access to the Pacific, then known as the South Sea. But though his territorial conquest now far outstripped those of the island viceroys of Cuba and Jamaica, his position was founded solely on force and still had no legal basis, so that his old enemy, Fonseca, was able to dispatch Cristóbal de Tapia with the apparent authority of the Emperor to oversee the conquered territories for the crown. He was a worse choice than Narváez, for he was not only weak, but venal as well, and he had no force to back him up.

Cortés countered with the legal argument that he had used before – that he was the elected captain-general of a properly constituted Spanish settlement. He backed it up with personal bribes; and that was the end of it. The fame of his conquests, supported by his dispatches to the Emperor and the weight of gold he had sent back from Vera Cruz, now at last bore fruit. On October 15, 1522, he received two letters from the Emperor that finally confirmed his position. He was legally appointed Governor and Captain-General of New Spain. His position was thenceforth unassailable.

Even so, Garay, acting against orders from Spain, again descended on the Pánuco river area. It was a repetition of the Narváez débâcle, and in the end

Cortés received him in royal state in Mexico, their long-standing quarrel was patched up, and they attended mass together. This was on Christmas Eve 1523. Garay caught pneumonia – Gómara calls it *dolor de costado* and says he died two weeks later. Cortés was accused by his enemies of murdering him, but since Garay had been several years in Jamaica and had come straight from the tropical coastal area to the 7,000-feet high plateau of Mexico, it seems not unreasonable that he did catch pneumonia.

By now Pedro de Alvarado was marching south into what is now Guatemala. Sandoval was pacifying the Pánuco river area, seizing the Indian town of Coatzacoalcos and subduing all the coastal area, including the warlike Tabascans. The great province of Oaxaca had already submitted; the Spaniards were advancing into the land of the Zapotecs; and four ships were being built for the exploration of the Pacific, 'which vessels – our Lord being willing – will sail down the coast at the end of July of this year 1524 in search of the same strait; for if it exists it cannot escape both those who go by the South Sea and those who go by the North Sea'. Cortés was dreaming the same dream that had motivated Columbus and all the other discoverers of that period – a strait that would lead through central America to the spice islands of the Moluccas. Far to the south Olid was marching into Honduras.

Meanwhile, the city of Mexico had been largely rebuilt and fortified, and gunpowder was being manufactured locally with sulphur taken from the crater of Popocatépetl. Mines were being opened, and breeding stocks of cows, sows, sheep, goats, she-asses, and mares brought in from the islands of the Caribbean. Grants of land and *encomiendas* of Indians were being allocated to the conquistadors on the basis that those granted up to five hundred Indians must have arms ready to serve at call as foot soldiers; above that number they must keep a horse and hold themselves in readiness to serve in the cavalry. Thus Cortés held New Spain on a feudal basis. By the beginning of 1524 he could write to his Emperor with complete confidence that, when Alvarado and Olid had completed their tasks, he would hold for the crown 400 leagues of the north coast and 'on the southern coast the country extends from one sea to the other, without interruption, for 500 leagues' – an area bigger than Spain itself. All this within eighteen months of the final destruction of the Aztec empire.

The Aztecs had indeed passed out of history. Their religion may have been a filthy one, their rites and practices abominable in our eyes, but their morality was no worse than that of many American and even South Pacific communities of that time. Their vanished civilization remains a remarkable one. In Mexico today there is no vestige remaining of the exquisite Venetian beauty of their waterborne city; the Spaniards destroyed it utterly. Worse, in their determination to root out idolatry and plant their own religion, their priests destroyed much of the Indian civilization, the idols, the featherwork, the jewelry, the libraries of their sacred records, the picture writings. And the people themselves were enslaved.

D.FRAN.^{co} PIZARRO.

PART THREE

Pizarro

Francisco Pizarro, conqueror of Peru.

8

The Gold Seekers

THE EMPEROR CHARLES was now beginning to realize that, though he might still regard Spain as the least attractive of his European dominions, the lands beyond the Western Ocean that his Spanish subjects were discovering and opening up had great possibilities as a source of much-needed revenue. Whilst Cortés was adhering to the policy implicit in the offer he had once made to Moctezuma, sending his captains on wide-ranging expeditions of conquest designed to enlarge the already considerable territory of New Spain, new horizons were beginning to open further south, in the small port settlement of Panama. Colonization of the isthmus had been a by-product of the ill-fated Nicuesa-Hojeda expedition of 1509. This was the expedition that Cortés would have joined if he had not been suffering from syphilis at the time it sailed. It is of particular interest because Francisco Pizarro did sail with it, and he is the man with whom we will now be concerned. It not only gives us the first clear record we have of his qualities in command, that quite remarkable courage and ruthless determination that was to take him to the pinnacle of power in Peru, but it also shows the penalties paid by the Spanish soldier adventurers for ineffective leadership at the top.

Both Hojeda and Nicuesa had made full use of their court connections to get themselves colonial appointments. As a result, the president of the Council of the Indies, Bishop Fonseca, had named them governors of two great slices of unexplored territory on either side of the gulf of Darién – Hojeda taking New Andalusia on the eastern side (the north coast of what is now Colombia and Venezuela) and Nicuesa Castilla del Oro on the western side (Nicaragua and Honduras). This was all very fine on paper in Castile, but three thousand miles away in Hispaniola the blood and sweat of Spanish settlers had still to translate these two new colonies into fact. Moreover, the appointments quite ignored the hereditary claims of Diego Columbus who, as soon as they began fitting out their ships, put legal obstacles in Nicuesa's way, singling him out no doubt because he was already a rich man. Thus, the impecunious Hojeda, who was backed by the cosmographer, Juan de la Cosa, sailed first, heading south across the Caribbean to Cartagena on the north coast of South America with about three hundred men.

Nicuesa, with a force of some seven hundred, finally got away ten days later, but by the time he reached Cartagena Hojeda had already fallen foul of the Caribs, Juan de la Cosa was dead, stuck full of poisoned arrows, and seventy men had been lost as well as many wounded.

It was a bad opening to what was to prove one of the most disastrous expeditions ever launched in the New World, and even when they had founded the settlement of San Sebastián, further to the east in the gulf of Urabá, they were little better off than on shipboard, since the hostility of the natives forced them to shut themselves up inside their wooden palisades. It was here, in a brush with the Caribs, that Hojeda got an arrow in his thigh and survived somehow his self-imposed treatment of white-hot iron sheets pressed to his inflamed flesh.

If we accept Las Casas' account of this as accurate, the story is a vivid illustration of the fortitude of the conquistadors. In this period, and for several centuries after, sailors accepted as normal the amputation of a limb without any form of anaesthetic, but this particular cure for a wound inflamed by poison was regarded as so drastic that Hojeda had to threaten to hang his surgeon before he would undertake it. He then applied the white-hot iron sheets to both sides of Hojeda's thigh, 'in such a way that not only did he burn through the thigh and leg and the fire conquered and expelled the evil of the herb, but it penetrated his body to such a degree that they had to consume a whole barrel of vinegar, imbibing sheets and wrapping his body in them'. And the patient suffered all this without being either held or tied. It sounds incredible, but there is little doubt that these men, born to the saddle and a hard life of fighting, were peculiarly scornful of pain. They were men of endurance and action, incapable of expressing themselves except by their deeds. Thus most of them remain shadowy figures who come to life for us mainly in their achievements, occasionally in personal incidents such as this.

Shortly afterwards the expedition had its one stroke of good fortune – a dubious character named Talavera, with seventy other desperadoes, came in from Hispaniola in a Genoese ship they had 'requisitioned'. It was full of cassava bread and meat, and Talavera was only too happy to trade this welcome change of diet with the settlers for gold. By then Nicuesa had left, and Hojeda followed as soon as he had recovered, sailing with Talavera to get help at Santo Domingo. It was a disastrous voyage and in the end they beached their vessel at the western end of Cuba. For a month they marched eastward, stumbling through swamps and cutting their way through jungle; at the end of four hundred miles only about a dozen of them were still alive. They were eventually taken off by a caravel commanded by Pánfilo de Narváez. Talavera was hanged in Jamaica. Hojeda died penniless in hospital at Santo Domingo.

Meanwhile, the little settlement of San Sebastián had been left in the charge of Pizarro. By the end of two months the situation had become desperate. Evacuation was the only answer, but he had sixty men and only two tiny brigantines. Coolly he decided to wait until poisoned arrows, disease and starvation had done their work. It did not take long, and within six months of their landing in the gulf of Urabá the settlers were sufficiently reduced in numbers for him to cram the survivors into the two vessels, one of which sank almost immediately. His own ship reached Cartagena safely, and there his incredible luck came to his aid: Enciso, an associate of Hojeda, who had sailed from Santo Domingo in 1511, had just arrived with a relief force of a hundred and fifty men. They sailed back again to Urabá, where Enciso promptly lost his ship on a sandbank. After this exhibition of incompetent seamanship Pizarro might have seized command if another, even bolder, adventurer from Estremadura – the man who was about to write his name in history as the discoverer of the Pacific – had not been there. Vasco Núñez de Balboa had shipped out in Enciso's ship, a stowaway hidden in a wine cask, escaping from his creditors. He had been in the gulf of Darién before and knew of an estuary where there was food to be had and the Indians were friendly and did not use poisoned arrows. Together Balboa and Pizarro sailed for Darién, where they founded a settlement they called Santa María de la Antigua. Here Nicuesa, having established the settlement of Nombre de Dios further up the coast, finally joined them with the pitiful remnants of his force. He attempted to assume command, and interfere with the gold trade, with the result that the settlers shipped him off in a leaking ship. They could then get on with the business of trading with the Indians, their gold lust having already been whetted by vague reports of a land to the south agleam with the metal they so urgently coveted.

So ended the Nicuesa-Hojeda expedition. Out of a total of some 1,250 men – more than treble the number Cortés had on his march to Mexico, more than six times the force Pizarro would command in his advance on the Inca stronghold of Peru – barely two hundred survived, most of them with Balboa and Pizarro in Darién. Disastrous as it was, it nevertheless produced the most startling result since Columbus had first crossed the Western Ocean.

On September 1, 1513, Balboa and a handful of men headed south from Nombre de Dios, hacking their way through the lush tropical green of the swamp edges, up over hills that were covered with some of the densest jungle growth in the Americas, and across the crocodile-infested Chagres river. Twenty-five days later they caught their first distant glimpse of the Pacific. The line of their march was well to the east of the present canal, east even of the Camino Real, the pack mule route that was to bring the gold from the Pacific to the Atlantic shore. Bearing in mind that 370 years later the French were to lose thousands to malaria and yellow fever in their abortive attempts to build the canal, and that the jungle density was a much greater obstacle than it appears today following the clearance operation that was the American preliminary to the canal, this first crossing of the isthmus was a remarkable achievement.

On September 25 Balboa is supposed to have waded into the waters of the Pacific, waving his drawn sword and claiming the ocean for his emperor. It is here, on the shores of the great South Sea – the Mar del Sur – that he is also supposed to have been given more precise information about a fabulous golden land to the south and to have been shown Indian drawings of a strange camel-like creature, the llama. With ships in sections, transported on the backs of Indians across the isthmus and assembled on the shores of the South Sea, he explored south; but as soon as he was beyond the gulf of Panama, he met adverse winds and currents. He got little further than the Pearl Islands, a fairly large group in the south-east part of the gulf.

Home politics now intervened. At this stage in the development of the New World the appointment of governors was a somewhat haphazard affair, expediency going hand-in-hand with both home and colonial politics. Pedro Arias de Ávila – usually referred to as Pedrarias – obtained the governorship of Tierra Firme as a result of court connections. This hasty, evil-tempered man, whose actions seem to have been largely motivated by concern for his personal position, was placed in command of one of the best equipped expeditions King Ferdinand ever dispatched to the Indies – 15 ships with 1,200 troops and no less than 1,500 gentlemen-adventurers. It was only after Pedrarias had arrived at Santa María de la Antigua and had taken up his position as governor that news of Balboa's discovery of the Pacific reached Spain. It created a sensation, for it gave fresh impetus to Columbus's old dream of a sea route to the Moluccas. As a belated reward Balboa was made *adelantado* of the South Sea itself and also of the small settlements he had established at Panama and Coiba. Pedrarias met the situation by betrothing him to his daughter, who was still in Spain. In 1517 he moved the seat of his government across the isthmus to Panama.

This is not the present Panama, but the old city whose ruins include the tower of its great cathedral on a small hill, the shell of the church of San José, the pack mule arch called the King's Bridge because it was the start of the three gold routes across the isthmus, and the dungeons where prisoners were left to be drowned by the incoming tide. These extensive stone ruins lie four miles to the east of the present town on a small promontory backed by swamp. There is a good berthing creek and a sand foreshore with shelter for shallow-draft boats behind rocks and a long line of submerged reefs. Pelicans fish here and the north wind barely ruffles the water. The site was a good one, the afternoon breeze keeping the temperature down to about 80°; it was only abandoned after Henry Morgan sacked it in 1671, malaria by then having become a serious menace.

Pedrarias's move to Panama was political, his object being to press the search for a strait connecting the Atlantic and the South Sea. The immediate effect, however, was a clash of personalities between himself and Balboa. Hot tempers, the heat, the isolation – it was the Cortés-Velázquez situation all over again, the little frontier port too small to hold them both. Within months of his arrival in Panama, Pedrarias had arrested Balboa on a charge of conspiracy. Some accounts name Pizarro as the officer who actually made the arrest, and this is not too improbable since Pizarro was at all times an opportunist, prepared to sacrifice old comrades to the needs of the moment. The wretched Balboa was executed, and the irony of it was that he was then on the point of setting out on a second voyage of discovery to the south; but for the jealous nature of his father-in-law he might have been the discoverer of Peru as well as the Pacific.

The urge for pure exploration seems to have died with Balboa. The expeditions of Pedrarias were all to the northwards. Spurred by orders from home to find the strait that would lead to the Spice Islands, and later by envy of the great empire Cortés was opening up, the governor occupied Veragua, Costa Rica, Nicaragua; finally, in Honduras, he clashed with Cortés himself. Five years passed before anyone attempted again to sail south from Panama, and then, like Balboa, Pascual de Andagoya left at the wrong time of the year. He reached Punta Pinas, the bold, wooded headland where adverse winds and currents had stopped his more intrepid predecessor. He almost certainly anchored in the bay of the same name, which has a white sand beach and is protected from the southerly swell by high rocky headlands and off-lying islands, but he got little further.

To understand the problem that faced the Spanish adventurers exploring south to Peru it is necessary to appreciate the meteorological conditions of the area. The prevailing wind in the gulf of Panama is northerly, so that at the outset the discoverer had a favourable breeze at almost any time of the year. But once clear of the gulf his primarily square-rigged vessel was faced with the great movement of air set up by the high pressure area of the South Pacific. This, revolving in the southern hemisphere in an anti-clockwise direction, produces a south-westerly airstream along the whole of the South American littoral northwards of about 40°S. In addition, the Humboldt current flows north throughout the year. The problem is emphasized by the directions given in the British Admiralty Pilot for sailing vessels proceeding south from Panama. *These passages are all slow and difficult on account of the contrary currents and persistently light southerly winds. . . .* And the Pilot goes on to give detailed instructions on how to avoid the calms, the tropical storms and the disturbed seas that arise where currents meet, all of which entail keeping a minimum of two hundred miles off-shore. The unfortunate Spaniards, however, had no such sailing directions. They were the first, and they had to learn as they sailed, by trial and error and bitter experience.

Whilst anchored at Biru on the Colombian coast, Andagoya had talked with Indians who were trading far to the south. His expedition thus achieved something, since it brought back the first specific information about the empire of the Incas. But to the adventurers gathering like birds of prey in the torrid little colonial capital of Panama it must have appeared as yet another of the many tall stories they were constantly hearing. And though Cortés' achievements in Mexico had revived the hopes of every hard-bitten soldier of fortune, offering them concrete evidence of the dazzling rewards that still awaited men of courage and

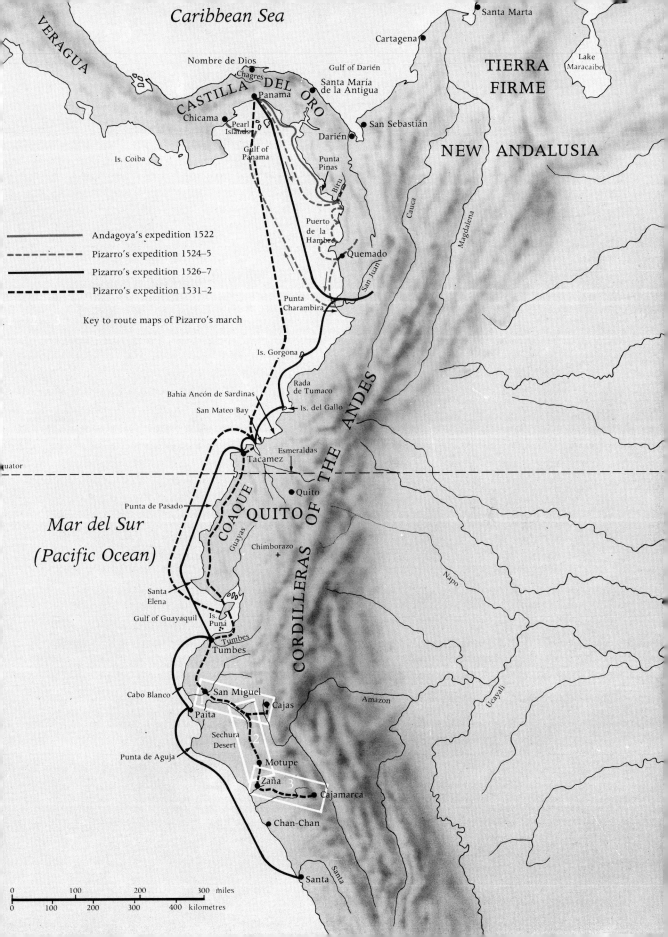

Caribbean Sea

VERAGUA

CASTILLA DEL ORO

Nombre de Dios
Chagres
Panama
Chicama
Pearl Islands
Gulf of Panama

Gulf of Darién
Santa María de la Antigua
San Sebastián
Darién

Punta Pinas

Biru

Puerto de la Hambre
Quemado

Punta Charambira

San Juan

Santa Marta
Cartagena

TIERRA FIRME

Lake Maracaibo

NEW ANDALUSIA

Cauca
Magdalena

Is. Coiba

Andagoya's expedition 1522
Pizarro's expedition 1524–5
Pizarro's expedition 1526–7
Pizarro's expedition 1531–2

Key to route maps of Pizarro's march

Is. Gorgona

Rada de Tumaco

Bahía Ancón de Sardinas
San Mateo Bay

Is. del Gallo

OF THE ANDES

Esmeraldas
Tacamez

Equator

Mar del Sur
(Pacific Ocean)

Punta de Pasado

COAQUE

QUITO

Quito

Guayas

Chimborazo

Napo

CORDILLERAS OF THE ANDES

Santa Elena

Gulf of Guayaquil
Is. Puná

Tumbes
Tumbes

Amazon

Ucayali

Cabo Blanco
Paita

San Miguel
Cajas

Sechura Desert
2

Punta de Aguja

Motupe
Zaña
3
Cajamarca

Chan-Chan

Santa

0   100   200   300 miles
0 100 200 300 400 kilometres

determination, few of them were sailors, and the land to the north and west offered safer prospects than the unknown perils of the great South Sea that stretched in limitless vastness beyond the southern horizon.

Francisco Pizarro, however, had sailed with Balboa. After thirteen years in the Indies he knew that the biggest prizes went to the boldest and to those who got there first. He had led at least one expedition northward, but all he had got out of his years of hardship and fighting was a tract of poor land and a *repartimiento* of Indians. He was already about fifty years old. Time was running out for him, as it was for his friend, Diego de Almagro, another tough soldier of fortune, who was probably older. The two of them approached a priest of Darién cathedral, Hernando de Luque, who was also schoolmaster and treasurer of the community's funds, and with his financial backing and the consent of the governor they began fitting out two small vessels for a voyage of discovery to Peru. Pizarro sailed as soon as the first of the ships was ready, leaving Almagro to follow later in the other vessel. The date of departure, according to his secretary, Francisco Xeres, was November 14, 1524, and he had with him 112 Spaniards and some Indian servants.

After clearing the headland of Punta Pinas, he put into what was then called the Biru river – it is possible that the name Peru may be a bastard form of Biru, since it was here that Andagoya had obtained his information about that country. Having no idea of the colossal ranges of mountains that stood between him and his objective, Pizarro made an abortive attempt to locate the Indian overland trade route, but the upper reaches of the river were a swamp fringed with dense jungle and backed by savage hills. The going was impossible, and after re-embarking and trying again a little further down the coast, he decided that the ocean was the lesser of two evils. He pushed seaward, attempting to find a more favourable wind off-shore, but his vessel got caught up in the calms and tropical storms typical of this area. After ten days, shortage of food and water forced him back to the coast, where the swamps, the dense jungle growth and the humidity completed the sea's demoralization. Faced with imminent famine, he did the only thing he could if he were not to yield to the wishes of most of his men and abandon the expedition; he sent the trouble-makers back under one of his captains, a man called Montenegro, with orders to re-victual the ship. The distance was short enough in sea miles, but it was over six weeks before Montenegro returned, and long before then Pizarro and his men were reduced to eating the shell-fish and sea-weed on the shore and the berries and roots of the forest.

Whilst they had been marooned in the humid swamps of what he called Puerto de la Hambre (Port of Famine) they had achieved limited contact with the natives, had got their first sight of crude gold ornaments, and had obtained vague accounts, probably in sign language, of a powerful, organized kingdom to the south that had been invaded by an even richer and more powerful state. Full bellies and the prospects of gold did much to restore their morale. They embarked

Spanish caravels of the type probably sailed by Pizarro. (See pp. 15 and 212.) Nineteenth-century watercolour reconstructions.

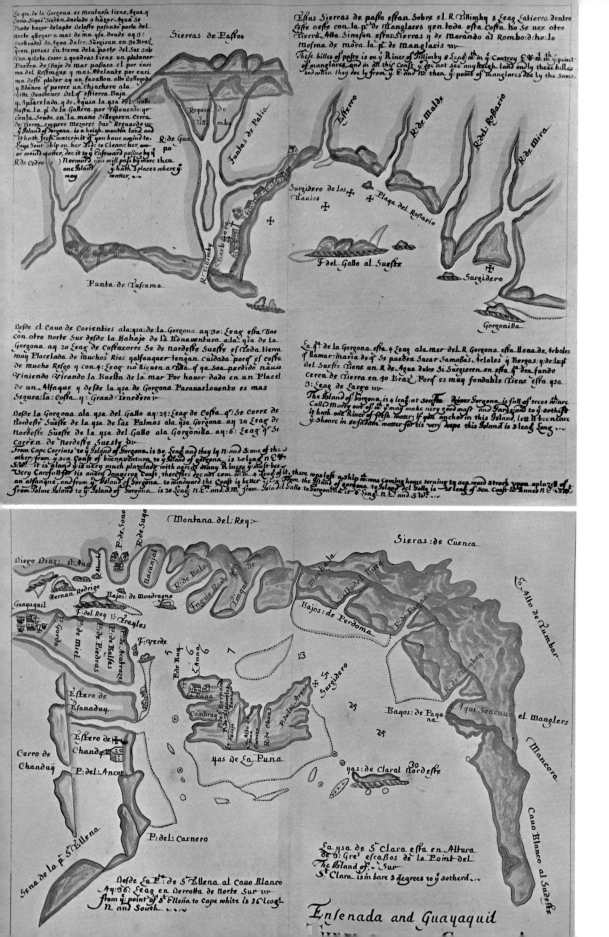

and headed south again, determined to push their luck to the very edge of disaster, their mood one of near-desperation. No word yet of Almagro, and those who had sailed back with Montenegro to the Pearl Islands for fresh provisions were still full of the headwinds and storms they had encountered in their voyage down the coast. Like most early discoverers Pizarro hugged the coast. He had to, for the coast was his only guide to what lay beyond. It was low and swampy, the rain almost incessant, with poor visibility. They made one landing, finding a village that had recently been deserted, which yielded a little food, mostly maize, and some crude gold ornaments. There were also clear indications of cannibalism. South again, into the thick of a violent storm. Finally, their ship badly strained, they rounded a headland to anchor against a shore fringed with mangrove swamps. Here they found a larger Indian settlement, but again it was deserted, so that it yielded no contact with the natives, only food and some more of the same primitive gold ornaments. Montenegro was dispatched inland, but was attacked in the foothills of the Cordilleras. It was a savage engagement in which Pizarro, coming to his rescue, was singled out for special attention as the leader – he received a total of seven minor wounds before the Indians were repulsed. Seventeen Spaniards were wounded and five killed in this brief battle.

Thus ended the first attempt to reach the fabled land of gold. The ship put her stern to the south, and with wind and current behind her, fled back to the Pearl Island archipelago in the gulf of Panama. Meantime, Almagro had sailed in the second ship. Following the coast, and locating by agreed marks the three places where Pizarro had landed, he penetrated as far south as the low, rain-clouded headland of Punta Charambira (4°16′N) before turning back. Apart from a brush with the Indians at Quemado, where Pizarro had been attacked, and the loss of an eye as a result of a javelin wound, his voyage seems to have been remarkably uneventful. This was to be the general pattern of discovery in South America, each initial thrust to the south being made slowly and with great difficulty, whilst subsequent voyages seemed relatively easy. Almagro, returning to the Pearl Islands, found his partner ashore at Chicama, a little place along the coast to the west of Panama.

Pizarro seems to have suffered from an inferiority complex in his dealings with the administration, probably because of his lack of education – he could neither read nor write. As a result, he had sent his treasurer, Nicolás de Rivera, with all the gold, to Panama to plead his case for a second and larger expedition. Almagro, who had brought back more gold, also departed for Panama. Though little better educated than Pizarro, he seems to have had no doubts about his ability to persuade the governor. But circumstances had changed. One of Pedrarias's captains was in revolt in Nicaragua and the governor needed every man he could muster for a punitive expedition. Besides, if Xeres is correct, the two partners had lost a hundred and thirty men on their abortive expeditions, a very high proportion indeed.

Seventeenth-century charts of the Pacific coast. The island of Gallo above, where Pizarro drew a line in the sand (see p. 213); the gulf of Guayaquil below, base for the conquest of Peru (see p. 217).

It was Fray Hernando de Luque, rather than Almagro or Rivera, who finally persuaded Pedrarias, though Oviedo, in his *Historia general de las Indias,* gives a highly imaginative account of a violent exchange between Pedrarias and Almagro, in which the governor is finally haggling over the amount he should get as compensation for withdrawing from the venture. Despite the gold they had looted, the first expedition showed a considerable financial loss. Nevertheless, Almagro agreed to buy Pedrarias out for 1,000 gold pesos, a sum he frankly admitted he did not possess. He managed to borrow it, however, and the luckless governor traded his share of the Inca gold for a small immediate gain. But in reluctantly agreeing to the second expedition, he sowed the seeds of later enmity, for he named Almagro as joint leader with Pizarro.

Pizarro had no alternative but to accept the situation, and the three partners – Pizarro and Almagro, now joint leaders of the expedition, and Luque, who had invested 20,000 pesos in it – entered into a most solemn contract, splitting the proceeds of the voyage and all territories conquered three ways. This contract, which was dated March 10, 1526, was signed by Luque and witnessed by three citizens of Panama, one of whom signed for Pizarro and another for Almagro. Both the leaders were required to swear on oath to keep it, and to clinch the matter, Luque then administered the sacrament. There is some doubt, however, as to Luque's position. Twenty thousand gold pesos was a great deal of money in a place like Panama, and the suggestion is that he was acting for a third party.

With Pedrarias preparing to march on Nicaragua, the resources of the small settlement were already stretched, so that it was with difficulty that the two commanders mustered about a hundred and sixty men, a few horses and a reasonable quantity of arms, ammunition, and supplies. They sailed in two vessels, piloted this time by a first-rate navigator, Bartholomew Ruiz. Like the pilots who had blazed the trail across the Atlantic with Columbus, he was from the little port of Palos de la Frontera near Moguer in Andalusia, and he was already one of the most experienced navigators in the seas off Panama. Indeed, the discovery and conquest of Peru is very largely due to the pioneering seamanship of this one man. Instead of following the coast, he stood out to sea, and as a result had a fast passage to latitude 4°N and the delta of the San Juan river, a great fifteen-mile span of jungle and mud flats that includes Punta Charambira.

This is one of the worst jungle and swamp areas of this very unpleasant coast. The shore is low and the estuaries full of mud banks at low water, with solid jungle growth extending into the flat delta interior. To the north it is all the same low country, a flat hell of jungle green, the rain swamps breeding a virulent insect life. Southwards lie the first of the Cordilleras, and, when the clouds lift for a while and the rain-washed air gives clear visibility, you can see the chain of tree-clad mountains extending south-westward along the coast, veiled with the white puffs and trailers of the clouds that cling to their slopes like mildew. These moisture-laden clouds are banked up by the prevailing northerlies to give

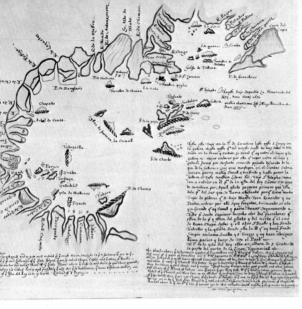
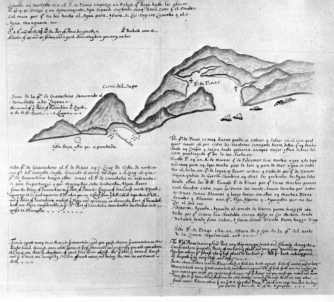
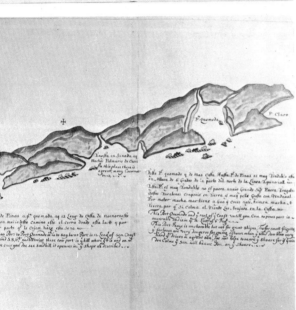
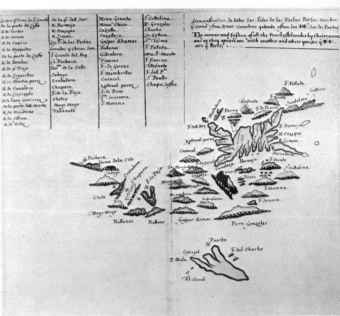

Seventeenth-century charts, combined with views from seaward, of the Pacific coast. The gulf of Panama top left, from which the Spanish expeditions set out; Punta Pinas top right, the furthest point reached by Andagoya; Quemado middle left, where Pizarro was wounded on his first expedition; the Pearl Islands middle right, to which the expedition returned; the delta of the San Juan river bottom right, where Pizarro made an unsuccessful attempt to penetrate inland on his second expedition.

Ruiz sailed on across the equator, and came up with a Peruvian balsa raft, making the first contact with the Inca civilization.

the flat lands one of the highest rainfalls in the world, about 350 inches per year, and though this helps to freshen the atmosphere (the air temperature is around 90°, rather higher than Panama), it does mean that the rain is almost incessant, particularly in the latter part of the day and during the night.

It is hardly the country in which to mount an expedition, yet Pizarro, with his ships anchored in the shelter of the sand banks, made a quick thrust inland and from one village alone collected a considerable quantity of gold in the form of ornaments, as well as capturing several Indians. The banks of the river had many small Indian settlements, their palm-thatched houses built on stilts over the swamps or in small clearings in the thick-fronded tree growth. It was clear from the number of these family settlements, and the movement of dugout canoes and log rafts on the estuary, that they had reached a more populated area of the coast where people had contact by water with the interior. Pizarro was no doubt conscious that he was now on the threshold of the powerful and well-organized people about which he had so often heard. It was decided, therefore, that the vessels should part company, Almagro returning to Panama to flaunt the precious booty they had so quickly acquired and drum up reinforcements, and Ruiz, in the other ship, to reconnoitre further to the south.

As soon as the two ships had sailed, Pizarro marched inland, where the Indians had told him he would find open country suitable for a permanent camp. They were probably referring to the high Andean plateau, and since even a twentieth-century peasant can be highly confusing in the matter of distance, it is hardly surprising that the Spaniards never reached their goal. Instead, they lost themselves in the impenetrable jungle growth of the tropical rain forest that clothed the foothills, their laborious progress constantly barred by deep ravines. Men died, became ill, sank with exhaustion, and in the end they struggled back to the coast, thankful to be out of the humid jungle hell in which they had become entangled, clear of the dangerous night life, the jaguars, panthers and other tropical beasts that were strange to them, the alligators and the snakes. Amongst the mosquitoes of the river swamps Pizarro and his men once again eked out a precarious existence on the edge of starvation, until at last Ruiz brought his ship back into the estuary.

He had a very different story to tell. His cruise had been as successful as Pizarro's march inland had been disastrous. He had had a favourable wind down the coast for fully 2° of latitude, had reconnoitred the island of Gallo, but finding the islanders hostile had sailed serenely on south-westward for a further eighty miles, across what is now called Bahía Ancón de Sardinas. Here, just to the east of the Esmeraldas river, he had found good shelter in a little bay he called San Mateo (St Matthew). All along the coast he had seen signs of increasing population, increasing civilization and, close-in to the shore, had seen the people watching without fear or any sign of hostility. It was whilst he was well off-shore, presumably to get a better slant of wind, that he came up with a balsa trading raft constructed on what we now know as the Kon-tiki pattern. Not only had it gold and silver articles on board, of more elaborate design than any he had seen before, and finely woven cloth embroidered with birds and flowers in bright vegetable dyes, but also two Peruvians from the Inca port of Tumbes. Their accounts of the flocks of llama and alpaca, of palaces sheeted with gold and silver, so excited his imagination that he continued on south as far as Punta de Pasado. He was then in latitude $\frac{1}{2}$°S, only 220 miles from Tumbes itself. But he was a prudent mariner and he did not push his luck. Instead, he turned back, content that he was the first Spaniard to take a ship across the 'line' in the Pacific and that he had seen the Cordilleras of the Andes marching on to the south'ard, a staggering infinity of peaks disappearing into the haze like some colossal rampart. Not only did he bring back to Pizarro and his starving and dispirited men news of wonderful discoveries, but he had with him the evidence – the gold and silver, the cloth, and, more important still, the two Peruvians and several other Indians he had taken from the trading raft. He had been absent seventy days.

And then Almagro came in from Panama. In place of Pedrarias, he had found Pedro de los Ríos installed as governor, and since the expedition showed promise the new governor was not disposed to interfere. Almagro had been free to recruit. Men just out from Spain, with little knowledge of the hardships involved in opening up new lands, had enlisted eagerly, so that, besides provisions, he had on board at least eighty reinforcements. Full bellies and new comrades once again lifted morale. The two ships sailed in company, first to the island of Gallo, where they spent a fortnight repairing storm damage, and then to St Matthew's Bay. The weather improved and they coasted as far south as Tacamez, now called Atacames, but at that time quite a large port with some two thousand houses, proper streets and other indications of a much higher standard of civilization. They were now on the very edge of the Inca empire, not Peru itself, but the recently-conquered state of Quito, the territory of which is broadly equivalent to present Ecuador. They were anchored off a country rich in gold and emeralds, with the evidence of an advanced system of agriculture plain before their eyes. Yet at this point they turned back, discouraged by the hostility of the natives. It is a decision that needs explanation in view of what Pizarro was to achieve later with an equally small force.

The hostility of the inhabitants was apparent the moment they anchored. Armed canoes full of warriors put out, with a golden mask as their battle sign, and when Pizarro landed in an attempt to parley in sign-language, his force was set upon by hordes of warriors. Pizarro only extricated himself because the Indians were shocked into momentary inactivity by the sight of one of his caballeros becoming separated from his horse.

That this one skirmish should have so discouraged his men that most of them clamoured to return to Panama was due in part to the conditions in which they were operating and in part to the quality of the men themselves. They were not much more than five hundred miles from Panama, but for most of them each mile had been a step into the unknown, and though five hundred miles is no great distance for a voyage of discovery, their shipboard existence was very different from that of the men who had sailed with Columbus and Magellan. They were not sailors. They were soldier-adventurers who had little to do with the handling of ships at sea. The exact size of the two vessels is not known, but it is unlikely that they were larger than Columbus's *Santa María*, which was $78\frac{1}{2}$ feet overall, and in addition to the crew, each vessel carried almost a hundred men, as well as their horses and stores. Anybody who has sailed in a drifter or trawler of this size will understand what discomfort this implies, and in storm conditions life on board must have been almost intolerable. Moreover, because the veteran colonists in Panama had known only too well what hardships the expedition would have to face, both Pizarro and Almagro had been forced to recruit their men from amongst the colonial failures or from new arrivals from Spain, men made redundant by the cessation of fighting in Europe, who had come overseas in a mood of near-desperation to seek their fortunes. Unlike Cortés, Pizarro had had no opportunity to weld this unpromising material into a disciplined and effective force. Faced with the determined opposition of the natives he knew he had little chance of survival.

The course of action finally decided upon was a repetition of what they had done previously. Pizarro would remain camped at some suitable point, whilst Almagro returned to Panama, and, with a display of the gold they had won, beat up reinforcements. It was not a prospect that appealed to Pizarro, and the two of them nearly came to blows over it, but in the end he agreed that there was no alternative. They hoisted sail, and with wind and current once again behind them, coasted north seeking a suitable place for a camp. But everywhere now the natives

This sixteenth-century model of a Catalan ship gives a good impression of the kind of vessel used by Pizarro.

were alerted and hostile. Rather than repeat his wretched experience in the humid mosquito-ridden swamps of the north, Pizarro landed on the island of Gallo. The two barren hills of this red-cliffed island are almost the only conspicuous features in the dreary flatness of the Rada de Tumaco; it did not take long for the desolation of the place to complete his men's sense of disillusion. Soldiers trained in obedience to authority, they were not yet openly mutinous, but several of them managed to smuggle a letter out in Almagro's ship, concealed in a specimen ball of raw cotton. The dispirited tone of this letter, and its implication that Pizarro was holding them on the island against their will, rapidly spread throughout the colony. As a result Almagro not only failed to get the governor's support for the reinforcements he needed, but two ships, under an officer named Tafur, were dispatched to Gallo to evacuate the rest of the expedition and bring them back to Panama.

When Tafur reached Isla del Gallo he found the remnants of the expedition in a state of near-starvation. Their numbers were much reduced, for soon after Almagro's departure Pizarro had rid himself of the most mutinous elements by sending them back with Ruiz in the second ship under the pretext that it was in need of repairs. Those that remained with him had finally been reduced to a subsistence diet of shell-fish. Drenched with tropical rain, their skin blotched with sores, burned by the sun, their clothes in rags and their bones staring, they had the appearance of animated scarecrows. Yet thirteen of them decided to ignore the governor's orders and remain with their leader in voluntary exile on this miserable, desolate island. Pizarro was learning from Cortés, and the tracing of his famous line in the sand with the point of his sword was a gesture every bit as dramatic as Cortés sinking his boats. His words, too: 'Gentlemen, this line represents toil, hunger, thirst, weariness, sickness, and all the other vicissitudes that our undertaking will involve, until the day when our souls will return to God. . . .' Prescott's version of the speech differs somewhat from Garcilaso's and it finishes even more dramatically: 'There lies Peru with its riches; here, Panama and its poverty. Choose, each man, what best becomes a brave Castilian. For my part I go to the south.' With that he stepped across the line.

This was not entirely an empty gesture of bravado. Almagro and Luque had both sent letters out to him imploring him to hold fast to the original plan, pointing out that to return like a beaten dog at the governor's order would mean the loss of all they had achieved at such cost of hardship and money, and they assured him that they would move heaven and earth to provide him with the means of going forward. Pizarro in this moment of history presents an indomitable, quite extraordinary figure, standing there on the sands of the island's foreshore in his ragged clothes with his drawn sword, and the two ships riding off, the ships that would carry him safely back to Panama, to historical oblivion. Something – the quest for power, the sense perhaps of frustrated energy and ability, of a life wasted, yet on the verge of fulfilment – something much more than mere lust for gold was driving him at that moment.

Ruiz, who had returned as pilot of one of Tafur's ships to rescue his captain, did not hesitate. He followed Pizarro across the line. The Crete-born Pedro de Candia was next, and after him stepped twelve others – Cristóbal de Peralta, Nicolás de Rivera, Domingo de Soraluce, Francisco de Cuéllar, Alonso de Molina, Pedro Alcón, García de Jarén, Antonio de Carrión, Alonso Briceño, Martín de Paz,

Juan de la Torre and Francisco Rodríguez de Villafuerte.* These forlorn, abandoned men stood and watched as the two ships set their sails and, with the south wind behind them, disappeared over the horizon. Tafur was not an adventurer. He was an officer to whom obedience was the cardinal virtue and he had no intention of encouraging them in their madness by leaving them one of his vessels. With him went Ruiz to impress upon the governor the urgency of supporting the expedition, at least as far as Tumbes.

Determination is something all men respect, and in the annals of discovery, as in the annals of war, the reckless pursuit of an objective without regard for personal safety is more often attended by success than by disaster. So it was with Pizarro. Representations by Almagro and Luque, supported by Ruiz, eventually prevailed, and in the end the governor reluctantly agreed to the fitting out of a vessel, provided that no soldiers were included in the expedition and that, whether they reached Tumbes or not, the pilot would return at the end of six months, bringing Pizarro and his thirteen comrades with him. Even this limited and reluctant consent had taken months to achieve, so that when Ruiz finally sailed, he had no idea whether he would find Pizarro alive or dead.

Yet this is the turning point, the moment of real discovery – the sailing of this one small ship, with no troops on board, only sailors.

Pizarro was no longer at Isla del Gallo. Quite early in their long, lonely vigil off the coast of South America he and his companions had decided to leave the island. For what reason we do not know. The probability is that the loneliness and desolation of the place, the sense of having been utterly abandoned, so played upon their nerves that anything seemed better than remaining to die ultimately of starvation. They still had with them the Indians Ruiz had taken, men who could build and sail a raft. Probably it was these Indians who advised them to move to the island of Gorgona, seventy-five miles back up the coast. This is a beautiful island with magnificent sand beaches in the south, and the virgin forests of the interior, which now provide logging work for the penal settlement on the eastern side, gave them material for solidly constructed shelters. Even more important, the island is high, with three peaks, the highest of which is 1,296 feet, and since it is still in the high rainfall belt of this coast there were numerous streams giving them a plentiful supply of fresh water. Bitter experience, and the help of the Indians, had taught them to live off the land, and when Ruiz found them they were sufficiently organized in their small settlement to be maintaining their morale with a routine of prayers in the morning and hymns in the evening. Despite the long period of privation only two of the Spaniards were

---

*Xeres says sixteen of Pizarro's companions crossed the line. Garcilaso gives thirteen, so does Herrera; Zárate nine. In the capitulation signed by Queen Joanna on July 26,1529, thirteen names are mentioned. The names given here are those recorded on a tablet in the Pizarro chapel in Lima cathedral. They are not necessarily correct, an obvious and very important omission being the name of Ruiz. And since one of them died on Gorgona, Xeres may well be right in giving the total as sixteen.

R: de Colanche

Isle de Colanche

✠
4: Braz.ˢ

P.º de la p.º de S.t Ellena

Aqui esta el Copie

Aqui: esta: la Sall

Por 15: Braz

P: de S.t Ellena al Sur Vna Legua

Sena de la p.º de S.t Ellena de
Morando al norte a: L: Leag

Sena de la p.º de S.t Ellena de
Morando al Sur a 2 Leag

Sena de la p.º de S.t Ellena al Norte
q.ta nordeste 4 Leag

Sena de la p.º de S.t Ellena al
Sur q.ta del Sueste a 4: Leag

y Paßando desuiado de la p.te Como 1 Leag Gouarnaras parra el Cauo
de S.t Franco Ea mita del Camino al Norte q.ta del nordeste parra darle
del nordeste parra darle Vista y no ay q.te tener miedo de tierra Alga
Porq.te estando Sobre tos Bajos de los Coximies en: 18: Braz.ª de fondo Sea
marco el Cauo de S.t Franco con el Abuja de Marear y Demora al
nordeste u:~

And when you are past cleare of y.e point of S.t Ellena about one league steere
for Cape S.t franco halfe of y.e waye N.e aquarter N.E.t to Come to y.e N.E.t and
when y.e see y.e Land y.e haue noe occeation to bee fearefull of y.e Land for when y.e
are on y.e Shoales of Coximies y.e are in 18 fadom water then with yo.r Compass
Marke Cape S.t franco y.t it may Ley N.E.t of you

Paßando por la p.º de S.t Ellena parra la ysa de la Plata mandaras
Gouernar al norte q.ta del noroeste y Paßaros cerca de lla por Eapt
de A fuera quentanse de Vna a estro diez y Seys Leag Ea P.º de
S.t Ellena este en Altura de 2: Greß ¼ de la p.º del Sur de la
Linea Equinoci all u:~

Pizarro sailed past the table-like promontory of Santa Elena above to come into the gulf of Guayaquil, from which the volcano of Chimborazo can be first glimpsed below.

III

so ill that they could not be embarked, and these were left in the care of the Indians. The two Peruvians, however, sailed with Pizarro.

South now. South again, into fair weather seas, the squalls all left behind – past Gallo, past Tacamez, the wind light, the sea calm. In a few days they crossed the equator and sighted Cape Pasado, the southernmost point previously reached by Ruiz. Barely three weeks out from Gorgona they reached the promontory of Santa Elena, a flat-topped mass of chert that is very conspicuous as you approach it from the north. Rounding the long, sandy point below it, they sailed into the great gulf of Guayaquil from which sometimes, in the morning on a clear day, before the usual rain clouds gather, you can see the 20,702-feet volcanic bulk of Chimborazo rising gigantic above the stratum of humidity that mists the lower slopes of the Andes. Here, in this shallow gulf, the flat mangrove-creeked delta is plugged at its seaward end by the sprawling green of the tree-clothed island of Puná, twenty-seven miles at its longest, from north-east to south-west, and fourteen miles wide. From seaward its flat fingers of mangrove merge into the similarly flat green of the delta, and since, on this first discovery voyage, they did not venture amongst the dangerous tide-swept shoals and muddy sandbanks of the Guayas river approaches, they could not have known that it was an island. Instead, they stood towards the high south-western end of Puná, which reaches over two thousand feet and is still to this day heavily wooded with laureola, the big Indian laurel which provides excellent timber.

So they came at last to the promised land, at the far southern end of the gulf, where they anchored for the night, clear of the reefs, in the lee of the shrouded, corpse-like bulk of the island of Santa Clara. In the morning they stood into the bay of Tumbes (3°30′S), with the town itself growing gradually larger, its towers and temples standing just above the irrigated green of the delta, a bright contrast to the dried-up brown of the hinterland. This Tumbes lies a few miles south-west of the present town, close to the río Corrales, which is the southernmost delta branch of the main Tumbes river. When Pizarro arrived there a fleet of balsa rafts was just leaving, packed with warriors, to raid the island of Puná. Filled with curiosity at the sight of his unusual vessel, they came alongside. Pizarro invited their chiefs on board, ordering his two Peruvians, whose long exile on Gorgona had given them a rudimentary knowledge of Spanish, to show them round. A request for provisions soon brought other rafts from the shore, loaded with game, fish, and vegetables, including sweet potatoes, also maize – and apparently several llamas. This is surprising for the llama is native to the high Andes and Tumbes is at least a hundred miles from the nearest natural grazing. If this report is correct, then these were the first living examples of Peruvian 'sheep' seen by the Spaniards.

One of these balsas had on board an Inca nobleman. He clambered over the side of the Spanish ship wearing a short tunic that covered his breech clout, with a llama wool cloak slung over one shoulder like a toga, so that he might have passed for a Roman patrician – except for the mahogany impassivity of his features and the large gold ear-lobe plugs. It is doubtful whether the two 'tongues' were as yet competent to explain that the Spaniards represented a distant and powerful king who claimed Peru as part of his domains, or to interpret Pizarro's sermon on the Christian faith; but at least Pizarro had made contact with a representative of the Peruvian government. The Inca chief dined on board, and when he left, mellowed by wine and the gift of an axe, he invited the Spaniards to visit the city.

The following morning Pizarro sent Alonso de Molina with a present of pigs and poultry to the city's *curaca*, or head-man. On his return Molina reported that the Peruvians had been childishly excited by the crowing of one of the cocks, by his own bearded appearance, and by the blackness of the negro who had accompanied him. He had been taken first to the chief's house, which was guarded and where he had been served from gold and silver dishes, and then on a tour of the city, including a fortress of great unmortared blocks of stone and a temple, which he described as 'blazing with gold and silver'.

Distrusting this account, Pizarro then sent Pedro de Candia ashore in full armour with his arquebus and instructions to demonstrate the power of this weapon to kill at a distance. Having duly impressed the inhabitants, he, too, was taken on a tour of the city, and on returning to the ship his report was, if anything, even more fantastic than Molina's. He described the temple as 'literally tapestried with plates of gold and silver', and his more detailed description of the fortress indicated that it was strongly guarded with a triple wall and a large garrison. He then went on to describe a convent that housed some Virgins of the Sun, where the gardens were decorated with gold and silver replicas of fruits and vegetables; moreover, he had been shown gold- and silversmiths working on such decorations for the religious houses.

Pizarro briefly went ashore to verify these accounts, meeting the chief and an Inca noble, then sailed once more. Ten miles to the south-west the lush green of the rain country ceased; the coast dry now, with cactus almost the only plant. They were approaching the Sechura Desert. There was a sea change, too, the temperature dropping abruptly, from around 84° to 64°, as they reached the northern limits of the cold Humboldt current. The frigate birds, with their bat-like wings and long stick of a tail that fans raggedly out as they swoop for fish, gave place to pelicans flying in long lines. Suddenly there was a great profusion of sea birds. They rounded Cabo Blanco, the high point of the cape all white with guano, and put into the port of Paita, which is flanked on three sides by tall, sandy bluffs. Again, the Spaniards were met by balsas loaded with provisions, and after a friendly exchange of gifts, they continued south along the arid shores of the Sechura, and, with the wind apparently still favourable, they rounded Punta de Aguja (6°S), the ship threading its way among the barren islets, with the coast now trending away south-south-eastwards. No problem of food now. They were sailing into seas brown with plankton, teeming with fish, and between the great

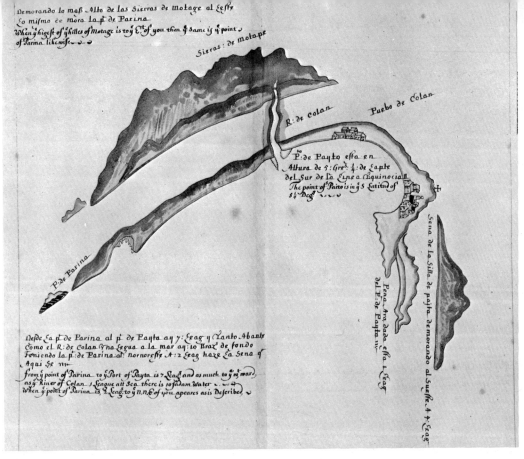

The Spaniards sailed on to Paita above *and rounded Punta de Aguja* below.

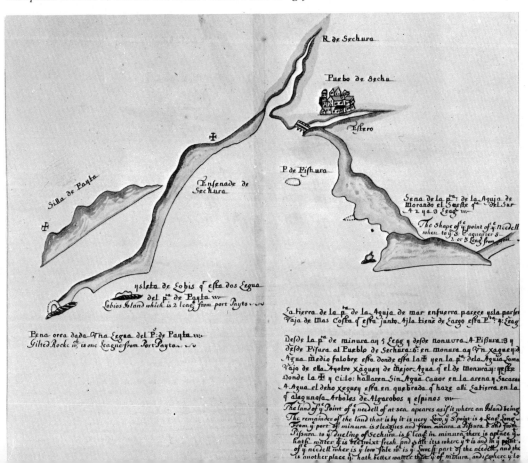

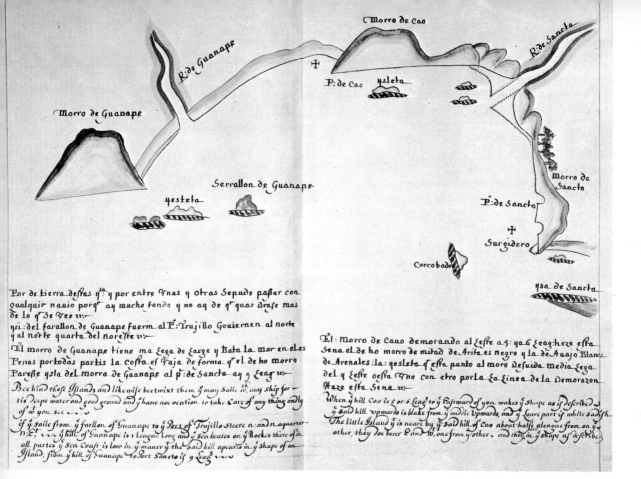

The river Santa, the furthest point reached by Pizarro's expedition above. *From this point they could see the mountain wall of the Andes lying inland beyond the low sea coast* below.

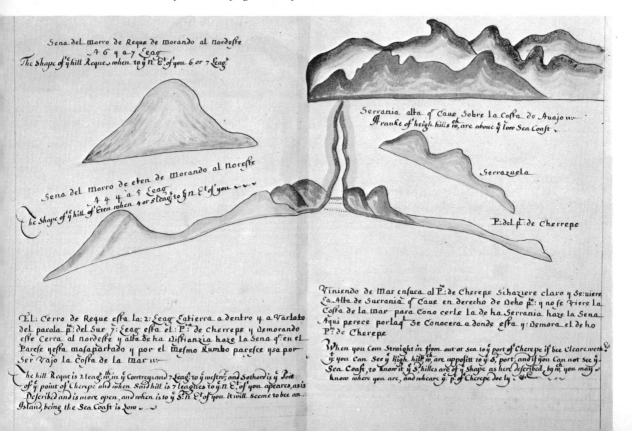

swathes of dead desert and rock were the green oases of the snow-fed rivers. It was water that was now the problem, for it seldom rains close in to the shore here, and both wind and current were against them, the wind having settled almost permanently out of a bearing of 211° and the long ground swell at about 235°.

These adverse winds held them up for a time. They called it a gale, but it is doubtful whether the wind speed rose much above 20 knots, for this is an area in which gales, and even squalls, are almost non-existent. It was probably the variance in direction of wind and swell, and the consequent rolling, that caused men with little knowledge of the sea to exaggerate the circumstances. When conditions eased they were able to beat slowly south-east past the great adobe complex of Chan-Chan.

Without knowing it Pizarro was now sailing past a fortune in gold lying buried with the mummified remains of the Chimú nobles. The burial chambers, or *huacas*, now mostly rifled, contained not only personal adornments, usually of gold, but also the most perfect of those beautifully designed and decorated ceramics that are now so avidly sought after by private collectors in Peru. In fact, from the Sechura south, great temple mounds, built of adobe – sun-dried mud bricks – and some of them as big as a fair-sized Egyptian pyramid, mark the irrigated areas of population, many of them the work of pre-Inca cultures. Further south-south-east he sailed past the place where he would later found the city of Trujillo, naming it after his birth-place. And so finally to the last river oasis of his coastal reconnaissance, the Santa. He had now reached latitude 9°S, 500 miles south of Tumbes, and all the way down the coast he had been received with friendliness mixed with curiosity. He had made no attempt to trade for gold. Indeed, he had seen little of it, except as the thin, beaten covering to temple walls, and his force was far too small to risk acts of desecration. Moreover, he had caught only occasional glimpses of the great mountain wall of the Andes which he would later have to scale, for though he was sailing in cooler waters and in a fair-weather area, here, in the cold current flowing up the coast from the Antarctic, it is always hazy, often foggy.

It was time to turn back, time to raise an army, to shed the cloak of discoverer, and assume the armour of conqueror, for he had now done what he had set out to do three hard years ago – he had discovered Peru. More, he had proved to his own satisfaction that the stories Andagoya had been told fell far short of the marvellous truth. The things he had seen, sailing south through 18° of latitude, had been sufficient to stir the imagination of the dullest. He had glimpsed the rain-green heights of the Andes piled up beyond the desiccated brown of the foothills, the wind-blown sand of the coastal desert reaching as high as six thousand feet, had seen the bright green of irrigated crops, where the rivers debouched from gorges cut in the frightful tumble of arid, disintegrating rock, the towns with their gold-hung temples, their palaces, their ordered, civilized life, and the great roads built like causeways through desert and over rivers. But this he now knew was only the periphery of a great Indian empire; the towns of the coast were mere outposts. All the way from Tumbes to the Santa river oasis he had been receiving accounts through his interpreters of the Inca king who ruled the high fantastic world of the Andes from a city of gold and silver that was remote as the stars, high as the hot, hazy, humid dome of the sky.

The Sun God king! It was enough, he felt, to set all Panama aflame with enthusiasm, to bring him the money and the men he needed to make this fabulous world his own. And in his haste to get back he stopped at few places - at Santa, at Tumbes, were he left Alonso de Molina and several others who had succumbed to the Indian way of life and the charm of the Indian women, at Gorgona to pick up the two sick men he had left there, one of whom had died. When his ship put in to Panama it had been away, not six months, but eighteen, and he and all his companions had long since been given up as dead.

That he had achieved so much with one small vessel was due in the main to the fact that it was not overcrowded with troops. Apart from himself and eleven of the thirteen soldiers of fortune who had crossed the sword-drawn line with him on the sandy shore of Isla del Gallo, together with several Indians, there had been only sailors on board, so that the ship, by accident rather than design, had been manned as for a true voyage of discovery. But if Pizarro thought that he had only to tell his story, and show the Indians and llamas he had brought back from Tumbes, for the whole of Panama to flock to his standard, he was bitterly mistaken. They were fêted, yes, and everyone duly marvelled at their achievements; but when he and Almagro proposed a full-scale expedition for conquest the veterans took the view that the task was beyond the colony's capacity. The conquest of Mexico was no longer a two-years' wonder, it was established fact, the territory of New Spain occupied by thousands of Spaniards. That Cortés had penetrated and held the city of the Aztecs with only four hundred men was now forgotten. And Pedro de los Ríos was not of the stuff of a conquistador. He baulked at the magnitude of the task and had no wish to be recalled to Spain to account for a disastrous expedition. He was, however, prepared to shift the burden of responsibility on to the home government, and when Luque proposed that they approach the crown direct, he put no obstacle in their way

Now the roles of Almagro and Pizarro are reversed. Whereas, on previous occasions, Pizarro had been content to remain in the background, it was now Almagro who was reluctant to be their ambassador. Perhaps he was conscious of his limitations. He was a typical Spanish soldier of fortune, a proud, boastful little man, a rough diamond who could talk bluntly and persuasively to a colonial governor, but who probably knew the sort of figure he would cut at court, his face maimed by the loss of an eye. Pizarro, on the other hand, seems to have gained vastly in confidence as a result of his long and highly successful voyage. In any case, as Almagro pointed out, the success of such a mission must depend on its presentation by one of those directly concerned; and of the three, Pizarro

Pizarro's standard.

was the only one who could give a first-hand account of Peru. He left Panama, overland for the north coast, in the spring of 1528, taking with him Pedro de Candia, several natives of Tumbes, some llamas, also examples of Peruvian gold and silver work and of their finely woven cloth.

The mission got off to a bad start. Pizarro had no sooner set foot on Spanish soil than his old comrade Enciso had him seized and clapped into jail for a debt contracted in the early days of the Darién settlement. Fortunately for him, the public outcry was backed by court officials; they had become very much aware of the New World now that Charles's hungry coffers were constantly being augmented by the great wealth arriving in ship after ship from Vera Cruz. The administration was, therefore, most sympathetic to a man who was said to bring news of another, even richer country. They ordered Pizarro's release and he was brought at once to Toledo, where Charles had his court preparatory to leaving for Italy to receive the crown of the Holy Roman Empire from the Pope.

In appearance Pizarro was probably much what court circles expected of the new-style colonial crusader – hard-bitten, uneducated, but a veteran with a commanding presence and the ability to talk directly and fascinatingly of a world which they had only read about in reports. He was granted a royal audience, and the result of it was that he left for Cadiz in a mood of great elation. This mood did not last long, for though Charles had given the enterprise his royal blessing, Pizarro now had to deal with the Council of the Indies, a bureaucratic machine grown fat on the energies and hard work of others. His partners in Panama had scraped together 15,000 pesos to finance his embassy. This rapidly disappeared as the expenses of delay mounted. It was not until July 26, 1529, almost a year after he had landed in Spain, that the Queen, who was acting for Charles in his absence, finally agreed the terms of the capitulation that appointed him governor and captain-general of yet another Spanish colony overseas – New Castile.

Details of the capitulation are important, for it contained in it the seeds of disaster and his own ultimate death. He was made Governor, Captain-General, *Adelantado* and *alguacil mayor,* or chief constable, for life, granted a salary of 750,000 maravedíes to cover the maintenance of law officers and an occupation force, given the right to erect fortresses and to assign *encomiendas.* But Almagro got nothing, except the governorship of Tumbes, the rank of *hidalgo,* and 300,000 maravedíes for the support of the necessary garrison. There is no reliable record that Pizarro did, in fact, press the claim of his associate, and if he did, it was probably done half-heartedly. He had been a year battling alone in the jungle of the Spanish court. He probably felt he had earned whatever he could get for himself. After all, Almagro had not been on the final voyage, which was the basis for the capitulation, and if Pizarro felt a twinge of conscience, it was readily squared by the memory of how very similar it had been when Almagro had been the negotiator and he had waited at Chicama.

The rest of his associates were better served. Luque was made Bishop of Tumbes

Peruvian head from a Mochica pot.

and 'Protector' of all the natives of Peru, Ruiz was given the title of Grand Pilot of the Southern Ocean with a salary to match its grandiloquence, Candia became commander of the artillery and the eleven* others were given titles such as *hidalgo* or *caballero*, though there is some reason to believe that Pizarro juggled a little with the names. All this, which sounded fine on paper, was subject to his raising a properly equipped force of two hundred and fifty men, a hundred of whom were to be drawn from the colonies; little more than token financial assistance was offered him by the home government. In other words, the expedition was to be self-financing, Spain retaining all the advantages of conquest without risking anything much in the way of money or even men.

Having finally got his capitulation signed by Charles's mother, Joanna the Mad, Pizarro left at once for Trujillo. To flaunt his success in the town of his birth was very natural. A foundling and a bastard, who had grown up as a swineherd, he was now a knight of the military order of Santiago, with the right to add to the Pizarro escutcheon an Indian city with a vessel standing off and a llama. More practically, he thought that the stock-grazing uplands of Estremadura, which had already produced some of the hardiest of the colonial settlers, would be a good recruiting centre. But Estremadura was already drained of its most enterprising men. A few joined him, and these included four of his kinsmen, Francisco Martín de Alcántara, who was a half-brother, and the three Pizarro brothers – Gonzalo, Juan and Hernando – 'all poor, and as proud as they were poor'. The only certainly legitimate one of the three was Hernando. Ruthless, arrogant, full of temper and courage, but without pity, this man was to become Pizarro's dreadful right hand.

It was not only men Pizarro lacked. He had great difficulty in raising funds. The rich were as chary of risking their money in such a wild enterprise as the poor were in risking their lives. Whether Cortés did, in fact, come to his aid is by no means certain. He was undoubtedly in Spain at the time, endeavouring to obtain full recognition from a none too grateful government and settlement of the many injustices that are part of the aftermath of any conquest. Only three weeks before Pizarro had finally obtained his capitulation Cortés had at last been confirmed as Governor and Captain-General of New Spain and granted the title of Marqués del Valle. He must have met Pizarro at court. Certainly he knew of his exploits. But it is unsafe to assume that, even at a time when he felt himself to be both wealthy and powerful, he would have given assistance to a man embarked upon a similar enterprise, even though he were from the same province. Pizarro might after all become a competitor for interest at court.

At the end of six months Pizarro had three vessels lying at Seville and rather less than the hundred and fifty men stipulated. Warned that the Council of the Indies proposed to inspect the vessels for their seaworthiness, he hastened his own

---

*In the capitulation Ruiz was included amongst the thirteen, but not Villafuerte.

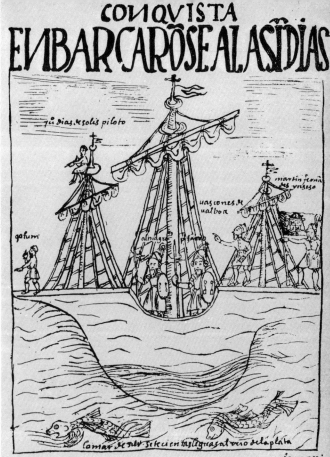

Pizarro returned to Spain to recruit volunteers left, *and formed a small fleet for the conquest of Peru* right. *Drawings from an early seventeenth-century Peruvian codex.*

departure, slipping down the river and out across the bar at Sanlúcar de Barrameda, leaving Hernando to follow him with the other two vessels if he could. Thus, when the Council inspected them, it was possible for Hernando to claim that the deficiencies, particularly in men, were due to their having already sailed in the first ship. The fleet rendezvous-ed at Gomera in the Canaries and thence proceeded to Nombre de Dios. It was here that Pizarro was joined by his two associates and had the difficult task of explaining to Almagro why he had failed to get him named as joint governor and chief constable. Almagro must have known it was not the policy of the Spanish administration to divide command in this way – they had long since discovered that this was always fatal to the success of an enterprise. But though he finally accepted the situation with an appearance of good grace, it rankled, and the behaviour of Hernando did not help, for he showed scant respect for the ageing veteran with his damaged face and slower ways. Thus from the start the three chief personalities were at odds.

Esta R de S: Tiagoa grande y Pueden entrar nauias por q en la
canal tiene 4: Braços ay en el mucha madera de cedro Bueno Roblo: y
de otros Generes tambien Suele hauer yndos de Guera :-

This greate Riuer of S't Tiago shipes may saile into it; it hath 4 fadam water
and in Said Riuer is agreatt dele of good timber of ceader and of other Soartes
Likewise vse to bee Indios of warr :-

Auiendo lo mas alto de la Bhia de S't matheo al Suesste q'a del Eeste
ay 17 Leag haze la tierra esta Sena de Ariba marcando el Lugar donde
esta la p'd:-
Esta Bahia de S't matheo esta en Ongrado y un q'd de la p'd del
norte de la Linea Equinociall :-

When y'e highest of y'e Coast of S't Mathew
is y'e quarter East distant from y'e 17 Leag
y'e Land makes this shape as aboue takeing
Notice of y'e place aboue where y'e it is.
This Coast of S't Mathew is in y'e North lat:
of 1 Degree and a quarter.

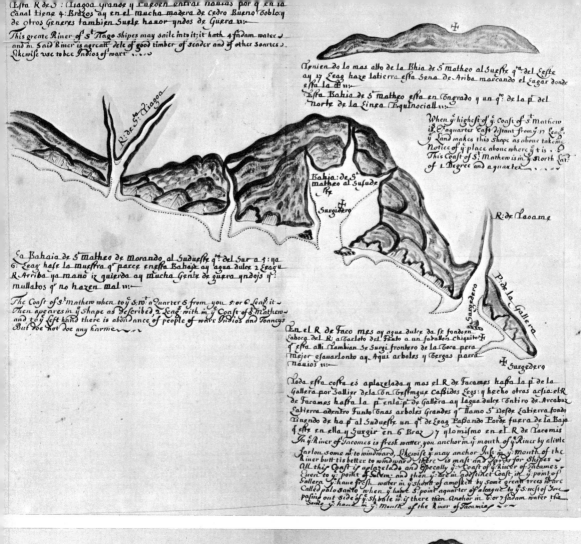

La Bahaia de S't matheo de Morando al Suduesste q'a del Sur a 4: ya
6: Leag hase la muestra q'e parece enessa Bahaia ay agua dulce 2 Leag
R Arriba ya mano iz quierda ay mucha Gente de guera yndojs y
mullatos q'e no hazen mal :-

The Coast of S't Mathew when to y'e S:w: a Quarter S from you 5: or 6 Leag: it
Then apeares in y'e Shape as described 2 Leag with in y'e Coast of S't Mathew
and to y'e left hand there is aboundance of people of warr Indios and Toancys
But doe not doe any harme :-

En el R de Taco mes ay agua dulce da se fondo en
laboca del R: a Tearloto del Punto a un farallon Chiquito F
q'e esta alli Tambian Se Surgi frontero de la Toca pera
mejor esauarlonto ay Aqui arboles y Lergas para
nauios :-

Toda esta costa es aplazelada y mas el R de Tacames hasta la p'd de la
Gallera por Sallier de la con crestmque Cassidos Legs: y hecho otras acsa: el R
de Tacames hasta la p'd en la p'd de Gallera ay agua dulce ontiro de Arcabuz
la tierra adentro Junto Unas arboles Grandes q'e llamo S't Neses la tierra fondo
Trayendo de ha p'd al Suduesste un q'd de Leag Passando Porde fuera de la Baja
q'e este en ella y Surgir en 6 Braz 7 ylomismo en el R de Tacemis :-

In y'e Riuer of Jacomes is fresh water you anchor in y'e mouth of y'e Riuer by a little
farlon some in to windward, Likewise y'e may anchor Iust in y'e mouth of the
Riuer butt tis better to windward where is mast and yards for Shipes
All this Coast is aplazelado and Specially y'e Coast of y'e Riuer of Tacames-
Euen to y'e point of Sollera: and then y'e are in a destinct Coast, in y'e point of
Sollera y'e haue fresh water in y'e shoure of amostch y'e haue some great trees there
Called palo santo when y'e haue S'point a quarter of a leage to y'e S: west of Ioe
posing out Side of y'e Sh vale in y'e there then Anchor in 6: or 7 fadam water the
Same y'e haue in y'e Mouth of the Riuer of Jacomia :-

Sierras coaque

R de Xama

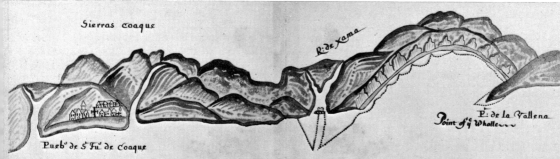

Puebo de S't Fu: de Coaque

Point of y'e Whotte

P: de la Vallena

Por estos Sierras de Coaque Baßa
La Linea Equinociall
In the aboue hilles of Coaque doe Run: y'e Equinocalline :-

Enestos Bajos del R de Xma Se perdio Domingo anto pilota
Con lo nao de Congo Alonso Beltran yendo a Virar cerca de
Tierra el Ano Domj 1612: Auisso :-
En el Rincon q'e haze, la p'd de la Vallena dio fondo P'e Luis: Pilote
con el nauio n'a S'a dell Rosareo m'e Iuo Dondaro y dejo Caer en
6: Braz el encla de Pleamar y quedo en Braja: y medio el meuio
y Se hizo pedajos proq'e tanto como esto Descarna: el Agua :-
La Playa q'e Descubre al pie delas parrancas Se parece de Baja
mar y dell Palemar Secubre y llega el Agua ad has: Barranca

On y'e aboue shoales of y'e Riuer of Xama was lost Congo Alonco Beltran in his
Ship Domingo Antonio Pilot, goeings tack about neare by y'e shoare. 1612
In y'e corner which y'e end of y'e Vallena or Whale doe make Peter Luis pilot of y'e ship
Nuestra Señora dell Rosario, Iohn Dondon Master, Came to Anchor there in y'e S't
Coarner and leeft drap his Anchor in hey water in 6 fadam Soe y'e when y'e water
fell y'e major part of y'e Ship laye on y'e Rockes in soe much y'e halfe of her was broken
In Small peeces; at low water you may see y'e Rinch y'e doe emptin to y'e sea but at;
full Sea they are Couered being y'e sea doe make vpeuen to them :-

9   *Expeditions to the Andes*

PIZARRO HAD SAILED from Spain in January 1530. It was January 1531 before the expedition finally left from Panama – three vessels, two large and one small, 180 men, 27 horses, arms, ammunition and stores. The force stipulated in the capitulation was small enough for the conquest of an empire that stretched two thousand sea miles south from Cabo Blanco, included one of the world's greatest mountain chains and extended inland to the rain forests of the Amazon. But Pizarro was seventy men short of even this totally inadequate number. Knowing the difficulties he faced, knowing that the whole enormous area of Inca territory was linked by military roads, that there were great fortresses heavily garrisoned, and that the whole country moved with absolute obedience to the command of a single ruler, it is difficult to understand what drove him on, how he thought he could possibly succeed. Was he so stupid, so unimaginative, that he could not comprehend the impossibility of such a gigantic task? It was not only the people who would be against him, but the fantastic terrain itself. Was he so puffed up with pride, so driven by greed for gold and power that he refused to see how the odds were piled against him? Nobody can say now. It is probably a mixture of all these things, plus the sense of mission, the same crusading zeal that had driven Cortés. The letters of Cortés to the Emperor had all been published, and, though he could not read them himself, Pizarro would undoubtedly have heard the full details of the conquest of Mexico whilst in Spain. He may even have got them direct from Cortés. In his pride and his new-found state he probably convinced himself that what one Estremaduran could do, another could emulate. His age may have had a bearing on it, too – the sense that time was running out and that he had nothing to lose; incredibly, he was bordering on sixty when he embarked on this third and final expedition.

There is no real basis for comparison, however, between Cortés and Pizarro. Pizarro was neither a diplomat nor a great general. The only characteristics they had in common were courage and determination of a very high order. Consider Pizarro's first positive action as commander of his new expedition. Ruiz had planned to sail direct to Tumbes, probably by the off-shore route; but gales, headwinds and adverse currents forced him, after thirteen days, to put in to San Mateo Bay. They were still one degree north of the equator and Tumbes almost 350 sea miles away, yet Pizarro disembarks his men and starts to march south with his ships keeping pace with him along the shore. After thirteen days cooped up in three small ships, plugging to windward in poorish weather, his troops were no doubt in a fairly dispirited state. Cortés would have got his men ashore, flexed their muscles and instilled a little discipline into them, and then re-embarked and proceeded to his original objective. He certainly would not have shown himself in his true colours by an unprovoked attack on a small town. For Pizarro, however, the bird in the hand seems to have been worth any number in the bush. After a difficult march across the swollen rivers of the Coaque district, he allowed his men to fall upon a small, undefended town. They were lucky in that they were able to loot gold and silver to the value of 20,000 pesos. Most of it was in the form of clumsily-wrought ornaments. There were also emeralds, but only Pizarro and a few others, including the Dominican, Fray Reginaldo de Pedraza, appreciated their worth. For this small immediate gain Pizarro traded the goodwill of the natives and any hope of achieving surprise. He sent the treasure back to Panama in his ships, hoping that the sight of such quick fortune would encourage others to join him, and then continued his march south.

They got no more loot. The few villages they came upon were deserted, empty of people and chattels. As in New Spain, all the troops wore protective clothing of quilted cotton, and the caballeros were in armour. The heat was appalling and their skin, soaked by the tropical rains, bitten by insects, broke out in great septic ulcers. Men died, dropped fainting in their tracks; it was the most senseless start to a campaign that any general could have conceived, and it says much for the toughness of Spanish soldiery that they did, in fact, reach the gulf of Guayaquil. Puná seemed to offer a suitable base. The warlike inhabitants were hostile to Tumbes, which lay only thirty miles beyond the high southern end of the island. Since they had made friendly overtures, Pizarro had his whole force transported across by balsas. Here, on this big, tree-covered island, safe from surprise attack, he set up camp to await reinforcements. Already, in the course of the march south, he had been joined by two ships, the first carrying the Royal Treasurer and other officials of the administration, who had been too late to join the expedition when it sailed from Seville, the other bringing thirty men under the command of a captain named Benalcázar.

Almost everything Pizarro does at this stage gives the impression of a bone-headed lack of imagination. Indians from Tumbes came over, and, though he knew they were bitter enemies of the inhabitants of Puná, he received them in his quarters. And then, when his two interpreters, who were themselves from Tumbes and had been with him to Spain, warned him that the Puná chiefs were meeting to plan an attack, he immediately surrounded them in their meeting place and handed them over to their Tumbes enemies. The result was a bloody massacre that stirred up the very revolt he had been trying to forestall. Several thousand Puná warriors fell upon his quarters. Cold steel and the cavalry eventually forced them to seek refuge in the forest. Casualties were relatively light – several men killed and Hernando Pizarro with a javelin wound in the leg – but thereafter the quarters were subjected to incessant guerilla attacks, all of which could have been avoided with a little tact and some slight recognition of the feelings of the Indian inhabitants of Puná. In the end, evacuation of the island became imperative, and when two more vessels arrived with a hundred volunteers and horses, under the command of Hernando de Soto, Pizarro felt himself strong enough to return to the mainland. By then the people of Tumbes seem to have recognized him for the sort of man he was, but the opposition to his landing was slight and was dealt with quickly by Hernando and the cavalry. The main body crossed the gulf in two vessels, and these were probably removed later to the sheltered anchorage we know as Puerto Pizarro, a few miles north-east of the present town.

The Spaniards were now at last in Tumbes – Tumbes of the Sun King's Virgins, of the gardens hung with golden fruit and the temples tapestried with gold and silver. The reality was utterly different. Tumbes was an empty shell. Nothing remained of the town except the fortress, the temple and a few of the more substantial houses. To men who had sailed seven hundred miles and then marched over three hundred miles through a dreadful hell of mangrove swamps and humid jungle, feeding their minds all the time on visions of a golden city, these pitiful ruins came as a tremendous shock. The suggestion that it also came as a shock to Pizarro is hardly tenable. The Peruvians, who had massacred Puná's captured war chiefs before his eyes, must have given him, through his interpreters, some explanation for their bloodthirsty vindictiveness. Though he had lost the quick profit that the looting of Tumbes would have yielded, he soon discovered, as he probed the reasons for its desolation, that he had gained much more – the key to conquest.

Pizarro's luck must surely be the envy of any general who has bothered to study his campaign. If he had attempted to conquer Peru on either of his earlier expeditions he would have failed. Indeed, if he had not been held up a year in Spain he would still have found it too tough a nut to crack with the forces at his command. He came to Tumbes at the precise moment when chance made his conquest of the Inca world just possible, at a time when the whole three thousand miles of empire was divided, yet on the verge, once again, of becoming docilely subservient to one man. This he learned when enquiring into the reasons for the derelict state of the city. It was the work of the people of Puná, they said; the Sun king – the Inca Huáscar – had been too busy warring with his brother Atahualpa to send them the help they needed; even the fortress garrison had been withdrawn.

This struggle for power had been resolved shortly before Pizarro landed at Tumbes. Atahualpa had won, and his army had captured Huáscar. The usurper from Quito was now Inca, but this did not mean that the people of Tumbes, and all the other regions that had supported Huáscar, approved of the change. It was the same sort of situation that had given Cortés his opportunity in Mexico. But in Peru, Pizarro did not have to exploit and build up the situation; it was already made for him. The Inca empire was split, and once he had grasped the full implications, his whole attitude changed. The bright vision of total conquest now filled his mind.

Leaving part of his force in Tumbes, he marched with the pick of his men into the interior. His object was two-fold – to weld his tiny force into a disciplined fighting machine and to win over the native population. For the first time he adopted Cortés' mode of pacification. No looting was allowed. Everywhere his Dominicans proselytized the Christian faith. The march became a crusade, re-kindling in his men the sense of a divine mission. The lust for gold was unabated, but concealed now under the cloak of the gospel of Christ.

As in their march down the coast, there was no difficulty about food. The sea provided them with all the fish they could stomach and, wherever the Incas had developed their marvellous system of irrigation, the tropical heat produced fruit and vegetables in profusion without regard for season. From May 16 onwards he kept his men moving from hamlet to hamlet, so that they had neither the time nor the energy to brood over the future. Indian chiefs who opposed him were burned as an example to others, so that, after a short campaign, the whole district was subdued and obedient to his commands. Here we see the first evidence of a policy of recruiting auxiliaries, and though Spanish accounts make no reference to Indian allies (nor does Garcilaso for obvious reasons) there is little doubt that, like Cortés, he took pains to augment his small force with local levies. In June he began work on a permanent settlement. The site chosen was at Tangarara on the Chira river, about eighty miles south of Tumbes. It was built on the usual colonial pattern, church, arsenal and law court all enclosed in fortifications. But though San Miguel was legally constituted with a proper municipal government, Pizarro did not have to descend to the political shifts that Cortés had employed, since his authority was already derived from Spain. This enabled him to grant each colonist a *repartimiento*, and as the Indians were accustomed to regimentation by their own government, they placidly accepted the situation. Later, the settlement

The Spaniards were now forbidden to loot and ordered to trade peaceably with the Indians far left; *Pizarro imposed pacts of alliance upon the local chiefs* left. *Pizarro's route map 1* right.

was moved a little further south to the Piura river for health reasons. All the gold and silver the Spaniards had obtained was now converted into ingots and, again like Cortés, Pizarro persuaded his men to forego their own share, so that, after deducting the king's fifth, he was able to send the treasure back in two vessels to Panama and thus settle the expedition's accounts.

It is not difficult to appreciate Pizarro's dilemma as he watched the sails of those two ships dwindle and drop below the horizon. The treasure they carried would surely substantiate the verbal reports of their commanders on the bright prospects now facing settlers in New Castile. Should he wait for the reinforcements that would undoubtedly pour in, or should he march with the force he already had? Three weeks went by whilst he tried to make up his mind, three weeks in which he discovered, as Cortés had before him, that inactivity breeds discontent. It was almost certainly the mood of his men that finally made up his mind for him. He decided to march.

This decision was reinforced by intelligence reports that Atahualpa was no longer at the Inca capital of Cuzco, but at Cajamarca. Cuzco was some thirteen hundred miles from San Miguel, and even today, using the fast Pan-American highway to Lima, the last stages of the journey through the Andes are so difficult that it would take several days' hard driving. In 1532, hampered by his baggage, it would have taken Pizarro several weeks, even though he kept to the Inca highways. Cajamarca, on the other hand, was only about three hundred and fifty miles away, and though it lies deep in the Sierra at a height of 9,000 feet, his newly-acquired Indian friends informed him that it involved no more than a twelve days' march. It was an opportunity not to be missed. Luck had put the reigning Inca within his reach.

On September 24, 1532, about six months after his first landing on the coast, Pizarro marched out of the tiny settlement, drums beating and his own standard and that of Castile fluttering in the sunlight. His force consisted of a hundred and ten foot, of whom not more than twenty were armed with either crossbows or arquebuses, and sixty-seven horse. It was a pitifully small array with which to confront the Inca, for though Atahualpa was reported to be taking a cure in the hot volcanic springs of Cajamarca – a wound received during the battles against his brother had turned septic – there is no doubt that he was also making a royal tour

of his new dominions to ensure their utter obedience to his rule, for he had with him an army that some reports put as high as forty thousand to fifty thousand warriors.

The Spaniards crossed the Chira river on rafts, spent the night at the Indian settlement of Poechos, and then marched south to the Piura river. Here they turned east, following the banks of the Piura inland. They had no alternative. Indian reports that the desert to the south represented an impassable barrier would have been confirmed by their own reconnaissance parties. This desert, the Sechura, is so utterly arid that not even cacti will grow there. It is the worst of the many desert areas along the Peruvian coast; it is also the widest, the distance from the Piura to the next river oasis being a hundred and twenty-five miles. The line of march along the river took the Spaniards in a wide north-sweeping curve, the flat country on either side green with the irrigated crops of many dusty Indian settlements. For those who had looked across the heat-miraged aridity of the Sechura, this was indeed a 'paradise of plenty' – an apt description of Prescott's, though he had never been there. And beyond the irrigated areas, the hills, too, were green with thick stands of algarrobo, a higher, denser forest than it is now, for it has been much cut over in recent years. These trees, the long bean-like fruit of which provides fodder for animals, must have reminded the Spaniards of the carob trees of the Mediterranean.

Despite the relatively pleasant conditions there was grumbling in the ranks. Some of the men were beginning to lose their nerve. At the end of four days, Pizarro halted to make 'preparations for the march'. The first thing he did was to parade his entire force and make the malcontents an offer. Any man whose heart was not in the enterprise could go back to San Miguel, and he would receive exactly the same grant of land and Indians as the men of the garrison. Whether he had prepared the ground as well as Cortés when he sank his boats, we do not know, for we have no equivalent of Bernal Díaz in the ranks of the conquistadors of Peru. The fact remains, however, that only nine men – four foot soldiers and five horse – opted to return to base. It was probably the setting, as much as Pizarro's speech of exhortation, that encouraged the remaining 168 to go on. They would then have been well past Tambo Grande, back on the main Inca road from Tumbes, probably about where the hacienda of Santa Leticia is now situated. Here the river is a broad, dried-out expanse of white stones, the rubble deposits of the hills after being rounded and polished by flood waters. But though the flat irrigated lands were already narrowing to the first foothills of the Andes, and ahead they could see the mountains that were the source of the Piura closing in, the slopes were still clothed in the green of the algarrobo and did not look impassable; the cold white peaks of the great ranges they would have to scale to reach Cajamarca were conveniently hidden from view.

In that place, where they stayed ten days, with the normality of settled Indian life all about them, mud brick and thatched villages huddled in the dust beside deep irrigation ditches, men's hopes outran realities. The promised land of temples hung with gold acted like the prospect of a heaven filled with houris upon the troops of Mohammed. Finally, rested, and with morale high, they marched on down the Inca highway to Zarán. Here a connecting road branched off to Huancabamba in the mountains to link up with the great Andean highway joining the colonial capital of Quito to the old Inca capital of Cuzco.

Pizarro was now faced with his first major decision. He did not have to make up his mind immediately, for the tambo at Zarán was a large one that included not only rest houses for the Inca, and the large retinue that invariably accompanied him on his royal tours, but also a store house and arsenal for supplying his army with food, clothing and weapons. His men were well provided for, and in any case he had to wait for de Soto, whom he had dispatched with a small force to reconnoitre the possibilities of the mountain highway and to establish contact with, and if necessary subdue, an Inca garrison at Cajas, about ten miles north-north-east of Huancabamba. To understand Pizarro's position at this time we have to remember that, as yet, he had no real knowledge or understanding of the mountain Indians. The information he possessed was all secondhand. His was a practical mind that dealt only in realities, and though he lacked the imagination to initiate and operate a war of nerves, he knew he had to make contact with the Inca. With none of the qualities of Cortés, or even any comprehension of the subtleties that had made that general so successful, he was preparing to follow blindly in his footsteps.

That de Soto was able to reach Cajas in two and a half days' hard climbing is due to the fact that here, at the northern end of the Peruvian Andes, the mountains are much lower, the pass giving access to the Sierra being little more than five thousand feet high. He was away eight days. At Cajas, which was 'in a small valley surrounded by mountains', he had found one of Atahualpa's tribute collectors. This official informed him that Cuzco was thirty days' march south along the Andean Highway and gave him a description of the Inca capital. Local Indians told him that Atahualpa had conquered the Cajas valley about a year previously, 'exacting great tribute, and daily perpetrating cruelties' – they had not only had to provide goods as tribute, but also their sons and daughters. There was a large building in the village occupied solely by women spinning and weaving cloth for Atahualpa's armies. There were also, by the entrance, some Indians hung up by their feet. At Huancabamba, a day's march from Cajas, de Soto found 'a fortress built entirely of cut stones, the larger stones being five or six palms wide, and so closely joined that there appeared to be no mortar between them'. This was the first indication the Spaniards had of the extraordinary stone-masonry of the Andean Indians, for the fortresses they had seen on the coast were all constructed of sun-dried bricks plastered over with mud.

On his return, de Soto was able to confirm that Atahualpa was still camped with his army by the hot springs at Cajamarca, for he brought back with him an Inca official who had instructions to welcome the Spaniards and to invite them to visit the

Overleaf The imposing stone-masonry of the Incas: a wall of the fortress at Sacsahuamán left.
Pizarro's route map 2 right.

Inca in his camp. From this it was clear that Atahualpa was fully informed of their movements, and though Pizarro was aware that the real object of the embassy was to discover his strength and intentions, he did not mind. He had achieved his purpose. He had made contact with the Inca and was already much further advanced towards his goal than Cortés had been when Moctezuma's envoys had met him in the sand dunes at San Juan de Ulúa. He accepted the gifts Atahualpa had sent him – two ceramic drinking vessels cast, symbolically perhaps, in the form of twin fortresses, some llama-wool cloth embroidered in gold and silver thread and, strangest of all, perfume made from dried and pulverized gooseflesh – and sent the man back with a present of a cap of crimson cloth, a shirt and two glass cups, and also instructions to tell his king that the Spaniards, who were on a mission from the most powerful emperor in the world, offered their services against his enemies.

Despite de Soto's report that the mountain highway was 'well made, being broad enough for six horsemen to ride abreast', Pizarro turned his back on the link road up through the mountains and marched south. This extraordinary decision can only be explained by adherence to the Cortés pattern of conquest. Pizarro needed Indian allies before committing his small force irrevocably to the mountains. This would also explain his four-day halt at Motupe, which would otherwise have to be put down to indecision, and indecision is certainly not characteristic of the man.

The march south had not been easy – three days without water, except for one poor well, and no sign of any habitation. They were skirting the edge of the Sechura, and where the windblown sand of the desert piled a quilted dune-scape against the flanks of the foothills, the comforting green of the deep-rooted algarrobo forest abruptly disappeared. They had entered the rainless belt that extends southwards along all the Peruvian coast for hundreds of miles. Everything was brown now; to the left the brown rock of arid, heat-eroded hills, to the right the paler brown of the desert, with outriders of the foothills standing miraged like islands in a sea of sand, and ahead the Inca highway shimmering in the heat. At the end of those three days they came to the flat land that had once been the home of the Olmos Indians. There was a fortress there, but the dykes were broken, there was no water, and it had been abandoned. Not until they reached

Motupe were they able to water their horses and slake their thirsts. But they were men accustomed to hardship, and though the march had been difficult, that in itself does not account for the four-day halt. Xeres gives no reason.

When the march was resumed it was at a leisurely pace. They were two days in 'well-peopled' valleys and a further day crossing a dry, sandy tract into another thickly populated valley. Here they were held up by a river in flood. Presuming that this is the Leche, it is clear that Pizarro was making the most of his opportunity of winning over the local people, for the distance from Motupe to the Leche is barely twenty-five miles. His brother, Hernando, swam the swollen river with an advance party, and though the welcome he received on the far side was friendly, he nevertheless tortured one of the chiefs in an endeavour to obtain accurate information about Atahualpa's intentions. As a result, he was able to send word back across the river to Pizarro next morning that the Inca's army was deployed in three divisions, one at the foot of the mountains, one at the top of the pass, and the third at Cajamarca. Xeres does not say where at the foot of the mountains, or what pass, and the information was almost certainly inaccurate.

When the army had crossed, which took nearly the whole day, swimming the horses and ferrying the baggage over on rafts made from felled trees, they were quartered in the fortress where Hernando Pizarro had spent the night. This was either Tambo Real or Batán Grande, three miles to the east. From here the Inca highway ran south for sixteen miles through a flat plain, between arid hills, to the Lambayeque river. It is now dry as a desert, but, skirting the hills for miles, is one of those deep-dug canals, and the criss-cross traces of old irrigation ditches, the remains of temple mounds and mud-walled fortresses suggest that the whole area was once green and fertile and thickly populated. This would explain why Pizarro halted for a further four days. His object was clearly pacification, a task made easy for him by the fact that the villages had suffered badly at the hands of Atahualpa. And here he found an Indian chief who was willing to go to Cajamarca to act the usual double role of spy and ambassador.

After his four-day halt Pizarro began his march in earnest. He crossed the Lambayeque and Reque rivers, and ignoring the Chongoyape route into the mountains, which trends north-east, pressed on due south, past what are now the haciendas of Pucala and Saltur, arriving after three days at Zaña. From here he had

South of Batán Grande; once irrigated by the Incas, it has now reverted to desert left. Pizarro's route map 3 right.

been told a track ran direct to Cajamarca. His information proved correct, and he now abandoned the main Inca highway, turning due east and following the Zaña river into a gap in the foothills. Since the Spaniards had no names then for the mountains and gorges, and even had great difficulty in recording the names of Indian villages, it is not surprising that the few accounts of the march are vague about the route taken. It is fairly certain that the Spaniards diverged from the Zaña river gorge, turning south-east into the narrower gap of the Nancho gorge. This was the most direct line to their objective, and once over the 12,000-feet pass and into the slightly lower uplands the going is relatively easy. Xeres describes the pass itself as so steep that in places they had to ascend by steps. Pizarro had gone on ahead with fifty horse and sixty foot soldiers, intending to try and force the pass if it were defended. But, though there was a strong fortress there, Atahualpa had left the gateway to his lair unbarred. The cold was intense, so much so that the horses suffered from frostbite. It was early summer now, but when it is summer on the coast, it is regarded as winter in the Sierra, for this is the rainy season and there is snow on the high ground.

He spent the night at a village where the house in which he lodged was protected by an Inca wall of unmortared stone. The following day he moved more slowly to allow his rearguard and the baggage to catch up. He was still climbing, and that night the whole army camped on the top of the mountain. Here he was greeted by messengers from Atahualpa, bringing a gift of ten llamas. They told him that the Inca had been waiting for him at Cajamarca for the last five days. Apparently they also gave him a garbled account of the wars between Atahualpa and Huáscar. In return, Pizarro is reported to have made a long speech, concluding with these words: 'If he [Atahualpa] should wish for war, I will make war, as I have done against the chief of the island of Santiago [Puná], and against the chief of Tumbes, and against all those who have wished to have war with me. I make war upon no-one, nor do I molest anyone, unless war is made upon me.'

Now that Pizarro was nearing his objective, the messengers moved more rapidly between the two forces. A long day's march across the mountains brought the Spaniards to a village nestled in a valley. Here the same chief that de Soto had brought to Zarán was waiting for Pizarro with half a dozen gold cups from which he offered the Spanish captains *chicha*, the Indian corn liquor. He had orders to

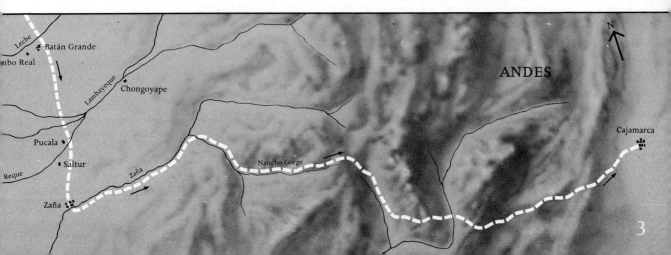

accompany them to Cajamarca. Another day's march and Pizarro decided to
rest his men for a day so that they would be fresh to cope with whatever lay in
front of them. Here his own messenger, dispatched from Tambo Real, arrived and
was so furious that they were giving hospitality to Atahualpa's emissary, whom he
regarded as a liar and a rogue, that he rushed upon the man and seized him by the
ears. His own life had been threatened in the Inca camp, he had been given no
food, and, though a chief himself, he had been refused admittance to Atahualpa on
the grounds that the Inca was fasting. Atahualpa, he said, was 'in warlike array
outside Cajamarca on the plain. He has a large army, and I found the town empty.'
He had then gone to the camp, had seen tents and flocks and many warriors,
'and all were ready for war'. In answer, Atahualpa's messenger said that if the
town was empty, it was to leave the houses free for the Spaniards, and that
Atahualpa was in the field because 'such is his custom after he has commenced
war', by which he meant the war against his brother. Like all exchanges between
emissaries it must have left Pizarro more confused as to Atahualpa's intentions
than before.

One more day's march and he was within striking distance of Atahualpa's
army. He camped the night on a grassy plain, made an early start the following
morning, and long before noon was looking down from the rounded hills that hang
over Cajamarca into what is perhaps the most beautiful valley in the Andes.
The stage was set for one of the cruellest acts of aggression and the wanton
destruction of a fascinating and remarkable empire. Throughout the long day's
march up the precipitous slopes of the Nancho gorge the Spaniards had been at
the mercy of Atahualpa's warriors. Suffering, as everybody does, from the
suddenness of the altitude, and caught breathless on the slopes below the pass,
they would have had no chance of survival against seasoned warriors attacking
from above. Even if they did have Indian auxiliaries with them, the fortress at
the top, had it been defended, would have stopped them in their tracks. And
afterwards, during the five days' march across the high Sierra, they were still
vulnerable. At any moment during that exhausting week Atahualpa could have
destroyed them. Why did he hold his hand? What was he afraid of?

Garcilaso insists that it was because of the instructions given by his father,
Huayna Capac, on his deathbed, and he quotes this last of the real Incas as saying
to his captains and curacas:

Our father the Sun disclosed to us a long time ago that we should be twelve Incas,
his own sons, to reign on this earth; and that then, new, hitherto unknown people
would arrive; that they would obtain victory and subject all our kingdoms to their
Empire, as well as many other lands. I think that the people who came recently by sea
to our own shores are the ones referred to. They are strong, powerful men, who will
outstrip you in everything. The reign of the twelve Incas ends with me. I can therefore
certify to you that these people will return shortly after I have left you, and that they
will accomplish what our father the Sun predicted; they will conquer our Empire, and

The terrain of Peru: the mountainous situation of the fortress of Ollantaytambo.

they will become its only lords. I order you to obey and serve them, as one should serve those who are superior in every way; because their law will be better than ours, and their weapons will be more powerful and invincible than yours. Dwell in peace; my father the Sun is calling me, I shall go now to rest at his side.

Garcilaso de la Vega is a highly imaginative writer. He was descended from the Incas on his mother's side, and it is natural that he should seek to establish a rational explanation for the failure of the Indian people to oppose the invader. Nevertheless, it is not unreasonable to imagine that Huayna Capac shared Moctezuma's sense of impending doom, and he may well have felt it expedient to warn his people on his deathbed not to fight against the inevitable; if so, he would certainly have done it in the Sun god's name. 'The news of this prediction', Garcilaso goes on, 'spread throughout all Peru, and the accounts of all chroniclers bear witness to its veracity.' The chroniclers he quotes are Cieza de León and López de Gómara, but they, like Garcilaso himself, were writing after the event. We must, therefore, regard these prophecies and instructions of Huayna Capac as unsubstantiated and decide for ourselves how it was possible for Pizarro, with so small a force, to overthrow a vast empire. To do this we must now take a look at the origins of the Inca empire, the religious beliefs and culture of this Indian people; above all, at the weaknesses inherent in the pyramidical structure of the state and the absolute subservience of all to the father figure of the supreme Inca.

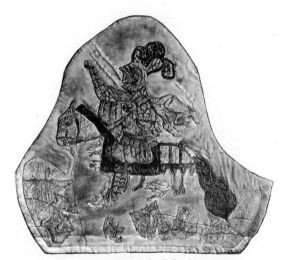

Pizarro's standard (back).

The terrain of Peru: the gorge of the Urubamba.

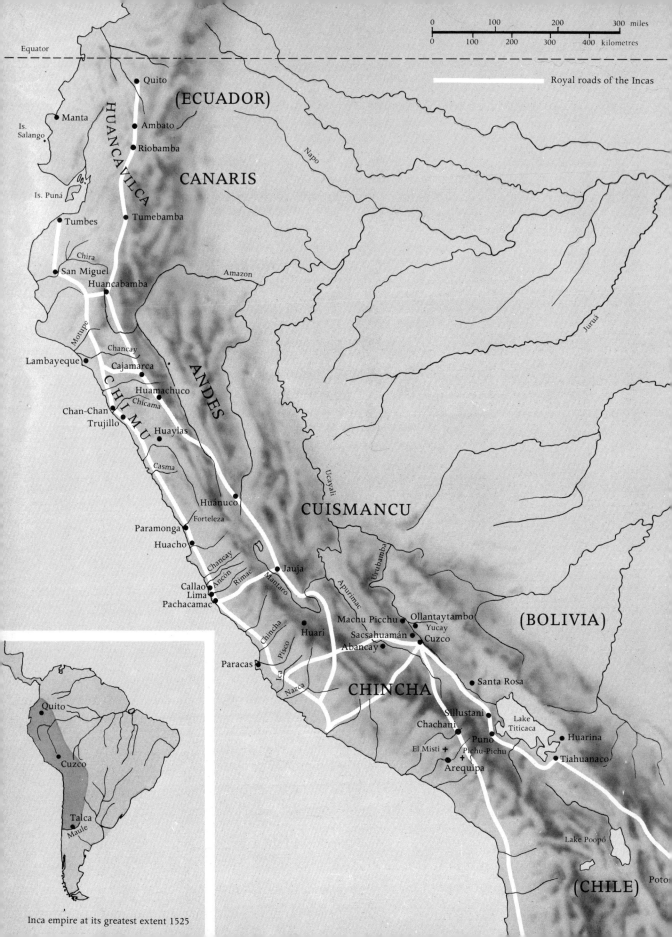

Equator

0   100   200   300 miles
0 100 200 300 400 kilometres

——— Royal roads of the Incas

Quito

(ECUADOR)

Manta

Ambato

Is.
Salango

Riobamba

HUANCAVILCA

CANARIS

Napo

Is. Puná

Tumbes

Tumebamba

Chira

Amazon

San Miguel

Huancabamba

Lambayeque

Chancay

Cajamarca

Motupe

CHIMU

ANDES

Jurua

Huamachuco

Chicama

Chan-Chan

Trujillo

Huaylas

Casma

Huánuco

Forteleza

Paramonga

Huacho

CUISMANCU

Chancay

Jauja

Ucayali

Callao

Ancon

Rimac

Lima

Mantaro

Pachacamac

Apurimac

Urubamba

Machu Picchu

Ollantaytambo

(BOLIVIA)

Chincha

Huari

Yucay

Cuzco

Sacsahuamán

Abancay

Paracas

Ica

Pisco

Nazca

CHINCHA

Santa Rosa

Sillustani

Chachani

Lake
Titicaca

Huarina

El Misti +

Puno

Pichu-Pichu

Tiahuanaco

Arequipa

Quito

Cuzco

Talca

Maule

Lake Poopó

(CHILE)

Potos

Inca empire at its greatest extent 1525

10

The Incas

FEW AREAS OF THE WORLD are as fantastic geophysically as the western littoral of South America; here geography is vertical and climate governed by height rather than latitude. As we have seen, man had certainly reached the central lake area of Mexico some eleven thousand years ago. We now know that he had also penetrated as far south as Patagonia at around this time, so that he may have been in Peru even earlier than 9000 B.C. However, the development from a hunting or fishing subsistence to even the most primitive agriculture was slow and it was not until about 2500 B.C. that some form of primitive civilization began to emerge. Indeed, agriculture only became an important factor in the life of the people about 1000 B.C. and then chiefly in the coastal regions, where geographical conditions were most suitable.

Here the Humboldt current, sweeping up from the cold southern latitudes, teems with fish. Its effect upon the warm air of the tropics is to reduce the temperature and produce cloud, high humidity, even fog in winter months (June to November) – but no rain, except when that curious phenomenon, the counter-current called El Niño, is running southward. The coastal plain is, in fact, so absolutely arid that in many places it is devoid even of cactus. But across it, almost forty river beds reach stoney fingers into the sea. All have their source in the melting snows of the Andes, and about thirty of them manage to maintain some sort of a flow all the year round. It was in the flat delta areas of these rivers that the first farmers began to harvest crops of gourds, beans, chile peppers and squash.

The altiplanos of the high Andes provide a complete contrast. There are six of these great upland basins – Cajamarca, Huaylas, Huánuco, Mantaro, Cuzco and Titicaca – all of them between 8,000 and 13,000 feet and walled in by mountains behind which loom the great snow peaks of the Cordilleras, ranges with names like Sierra Blanca and Sierra Negra. In the south, towering above the present city of Arequipa, three great volcanic masses – Chachani, Misti and Pichu-Pichu – rise to a height of 20,000 feet. El Misti, a cone so perfectly shaped that it matches Fuji Yama, is still active. Indeed, most of Peru is subject to

Peru at the time of the Conquest.

earthquakes – Huacho, on the coast just north of Lima, was badly damaged in October 1966. Even the altiplanos are not immune, which is why the Inca and pre-Inca people sometimes keyed the stone of their walls, sometimes built them of uneven courses. Much of the best colonial architecture in Cuzco itself has been destroyed because the Spaniards did not appreciate the severity of the shocks their buildings would have to withstand.

At what date man first established himself in these upland basins, which are now called *punas*, we do not yet know for certain, but carbon-dating of finds from one cave-shelter suggests that it may have been as early as 9,500 years ago. Here the geographical accident of optimum conditions for a nomadic herding people at a high altitude resulted in the development of physical characteristics that are virtually unique. The small stature and stocky build is typical of any highland people, the men on average about 5 ft 2½ ins tall, the women 4 ft 9½ ins. What is unique is the lung development, which is almost a third greater than the normal human, the blood volume about four pints more, the haemoglobin about double, the red corpuscle count up from five million to about eight million, and a much slower rate of heart beat. Surprisingly, these characteristics are not inherited, but are developed individually in youth.

Because of the semi-isolation imposed by the terrain there has been little dilution of the basic stock, so that the Quechua Indians you see today, particularly in the south – squat, broad-featured, the women with their provocatively-tilted, round felt hats and llama wool mantas, the men with their coloured woollen caps and ponchos – are basically the same as Pizarro faced in 1532. They are a people accustomed to the solitude of vast spaces, their bodies and their minds moulded by the country in which they live – a world of rock and rain and rushing rivers, with every vista of the sere grass that gives them life blocked by mountain walls. Even their movements are different. They either stand so quiet and still that they seem to merge like animals into the landscape, or else they are moving in a light-footed shuffling trot like leaves blown by the wind. They seldom walk as we do unless they have drunk too much *chicha*.

Traces of permanent habitation have been found as high as 17,500 feet and the characteristics developed to cope with the extraordinary altitude have remained unchanged down the millennia. The conquistadors probably had an advantage in stature, but anybody who, whilst gasping for breath on the shores of Lake Titicaca, 12,648 feet up, has watched Indians playing a violent game of football, must wonder at the speed with which the Spaniards acclimatized themselves, coming straight up from the coast and almost immediately prepared for the exertion of fighting. Here, 150 miles south of Cuzco, the high valleys open out into a broad plain, and suddenly to the south-east you have a prairie vista – no mountains, nothing but emptiness. The clear, thin air on the shores of Lake Titicaca is dazzlingly bright, and the rain storms, clinging to the distant heights, circle you with a fantastic cloudscape. Cajamarca is the complete opposite; a

The Peruvian Indians today are little changed from the time of the Conquest.

narrow valley, between rounded, almost down-like hills, it is barely six miles wide, and in place of the sere, yellowed grasses of the upper valleys are the lush meadows normally associated with the English countryside – grass that is knee-high, buttercups and clover, and willows growing in the hedges. Only the presence of the occasional cactus, a smaller version of the maguey, reminds one that the valley lies a few degrees from the equator.

It was in this temperate zone of the high altiplanos that the main, or Imperial, Inca civilization emerged – very late, only just over a hundred years before Nemesis in the form of Pizarro and his adventurers arrived to destroy it. Since they developed no form of writing, not even picture-writing, there is no record of the cultures that preceded them. Nor was any verbal account of pre-Inca history passed on to the Spaniards, for, like the modern Soviet and Chinese communists, they re-taught the history of the Indians they conquered so effectively that, in the space of a single generation, all believed that the culture and life of the people stemmed solely from the Incas.

Thus it is only through the painstaking sifting of the evidence of numerous archaeological finds that we have gradually come to realize that the Incas, like the Aztecs in Mexico, absorbed and took credit for a relatively advanced culture already in existence. In fact, the Inca civilization, like most other civilizations, was the product of the past; both the building techniques and the highly organized, bureaucratically-controlled empire-cum-welfare state were developments of the Chimú and earlier cultures.

A visit to the *chullpas* of Sillustani, for instance, provides immediate evidence that even the technique of building with unmortared stone blocks was not an Inca development. The *chullpas* are tall stone burial towers of the late Tiahuanaco period. They cover a promontory overlooking Lake Uyamú, about thirty miles north-west of Puno, and the stonework of the few that still stand virtually complete shows the edge of the top course flared inwards to reduce wind resistance, the circumference of the top greater than the base, so that the whole tower looks rather like a tall drinking glass. Moreover, fallen blocks of stone show that the secret of stability without the aid of mortar, and the fact that they have withstood centuries of earth tremors, is a boss locking into a socket in the stone above, sometimes even a protuding rim. This is workmanship of an even higher order than anything in Cuzco, and it was done without the aid of metal, the stone being beaten into shape by primitive hammer tools of a harder stone.

In ceramics, too, pre-Inca cultures were superior, a fact which the Brunning collection of *huacos* (the pottery looted from the burial chambers of old cemeteries), newly housed at Lambayeque, demonstrates very clearly. Even in textiles, Inca design and weaving was not comparable with those old ceremonial mantles and head-dresses found preserved in the dry-air burial chambers at Paracas and now filling one of the most interesting rooms in the Archaeological Museum in Lima.

The Huaca Prieta midden in the Chicama valley of Northern Peru, the lowest

One of the chullpas *of Sillustani.*

levels of which go back some 4,500 years, show the people of the coastal plain living off sea and land, with little leisure for anything more complicated than the struggle for existence. This is confirmed by many other discoveries in the coastal desert area; yet, little more than 2,000 years later, there is plentiful evidence of ceramics, of personal adornments – the earplugs that are such a peculiar characteristic of the Inca hierarchy, necklaces, bracelets, rings, crowns, the materials ranging from bone and shell to stone and gold – of metalwork, mainly in gold, which later developed techniques so advanced that they included welding and soldering, of weaving, and of stone carving. Agriculture covered many types of plant, used irrigation, and had, in fact, reached the stage where man had leisure for craftsmanship and design. He also appears to have had leisure for some form of religion, for it is in the finds of this pre-Christian period that the Chavín cat design appears, and by then he was building non-utilitarian structures of considerable size and complexity that can only have been temples used for religious purposes.

Development is now rapid, but always along the same lines. Ceramics pass through periods of distinctive patterns and designs. By the first millenium A.D. systems of irrigation have become very advanced, with aqueducts up to fifteen hundred yards long and almost fifty feet above the ground. Metalwork has reached the stage where gold is alloyed with silver and copper to produce complex designs. But it is in public works that we now see the development that led to the massive temples of the 'Classic Period'. On the coast these temples were of adobe, with platforms, approach causeways and pyramids requiring a large organized body of labour. In the highlands, the construction was of dressed stone.

It is these temple structures, and the *huacos* found in the burial chambers, that have enabled archaeologists to achieve some success in defining the various cultures, many of them extremely local, as might be expected in the development of desert territory wholly dependent upon mountain water delivered by river. Each of the coastal cultures was, in fact, an oasis separated from its neighbour by sand and bare rock hills of absolute aridity. Neither Inca rule, nor Spanish rule, not even independence, has changed the situation. The city complexes have now become big hacienda complexes – that is all. And since the materials for pottery were ready to hand it is hardly surprising that, here on the coast of Peru, the potter's art was developed to a very high degree, producing some of the most remarkable ceramics to be seen anywhere in the world. Not only are the designs intricate and unusual, including the uninhibited use of erotic forms, but the polychrome colouring, possibly affected by differences in firing and ageing, includes a great variety of tints. The cemeteries have yielded up a golden harvest of these ceramics, many of them in mint condition, and dedicated private collectors have opened their own museums. Grave robbing on such a scale, however, has greatly complicated the archaeologist's task.

Prior to the Inca empire only two cultures appear to have spread throughout Peru. The first was the Chavín culture, with its cat motif, covering the middle of

Peruvian gold. Opposite A mummy from the Paracas cemetery, wearing a gold nose ornament, collar and necklace. Overleaf left Ceremonial knife, surmounted by a male idol, in gold and turquoise. Overleaf right Ceremonial knife, surmounted by a llama, in gold and turquoise. Chimú culture.

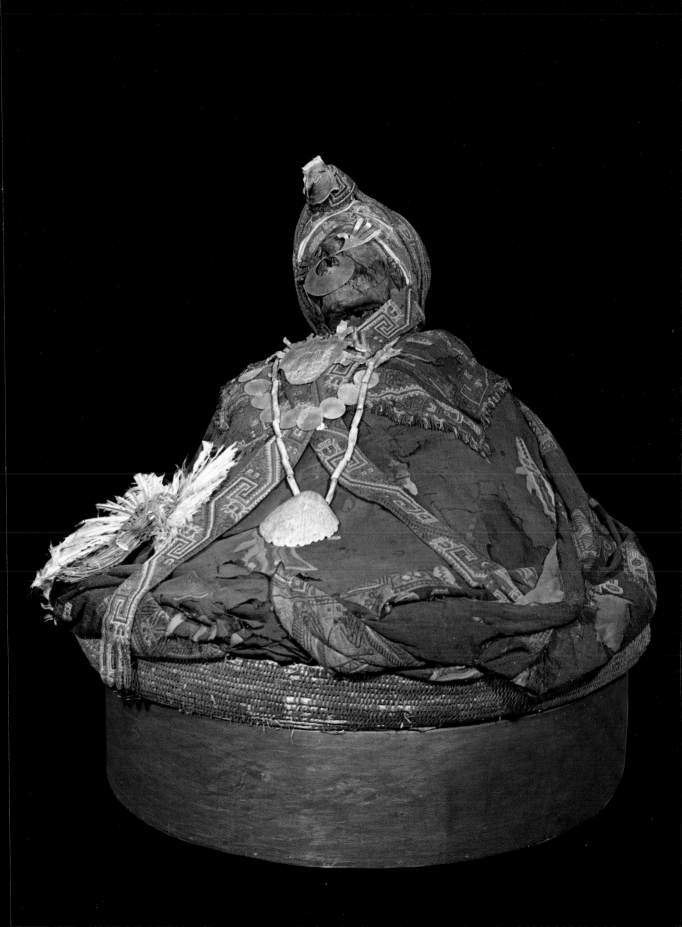

DON P. ZZA S.

the first millenium B.C.; the second was the much more pervasive Tiahuanaco culture, covering almost the whole of the first millenium A.D. It spread through Huari to the coast around 800 A.D., and during the next two centuries overlaid and virtually obliterated the art of that area. This was a dynamic period in which the artistic aspirations of the Indian people reached their peak, in ceramics, jewelry and textiles, in architecture on the grand scale, all indicating a degree of political and economic unity sufficient to liberate a large labour force for non-productive work.

In the Sierra the evidence of a very advanced stone-masonry craft is still there for all to see, particularly at Tiahuanaco. The setting of this megalithic complex is unique, for it lies twelve miles south of Lake Titicaca on a bleak Bolivian *puna* 13,000 feet above sea level – an extraordinary place in which to find the ruins of a civilization. The terraced pyramid of the Acapana and the great courtyard of the Calasasaya suggest a ceremonial centre. The standing stones of these and other buildings are boldly carved; so, too, is the 'Gateway of the Sun', which is a single ten-foot high block of masonry. There are more remains in the lake itself, on the islands of the Sun and the Moon, and to the north-west of the lake stand the much later *chullpas* of Sillustani; all stone, nothing but stone, in a flat grass land at breathless altitude, and overhead the wide clear skies so typical of the Titicaca area. It is hardly surprising that archaeologists have taken Tiahuanaco as descriptive of the whole period, for the artistic influence of these people is noticeable in most areas of Peru. The pyramid-courtyard sites of the coast indicate a highly organized society, but they were still no more than the ceremonial centres of relatively scattered communities, for it is only in the period immediately preceding the Inca empire that they became a part of large city complexes. The most outstanding example of this development is Chan-Chan, just north of Trujillo in the coastal desert. Though it was conquered by the Incas and is much damaged by rain and the passage of time, you can still drive for a long time through the six square miles of its ruins, the mud enclave walls of the ten units still towering above the flat expanse of gravelly desert to which, in the absence of water, the whole area has reverted. The little grave cubicles of the cemetery areas have all been raided, and the adobe covering of the mud-brick walls is runnelled by the erosion of occasional rainstorms. It is a very dead city, echoing to the sad sound of the waves, as though the Pacific were beating against the last great wall, instead of nearly two miles away. It is difficult, in the eerie solitude of the place as it is now, to visualize what it was like when the reservoirs were intact and the carefully-planned streets, with their houses, terraces, and gardens, were full of people.

Chan-Chan was the capital of the Chimú coastal empire, which at the time of the Inca conquest included most of the northern valleys. From the Motupe, south as far as the Casma, these river oases were linked by roads spanning the desert areas that had previously isolated them. Other, smaller states, developed further south.

An Ecuadorian from Quito wearing nose and ear ornaments and a necklace of gold. A detail from the earliest known painting from South America.

Featherwork ceremonial shield from the coastal region, probably representing the Sun god top left. Recuay pot, from a highland site of the seventh to eighth century A.D., representing a man being seized by a puma bottom left; Mochica pots of the fifth to seventh century A.D.: a sleeping soldier above left; a bearded man or priest above right.

They, too, had their inter-linking roads and centralized forms of government. It was this that enabled their Inca conquerors to weld the whole country so rapidly into a single empire under a pyramidical governing bureaucracy whose apex was the Sapa, or Unique, Inca.

The first Inca was Manco Capac. We have no date for this ruler, or for the seven Incas who succeeded him; it is generally assumed that they covered the period 1250 to 1438. They are believed to have originated at Cuzco in the Central Highlands, though there is a local belief that they came from the islands of Lake Titicaca. Bingham's theory that they came from Machu Picchu has now apparently been disproved, the mountain city being attributed to the late Inca period. Throughout the whole period of empire Cuzco remained their capital. The basis of conquest was organization, the Inca himself the divine symbol of the sun god they worshipped, his tight bureaucratic circle of officials belonging to the eleven royal *ayllus* and in part the product of his own loins through concubinage, the line of descent continuing through incestuous marriage with one of his sisters – the Coya or legal queen.

There is no evidence that the Inca empire was in any way the result of population pressure. As with the Nordic races, the expansionist urge was probably the result of climatic conditions. They were highlanders, with an excess of vitality and energy, and their animal resources were limited to the llama, the alpaca and the vicuña. Where the coastal people developed a moon cult, having a natural fear of the sun in the desiccated aridity of their desert strip, the Incas on their high grasslands looked to the sun as the source of warmth and light, of the melted snow water that kept the grasslands green for their flocks. Economic gain was almost certainly the original motivating force, reinforced by the development of a power complex under their great empire-builder, Pachacuti. The perfection of their organization, both political and military, really begins with this Inca, who incorporated, and developed to suit his own purposes, the patterns of culture already existing, particularly that of the Chimú empire.

It was in 1445, less than a hundred years before the Spaniards arrived, that Pachacuti Inca Yupanqui (the ninth Inca) began the conquest of the Titicaca regions. Thereafter, expansion proceeded at a fast rate. Propaganda was used and the system of military roads provided the life line. But organization was the basis of conquest. Conscription provided an army in which discipline was severe. The officers were all from the élite of the Inca's own household, and since they looked to him as the patriarch of the family and were dependent upon him for their position in a tight-knit society, he could count on their absolute loyalty. The common soldiers were well armed with bronze battle axes, or maces, with wooden hafts and stone or bronze heads, with slings, lances and throwing spears, and bows and arrows in the case of those from the eastern lowlands; for protection they had wooden shields covered with leather or cloth, cotton or cane helmets, and quilted armour.

Each newly-captured province was reorganized on the Inca pattern, with Inca officials superimposed upon the existing local officialdom, whose loyalty was assured by the removal of their sons as hostages to Cuzco. Quechua became the official language, sun worship, with the Inca the divine incarnation of the deity, the official religion. If, in the face of these abrupt changes, the population proved recalcitrant, they were removed en bloc and re-settled in an area that had already been pacified and which, through indoctrination, had become entirely docile;

Inca soldiers were well armed with bronze battle axes and leather-covered shields far left. *The empire was linked by a network of highways* left, *which crossed rivers by rope bridges* right.

their place was taken by hard-core settlers, absolutely loyal to the regime, known as *mitimaes*. The system was virtually foolproof, particularly as the Incas were conquering first a mountain people, valley by valley, and later, the more thickly populated coastal strip, where each river oasis had developed its city-state, or at least some central organization controlling irrigation and water supplies. Taxation followed conquest, and since one-tenth of the population was conscripted for the Inca armies, and it has been estimated that their bureaucratic system required 1,331 officials per 10,000 of population, increased productivity was essential.

This was achieved by ruthless exploitation of the labour force, by rapid development of the irrigation and terrace cultivation systems already in existence, and by intensive use of fertilizers, particularly the deposits of guano on the coastal islands where the seabirds that produced this vital form of land-enrichment – mainly a species of pelican and gannet, also cormorant – were protected. As in all agrarian societies dependent on large-scale irrigation systems, the social system required severe authoritarian government backed by ritual and divine compulsion. Thus, temples and fortresses buttressed each newly-acquired province, side by side with the municipal buildings of the bureaucracy. But though Inca building was on a huge scale, it was essentially functional, and neither in the quality of its masonry, nor in its artistic design, did it surpass, or even equal, the work of the earlier cultures.

In road building, however, the Incas were supreme. Paradoxically, it was their superb network of highways that made the Spanish conquest possible. The royal roads of the Incas finally extended 3,250 miles from Quito in the north to Talca in central Chile, spanning 35° of latitude. They were military roads every bit as vital to the maintenance of the empire as the roads constructed for the Roman legions. In the coastal area the roads of the Chimú and other city-states were developed and extended until the main artery was 2,520 miles long and up to about 24 feet wide, with lateral link roads connecting it to the Andean highway. Pack llama stairways climbed as high as 15,600 feet. Rope cables, some of them as thick as a man's body and renewed each year, slung the roads across deep river gorges. Road markers were set up at each *topo* (4½ miles) along their entire length and there were rest houses (*tambos*) about every twelve miles for the Inca and his retinue as

he travelled his empire; some of these were, in fact, fortresses with magazines containing arms and everything else required for the equipment of armies travelling light to deal with insurrection. Small post houses about every five miles housed runners (*chasquis*); these men, with their distinctive chequered tunics, were used for the relaying of dispatches at the incredible rate of 150 miles per day. Verbal dispatches were often supplemented by the *quipu*, and though these knotted strings were primarily for recording taxes and the contents of Government storehouses, it is probable that there was some sort of code in existence based on numbers. Certainly a strand of the royal fringe marked the dispatch as emanating from the Inca himself.

The knotted strings of the *quipu* were the exact equivalent of the notched sticks of the old tally system used in Europe. Pedro Cieza de León, writing immediately after the conquest, states that 'in the capital of each province there were accountants whom they called *quipu-camayocs*, and by these knots they kept the account of the tribute paid by the natives of that district in silver, gold, clothing, flocks, down to wood and other more insignificant things, and by these *quipus* at the end of the year, or ten or twenty years, they gave a report to one whose duty it was to check the account so exact that not even a pair of sandals was missing'. By this means the cacique of Huacara-Pora could account for every item he had given to the Spaniards since Pizarro arrived in that valley 'without a single omission . . . and I was amazed thereby'. And he adds, 'the wars, cruelties, pillaging and tyranny of the Spaniards had been such that if these Indians had not been so accustomed to order and providence they would all have perished. . . . After they (the Spaniards) had passed through, the chieftains came together with the keepers of the *quipus*, and if one had expended more than the others, those who had given less made up the difference, so that all were on an equal footing.'

This 'equal footing' was the cornerstone on which the empire was based. 'No-one who was lazy or tried to live by the work of others was tolerated; everyone had to work. Thus on certain days each lord went to his lands and took the plough in hand . . . even the Incas themselves did this to set an example.' This was, of course, a purely symbolic ritual intended to give a lead to the rank and file. If a man was fit 'he worked and lacked for nothing; and if he was ill he received what he needed from the storehouse'. Nevertheless, the 'equal footing',

as in all centrally-controlled, bureaucratic, or communist, states, was a façade supporting a two-caste system. The fact that penalties for transgression of the Inca laws were less severe for the bureaucratic élite only emphasizes the importance of the upper caste in the maintenance of the system. In modern communistic terms they were the 'party' members.

The basis of the Inca state was the worker, and the basic unit of the worker was the *ayllu*. This was a village grouping of families, a virtually self-sufficient unit that varied in size with the nature of the terrain. The grouping was historic, a natural development in mountainous country where each valley or grassy upland was almost completely isolated. The difference under the Inca system was that the isolated communities were connected by royal roads. These, designed for conquest in the first place, became subsequently the lines of communication that made central planning and organization possible. The other fundamental change was that the *ayllu* or clan land was appropriated by the state and reallocated, part to the people, part to the state, and part to the sun god, the *ayllu* paying a form of labour tax by tilling and harvesting the state and religious lands. It also washed the gold from the placer deposits in the rivers and got the silver from the mountain mines, refining it from the lead and tin and sulphur with which it was mixed by 'burning the hill, and, as the sulphur stone burns, the silver falls in lumps'.

Each autumn that part of the land loaned by the state to the commune was re-allocated, each married couple being entitled to a *topo*. This varied in size according to the number of mouths the family had to feed; in general it was about an acre. Each able-bodied worker had to marry by the age of twenty, otherwise a bride was chosen for him. Since the *puric*, or worker, was the basis of Inca society, the reproduction of this essential raw material of empire was encouraged; marriage was simply a matter of joining hands and exchanging sandals. The labour force for working state and religious lands was based on the decimal or *quipu* system; ten workers made a field unit under a leader, ten of these units had a foreman, ten foremen a headman. And so it went on, from the village unit to the tribal unit, from the tribal to the provincial, from the provincial to the regional, and finally from the regional, which was one of the four quarters of the empire, to the Inca himself.

Relays of chasquis *carried messages rapidly throughout the country* far left; *although writing was unknown, the knotted* quipus *enabled accounts to be kept* middle left; *agriculture was based upon the* ayllu, *which was state-owned* left; *transport was by llamas* right.

There was almost no way by which a male child could escape from his *ayllu*. As he was born, so he died. Garcilaso tells us:

Children were brought up very severely, not only among the Incas, but among simple people as well. From birth, they were washed in cold water every morning, then wrapped in swaddling covers . . . This custom of a cold dip was said to strengthen the child's legs and arms and give him greater resistance to the severe mountain climate. His arms were kept tightly bound until the age of four months. Indeed, during the entire first cycle, he remained attached night and day to a netting that was as hard as wood, and which was stretched across a chest with only three legs, to make it rock like a cradle. In order to nurse her child, the mother leaned down to him, without ever untying him or taking him up in her arms. He was fed the breast three times a day, morning, noon and night, and never at other hours, even if he cried and called his mother. The women always nursed their own children, no matter what their rank; they abstained from all relations with their husbands as long as they were nursing, and until the child was weaned, it received no other food than its mother's milk. When the time came to take the child out of its cradle, in order not to have to take it into their arms, the mothers put it in a hole, dug in the ground, which was as deep as the child's chest. When he reached the age where he could walk on his hands and feet, he nursed kneeling, and walked round his mother to change breasts, without her giving him any help whatsoever. At the birth of the baby, the mothers took less care of themselves than they did of their children: after having given birth, either in their homes, or beside a river, and having washed the new born baby, they washed themselves and went back to work as though nothing had happened. There were no midwives, properly speaking, and those women who served in this function were more like witches than anything else. This was the common custom among all the Indians in Peru, whether rich or poor, nobles or commoners.

At puberty the male child assumed the breech clout. Thereafter his life was spent working for his family and for the state, or in the armed services, either fighting or doing garrison duty, or in the labour corps building roads and cities.

Because of the vertical variations of climate, the crops the worker grew were incredibly various. Cotton on the coast complemented the llama wool of the Sierra as the raw material of clothes, even armour and a sort of war helmet. The dominant food was maize and potatoes – there were twenty varieties of maize and no less than 240 varieties of potato. Terracing and irrigation were developed on a grand scale, the water being channelled from as much as forty miles away. Game was protected, being rounded up, region by region, in the royal hunt, which was a yearly event involving anything up to thirty thousand warrior-beaters. The predators were slaughtered, poor stock culled to provide meat for the villages, and the vicuña and the guanaco, the wild llama, shorn for their fine wool. Yet, though their pastoral-agrarian economy was extremely advanced, the only form of plough was a copper-shoed digging stick; if they knew about the wheel, they did not use it. An abundant supply of docile labour, the terracing system in the

Death mask of gold on copper, the eyes inlaid
with shell. Mochica culture.

mountains and intensive cultivation in the irrigated areas discouraged the development of more mechanized farming methods, just as the mountain terrain of their natural habitat discouraged the development of any form of wheeled transport. They had the *puric* for cultivation, the llama for transport. That was sufficient. Man hours were the basis of their civilization. And though the *puric* had security, he had little freedom.

This was true also of the élite. The *orejones* (the big-eared ones) were born of the blood royal; they lived and died within the *ayllu* of the Inca. Their life, however, was very different. They were given a good education – mathematics, religion, language and the Inca version of history – culminating in tough examinations. To mark them out from the rest of the population their ears were pierced and the hole enlarged until it would take the gold or jewelled earplugs that indicated their station. There was also a second class of administrators – the *curacas* – necessitated by the rapid growth of empire. It was Inca policy to administer newly-acquired territory through the existing administrative machinery – under supervision, of course, and after suitable indoctrination of the local ruling class. A man could climb to the privileged position of *curaca* by ability. This was his limit. But a woman could go further. At puberty there was a hair-combing ceremony, and if a girl were particularly beautiful or showed exceptional ability in weaving or other feminine craft, she could be chosen to attend a school at Cuzco or at one of the provincial capitals. She had a chance then to marry into the nobility or to become one of the 'daughters of the sun', a royal concubine, living a life of segregation and at the disposal of the Inca alone.

The position of women generally is covered in great detail by Garcilaso in his *Royal Commentaries*. The Virgins of the Sun were the élite, the chosen of the royal blood. At Cuzco they were housed in a 'convent close by, but not within the Temple of the Sun'. They were chosen for their beauty and lineage at puberty so that there should be no doubt about their virginity. There were about fifteen hundred of them. At maturity they became *mamacunas*, and there were five hundred or so virgins in service to look after them. 'All the table service in their convent, as well as that in the Temple of the Sun, was either gold or silver. They also had the privileges of a garden of precious metals, similar to that of the temple.' If one of the Virgins was so misguided as to ignore her vow of chastity and get caught, the law demanded that 'she was to be buried alive and her accomplice hung; he, his wife, his children, his servants and all his close relations; and, in order that the punishment should be complete, his llamas were also to be put to death, his fields destroyed, his house razed to the ground, and the entire place was to be strewn with stones, so that nothing could grow there again'. The main occupations of the Virgins of the Sun was to spin and weave the garments of the Inca and his Coya, and also the cloths that were offered up to the Sun at the time of sacrifice.

The provincial 'convents' (there is now a reconstruction of one of these

Inca stone-masonry: the bath at Tambo Machay.

at Pachacamac near Lima) were organized on the lines of the Cuzco establishment, but since these virgins were not of the blood-royal, the materials they wove could be distributed by the Inca to those he wished to reward. Moreover, Garcilaso tells us, they were the Inca's concubines and

> when the Inca wished to possess one or other of these women, he had her summoned and she was brought to wherever he happened to be. . . . Those who had once had relations with the king could not go back into the convent. They were brought to the royal palace, where they served as attendants or ladies-in-waiting to the Queen, until the day they were sent back home to their provinces, richly endowed with land and other benefits. . . . Each convent had a governor, who had to belong to the Inca class, and who was surrounded by a majordomo and numerous other assistants. The tableware in all these convents was also of gold and silver. In fact, it might be stated that all the precious metal that was dug in the imperial mines served no other purpose than that of decorating the temples, convents, and royal palaces. . . . Other women of royal blood lived in the palace, and observed the vow of perpetual chastity, without, however, adding to it that of confinement. . . . They were called *occlos* and were treated with the greatest consideration. Nor was their chastity feigned. . . . Married women were generally dedicated to the care of their homes; they knew how to spin and weave wool or cotton, according to whether they lived in cold or hot regions. They did little sewing, however, for there was hardly any needed, Indian garments, both masculine and feminine, being generally woven in one piece in the proper length and width. . . . All the men and all the women worked together in the fields.

Prostitution was allowed, but these women 'lived in the country in wretched thatched huts, each one separately, and they were forbidden to enter the towns and villages in order that no virtuous women should ever encounter them'.

The division between commoners and nobles was absolute, the gulf between them widening as the empire grew and the need for rigid obedience became more imperative. The *orejones* and the *curacas* had a monopoly of the high administrative and religious appointments. They paid no taxes and lived in considerably luxury, eating off gold and silver in fine houses, dressed in fine cloth and having several wives. The price they paid was complete subservience to the Inca. If they entered his presence they changed into poorer clothing and bore on their shoulders a burden symbolic of that subservience. The loyalty of

Weaving was the basic occupation of women left. The virgins of the Sun right were girls of royal blood who spun and wove only for the Inca and his Coya.

the ruling class was thus assured, and it was from them that the standing army, the personal bodyguard of the Inca, was drawn. This army may have numbered about ten thousand and was the cadre for the build-up of the much larger local forces in the event of war. The dependence in these circumstances upon the regional militia was one of the weaknesses of the empire when faced by the Spaniards. Such an army could only keep the field for a limited time, the normal period being not more than twenty days. But though such central organization had its weaknesses in the face of invasion from the outside, within the fabric of the existing Andean culture its supremacy was complete, its ruthless efficiency still evident today in such great works of construction as the road system, the fantastic hanging cities like Machu Picchu, or the huge fortress complexes like Sacsahuamán at Cuzco. Their system of agriculture produced food for all in abundance and a sufficient surplus to feed the enormous number of workers employed in these unproductive projects.

Though the function of many of their public works was partly religious and ceremonial, religion never acquired such complete ascendancy as in the Aztec empire. Captives were sometimes sacrificed, so too were children offered by their parents, but this was usually associated with some crisis, such as lack of rain. The normal sacrifice was a llama or an alpaca, the heart of the beast being wrenched out and offered to the gods. More often the Indians were content to make an offering of meat and burn a candle to the gods in the form of a ball of wool floating in oil or fat.

The simplicity of their rites has not changed in the last four hundred years; they have simply been transferred to the Roman Catholic faith, so that it is not unusual to see an offering placed at the foot of some statue whilst the Indian family, holding their candles, kneel before it. And in the high Sierra a Christian version of the old household gods will be carried to the church to the accompaniment of the age-old sound of the hand drum, the reed flute and the twelve-foot-long bamboo trumpet. At carnival time, after the rains, the misery of their life deadened by *chicha*, they will erect tall branches of willow or eucalyptus, festoon them with paper streamers and, to the sound of firecrackers and music, dance round them. The site chosen for this version of the maypole dance is sometimes macabre. At Cajamarca, for instance, they dance on the graves of their ancestors, on the hill known as the Necropolis of Otuzco, where the exposed rock is punctured by little window-like sepulchres.

Water was almost certainly a part of Inca religious ceremonial – hardly surprising since they lived in a world of rushing rivers, cascades and springs, with here and there a bubbling eruption of mineral waters out of the bowels of their volcanic terrain. Tambo Machay, near Cuzco, a sanctuary built around a mountain spring, almost certainly had religious significance, and the strange runnels cut into the rock of that extraordinary observatory site just beyond the fortress of Sacsahuamán, the similar runnels of Rumy Tiana above Cajamarca and at the central water point, the fountain, at Machu Picchu suggest that divination by water formed some part of their religious ceremonies.

Their gods were not as numerous as the Aztec gods, but, like the Aztecs, they worshipped the natural phenomena of the world in which they lived, except for Viracocha, the Supreme Being, the Creator. The enormous religious complex twenty miles down the coast from Lima still bears the name of the older god, Pachacamac, which the Incas equated with their own Viracocha. But though they incorporated him into their own mythology, they nevertheless felt the need to overtop the Pachacamac temple with a larger pyramid. This Temple of the Sun, looking east over the green Lurín valley, west over the Pacific, is the largest religious structure in Peru, larger even than the great fortress pyramid at Paramonga rising abruptly above the sugar-cane green of the Forteleza river two hundred miles to the north. Now partly restored, it dominates the ruins of the Temple of Pachacamac, dominates the whole fantastic adobe site.

The Viracocha of the Incas is believed to have originated in the Inca of that name – the eighth in line – who was regarded as a sort of oracle. He is supposed to have foretold the coming of the Spaniards and, according to Garcilaso, this was the reason they called them Viracochas, in the same way that the Aztecs called their invaders *teules*. 'There was never in the Empire any other recognized god than the Sun, and Pachacamac, the Invisible God.' This is an over-simplification. The Sun was their natural god, since it was upon the sun that their crops depended. The Moon was the Sun's wife. Second in importance was Thunder, the god of war and weather. The Earth, the Sea, even some constellations, were worshipped. Gods peculiar to a conquered tribe were not obliterated, simply incorporated, and in addition to the formal priesthood there were wise men, some of whom had a considerable reputation.

Pachacamac, the 'invisible God', is always referred to as Tici-Viracocha by Cieza de León, and his explanation of this Supreme Being is of particular interest since the legendary origins of his Tici-Viracocha are similar to the Aztecs' Quetzalcoatl: 'Before the Incas came to reign in these kingdoms or were known there, these Indians tell a thing that far exceeds all else they say. They state that a long time went by in which they did not see the sun. . . .' It finally emerged out of Lake Titicaca and shortly afterwards 'out of the regions of the south there came and appeared among them a white man, large of stature, whose air and person aroused great respect and veneration'. Because he could work miracles, 'making plains of the hills and of the plains mountains, and bringing forth springs in the living rock', they called him 'the Maker of all things, their Beginning, Father of the Sun. . . . They say that in many places he instructed people how they should live and spoke to them lovingly and meekly, exhorting them to be good and not do one another harm or injury, but rather to love one another, and use charity to all.' And Cieza de León goes on to tell of another similar man who, by the words he spoke, healed the sick and restored sight to the blind. Threatened with stoning in

A primitive stone sculpture, believed to be of Viracocha, the Supreme Being of Indian religion.

the village of Cacha, he knelt, with his arms upraised to heaven, and fire appeared in the sky; this was an eruption, since the stones it scorched became 'so light that even a big one can be picked up as though it were a cork'. On leaving Cacha he journeyed to the coast where, 'spreading his cloak he moved over the waves, and never again appeared'.

Who was this man who sailed away into the west and whose name Viracocha means 'foam of the sea'? Some Spaniards believed he was one of the apostles and claimed that the idol the Indians erected in a temple at Cacha held a rosary in its hands. Cieza de León visited this statue. There was no rosary, but the clothes had marks on them suggesting they were fastened by buttons.

Cieza de León goes on to describe the origins of the Incas. His chapter headings suffice to give an idea of the story: 'Of how certain men and women appeared in Paccuric-Tampu (the "origin-tambo"). . . . How the two brothers when they were in Tampu Quiru saw the one that they had lured into the cave emerge with wings of feathers, who told them to go and found the great city of Cuzco. . . . How, after Manco Capac saw that his brothers had been turned to stone, he came to a valley where he found certain peoples and founded or built the ancient and vastly rich city of Cuzco, which became the capital of the whole empire of the Incas. . . . Of how the Lord-Inca, after assuming the royal fringe, married his sister, the Coya, which is the name of the Queen, and how he was allowed to take many wives, although, of them all, the Coya was the only legitimate one, and the most important.'

Beginning around the middle of the thirteenth century, the first eight Incas were: Manco Capac, Sinchi Roca, Lloqui Yupanqui, Mayta Capac, Capac Yupanqui, Inca Roca, Yahuar Huacac, and Viracocha. But accurate dates only begin with the two great empire builders – Pachacuti Inca Yupanqui (1438–71) and Topa Inca Yupanqui (1471–93). These two, in the short space of just over half a century, conquered the whole of Peru, parts of Bolivia and Ecuador and most of Chile – an area of about 380,000 square miles. The initial phase – the subjugation by Pachacuti of the tribes in the Cuzco and Urubamba area – can have presented no difficulties. From its source, a hundred and thirty miles south of Cuzco, to the point where it enters the Sacred Valley forty miles to the north, the Urubamba flows through a continuous, but quite narrow grazing valley. It is beyond these two limits that conquest became a major operation. Southward over the height of land, where the little railway station of Santa Rosa (13,000 feet) now stands, the whole country changes, gradually widening out into the open grass plains of the Titicaca region. Northward, the reverse happens, the mountain walls close in, the valley becomes suddenly constricted to a gorge, the Urubamba a raging brown torrent. This would later be the gateway to the Amazon, and, here, to dominate the Indians of the *selva* and to ensure continuity of the rain forest's wealth of exotic produce, the Incas built the stone city of Machu Picchu. To guard the entrance to the Urubamba gorge they also built the cliff-hung fortress of Ollantaytambo.

The trapezoidal Inca gate and niches at Ollantaytambo.

But this, like the great move southward to Bolivia and Chile, lay in the future. Pachacuti's interest was the conquest of the existing tribes of the Sierra. Mountain barriers meant nothing to his warriors. They moved steadily north, from valley to valley, until they had occupied the richest valley of all, Cajamarca. It was at this point that Pachacuti executed his brother, Capac Yupanqui, for letting his warriors advance beyond the limits he himself had set. Pachacuti's genius was administrative. The task of continuing the expansion of empire he now passed to his son, Topa or Tupac, whilst he concentrated on consolidating the conquests and organizing Cuzco as the capital of empire.

Topa's marches rank amongst the greatest in military history. His first long march was northwards, with over two hundred thousand warriors, across the heights of the Andes to conquer the Cañari Indians, and having incorporated these fierce warriors into his army, he went on to subdue the Quito people of Ecuador. Down to the coast then, conquering more tribes and making a seaborne expedition, presumably first to Salango island and then to Puná; the latter would certainly have had to be subdued if he were to safeguard his line of march, which was now south along the coastal desert strip.

The defence works of the Chimú cities were supposed to have been prepared on the basis that the attack would come from the south, from the direction of Cuzco – presumably on the assumption that, coming from the north, Topa Inca took them by surprise. Even the briefest examination of Chan-Chan makes nonsense of this theory. In that flat desert country anything but an all-round defensive system could easily have been turned. In fact, the ruins show that each walled unit was in the form of a rectangle. The reason for the downfall of these cities was almost certainly the vulnerability of the water supply and the physical contrast between these rich farming communities and the hardy warrior race from the Sierra, together with the fact that they were separated from each other by broad stretches of desert.

Topa Inca overran them one by one, then crossed the Andes and launched his armies into the lowlands of the Amazon basin. A swift turn-round to meet an uprising in the Titicaca region, and after subduing the tribes there in two big battles and gaining control of the central Bolivian Highlands, he crossed the Andes again, descended into the coastal plain and attacked into Chile, the territory of the warlike Araucanian Indians. This fighting march took him as far as latitude 35° south, to the río Maule, which became the southern limit of the Inca empire. The total distance covered by the armies of Topa Inca in their sweep north and south was in the region of ten thousand miles, and it was made through some of the most difficult country in the world, fighting sometimes on the edge of the snowline at anything up to 13,000 feet, sometimes in the humid heat of the Amazon rain forest, sometimes in the arid desert country of the coast.

All these conquests he consolidated by the benevolent despotism laid down by his father and by the communication system he built himself. He came to the throne very young, probably at the age of eighteen, for his father handed the

Opposite *Chimú necklace of gold and turquoise.* Overleaf *Chimú gold cat.*

royal *borla* on to him in 1471, a few years before his death. When Topa died in 1493 his army is said to have numbered three hundred thousand and the empire of the Incas was complete.

Where, or in what place, he is buried they do not say. They tell that a large number of women and servitors and pages were killed to be laid with him, and so much treasure and precious stones that it must have amounted to more than a million [gold pesos]. Even this figure is probably less than it was, for there were private persons who were buried with over a hundred castellanos. Aside from the many who were buried with him, many men and women in different parts of the kingdom hanged themselves and were buried, and everywhere mourning went on for a whole year, and most of the women cut off their hair, binding their heads with hempen ropes; and at the end of a year they did him his honours. What they say they used to do, I do not choose to set down, for they were heathenish things.

He was succeeded by his son Huayna Capac, and Cieza de León goes on to give a very clear picture of this last of the great Inca-emperors:

Huayna Capac, according to many Indians who saw and knew him, was not large of stature, but strong and well built, of grave, goodly countenance, a man of few words and many deeds; he was stern, and unmerciful in his punishments. He wanted to be so feared that at night the Indians would dream of him. . . . Young men who succumbed to the temptations of the flesh, and slept with his wives or concubines or with the women of the temple of the sun, were given instant death, and the women, too. Those who had a part in riots or uprising were punished by being stripped of their property, which was given to others; for other crimes the punishment was only corporal. . . . The mother of Huayna Capac . . . loved him so much, she begged him not to go to Quito or Chile until after her death. And they tell that to please and obey her, he remained in Cuzco until she had died and was buried with great pomp, much treasure and fine clothing, some of her ladies and servitors being placed in the tomb with her. Most of the treasures of the dead Incas, and their lands, which are called *chacaras* (*huacas*), were kept intact from the very first one, and none ventured to touch or spend any part of them, for they had no wars or needs which required money. For this reason we believe that there are great treasures lost in the depths of the earth, and will remain there unless someone, building or doing some other thing, should by chance stumble on part of the much that there is.

Huayna Capac summoned to appear before him the principal native lords of the provinces, and when his court was teeming with them, he took to wife his sister, Chincha Occlo, with great festivities omitting the customary mourning for the death of Topa Inca. When these were concluded, he ordered some fifty thousand troops to accompany him in a progress throughout his kingdom. As he ordered it, so it was done; and he set out from Cuzco with more pomp and majesty than his father, for his litter was so rich, according to those who carried the Inca on their shoulders, that the many and large stones with which it was set were priceless, not to mention the gold of which

Inca female idol in gold.

it was made. . . . From these regions he returned to Cuzco, where he occupied himself in making great sacrifices to the sun and to those they held as greater gods.

It was Huayna Capac who completed the huge fortress of Sacsahuamán that his father had begun. 'A great cable of gold was put around the square of Cuzco, and great dances and drinking feasts took place . . .' Sacsahuamán was the greatest of all Inca architectural feats. The huge stones of the outer wall, weighing up to a hundred tons each, still stretch for a third of a mile; grey and glistening in the rain, their uneven-edged, tightly-fitted rampart of monolithic blocks constitute one of the most extraordinary sights in the world. Above it are two further walls enclosing the ruins of the whole massive fortress complex. Cuzco, at the time when Huayna Capac was building this gigantic monument to the stone-mason's craft, must have been a strange place, thousands of men quarrying and dragging stones on rollers, levering them into position, and inside the angled outer walls constructing reservoirs, towers, buildings. The city itself had already been completed, the extent of it still evident today in the long stretches of Inca walls that have been incorporated as the indestructible foundations of later Spanish buildings. These have crumbled to the battering of earthquakes, so that Cuzco now has a sad atmosphere, the ruins of superimposed Spanish colonial architecture combining with the solid Inca remains to give it the feel of a ghost city.

Huayna Capac's enthusiasm for architecture on the grand scale did not wane with the completion of Sacsahuamán, for he then toured the empire and 'wherever he went he ordered lodgings and fortresses built, drawing up the designs with his own hand'. The triangular courtyard at Cajamarca, the only one of this shape ever built by the Incas, reveals his individual approach to architecture. But, like his grandfather, he was also a brilliant administrator. Cieza de León records that:

> he revised the boundaries of many provinces so that they would not seek to better them by force of arms. His troops, despite their number, were so well disciplined that they did not set foot outside their camps; wherever they went the natives provided for their needs so fully that more was left over than they used. In certain places he built baths; in others he established hunting preserves, and in the deserts he had large houses built. Wherever the Inca passed, he left behind such noteworthy accomplishments that their mere relation arouses wonder.

The fortress at Sacsahuamán: as it is today left, *and in construction* right.

It had been an orderly and obedient empire that Huayna Capac inherited from his father, and the system was so successful, the empire by then so firmly established, that the only real opposition to Inca rule seems to have come from the recently conquered north. The Quito people of Ecuador were fully as advanced and quite as warlike as the Incas; Prescott describes their incorporation into the empire as 'the most important accession yet made to it since the foundation of the dynasty of Manco Capac'. In fact, though continuing to develop the organization he had inherited – particularly the introduction of Quechua as the dominant language, the improvement of agricultural methods and the completion of the Andean Highway from Quito to Cuzco – Huayna Capac spent much of the thirty-four years of his reign in the north. Thus at the time of his death in 1527 his two greatest generals, Quizquiz and Challcuchima, were with him in Quito, together with all the empire's most experienced and battle-trained warriors.

Prescott states that Huayna Capac had already divided the empire. Some chroniclers seem to take the view that he died without naming his successor. The results were the same in either case. The empire was split, Atahualpa taking the new territory in the north, Huáscar the old empire centred on Cuzco. 'Huáscar was the son of Huayna Capac, as was Atahualpa. Huáscar was the younger, Atahualpa the elder. Huáscar was the son of the Coya, the sister of his father; Atahualpa was the son of a woman of Quilaca, by name Tapac Palla. Both of them were born in Cuzco, not in Quito, as some have said and even written, without knowing the facts.' Cieza de León goes on to say that 'this is borne out by the fact that Huayna Capac was engaged in the conquest of Quito and those lands for some twelve years, and Atahualpa was over thirty when he died'. And he adds: 'Huáscar was born in Cuzco, and Atahualpa was four or five years older than he. This is the truth, and so I believe it.' Nevertheless, the belief that Atahualpa was born in the north, possibly in Quito itself, still persists.

It was inevitable that Huáscar should succeed to the *borla*, the royal fringe, since he was unquestionably the lawful heir, and was in Cuzco at the time of his father's death, surrounded by all the bureaucratic hierarchy of empire. Atahualpa, on the other hand, was in Quito with his father when he died. 'He was well set up for an Indian, of good presence, medium figure, not over stout, comely of countenance and serious withal . . .' In one succinct paragraph Cieza de León describes the inevitability of the struggle for power that was to open the door to the Spaniards: 'Atahualpa was loved by the old captains of his father and the soldiers, because he went to the wars with him as a child, and because Huayna Capac had so loved him during his lifetime, allowing him to eat nothing except what he left on his plate. Huáscar was clement and pious; Atahualpa, ruthless and vengeful; both were generous, but Atahualpa was a man of greater determination and endeavour.'

It is impossible to know what was in Huayna Capac's mind when he either made this division of empire, or, by dying without actually naming his successor, allowed it to happen. During the last few years of his life, raft traders and others must have given him some inkling of what was happening beyond his borders to the north. However inaccurate this intelligence, he cannot have been unaware of the threat posed by the Spanish thrust into Mexico and south into Darién. Vague reports would also have been brought to him of ships full of these bearded men sailing the seas. That the mood was one of foreboding, and that, like Moctezuma, he was faced with a series of ill omens, is evident from the writings of Garcilaso. His wise men were already prophesying evil because of the death of an eagle that fell out of the sky after being harassed by buzzards during the feast of the Sun.

> There followed earthquakes and such unusual violence that great rocks were shattered in pieces and mountains collapsed. The sea became furious, overflowed its shores, invading the land, while numerous comets streaked the heavens, sowing terror in their wake. A curious, mysterious fear had seized upon all of Peru, when one unusually bright night the new moon appeared with a halo of three large rings; the first one was the colour of blood, the second a greenish black, and the third seemed to be made of smoke.

The soothsayers claimed that the blood-coloured ring foretold war between the Inca's descendants, and they added: 'The black ring threatens our religion, our laws and the Empire, which will not survive these wars and the death of your people; and all you have done, and all your ancestors have done, will vanish in smoke, as is shown by the third ring.'

But, despite these forebodings, it is difficult to accept, as Prescott seems to, that Huayna Capac did, in fact, order his chieftains to submit to the bearded strangers, whose coming had been foretold by the Inca Viracocha. Though superstitious and fatalistic, he was, after all, absolute ruler of the entire Inca world, and that world had not yet been seriously threatened or even penetrated. His splitting of the empire, however, is much more understandable. Realizing that the threat would come from the north, he did what he could to ensure that it would be met by the full flower of his army under the only son on whose ability as a leader in time of war he could rely.

The year of Huayna Capac's death was the year Pizarro's tiny vessel called at Tumbes.

It is possible that Huayna Capac hoped Atahualpa would at once use the weapon of his battle-trained army and establish himself as Inca, supplanting Huáscar as Pachacuti had supplanted his brother Urco. But Atahualpa seems to have been uncertain of the support he could rely upon. He evidently felt he needed time to consolidate his position; and Huáscar was too easy-going to precipitate the clash by challenging his half-brother's hold on the north. It was not until five years after his father's death that Atahualpa finally felt himself strong enough to move.

Even then his ruthlessness reveals his sense of doubt at not being of the true Inca descent.

His first victory, early in 1532, was at Ambato, about sixty miles to the south of Quito. He then attacked the city of Tumebamba, slaughtered the inhabitants, and razed it to the ground. He went on to lay waste the whole province of Cañaris as an example to the rest of Huáscar's adherents. He behaved, in fact, like a man who must command by force or lose all. Advancing by the coast road, he was checked by the Puná islanders, left them to be dealt with by the people of Tumbes, and took the lateral road up into the Andes. It was spring now, and Pizarro was already landing his troops behind the Indian line of march when Atahualpa sent his generals and the army forward to the final battle near Cuzco, holding himself in reserve at Cajamarca. The discipline of his seasoned warriors proved superior to Huáscar's hastily conscripted levies. Nevertheless, the battle lasted all day. Thousands were killed. Huáscar himself was captured.

Spanish writers, seeking some justification for what their countrymen did later, claim that Atahualpa was so absolutely ruthless that he slaughtered the whole *ayllu* of the Inca. Garcilaso himself says that he 'immolated his two hundred brothers, the sons of Huayna Capac', and that 'some were massacred, some were hung, while others were thrown in the river or lakes with a stone tied round their necks, or hurled from high rocks or steep peaks'. He claims that the wretched Huáscar was forced to watch the massacre, but the account is a little confused here in that it says that Huáscar was forced to walk amongst his relatives, drawn up in two lines in the Sacsahuana valley, dressed 'in mourning garb, his hands tied together and a rope round his neck. . . . This was the last opportunity they had to manifest their loyalty and their devotion to a lost cause, because they were immediately massacred with hatchets and swords.' Not content with this, Garcilaso adds that 'when there was not a single adult man left of all Huáscar's line, or of his principal vassals, Atahualpa turned his vengeance upon the women and children of royal birth'. All who could be found were placed in a large enclosure on the Yahuarpampa plain. 'They were first subjected to severe fasting. Then, all Huáscar's wives, sisters, aunts, nieces, cousins, mothers-in-law were hung, now to trees, now to gallows built for the occasion, some by their hair, others by both arms, or by one arm, or by the waist, or by still other ways that decency forbids me to relate. They were handed their small children whom they clasped tightly in their arms until the children crashed to the earth. The longer the torture lasted, the more delighted were the executioners, who would have considered it a favour to grant a rapid death to their innocent victims.'

As confirmation of Atahualpa's cruelties, Garcilaso quotes chapter five of the third book of the second part of the *History of Peru* by Diego Fernández, adding, 'and it will be seen that I have not invented anything'. Not only does he make Atahualpa destroy the whole *ayllu* of the Inca, but he claims that 'the porters, paymasters, cup-bearers, cooks and, in general, all those who, because of the nature of their service, came in daily contact with the Inca, were pitilessly slaughtered with their entire families; in addition to which their houses were burned and their villages destroyed'. This is too much, since vengeance on this scale would have meant the destruction of the whole machinery of government. And if he was prepared to destroy the whole *ayllu* of the Inca, why did he not kill the Inca himself?

At the time Huáscar was defeated and captured, Pizarro and his Spaniards were already constructing the first colonial garrison town of San Miguel. Time was short, and clemency would seem to have been a political necessity for Atahualpa. The weeks passed: Atahualpa at Cajamarca, the Spaniards on the coast. Finally, in September, Pizarro marched. By mid-November his tiny force was emerging from the defiles of the Andes and descending into Cajamarca, where Atahualpa, waiting with his tented army by the hot springs two leagues from the town, meditated upon his course of action. He knew every detail of the Spanish force, for he had sent an embassy to Pizarro when he was still climbing laboriously through the defiles and another when he was advancing across the high ground. Both were embassies of welcome.

Was it a trick, as Pizarro believed, or was the welcome genuine?

For the answer to these questions we must see the situation from Atahualpa's point of view. Not Stalin, not Napoleon, not any dictator since the days of Rome, was so absolutely supreme as Atahualpa, now that he had assumed the royal *borla* and was Sapa-Inca of Peru at the peak of Inca power. He had only to speak and what he commanded would be done, his *chasquis* carrying the word through the whole three thousand miles of his fantastic empire. He might be apprehensive about what the incursion of this force represented for the future, but of the force itself he had nothing to fear; he could blot it out, or not, as he wished. Meantime, he was consumed with a sort of arrogant curiosity. So many reports, some of them conflicting, had been sent to him – about the ships, which he could probably just comprehend, about firearms and guns, which must have seemed to him highly exaggerated, about troopers who rode animals much larger than the llama. There was talk of a powerful prince across the water and of a new religion, with the cross as its symbol and a man-god who was killed by his own people. Pizarro had not gone to the same lengths as Cortés in giving invasion the semblance of a crusade, but the Dominican Friar, Valverde, was a dedicated missionary, and Atahualpa must have wondered about this Jesus, who, like himself, was the son of a god. So he waited with his army by the hot springs, letting the Spaniards struggle to the top of the defiles unmolested, letting them cross the high Sierra country without opposition, even giving them the stone-built security of Cajamarca for their rest camp. He was like a child mesmerized into inactivity by his curiosity.

11   *Massacre, Gold and Civil War*

EARLY ON THE MORNING of Friday, November 15, 1532, Pizarro arrived on the heights overlooking the town and saw for the first time the strip of lush meadowland beside the river, the tented camp sprawled out below the mountain on the far side of the valley. The slopes by which his army had to descend were grass-grown and not too steep; it was, in fact, relatively easy going and by noon he was within a league of Cajamarca. Here, Xeres says, he waited for his rearguard to catch up – 'all the troops got their arms ready, and the Governor [Pizarro] formed the Spaniards, horse and foot, three deep, to enter the town'. Prescott says he marched in three divisions, which would seem more realistic since he could see for himself the size of the Inca's army and needed to make as brave a show as possible.

Cajamarca was empty and waiting for them, an extraordinary gesture on Atahualpa's part since it gave the Spaniards the advantage of a strong defensive position. Xeres gives us a very detailed picture of this Indian town of two thousand inhabitants.

> The houses are more than two hundred paces in length, and very well built, being surrounded by strong walls, three times the height of a man. The roofs are covered with straw and wood, resting on the walls. The interiors are divided into eight rooms, much better built than any we had seen before. Their walls are of very well cut stones and each lodging is surrounded by its masonry wall with doorways, and has its fountain of water in an open court, conveyed from a distance by pipes, for the supply of the house. In front of the *plaza*, towards the open country, a stone fortress is connected with it by a staircase leading from the square to the fort. Towards the open country there is another small door, with a narrow staircase, all within the outer wall of the *plaza*. Above the town, on the mountain side, where the houses commence, there is another fort on a hill, the greater part of which is hewn out of the rock. This is larger than the other, and surrounded by three walls, rising spirally.

Having positioned his men in the main courtyard, Pizarro waited for some time, but as no messenger arrived from the Indian camp he sent de Soto with twenty horse to invite the Inca to meet him. He then went up to the top of the fort, was appalled at the number of Indian warriors gathered in front of their tents and at once ordered his brother, Hernando, to follow de Soto with a further twenty horse. By then the usual afternoon clouds had gathered; it was raining and bitterly cold, with some hail. Because the dirt road between Cajamarca and the hot springs had been cut by the Indians, Hernando had to make a detour. This brought him to a bridge, where he found the first troop facing a group of warriors across a small stream. De Soto had gone on ahead with the interpreter, Felipillo. Hernando followed at once, fording the stream and pushing his horse straight through the Indian force on the further bank. He found the Inca seated at the door of his quarters on a small stool or throne, with his *orejones* and *curacas* about him, women squatting on the ground at his feet and a bodyguard of some four hundred armed warriors standing behind him.

The hot springs, now called the Baños del Inca, have hardly changed in more than four centuries. They still bubble out of the grass, steaming pools of sulphurous water covering about a quarter of an acre, and at week-ends the Indians come in bus-loads to immerse themselves in the public baths erected on the spot where Atahualpa had his quarters. These, according to Xeres, consisted of four rooms surrounding a courtyard with a bath to which pipes supplied both hot and cold water. There was another bathing pool outside. Both had stone steps leading down into them. 'The room in which Atahualpa stayed during the day was a corridor leading into an orchard, near it there is a chamber where he slept, with a window looking towards the court and the ponds. The corridor also opens on the court. The walls were plastered with the red bitumen, better than ochre, which shined much, and the wood, which formed the eaves of the house, was of the same colour. Another room is composed of four vaults, like bells, united into one. This is plastered with lime, as white as snow. The other two are offices. A river flows in front of this palace.' This was the stream where de Soto had left his troop, and it still exists.

Since Xeres must have seen Atahualpa on many occasions, his description of him is probably more accurate than that of Cieza de León already quoted: 'Atahualpa was a man of thirty years of age, good-looking, somewhat stout, with a fine face, handsome and fierce, the eyes bloodshot. He spoke with much dignity, like a great lord. He talked with good arguments and reasoned well, and when the Spaniards understood what he said they knew him to be a wise man. He was cheerful; but, when he spoke to his subjects, he was very haughty, and showed no sign of pleasure.' He was not talking at all, however, when Hernando saw him for the first time at the hot springs. He was wearing the *borla* 'which looked like silk, of crimson colour, fastened to the head by cords', and he was very much on his dignity – 'his eyes were cast on the ground, without looking in any other direction'.

De Soto, still mounted, towered above him, his armour gleaming dully in the cold altiplano light. According to some accounts, he had forced his horse so close

to the Inca that the breath of its nostril stirred the fringe of the *borla*. This Atahualpa ignored, though he had never seen a horse before, remaining absolutely still and not speaking a word. Other accounts of this episode say that de Soto, seeing Atahualpa's natural interest in the beast on which he was seated, suddenly wheeled about and began showing off his superb horsemanship, the display culminating in his bringing his charger on to its haunches right in front of the Inca. In this account Atahualpa is supposed to have sentenced to death several of his chiefs who had flinched before the final charge. Whichever is correct – and the latter is certainly in keeping with the high-mettled character of de Soto – there is little doubt that the armoured caballero made a deep impression on both Atahualpa himself and his assembled chiefs, and that this was the cause of the indecisiveness on the following day.

At the time Hernando arrived de Soto had already delivered Pizarro's message requesting Atahualpa to visit the Spaniards in their camp. He had been answered indirectly by one of the *orejones,* who declared that Atahualpa was fasting, but would visit the Spaniards the following day. But when de Soto introduced Hernando as the Spanish commander's brother, Atahualpa broke his silence and began to complain that his chiefs in the Chira river had been ill-treated. He had had word of it from his local governor, who claimed that he had personally killed three Spaniards and a horse. Hernando immediately and hotly denied it – 'neither he, nor all the Indians of that river together, could kill a single Christian'. They argued for a moment through the interpreter, Hernando bragging about what the Spaniards would do to Atahualpa's enemies and Atahualpa himself saying, 'A chief refuses to obey me, my troops will go with yours, and you will make war on him.' To which Hernando countered quickly: 'Ten Christians on horseback will suffice to destroy him.'

Women appeared with gold vessels filled with *chicha,* were sent back for larger ones, the Inca thus overwhelming the Spaniards with the traditional hospitality of the Sierra. They left finally, expecting Atahualpa to visit Cajamarca the following day. Xeres adds: 'His camp was formed on the skirts of a small hill, the tents, which were of cotton, extending for a league, with that of Atahualpa in the centre. All the men were on foot outside the tents, with their arms, consisting of long lances like pikes, stuck into the ground. There seemed to be upwards of thirty thousand men in the camp.'

Though Atahualpa had said he would visit the Spaniards the following day, it was quite late on that fatal Saturday, November 16, that his state procession got under way. Since he was camped with all his warriors around him, the delay could not have been due to the time necessary to assemble the procession; it can only have been caused by a council of war in which the opinion of his advisers was either divided or contrary to his own. This is confirmed by the fact that, when he finally decided to make the move to Cajamarca, he sent a messenger to Pizarro to say that he would come armed as the Spaniards had into his camp. This was

Mochica pot: a man in a deerskin with a rope round his neck – perhaps acting a sacrificial role.

clearly a concession to his military chiefs, who were probably disturbed at the strange lack of movement in the Spanish camp, no horses being exercised, not a soldier to be seen. As a precaution they lined the causeway with their warriors, sent thousands more into the grasslands on either side of the procession.

Though the main body of Atahualpa's army was in the Cuzco region, it was still a formidable array. First came a squadron of what might well be *chasquis*, since they were dressed in a chequered livery of different colours, who moved slowly down the causeway sweeping the road ahead of the Inca. Behind them came three squadrons in different dresses, singing and dancing, followed by 'a number of men with armour, large metal plates, and crowns of gold and silver'. These were presumably the eighty or so chiefs who are described as carrying the Inca's litter, for it was amongst this group that Atahualpa appeared 'in a litter lined with plumes of macaws' feathers, of many colours, and adorned with plates of gold and silver'.

Atahualpa was apparently dressed much more richly than on the preceding evening; besides the *borla*, his short hair was covered with golden ornaments, and round his neck he wore a collar of large emeralds – these were more probably turquoise. The state in which he moved, the whole cavalcade blazing with gold, was calculated to impress, for Atahualpa, in his march south, had grown accustomed to using the trappings of state as the visual symbol of power to consolidate what he had gained by force. His personal retinue was of the north, *orejones* from Quito determined to impress upon the old empire their power and wealth. To them Atahualpa was more than Inca – he was the conquered North reborn. He was, in fact, surrounded by men who were devoted to him personally and for whom he represented the glorious future.

His warriors, however, were almost certainly levies from the territories he had conquered, a fact that may have had a bearing on his subsequent behaviour. The distance to be covered was not great – six kilometres, in fact – but it was long enough for Atahualpa to have second thoughts. Alone there, seated high above the crowd, he had a clear view down the causeway to the silent, empty-seeming buildings ahead. Did he feel the menace of that dead, empty town – did he sense the plot that had been hatched, the slayers waiting at their posts? He was not, like Moctezuma of the Aztecs, a member of the priesthood. He was the son of the Sun, a god himself. A god cannot shrink from such small fears. But he was also human.

 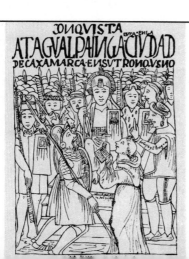

De Soto and Hernando Pizarro ride up to Atahualpa to deliver Pizarro's message left; Atahualpa enters Cajamarca, and a Spanish friar hands him the Bible right.

Half a mile short of Cajamarca he halted, gave orders for the tents to be pitched, and sent a message to Pizarro to say that he would stay there the night and enter Cajamarca in the morning.

The last moments of Inca power were now falling away like sand in an hour-glass. Some instinct, some sixth sense may have warned him of this. We do not know whether he called a council of war, but he had clearly come to the decision that he needed more time, a night at least, in which to reflect upon the situation.

The extraordinary thing is that, on receipt of a reply from Pizarro, he changed his mind again, struck his half-pitched tents, and resumed the march, this time unaccompanied by the main body of his warriors and going forward with only some six thousand Indians, all unarmed. It makes us wonder what was in that message from Pizarro. What had so goaded him that he delivered himself helpless into the hands of the Spaniards? Did Pizarro, with the deadly insight of a peasant soldier, impute cowardice and a lack of true nobility and royalty?

Atahualpa's real difficulty was that the two generals he had grown up with and trusted, Quizquiz and Challcuchima, were in the Cuzco region. Had they been with him at Cajamarca, he would probably have accepted their advice, and even in the face of such a small force, taken military precautions. But the usurper never has that innate confidence that enables him to act without regard to appearances, and though the empire was so absolutely subservient to the Inca that even the most outrageous commands, as we shall see later, would be obeyed without question, Atahualpa, at that moment of time, could not be sure. It was almost certainly lack of self-confidence, the desire to make public demonstration of his fearlessness and his godlike command of the situation, that was his undoing.

The lay-out of the Indian town was on the neat, orderly Inca state pattern – houses, streets, alleys, all in straight lines. The big triangular courtyard was in the centre, surrounded by a wall with two gateways opening on to the streets. Inside the courtyard walls were the local government buildings. These were single-storey and included, on the south-eastern side, the palace of the local *curaca*, Angasnopo. The westernmost point of the triangle touched the foot of the sacred hill of Rumy Tiana (now called the Sanctuary of Santa Apolonia).* On entering this courtyard the procession split into two parts, so that the chiefs bearing the Inca on his litter moved to a central position. There was no sign of the Spanish force, and it was Valverde, not Pizarro, who came forward to greet Atahualpa with the Bible and Crucifix and a long discourse on the Christian faith.

There are various accounts of what happened then, Garcilaso's being quite extraordinarily detailed, but since they are from Spanish sources it seems unlikely that the actual words spoken by Atahualpa would have been correctly reported –

*Records in the Biblioteca at Cajamarca show that the confusion over the shape of the 'square' was due to the fact that orders were given early in the nineteenth century for the demolition of the old triangular plaza and its replacement by a new rectangular one. Hernando Pizarro, in his letter to the Royal Audience of Santo Domingo, confirms that it was triangular.

Valverde's discourse and the Inca's replies were all passing through the Spanish 'tongue', Felipillo. Visual reporting is less open to doubt, and it seems likely that the friar did hand Atahualpa the Bible, as the authority upon which the Christian faith was based, and that the Inca did throw it to the ground. However difficult he may have found it to follow the Dominican's theological argument, he can have been under no illusion as to the intention: this miserable stranger, with his tonsured head and his cross, was urging him to renounce his own divinity in favour of a god who had been stupidly killed by his own people, and at the same time to acknowledge, in the Emperor Charles, a king greater than himself. He was to forfeit, in other words, all that he had just fought so hard to attain. His anger at this effrontery was immediate, his rejection of the Book inevitable. The proud gesture as he pointed to the sun, and the words, 'My God still lives', are probably correctly reported.

The Dominican Friar retrieved the Bible and scuttled away. The square, packed with Indians, click-clacked with the staccato sound of the Quechua language.

Atahualpa, seated head and shoulders above the clatter of speculation, may have seen the handkerchief dropped by Pizarro. He certainly saw the smoke from the cannon as it boomed out, cutting a swathe through the crowd. It was the signal, followed instantly by the battle-cry – 'Santiago!' The fire of the arquebuses was sharp and clear, like the crackle of fireworks, above the sudden din of cavalry charging; the Spanish foot poured into the square, their swords flashing in the late afternoon sun – steel at first, then dripping crimson as they hacked and hacked at the helpless wall of human bodies.

The Indian chiefs died fighting with their bare hands in defence of Atahualpa. The attendants and some of the unarmed bodyguard pressed with such panic at one part of the courtyard wall that they broke it down and fled into the country beyond, pursued by the cavalry. The butchery of those that remained trapped in the square was such that even Spanish eye-witnesses say they were hacking at the defenceless Indians for a full half hour and did not desist until the sun was behind the mountains and it was almost dark. Before then, Atahualpa's litter had crashed to the ground. Such was the blood lust of the Spaniards that it was only the intervention of Pizarro himself and some of his cavaliers that saved the Inca.

The massacre at Cajamarca on that fatal evening of November 16, 1532, has disgraced Spanish chivalry in the eyes of the world. The attack can possibly be justified in the circumstances – what else could a small, determined force do to gain the ascendancy, faced as it was by overwhelming odds? It was the brutal stupidity of the Spaniards and the whole foul record of their behaviour in Peru that history cannot stomach. The massacre has thus become symbolic of what happened later, so that the assessment of history, which has accepted without such revulsion so many similar cruelties ordered by generals far greater than Pizarro, is a correct assessment.

For the Spaniards, who had just completed a long and exhausting march across an unknown mountain range, the waiting that Saturday must have seemed interminable. It is hardly surprising that some of them had lost heart at the sight of the enormous army of Indians camped by the hot springs. But, as Pizarro bluntly told them, it was too late to retreat; their only hope was to emulate Cortés and secure the person of the Inca. This had been his plan from the beginning, and on the Friday evening he had put it to his officers in council. Zárate says the Spaniards were outnumbered by two hundred to one – 'But notwithstanding, he and all his company being haughty minded, and also of great stomach. The night following they comforted one another, putting their only confidence in God, so that then they occupied themselves in trimming their armour and other furniture, without taking any rest of sleep the whole night.' In fact, they slept, as they always did, with their arms beside them, and sentinels posted. But there was no movement from the Indian camp and the night passed quietly. At dawn Pizarro made his dispositions. The public buildings were open-doored halls, ideal for the concealment of troops. The cavalry, in two divisions under Hernando Pizarro and de Soto, occupied two of these halls, the foot soldiers a third, and Candia, with a few soldiers and the two falconets, was posted on the lower slopes of Rumy Tiana, thus commanding the open triangle of the courtyard. Pizarro kept twenty picked men to act as an independent force under his personal command.

The dispositions completed and every soldier briefed, mass was celebrated, 'and all joined with enthusiasm in the chant, *"Exsurge, Domine"* – "Rise, O Lord! and judge thine own cause" '. After that everyone went to their posts. The hours passed slowly, and as the soldiers waited, they had ample opportunity to reflect on the odds against them. It was mid-day before the look outs reported the Inca's army on the move. And then, when the procession was still half a mile away, it stopped. Tents began to be pitched. Finally the news was brought that the Inca would not enter Cajamarca till the following day. By then the tension of waiting had become intolerable.

Pedro Pizarro, the general's kinsman and page, says that the answer his master returned to Atahualpa 'deprecated his change of purpose', and added that 'he had provided everything for his entertainment and expected him that night to sup with him'. But there must have been something more to it to persuade Atahualpa to come unarmed into Cajamarca. Prescott says, 'He was too absolute in his own empire easily to suspect, and he probably could not comprehend the audacity with which a few men meditated an assault on a powerful monarch in the midst of his victorious army.' Sombrely the great historian adds, 'He did not know the character of the Spaniards.' This failure of the Indian to appreciate the single-purposed drive of the invader is a recurring theme in the Spanish conquest of the Americas, and it is difficult to understand, since both the Aztecs and the Incas had also been small in numbers when they themselves began the subjugation of their neighbours. The only explanation is that even a century of absolute power blinds the despot to the history of his own race.

And so, as the sun of the Incas set over the Andes, Atahualpa came unarmed into Cajamarca. And that night he supped with Pizarro as his captive, in one of the halls of the great courtyard where his people had been slaughtered, the smell of death and the reek of blood still in the air. 'It is the fortune of war', he is supposed to have said, much as the Moors of Granada would have said, 'It is the will of Allah.' But this, and the suggestion that he expressed admiration of Pizarro's cunning, is, of course, a Spanish version, intended to support the contention that, in doing what he did, Pizarro was only forestalling Atahualpa's own cruel intentions. Xeres is most careful to explain that the Inca's attendants had all carried arms under their cotton tunics, including stones and slings, 'all of which made it appear that they had a treacherous design'.

Whatever those intentions may have been, and there is no certainty that he was planning to destroy the Spaniards, his behaviour in captivity induces in us none of the sympathy we feel for Moctezuma. Nevertheless, we cannot avoid a sense of sadness, for the passivity of the Peruvian Indians was so ingrained that they lacked all initiative and so had no will to resist. At Cajamarca the Spaniards were allowed to loot the camp and to drive off the great flocks of Peruvian 'sheep' collected by their herdsmen to feed the Inca's army. The Indian warriors seemed stunned into immobility; finally they melted away without making any attempt to rescue Atahualpa.

It was unbelievable. Pizarro suddenly found the great empire wide open. It had all been achieved by a stroke of luck in which not a single Spaniard had lost his life. Indeed, none of them had even been wounded, except Pizarro himself, who had received a sword cut on the hand whilst defending Atahualpa from the blood lust of his own men.

> In the royal baths, they found five thousand women, of whom they did not fail to take advantage, despite the fact that the women were sad and weary; they also took possession of many fine, large tents and all kinds of provisions; clothing, household linens, valuable tableware, and vases, one of which weighed one hundred kilograms in gold; Atahualpa's tableware alone, which was entirely of gold and silver, was worth one hundred thousand ducats.

With the wives and attendants of Atahualpa, they brought in so many Indian men and women that even the foot soldiers found themselves with a retinue of servants. They were more interested, however, in the gold and silver looted from the pavilions of the Inca and the tents of his *orejones*; there was a great deal of very large, very heavy plate, also some unusually large emeralds.

Atahualpa, who appears to have made no attempt to get a message out to his generals at Cuzco to destroy the Spaniards, presumably because he had been warned that such action would cost him his life, was quick to take advantage of their greed at the expense of his people. He proposed that, in exchange for his freedom, one of the halls should be filled with gold 'as high as he could reach'. Thus Pizarro was offered the same very advantageous deal that Ferdinand had proposed to the Moors after the fall of the city of Málaga forty-five years before. Like Ferdinand, he was convinced that such a huge ransom could never be met, for the hall was twenty-two feet long and seventeen feet broad, and the line he drew in red around the walls was over seven feet above the floor. The plan, however, would mean that, instead of secreting the empire's wealth, the Indians themselves would collect it and transport it to the Spaniard's camp. To make absolutely certain that the terms of ransom would never be fully met, Pizarro insisted that an adjoining hall, rather smaller in size, be filled twice over with silver. Atahualpa agreed, only insisting that the gold and silver should be piled in the form in which it arrived and that his people should be given two months in which to deliver it. The terms of ransom were recorded by the notary, and Atahualpa immediately issued the necessary instructions to his *chasquis*.

In this way Atahualpa bought time. Strangely, he never seemed to doubt that Pizarro would keep his side of the bargain. Presumably he thought that somehow in those two months he would be able to escape, rejoin his main army, and kill the Spaniards – hopes that were presumably based on his experience of Indian levies. In this again he underrated the Spaniards, and particularly their leader, whose peasant cunning matched his own.

Once the order for the delivery of the treasure had gone out, Pizarro played his second card. Atahualpa's freedom was one thing, but if he had to free him, there was no reason why it should be as Inca. The true-born Inca was still alive, and Garcilaso may be right when he says that de Soto and del Barco visited Huáscar on their way to Cuzco, and that, after speaking of the injustice done him by his brother, Huáscar offered three times the ransom Atahualpa had contracted to provide – 'it will not be up to any line drawn on the wall, but up to the ceiling that I shall fill the room, because I know where the incalculable riches amassed by my father and all his predecessors are hidden; whereas my brother does not know this, and he is therefore reduced to stripping our temples of their ornaments in order to fulfil his promise'.

Atahualpa was kept in captivity left; *but he managed to send out orders for the rival Inca, Huáscar, to be put to death* right.

This suggestion, reported back to Pizarro, would almost certainly have reached Atahualpa, and Zárate may be correct in suggesting that Atahualpa endeavoured to discover the reaction of the Spanish general to Huáscar's death by pretending that it had already happened and feigning sadness at the news:

> The Governor hearing his sorrowful complaint, comforted him, and bid him be of good cheer, saying moreover, that death was a thing natural. . . . When Atahualpa perceived that the Governor took the matter so slightly, he then fully determined to execute the thing which he had devised, and sent privily to the Captains, who had the keeping of Huáscar, express commission to kill him, which was forthwith committed with such speed, that it was never certainly known whether he was slain in the time that Atahualpa made his feigned mourning, or afterwards, of which evil success the principal fault was laid to Captain Soto and Pedro de Barrio, who were so precise in their determined journey to Cuzco.

Whether this is correctly reported or not, it was obviously to Pizarro's advantage to play the Inca-maker, and it was undoubtedly his decision to set up an arbitration court to decide who was the rightful Inca that was the direct cause of Huáscar's death. When it was reported to him that Huáscar had been murdered Pizarro was at first incredulous, then furious. By this stroke Atahualpa had ensured that the Spaniards were dealing with the one and only Inca. However surprised and indignant Atahualpa may have pretended to be at the news of his brother's death, there can be little doubt that he ordered it. Fratricide, as Prescott points out, was not a particularly heinous crime in the Indian world, since the Lord-Incas were polygamous and fathered many sons. For the Christians, however, it was different, particularly if Garcilaso is right in saying that Huáscar 'was put to death in a very cruel manner. His executioners cut him to pieces, and it is not known what they did with him afterwards. According to Indian folk legend, they ate him, out of rage. However, Father Acosta writes that his remains were burned.' That he was burned is most unlikely, since in the Indian religion he would then have had no life after death. However it was, the memory of Atahualpa's action no doubt helped to salve the consciences of the Spaniards when the final act in this tragedy came to be staged.

Several weeks passed, the tension mounting in the Spanish camp, before the treasure began to trickle in. The distances were long and every sheet of gold had to be transported by llama or on the backs of the Indian carriers. First came sheets ripped from the nearer temples and great gold plates weighing a quarter of a hundredweight. Packed down tight they took up little space, and the ransom pile grew slowly. The soldiers, with nothing to do but guard the Inca and gamble on their prospects, began to complain. As a result of representations to Atahualpa that he was not keeping his side of the bargain, it was agreed that three Spaniards should be sent to Cuzco to oversee the dismantling of the gold plating of the great Temple of the Sun. This was the most important temple of the Inca world and part of it can still be seen in the cloisters of the church of Santo Domingo. Garcilaso has has described it in detail:

> The main door of the temple opened to the north, as it does today, and there were several others, of less importance, which were used for services in the temple. All of these doors were covered with plaques of gold and the walls of the building were crowned on the outside with a gold band, three feet wide, that went all around it.
>
> The temple was prolonged by a square cloister with an adjoining wall, and crowned by a gold band like the one we have just described. The Spaniards replaced this by a plaster band of the same width that could be seen on the walls, which were still standing, when I left Peru. The three other sides of the cloister gave on to five large square rooms, that had no communication between them, and were roofed over in the form of a pyramid.
>
> The first of these rooms was dedicated to the Moon, the bride of the Sun, and for this reason it was nearest to the main building. It was entirely panelled with silver, and a likeness of the Moon, with the face of a woman, decorated it in the same way that the Sun decorated the larger building. The Indians offered no sacrifices to her, but they came to visit her and begged her intercession, as to the sister-bride of the Sun and to the mother of all the Incas. They called her Mamaquilla, which means our mother the Moon. The bodies of queens were laid away in this Temple, just as those of the kings were kept in the other. Mama Occlo, the mother of Huayna Capac, occupied the place of honour, before the likeness of the Moon, because she had given birth to such a son.
>
> The room nearest that of the Moon was devoted to Venus, to the Pleiades and to all the stars. As we said before, Venus was honoured as the Sun's page, who accompanies him on his way, now following him, now preceding him. The Indians considered the other stars as servants of the Moon, and this was why they were represented near her. The constellations of the Pleiades was particularly revered because of the regularity and perfection of its well-grouped design.
>
> This room was hung with silver, like that of the Moon, and the ceiling was dotted with stars, like the firmament. The next room was dedicated to lightning, and to thunder, which were both expressed by the single name, *illapa* . . . The fourth room was devoted to the rainbow, which they said had descended from the Sun . . . the fifth and last room was reserved for the high priest and his assistants.

The three emissaries sent to Cuzco were treated like gods and, according to some accounts, behaved abominably, even ravishing the Virgins of the Sun. Zárate was one of them and it seems most unlikely that he and his two companions, alone in the great city of the Incas, would have risked their lives so unnecessarily. True, Pizarro dispatched de Soto and del Barco to Cuzco, but this was probably because he felt the gold was not coming through fast enough. In any case, it was primarily an embassy to Huáscar. Meanwhile, though the Indian chiefs had been coming in from further and further afield to demonstrate their loyalty – even the chief and high priest of Pachacamac, two hundred and fifty miles away on the coast – the Spaniards were in a state of nervous tension, rumour was rife in the camp and there was talk of an attack gathering at Huamachuco sixty miles to the south.

On January 14, 1533, Hernando Pizarro was dispatched with twenty horse and ten or twelve foot soldiers 'to ascertain the truth of these reports, and hurry the arrival of the gold'. The reports proved unfounded. He sent gold off under escort and then set out on the first of those fantastic marches that the Spaniards make so light of in their reports. His first objective was Pachacamac itself. 'It took us twenty-two days', Hernando Pizarro reports laconically, and he follows this with a brief account of the mountain roads – 'a thing worth seeing' – the stone bridges, the mines, the towns. 'It is a cold climate, it snows and there is much rain.' It was 'winter' in the Sierra, yet he says nothing about the difficulties, the hardships – in fact, the horses' shoes wore out on the mountain roads and for lack of iron they re-shod with silver. Miguel de Estete's report – he was inspector of gold on the expedition – gives the full itinerary; they stopped at seventeen towns in the thirty days which, by his reckoning, it took them to reach Pachacamac, and at twenty-two towns on the return journey, which took much longer – fifty-four days – because they doubled back across snow-covered passes to Jauja.

It never seemed to occur to Hernando Pizarro that he was being over-reckless, yet Jauja had a population of a hundred thousand and was where Atahualpa's general, Challcuchima, was camped with 35,000 warriors. Jauja, he thought, would be a good place for a settlement – 'in all my travels I did not see a better site'. He remained there five days, and 'during all that time they did nothing but dance and sing, and hold great drinking feasts'. This carnival of drinking and dancing is still held to celebrate the rainy season. And all he says about his 'capture' of Atahualpa's general is: 'The captain did not want to come with me, but when he saw I was determined to take him, he came of his own accord.' Even allowing for Hernando Pizarro's incredible self-confidence, and for the fact that the Spaniards were received by the Indians as though they were gods, it seems hardly possible that he could have secured the person of one of Atahualpa's most formidable chiefs and immobilized an army of 35,000 warriors with a force of no more than thirteen horse and about nine soldiers. He must surely have also had the support of pro-Huáscar warriors, though the presence of Indian auxiliaries is not admitted until the Spaniards themselves were at each other's throats.

The Spaniards scoured the countryside for gold, making fantastic marches across the mountains left. *Peruvian ornaments of precious metal: a gold whistling vase* right; *a silver alpaca* far right.

Meanwhile, at Cajamarca, Pizarro had at last been joined by Almagro, with the reinforcements for which he had waited so anxiously before his desperate march into the Andes. Almagro had reached the Spanish settlement of San Miguel in December 1532 with a hundred and fifty troops and eighty-four horses, the three large vessels with which he had sailed from Panama having been joined by three small caravels from Nicaragua. Prescott states that he joined Pizarro in Cajamarca 'about the middle of February, 1533', but according to Xeres the link-up did not occur until April 14. The latter seems more likely since otherwise Pizarro's failure to march with his army on Cuzco is difficult to understand; unless, of course, current Peruvian thinking is correct – that his immobility at this stage was primarily due to the need to wait upon the support of tribes hostile to Atahualpa.

It was certainly April by the time Hernando and the Cuzco emissaries had returned to Cajamarca. By then the combined forces of the two commanders were becoming very restless. Over five months had passed since Atahualpa's capture and still the gold room had not been filled to the ransom height. Nevertheless, the treasure amassed was enormous, a total of 1,326,539 gold pesos, and Pizarro felt that the division of the spoils could not be delayed any longer. Almagro's soldiers inevitably wanted a share, but it was finally agreed that, since they had not been a party to the original contract with Atahualpa, they would only share in future spoils. It was then generally assumed that further great quantities of gold would be acquired when they occupied Cuzco.

This arrangement was undoubtedly facilitated by the decision to dispatch Hernando to Spain. Almagro, the bluff, dedicated soldier, had always disliked the arrogant, much flashier Hernando; and to send him back to report to the Emperor, with a part of the royal fifth in the form of the finest examples of Indian craftsmanship, was not only sensible, but followed the precedent set by Cortés. The total value of the consignment was 100,000 gold pesos; but what happened to this nobody knows. Like the consignment Cortés sent, which fell into the hands of the French, it has disappeared without trace. There were 'goblets, ewers, salvers, vases of every shape and size, ornaments and utensils for the temples of the royal palaces, tiles and plates for the decoration of public edifices, curious imitations of different plants and animals. Among the plants, the most beautiful was the Indian corn, in which the golden ear was sheathed in its broad leaves of

silver from which hung a rich tassel of threads of the same precious metal.' There was also a fountain 'which sent up a sparkling jet of gold, while birds and animals of the same material played in the waters at its base'.

With Hernando's departure the two commanders were, temporarily at least, reunited. The work of rendering down into ingots the contents of the ransom halls now began. The final division of the spoils, after deduction of the royal fifth, was as follows: Pizarro – 57,222 pesos of gold and 2,350 marks of silver, plus the Inca's throne of solid gold valued at 25,000 pesos; Hernando – 31,080 pesos of gold and 2,350 marks of silver; de Soto – 17,740 pesos of gold and 724 marks of silver; the sixty cavalry men shared 532,800 pesos of gold and 21,729 marks of silver; the hundred and five soldiers shared about 202,020 pesos of gold and 8,190 marks of silver. Almagro's men got 20,000 pesos, but the poor wretches who had been left to garrison San Miguel – apart from the nine who had turned back from the march into the Andes, they were all men who had been wounded or lost their health in the march down the coast – got a miserable 15,000 pesos. After allowing for the royal fifth and 2,000 pesos donated to the church of San Francisco in Cajamarca, there is 178,369 gold pesos unaccounted for. Presumably this covered the costs of the expedition and the share due to Almagro and Espinosa (for whom Luque had been acting) as the original partners.

An interesting sidelight to this division of the spoils was its effect upon the cost of living amongst men isolated in the Sierra who had to maintain themselves at their own expense. Horses changed hands at from 2,500 to 3,300 gold pesos. A jar of wine cost 60 pesos, a pair of high boots or a pair of shoes 30 to 40 pesos, a cloak 100 to 120, a sword 40 to 50 – even a string of garlic fetched half a peso and a sheet of paper was 10 pesos. Little store was set by the gold and silver now it was in circulation; 'If one man owed anything to another, he paid it in a lump of gold, without weighing the gold, and being quite indifferent whether it was worth double the amount of the debt or not.'

Now that the ransom room was empty there remained only the problem of Atahualpa. Through the good offices of de Soto, who seems to have been more of a gentleman than the rest of the adventurers, he reasonably demanded his release on the grounds that he had acted throughout in good faith, even though the full amount of the ransom had not been collected. Pizarro was apparently prepared to accept this, since he had his notary record that the Inca was acquitted of 'further obligations in respect of the ransom' and had it proclaimed publicly throughout the camp. But that was all. He ignored his side of the bargain and continued to hold the Inca captive on the grounds of security.

Who started the rumour of an Indian uprising at this stage is not certain. Prescott makes the point that there were Indians in the camp who had supported Huáscar and were, therefore, hostile to Atahualpa, and he also refers to the 'malignant temper' of the interpreter, Felipillo, who was supposed to have been engaged in a love affair with one of the royal concubines. But in view of what followed, the real source was almost certainly Pizarro himself. Challcuchima was interrogated and flatly denied that there was any substance in the rumours. Nevertheless they continued, and the soldiers, imputing to the Indians their own motives, conceived that they were after the gold. Gold has always been a basis for bloodshed amongst those who value it; and men of property, as each soldier now was, are sensitive to the slenderest rumour that may rob them of their wealth. The guards were increased, the men slept with their arms beside them and kept their horses saddled and bridled. And for Almagro's men, who had got so little reward for helping to guard the Inca, the duty was irksome – their golden future lay in Cuzco, and they wanted nothing but to begin the march.

The mood of the camp was rapidly building up to the point where the men themselves would demand what Pizarro wanted most – to be rid of Atahualpa. The Inca had now become an encumbrance. He had served his purpose. The expedition had paid off. Pizarro had the gold. Now he wanted power. An empire was within his grasp, but as long as the Inca lived he constituted a rallying point for Indian resistance. His death had become both a political and a tactical necessity.

Pizarro's first move was to dispatch de Soto, the one man who might effectively oppose his plan, with a small force to Huamachuco, which rumour had again given as the place where the Indian forces were gathering. De Soto almost certainly undertook this mission voluntarily, since he was well disposed to Atahualpa and presumably took the view that the rumours were unfounded. With his departure the way was clear for Atahualpa's murder. But for the record Pizarro had still to make it appear that he was yielding to the demands of his men, and there must be legal justification. The first was not difficult to achieve. Rumour is an insidious weapon where men have been locked up too long in a camp high in a lonely, hostile world. For the second, the Inquisition had already provided the precedent. Thus, yielding, apparently reluctantly, to the clamour of his men, he set up a court, with himself and Almagro as judges. The twelve charges included usurpation of the royal *borla* of the Incas, the murder of Huáscar, incitement to insurrection, even misuse of the revenues of the crown following the conquest of his country by lavishing them on his family and friends. But the really vital charges were that he was an adulterer, in that he had many wives, and that he worshipped idols. Thus the case was given a religious twist – 'a badly contrived and worse-written document, devised by a factious and unprincipled priest, a clumsy notary without conscience, and others of like stamp, who were all concerned in this villainy': that is the verdict of one Spanish writer. But he does not accuse Pizarro, the prime mover and stage manager of the whole horrid farce.

The 'trial' was a summary one, the result a foregone conclusion. Atahualpa had the benefit of a 'counsel', but the prosecutor had the benefit of Felipillo, who interpreted the answers given by Indian witnesses for his own ends. Atahualpa was found guilty, but of which charges we do not know. Certainly the religious charges were proved, since the sentence was one of death by burning. However, Pizarro did not have it all his own way. Twelve of the Spanish captains, headed by the Chaves brothers of Trujillo, protested at this travesty of justice. They eventually acquiesced on grounds of expediency. 'I myself saw the general weep', Pedro Pizarro writes. He could afford a few crocodile tears, for two hours after sundown on July 16, 1533,* Atahualpa was carried by torchlight to the stake.

It was a true *auto de fe*, for when he realized that his body was to be consumed by fire – a fact which would damn him utterly in his life after death – he agreed to become a Christian in return for the kind favour of being garrotted. He was christened Juan de Atahualpa, and then strangled like a common criminal. Even his request that his body be taken to Quito was ignored. It was buried in the newly-constructed cemetery at Cajamarca, and his women, who according to Inca custom wished to die with him, were excluded from the funeral, which was held in the church of San Francisco, Pizarro and his officers all in deep mourning.

A few days later de Soto returned. There had been no gathering of Indian warriors at Huamachuco. No uprising had been planned. 'I have met with nothing on the road but demonstrations of good will, and all is quiet.' Angrily he pointed out to Pizarro that if Atahualpa had to be brought to trial, then he should have been sent to stand his trial in Spain before the court of the Emperor. The argument was pointless. Atahualpa was dead.

Now at last the Spaniards were free to march on Cuzco. But it was as though at Cajamarca they had called down a curse upon themselves. The manner of Atahualpa's capture, the charade of his trial and execution may have been expedient, but it was also symbolic of the nature of these gold-hungry adventurers. Throughout the months when they had been waiting on the arrival of the ransom gold they had been living off the prudently accumulated wealth of the Indians, slaughtering something around 150 llamas a day as though there were no end to the flocks of these animals, plundering the army supply depot at Cajamarca for cloth, demanding and getting a steady supply of food from local chiefs. They

---

*Prescott gives the date as August 29. The earlier date is that given by Padre Rubén Vargas Ugarte of Lima in his *Historia del Perú* Vol I and is based on MSS in the hands of Dr Rafael Loredo.

After the murder of Atahualpa left, *the Spaniards completed the conquest of the country* right.

were men without thought to the future and the curse they carried with them was the curse of their own greed. They were embarked now upon the destruction of a whole brilliant civilization without possessing the organization to replace it with anything comparable.

At Jauja, Pizarro had Challcuchima put in irons on the grounds that it was he who had raised the country against them. The Spaniards were meeting with organized resistance now, but it was Atahualpa's death, not Challcuchima, that was the cause of it. Pizarro's proposed puppet Inca, Toparca, died mysteriously. Again Challcuchima was blamed. High in the lonely valley of Xaquixaguana, about a dozen miles north of Cuzco, Pizarro had him 'tried' and burned at the stake.

On November 15, 1533, just a year after they had arrived at Cajamarca, the Spaniards entered the Inca capital. Here, and on the march, they accumulated a further 580,200 gold pesos' worth of loot, including ten planks of silver, twenty feet long, one foot broad and two or three inches thick. But now in their greed they were beginning to defraud their own Emperor, for the loot must have been considerably more valuable if, as Pedro Pizarro says, each of the 110 horsemen got 8,000 and each of the 460 soldiers 4,000 pesos. At Cuzco another puppet, a legitimate son of Huayna Capac, named Manco, was crowned with the *borla* as Inca, and shortly afterwards, on March 24, 1534, Cuzco was inaugurated as a Spanish settlement by the election of municipal officers. Two of Pizarro's brothers were among the eight *regidores*, Valverde became Bishop of Cuzco and Pizarro himself Governor of the whole province. Meanwhile, the war clouds were gathering. Quizquiz, the last of Atahualpa's generals, was finally moving to the attack. Almagro went out to meet him, accompanied by a large levy of warriors led by the new Inca. Since Quizquiz's force was composed mainly of men from the north, Manco and his warriors were eager for battle. Quizquiz retreated to Jauja, and there Almagro, that old war horse of countless battles, destroyed his army utterly. The wretched general fled to Quito and was finally murdered by his own men because he insisted on continuing a war which they regarded as futile.

His destruction should have marked the final pacification of Peru. Instead, the curse of Spanish greed was only just beginning to work.

The first sign of the terrible retribution to come was the sudden appearance of Pedro de Alvarado in the north. This was the same red-bearded, reckless captain who had lost Cortés the city of Mexico, the hero of Alvarado's Leap. Now, in March 1534, he arrived off the Ecuador coast with a large fleet which had been fitted out for yet another attempt to reach the Spice Islands. Peruvian gold, however, had proved a greater lure than pepper, and he was secure at home in his recent marriage to a noble heiress. He had with him two hundred and fifty horse and the same number of foot soldiers, and after crossing the Andes in the depth of winter and in the face of an eruption, he marched on Quito. But whilst he had been struggling through the Andes, Benalcázar, who commanded the

garrison at San Miguel, had taken to the Andean highway with a hundred and
forty Spaniards and a large force of Indians, and by an incredible forced march
reached Quito before him. Whether Benalcázar ever considered joining him is
by no means certain, but if he did, he changed his mind when Almagro appeared
on the scene. Pizarro had sent his partner to reinforce the garrison at San Miguel
as soon as he received the news of Alvarado's landing, but, finding the city
almost empty of troops, Almagro had immediately started out in pursuit of
Benalcázar. The two captains joined forces at Riobamba, Benalcázar maintaining
he had no intention of deserting to Alvarado. When Alvarado arrived the two
forces mingled amicably and the final result was that for 100,000 pesos, to be
paid ostensibly as the price of his arms, equipment and fleet, Alvarado would
gracefully retire.

The effect of this settlement was to make Pizarro absolute master of Peru. But
the writing was on the wall. Where Alvarado had led others would follow. The
lure of gold was drawing the adventurers south, and the gifts Hernando had
taken to Spain would bring more adventurers, as well as government officials in
droves to administer laws that would gradually strip the conquistadors of most
of what they had fought to gain.

Nevertheless, Pizarro was lord of the greatest of all the Spanish American
provinces for eight years. Had he been possessed of any real administrative
ability, he could have had the whole-hearted co-operation of the Indians. They
were a stoic race, accustomed to passive subservience rather than active loyalty
to the central government of their Incas. With little effort, he could have turned
their indoctrinated obedience to the support of his own administration, and,
standing as he was at the uttermost limits of the home government's reach, could
have made his position impregnable. But the seeds of disaster were ingrained in
his own nature and in the nature of the men who had come out with him. His
soldiery mistook Peruvian subservience to authority for cowardice, and just as
cringing encourages the bully, so the passivity of the Indians brought out the
worst in them.

No provision was made for the maintenance of the advanced system of irrigation
on which the country depended for its crops. The flocks of llamas were slaughtered
in feast after feast without regard for the future. Wherever the Spaniards went the
story was one of looting, rape and murder, and the profligate waste of the carefully
accumulated wealth of the Inca storehouses. Worse still, from the Spanish point of
view, the differences between Almagro and Pizarro had only been driven under-
ground in the obvious need to present a common front to an enemy numerically
vastly superior.

In the following year, the country appearing more or less settled, the differences
between the two partners came out into the open once again. Whilst Pizarro was
on the coast, founding his new capital of Lima, Almagro was governing in Cuzco.
His agents had accompanied Hernando Pizarro to Spain, and as a result he was now

Machu Picchu, the last refuge of the Incas.

informed that the Emperor Charles had given him command of a huge slice of
territory extending for two hundred leagues to the south of Pizarro's province.
He was thus by royal command made independent of Pizarro. Charles and his
advisers had little real knowledge of their distant empire. At this early stage
there was almost certainly no map, so that the spheres of influence – distances
were all measured from the island of Puná – were extremely vague. Almagro
claimed that Cuzco was in his sphere. Pizarro ordered his brothers, Gonzalo and
Juan, to resume command. The city was split into factions. Even the Indians took
sides. Not until June 12, 1535, was the matter finally resolved and their differences
patched up, the two contracting to pursue their aims amicably, sharing the costs
and the rewards of all future conquests. Almagro thereupon advanced into Chile
and for nearly two years disappeared from the scene as he endeavoured to take
command of the area his Emperor had allotted him and, at the same time, to satisfy
the demands of his own men for their full share of the loot of conquest.

Meantime, at Cuzco, the patience of the Indians was finally exhausted. Manco
himself was involved. He escaped from the city and joined the insurgents. Peru
was at last in revolt against the senseless brutality of its foreign masters. Juan
Pizarro, searching the surrounding country for the missing Inca, was forced to
retreat from the banks of the Yucay river. Swarms of armed warriors now advanced
on Cuzco, and for the first time the Spaniards in Peru were faced with the same
fanatical opposition that Cortés had battled with in the Aztec city of Mexico.
The siege, which began in February 1536, lasted for nearly six months. Most of
Cuzco was destroyed by fire. Repeated attempts by Pizarro to relieve the garrison
failed. The whole country was in revolt, and it was only the impregnable strength
of the great fortress of Sacsahuamán that enabled the Spaniards to hold out.
Then, in August 1536, the revolt subsided as suddenly as it had begun, the
young Inca having exhausted the supplies of the storehouses which had kept his
army in the field for so much longer than the traditional three weeks. But the
country remained in arms, the Spaniards mured up in Cuzco and isolated on the
coast.

This was still the situation when Almagro returned from Chile by way of the
Atacama desert. His march is not to be compared with that of Topa Inca Yupanqui,
but it was still a considerable achievement for a force that numbered about five
hundred soldiers, and his men had got little reward for the incredible hardships
they had suffered. Hernando Pizarro was now back from Spain and acting as
governor of Cuzco. Discovering that the young Inca Manco was camped with a
considerable force of warriors not far from Cuzco, Almagro immediately arranged
a meeting. He probably had some sort of an alliance in mind, but Manco, with the
memory of what had happened to Atahualpa, suspected a trap; he attacked
Almagro's men with fifteen thousand warriors. He was defeated and Almagro
turned his attention to Cuzco itself. Even now he seems to have been unwilling to
be the cause of internecine strife between men of his own race, particularly with

*Baroque churches: the legacy of Spanish rule. The Capilla del Rosario in the church of
Santo Domingo, Puebla, Mexico.*

the whole country still in arms. His men, however, thinking in more personal terms, broke the uneasy truce agreed between Hernando and their leader, and on the night of April 8, 1537, they invaded the city. The Pizarros and more than a dozen other Spanish captains were imprisoned. Almagro, now in command of Cuzco, sent emissaries to demand obedience of the only Spanish commander who could threaten him – Alonso de Alvarado, who commanded a force as big as his own at Jauja. His emissaries were arrested. Almagro marched and at the battle of Abancay on July 12 forced Alvarado to surrender. But Pizarro himself was now moving up from the coast with 450 men, half of them cavalry. Almagro had a thousand men, but despite his advantage in number, he did not fight. Once again the quarrel was patched up; Almagro would take over in Cuzco and Hernando Pizarro would be released on the understanding that he left for Spain again within six weeks.

This is one of the dirtiest double-crosses of the conquest. Hernando did not leave for Spain, and the uneasy agreement, arranged on November 13, 1537, lasted only long enough for Pizarro to gather his forces. He left the conduct of the campaign to his brothers, and on April 26, 1538, at the battle of Las Salinas, Almagro was defeated. This bloody battle, in which a hundred and fifty Spaniards died, lasted a short two hours. Almagro himself was captured alive. He was tried on July 8 and subsequently executed. Zárate says Hernando Pizarro 'caused his throat to be cut', but there is reason to believe that the means of death was the same as that used for the murder of Atahualpa – the garrotte. In any case, it was a nice reward for fighting his partner's battles for him over a period of almost five years. For this nasty expression of his long enmity of Almagro, Hernando Pizarro was ultimately arrested when he paid a second visit to Spain. He was imprisoned in the fortress of Medina del Campo, and it was twenty years before he was finally released.

The home government was now actively interesting itself in Peru. Every report coming in from this outpost of empire indicated that conditions there were chaotic. The chief sufferers, as in all Spain's colonial territories, were the wretched Indians. The Inca Manco was still in revolt, moving from one hidden and impenetrable fortress city to another. One of his hide-outs was undoubtedly Machu Picchu, and anyone who has visited the remains of this 'lost' city will readily appreciate how impossible it was for the Spaniards to deal with a leader who had now learned the lesson of guerilla tactics. Typical of the period is the story of Pizarro's attempted meeting with Manco. The Inca had again suggested the Yucay valley, and Pizarro, before going with a strong bodyguard to the meeting place, had sent an African slave to Manco with the customary gifts. This man had been taken by Manco's warriors and murdered. On hearing of this, Pizarro had one of the Inca's wives, a young and very beautiful girl, bound naked to a tree in front of his assembled army, beaten half to death and then shot full of arrows. As Manco was believed to be extremely fond of the girl it was hardly the most sensible way to bring about a settlement.

The terraces of Machu Picchu, the inaccessible Inca fortress that was never discovered by the Spaniards.

However, during the next two years, Pizarro did manage to tighten his grip on the country. Two expeditions, in particular, stand out: Pedro de Valdivia's march into Chile and Gonzalo Pizarro's two-year expedition in the north. This latter included a piece of original exploration that is almost incredible, and emphasizes once again the quite extraordinary fearlessness of the Spaniards in their driving urge to explore new territory. Having discovered the Napo river, one of the headwater tributaries of the Amazon, Gonzalo built a small brigantine and sent one of his captains, Francisco de Orellana, ahead by this means, to forage for food, whilst the main body continued to fight their way along the river bank. But Orellana 'found the current of such force, that in short time he came to the meeting of the two great Rivers, without finding any kind of sustenance: and also considering what way he had made in three days, he found that in a whole year it was not possible to return that way again . . .' He not only reached the mouth of the Amazon, but took his forest-made vessel out to sea, sailing north to the island of Cubagua in the Caribbean – an almost unbelievable feat. Gonzalo was furious. His men were starving and he was in bad country, amongst a people so primitive that they 'used the forepart of their privy members, to be tied with a string of cotton wool betwixt their legs, and made fast at their girdling: and the women had certain rags to cover their secrets, but no other kind of clothing'. It took the main body of the expedition over a year to struggle back to Quito, where they arrived in June 1542 – 'almost naked, for long since with the great waters of rain, and otherwise, their clothes were rotted from their bodies, so that now each of them had but only two small deerskins, which covered their foreparts, and also their hinder parts: some had left old rotten breeches, and shoes made of raw deerskins: their swords wanted scabbards and were spoiled with rust: they came all on foot, their arms and legs were scratched with shrubs and briars, their features seemed like unto dead men, so that scarcely their friends and old acquaintance knew them . . .' Eighty of them had perished, and of the four thousand Indian auxiliaries that had accompanied them more than half were dead.

This extraordinary expedition is perhaps the highlight of Pizarro's administration in Peru, for it shows the Spaniards at their best – brave, fearless and possessed of remarkable fortitude in adversity. But whilst Gonzalo's Spaniards were staggering up out of the streaming forests of the Amazon, the fortunes of the Pizarro family were reaching their inevitable climax. Almagro's men – the men who had marched into Chile and had got so little for their hardships – were becoming increasingly restless. The focal point for their disaffection was Almagro's son, whom Pizarro had stripped of the lands and Indians he had inherited from his father. There was news of a royal commission headed by a judge being sent out to examine the situation in Peru, but it did not arrive until August 1541, two years after Almagro's death. Pride was all that was left to the adherents of the Young Almagro as they walked the streets of Lima, ragged, consumed with hatred for Pizarro and plotting murder.

Sunday, June 26, 1541, was the day appointed. Like the plot against Cortés two decades earlier, everything seems to have gone wrong for the conspirators. Their plot was disclosed to Pizarro, but there had been so many others that he took little notice of it. He told his judge, Velázquez, and decided not to attend mass; that was all; and though Velázquez made no effort to arrest the conspirators, they guessed that their plan was discovered when Pizarro failed to attend the church service.

They were too embittered, however, to be turned from their purpose. About mid-day they entered the Governor's palace. Pizarro was at dinner with a number of his captains, the bishop elect of Quito, the judge Velázquez and his half-brother Martín de Alcántara. They were unarmed and most of them escaped into the garden. Pizarro called to one of his officers to bar the door. Instead, the man tried to parley with the assassins. He was cut down, and Alcántara, who was helping Pizarro into his armour, went with two pages to defend the entrance to the inner room. Pizarro flung aside his unfastened cuirass, seized his sword, and wrapping a cloak round his left arm, went to their assistance. But they were already wounded. Alcántara collapsed. The assassins then turned on Pizarro,

> who fought so long with them that with very weariness, his sword fell out of his hands, and then they slew him with a prick of a rapier through his throat: and when he was fallen to the ground, and his wind failing him, he cried unto God for mercy, and when he had so done, he made a cross on the ground and kissed it, and then incontinent yielded up the ghost.

It is very doubtful whether he was given time to thus make his peace with God since other accounts suggest that the assassins immediately closed in for the kill, plunging their swords into the body of the man they hated.

It was a fitting end to the least well equipped of all the great conquerors of history. In the name of Christ, he destroyed a fruitful empire, bringing nothing but disaster, contributing nothing. He represents the dark side of man – Man the Destroyer. And yet we cannot help having a sneaking admiration for him – his blind determination, his courage and endurance, his incredible luck. The odds he faced were fantastic – in the numbers of his opponents, in the climate and terrain, above all in the unknown seas which his three expeditions penetrated. Despite his base qualities, Francisco Pizarro remains a perversely heroic figure.

PART FOUR

The
Aftermath

Symbol of Spanish conquest. A detail from the facade of San Agustin, Lima, Peru.

The Aftermath

THOUGH PERU AND CHILE were the furthest reaches of the Spanish colonial empire, much of the interior of South America still remained to be subdued and pacified. Nevertheless, with the assassination of Pizarro in 1541, the age of the conquistadors was drawing to its end. The period of discovery and conquest had been relatively short. In half a century a whole new world, vast in size and covering two continents, had been opened up. But most of the men whose qualities had made such extraordinary achievements possible were not of the stuff of empire-builders. Even the role of explorer had been purely incidental. Their business was fighting; and success did not break them of the habit – most of them died violent deaths in the power struggles that followed upon each new conquest. Consolidation of the empire they gained devolved upon others.

In Peru, the death of Pizarro created a power vacuum that was filled first by the Young Almagro and then by Gonzalo Pizarro. Both these men set themselves up as warlords, not only in defiance of orders from Spain, but in armed opposition to the crown's representatives. Almagro's youth and lack of experience was against him, and he was inhibited in his conflict with Vaca de Castro, who had officially been designated governor in the event of Pizarro's death, by his inherent loyalty to the crown. When it came to the crunch he was faced with one of the most terrible of the old-type conquistadors – Francisco de Carbajal. Carbajal was old and fat. He 'had a jest for everything – for the misfortunes of others, and for his own. He looked on life as a farce – though he too often made it a tragedy'. He is credited with a fantastic number of executions, but men followed him recklessly, and it was this that turned the tide of battle on the plains of Chupas. Young Almagro was defeated and executed, and under Vaca de Castro's firm administration the country had peace for a time.

The authorities at home, however, did not know this, for communications with Peru were very slow. The reports they had were all of civil wars, murder, and the reckless destruction of Indian life and property. To deal with the situation they appointed Blasco Núñez Vela as viceroy, and sent him out with a Royal Audience of four judges to administer a new and moderate code of laws, the result of Las

Casas' pleadings. But by the time the viceroy reached Lima, Gonzalo Pizarro had abandoned his exploitation of the silver mines at Potosí and had moved to Cuzco as the acknowledged leader of all the dissident conquistadors. Supported by Carbajal, he advanced on Lima. The coup d'état that followed was utterly bloodless, the four judges of the Audiencia appointing Gonzalo governor-general and rescinding the New Laws until they could receive further instructions from Spain.

Every boat from the Indies was now carrying to Spain rumours of the disaffection in Peru; and in 1545 the Emperor appointed a new viceroy, Pedro de la Gasca. But it was July before Gasca reached the Isthmus of Panama and by then Núñez had been defeated, his head lopped from his body on the field of battle. Gonzalo Pizarro was lord of Peru, Ecuador and Chile, with a first-class colonial army committed by self-interest to his support, and a fleet under Hinojosa commanding the whole western littoral of South America. Gasca played the only card he possessed – the personal authority of the Emperor. Time and his quiet confidence did the rest. His political methods were devious and, as Prescott says, he possessed 'a moral power stronger than his (Gonzalo's) steel-clad battalions'. Letters dispatched to Lima offered pardon, but no guarantee that Gonzalo would be confirmed in his acknowledged position as governor-general. The terms were rejected, but when Aldana reached Panama with the reply, he was persuaded by Gasca to a loyal acceptance of the Emperor's authority. His example was followed by the admiral, Hinojosa, who handed over the fleet and, with his officers, took an oath of allegiance to the crown in exchange for a free pardon. The way to Lima was now open, but Gasca, whose Inquisition experience had made him an adept in psychological warfare, allowed time for conciliation, and the power of his royal authority, to undermine Gonzalo's position. His agents were with the fleet which sailed to Callao, the port of Lima, in February 1547, and as Gonzalo's men began to defect Carbajal was moved to repeat in jest the words of a popular ditty – 'The wind blows the hairs of my head, mother; two at a time it blows them away.'

When Gasca landed at Tumbes, on June 13, Gonzalo retreated to Arequipa in the south. Appalled by the steady build-up of Gasca's forces, he decided to negotiate on the basis that he would abandon Peru in exchange for Chile. He marched to Lake Titicaca and sent his proposals to Diego Centeno, an old comrade-in-arms, who was holding the passes for Gasca. But Centeno replied that he served the king, and advised unconditional surrender. Gonzalo had no alternative then but to fight, and on October 26 the two forces met at Huarina, an Indian town on the south-eastern shore of Lake Titicaca. Centeno had about a thousand men, Gonzalo less than half that number, and the battle was fought at the breathtaking height of over 13,000 feet. Fortunately for Gonzalo, Centeno was ill with pleurisy and could not direct the battle himself. Even so, Gonzalo and the cavalry were routed, and it was Carbajal, old and indomitable and quite immovable, who won the day for the insurgents with his infantry.

It was almost six months before Gasca had recovered sufficiently to resume his march on Cuzco. By then his force had increased to nearly two thousand. Gonzalo's failure to react with the necessary speed lost him control of the Apurimac and Gasca's army crossed the gorge by balsa raft. On April 8, 1548, the two forces met at Xaquixaguana. Gonzalo was supported by a large number of Indians, but they were hardly effective, and the issue was really decided before the battle by the defection, in full view of both armies, first of Cepeda, who commanded part of the infantry, and then by Garcilaso de la Vega, the father of the writer. Their example was followed at once by a detachment of arquebusiers. The rot, once started, proved contagious, and Gonzalo's forces melted away. He himself was captured. So was Carbajal, who was unhorsed crossing a stream. Only the intervention of Centeno saved him from a rabble of soldiers, but Carbajal affected not to know him, and when Centeno told him his name, the old warhorse is supposed to have replied: 'I crave your pardon; it is so long since I have seen anything but your arse that I have forgotten your face.' The old man was then eighty-four. He was sentenced to be drawn and quartered – it was his remains that Garcilaso the writer says he played with as a child. Gonzalo was beheaded.

It was the end of an era. The swarm of officials that had plagued Cortés in New Spain now had access to South as well as Central America. But the new laws they introduced came too late to save the Indians. Manco, Pizarro's 'puppet' Inca, who had so nearly succeeded in destroying the Spaniards at Cuzco in 1536, carried on a guerilla resistance until his death at the hands of the Young Almagro's forces eight years later. Thereafter, the few Indians who continued to resist were forced to retreat deeper and deeper into the Andes. Their last strongholds were in the mountains between the Urubamba and the Apurimac. Machu Picchu was almost certainly one of them. The impenetrable nature of these mountains offered no incentive to Spaniards intent upon the rapid acquisition of wealth, and it was their failure to penetrate this area that gave rise to rumours of lost cities and hidden hoards of Inca gold. The majority of the Indians, however, passively accepted the destruction of their civilization and the condition of virtual serfdom that followed. For the *puric*, the *encomienda* system was not very different from that of the Incas; both involved the exploitation of their labour.

Not all the viceroys and governors who administered the colonies for the crown were of the calibre of Gasca and the two Mendozas who followed him in Peru. In any case, the colonial régime, based on the theory of supreme royal authority, was never rigidly uniform. The Indies were, in fact, a collection of kingdoms attached to the Crown of Castile, not to Spain, and its laws were issued in the Sovereign's name by the Royal and Supreme Council of the Indies. The King's *alter ego* was the Viceroy, and the legal side of the Council of the Indies was represented by the *audiencias*, high courts of law, established in colonial centres. The colonial *audiencia* was an exceedingly powerful combination of Court of Appeal, administrative council, local legislature and royal fifth column. It acted as watch-dog over all officials and as protector of the Indians. It was undoubtedly the most important link in the chain of checks and balances which were built into the legislation for the Indies, and through its strength intolerably bad government was made rare and relatively short-lived; more important, the loyalty of the Indies was assured to the distant and frequently perplexed crown.

It has to be remembered that Spain had no precedent on which to base her administration of such large and distant territories. It is, therefore, somewhat remarkable that her empire lasted longer than most – for three centuries. This was largely due to the fact that she had two highly developed instruments of bureaucracy ready to take over from the conquistadors – the Church and the Council of the Indies.

The power of the Catholic Church was at its zenith in Spain, following the defeat of the Moors and the development of the Spanish Inquisition under Torquemada. Its seminaries turned out a dedicated cadre, skilled in diplomacy and organization; and since it was the chief fount of education its doctrines permeated every section of Spanish administration. Unfortunately, the attitude and behaviour of some of its representatives in the Indies was distorted by early training, based on the need to root out Moslem and Jewish influence at home, and the spiritual brief of the more bigoted was too often interpreted as requiring the complete obliteration of all Indian culture and civilization. Nevertheless, without the Church the position of the native American Indians would undoubtedly have been much worse; Las Casas is the best known of many dedicated priests who worked unceasingly to spare them the extremes of exploitation that followed upon the granting of *encomiendas*.

Peru was too distant and too new a conquest for conditions there to influence decrees governing the Indians. It was the older colonies that provided the basis for the New Laws, particularly Mexico, or New Spain, where the blatant abuse of the *encomienda* system, introduced of necessity by Cortés, and continued by the crown's representatives as the only means of satisfying the labour requirements of the settlers, made legislative control essential. And it was primarily in Mexico that, hand-in-hand with forced conversion, the Inquisition, the destruction of temples and all Indian religious institutions, pious and charitable priests fought against the worst excesses of a brutal conquest.

The Council of the Indies was primarily based on the personal bureaucratic machine developed by Bishop Fonseca. He had been appointed head of the Committee of the Council of Castile shortly after Columbus's first voyage, and in 1503 established the *Casa de contratacion de las Indias* to regulate the trade, navigation and settlement of the New World. This prototype of colonial administration, which had its headquarters in Seville, was sufficiently well organized by the time Charles came to the throne for it to be expanded into a fully-fledged government department. In 1524 the administration of the colonies ceased to be the personal prerogative of one man and became a committee of six councillors and a secretary.

With the committee dominated by such powerful personalities as the Chancellor Sauvage and Cardinal Adrian, the newly-styled Council of the Indies was strong enough to begin the task of wresting control of the New World from the men who had won it for their king. The methods employed were the ones we know only too well in this bureaucratic century – the proliferation of laws, taxes, officials and paperwork, bureaucratic procrastination and the usual official ingratitude. Vaca de Castro's case was typical. Had Núñez Vela not been appointed viceroy over his head, his sound administration in Peru might have saved that country from the anarchy that followed. Yet on his return to Spain, he was arrested, and spent twelve years in prison before he was finally cleared of all the blatantly false charges brought against him. The Council's relations with Cortés and their takeover of Mexico are even more revealing of the power of the bureaucratic machine. The last pages of Gómara's *Historia* make sad reading.

When Cortés died on December 2, 1547, at the age of sixty-three, he was a pathetic old man, broken in health and seeking endlessly and hopelessly for redress of his grievances. It is a startling metamorphosis, considering the position of absolute power he had held after the fall of Tenochtitlan twenty-five years before. It shows how envy can tarnish, and faceless stonewalling of official 'policy' ultimately destroy, a great reputation. Cortés could have done what the Pizarros did, what his detractors at the Emperor's court accused him of planning: he could have founded an independent kingdom, for in 1524 he controlled most of Central America, the Indians and the Spanish alike deferring to him as the absolute ruler. Instead, inhibited by family upbringing and the ingrained loyalty of his class to the crown, he abided by the rules, accepting the indignities heaped upon him by upstart officials sent out from Spain, and seeking only constitutional redress. It was partly his own fault, for when Olid mutinied in Honduras, he decided to lead his forces himself, instead of sending one of his lieutenants. 'I bethought me that my own person had now long been idle', he wrote at the opening of his fifth letter to the Emperor. The spirit of the conquistador was obviously restless, but at the same time he may have been conscious of a similarity between Olid's action and his own behaviour towards Velázquez. He was away almost two years, and it was only reports of dissension amongst the officers he had left in charge in Mexico that prevented him from marching into Nicaragua, and possibly adventuring even further south. Those two reckless, arduous years damaged, not only his health, but his whole position. Rumours of his death, and reports of the chaotic situation in Mexico, sowed doubts, even grave suspicion, in the minds of Charles and his councillors. As a result, the Council of the Indies considered the appointment of Diego Columbus as governor in his place.

Fortunately for Cortés, it was at this moment that Diego de Soto reached Spain with the considerable treasure got together before the Honduras adventure. 'I am sending in addition', Cortés wrote in his fourth letter to the Emperor, 'a silver culverin cast from $24\frac{1}{2}$ cwts of silver which cost me some 24,500 pesos for the metal.' It was decorated with a phoenix motif and bore an inscription that was perhaps a little too indicative of a sense of his own importance for home consumption – 'Peerless this bird is by birth, Peerless you are on earth, Peerless is my service's worth.' The culverin was melted down for Charles's ever-hungry exchequer, but the treasure did the trick. Columbus's appointment was not confirmed; instead, Ponce de León was sent out as judge of a *residencia*, or Royal Commission of Enquiry, and also as governor. He died almost immediately on his arrival in Mexico, and, as in the case of Garay's death, Cortés was inevitably accused of poisoning him. The indignities that followed forced him to retire from the city into voluntary exile on his estates.

The fifth, and last, of his letters to the Emperor concludes with a bitter attack on 'various and powerful rivals and enemies' who have 'obscured the eyes of your Majesty . . . declaring that I have refused obedience to royal decrees and hold this land not in the might of your name but in a tyrannical and abominable manner, to which end they give base and diabolical reasons which are nothing more than false and idle conjectures'. Concluding his reply to this charge of treason, he writes: 'But of late the malice of those who have made such accusations has been more clearly and openly revealed, for were their accusations true I should never have journeyed six hundred leagues away from this city through uninhabited land and by dangerous roads nor left the land in charge of your Majesty's officials, whom one might have thought the persons most likely to display the greatest zeal in your Majesty's service, although their actions were far from corresponding to the trust I reposed in them'. The rest is a detailed answer to the charge of pilfering for his own purposes the revenues of the crown. But his statement that he remains a poor man and in debt to the tune of over half a million gold pesos, 'without so much as a castellano with which to pay it', hardly squares with the magnificence of his entourage when he returned to Spain in 1528 to put his case before Charles V in person.

In fairness to the Council of the Indies, there was another side to the picture, represented by the equally bitter complaints of Diego Velázquez. Fonseca was not only financially involved, but, until his fall from power, had strongly supported the governor of Cuba as the official best suited to govern the mainland in the interests of the crown. One of the most revealing passages in Cortés' dispatches occurs in the Fourth Letter: 'I propose to send a force over to Cuba, arrest Diego Velázquez and send him as a prisoner to your Majesty; for once the root of all evils has been cut, and truly this man is such, all other branches will wither.' Fonseca regarded Velázquez as safe, Cortés as dangerous, and this passage, showing as it does how absolute power had affected Cortés, suggests that, from the official and long-term point of view, Fonseca was probably right. In any case, a man like Cortés inevitably attracts the suspicion and envy of civil servants at home.

Success, however, and Charles's desperate need of money, won Cortés most of what he demanded. He was received by Charles at his court at Toledo, was created Marqués del Valle de Oaxaca, confirmed in the title of Captain-General, and given large tracts of land that included, among many others, the towns of Oaxaca and Cuernavaca. But instead of being created Commander of the Order of Santiago, he received only a knighthood – a title he never used. The governorship of New Spain, the one title that would have made him absolutely secure, was denied him. Thus, it was not as absolute ruler that he returned to New Spain after his marriage into the ducal family of Zúñiga. He reached Vera Cruz on July 15, 1530, to find that Nuño de Guzmán, president of the *audiencia* or high court of law governing Mexico, had reduced the country to a state of anarchy and had encouraged every sort of accusation against him, even including that of murdering his previous wife, Catalina. He was threatened with arrest, and at Texcoco, according to Gómara, he was ordered not to enter Mexico 'on pain of confiscation of his property and the displeasure of the king'. Nevertheless, as Captain-General, he appears to have exerted his authority again, until the arrival, in 1531, of the new *audiencia*, agreed upon before he left Spain. But though this was composed of more sensible officials, a legal wrangle developed over exactly what the Emperor had granted him in the way of land and vassals. The result was a compromise, and Cortés withdrew to Cuernavaca, where his palace remains to this day. Shrewdly, Charles had given him an outlet for his energies by granting him a capitulation covering the South Sea coasts. For the next eight years, till his final return to Spain in 1540, following disagreements with the viceroy, Cortés concentrated on Pacific exploration, his ships ranging from Tehuantepec to California.

By the time he left Mexico, control had passed absolutely into the hands of the bureaucracy, and the Indians were, legally at any rate, free people; forced labour was prohibited and the death penalty had been introduced for the branding of slaves. The first viceroy, who took office in 1535, was the sagacious Antonio de Mendoza; later he was sent to replace Gasca in Peru. Thus the two most important of Spain's colonies had the benefit at an early stage of fairly liberal administration. With the death of Cortés in 1547, and the execution of Gonzalo Pizarro the following year, the Council of the Indies had finally taken over the colonies, and some at least of the injustices that had followed upon the conquest of the Aztec and Inca empires were ended. This was important for Spain, for it was the wealth of Mexico and Peru that supported her dominant position in Europe and made the wars of Charles V and Philip II possible. In spite of this, the Council continued to maintain its headquarters at Seville, and to control the Atlantic trade exclusively in the interests of Spain.

The importance of this trade, and its rapid growth, can be gauged from the record of sailings – seventy-nine ships outward, forty-seven homeward, by 1540. By the middle of the sixteenth century European wars were making big inroads into the traffic. This led to the adoption, in 1564, of the convoy system. Even so, at the end of the century the whole economy of Spain, and her standing in the European power complex of nations, was dependent upon bullion from the New World. By then the rigidity of the colonial system was such that the colonies were virtually sealed off, not only from foreign countries, but also from each other. A mass of laws denied them the right to trade, to grow certain crops, even to manufacture for themselves. Raw materials had to be dispatched to Spain in Spanish bottoms. It was only the Spanish colonists' intense loyalty to the crown that enabled such bare-faced exploitation to continue for three centuries.

A saying presently current in Mexico has the ring of truth: the Indians made the conquest, the Spaniards made the revolution. In 1810 Hidalgo raised the cry *Viva, viva* in Mexico; in 1811 Bolívar became an active revolutionary in Caracas and began his attack on the Spanish garrisons in South America. In little more than ten years colonial independence had been established, sometimes with the help of 'mercenaries' released from European service by the defeat of Napoleon. But, as in Africa today, the colonists found they had no experience of self-government and little machinery of administration. The result was anarchy again, a situation that was exploited by the most powerful Spanish colonial families. The rich Creoles became richer; the Indians were reduced to the level of serfs on the big estates, and those of mixed blood were little better off. The degree of integration in Mexico, where conditions were particularly bad, produced an explosive situation. This led inevitably to the blood-bath of the 1910–17 revolution and to the obsessive nationalism of today. In Peru, as in other South American colonies, liberation from Spain was followed by military dictatorship. There was not the same intermingling of blood, and centuries of forced labour imposed by Inca and Spaniard had reduced the Indians to a state of passive acceptance of authority and exploitation. Independence took a different form, and it was war that bedevilled the new republics.

The traveller in Central and South America today, who looks beyond the great monuments of the Indian past, will be conscious that the history of the last four and a half centuries has left much more than a legacy of grandiose churches and elaborate mansions. In Mexico the mixture of Spanish and Indian blood is almost total, resulting in a new and volatile race of considerable energy. As a result of this, and the proximity of the United States of America, she is the first Latin-American republic to achieve the breakthrough to a financially sound economy. Peru may well be the next, but the Andes make communications costly and hinder the development of her mineral wealth, and her large Indian population, many of them outside a money economy, presents a problem that only time will solve. Like Panama, which is only viable because the American-owned Canal has replaced the Spanish mule trains, the condition of each of these countries has its roots in geography and the past.

Symbolic, and most significant, is the divergence of their attitudes to their Spanish founders. In Mexico, Cuauhtemoc, the Aztec leader executed by Cortés on his march into Honduras, is a national hero, Cortés himself execrated. By the standards of the day he was a liberal and just man, yet almost every trace of him has been expunged, his statues broken up, the streets renamed, his palaces at Tlaxcala and Cuernavaca filled with Mexican versions of the conquest, his personal image made grotesque by the murals of Diego Rivera.

Yet, in Peru, no stigma seems to attach to the much more brutal conqueror who founded Lima – Pizarro, mounted on his charger and looking very like the statue in his native Trujillo, still faces the Plaza de Armas; and the chapel to his memory, in the great cathedral opposite, is unmolested and full of visitors, Peruvian as well as foreign. Moreover, in Peru, Spanish colonial architecture, though pretentious and even more grotesquely ornate than in Mexico, has not been overlaid by any pseudo-Indian revival. This reflects the different political set-up; Peru is still largely governed by, and for, the white minority, many of them descended, without mixed blood, from the Spanish colonists.

The contrast in Mexico is startling, modern sculpture and architecture having reverted to the Aztec in an almost paranoic attempt to recreate a pre-Spanish mood and obliterate four and a half centuries of history. The Mexican attitude oddly echoes the Spanish conquest, and down the centuries one seems to hear faintly the words of Cortés at the end of his last Letter – *'for it is impossible but that in time your Majesty will come to recognize my services; and even though this time never comes, yet I am satisfied in doing my duty and in the knowledge that I hold myself in debt to no man . . .'* From this city of Tenochtitlan, the 3rd of September, 1526.

Author's Notes

INDIAN NAMES

Picture-writing could not, of course, define the spelling of Aztec names, and Cortés in his dispatches, and the Spaniards who wrote about the Conquest afterwards, had to reproduce the strange Indian sounds as best they could. It was not, in any case, a period in which spelling was notable for its uniformity. However, place names at least have now become reasonably established, and wherever possible I have adopted the local spelling. This applies also to the leading Indian figures. It would obviously be wrong to continue to use the form Montezuma, which Prescott established as general usage a century ago, when throughout Mexico he is now referred to as Moctezuma and this spelling is every-where displayed in lights as the brand name of a popular beer! When in doubt I have tried to combine simplicity of spelling with uniformity. The result is not always satis-factory. For instance, Moctezuma was succeeded by Cuitlahuac, and when he died of smallpox it was Cuauhtemoc who defied the Spaniards. This is not as simple as Guatemoc – though better than the alternatives: Quauhtemoc, Guatemozin, Quatemucin, Guatemuza, Guatemuz – but it is at least consistent. For those who like to be able to pronounce the names they read, with reasonable accuracy, the rules are simple: X = sh; Qu = k; Hu and Gu = w. Once these rules are applied, the alarmingly strange juxtaposition of consonants and proliferation of vowels is reduced to a more sensible pattern since all the rest is phonetic. This applies also to Peruvian Indian words.

BIBLIOGRAPHY

A great deal has now been written about Cortés and his conquest of Mexico, and the archives at Madrid and Seville have yielded a mass of documents. Scholars have found these last a fruitful field for research, but the resulting information is more germane to a study of the Indian civilization and the after-effects of the Conquest than to the Conquest itself. For this, the main sources will always remain the same – Cortés himself, Gómara, and Bernal Díaz. All three suffer from some degree of bias, and include, as a result, errors of statement, even of fact. But though facts are twisted to suit their purposes, misrepresentation is much less blatant than in the work of later chroniclers. Oviedo, who went to the Indies as royal inspector of gold smelting, had completed his vast *Historia General de las Indias* by 1535, and Sahagún, who was in Mexico by 1529, primarily concerned with the conversion of the Indians, and who lived amongst the people of Texcoco for some years, actually wrote his manuscripts in the Náhuatl language. There were several Indian writers: Tezozomoc within forty years of the Conquest, and the best known, Fernando de Alva Ixtlilxochitl, had completed his *Horribles Crueldades de los Conquistadores de Mexico* before the end of the sixteenth century. Only Fray Bartolomé de las Casas had actually been on the spot at the time of the Conquest. He went out to the New World with Ovando in 1502 and was there when Cortés arrived two years later. He was in a better position than any other to write a true history, but he was a Velázquez man and inimical to the upstart conqueror. His *Historia General de las Indias* fails as a proper source, partly on this account, but chiefly because he belonged to what might be termed today an extreme left-wing group of ecclesiastics who became more Indian than the Indians. His hostility to Cortés, and his terrible indictment of his own people for their treatment of the Indians, made his work attractive to Spanish writers of a later age who wished to throw the blame for the decline of empire on those who had originated it. Though his attitude is partly justified by the events that followed the Conquest, reference to Cortés' brief defence of the *encomienda* and *repartimiento* systems given at the end of his third dispatch to the Emperor reveals his own repugnance and clearly indicates that his promotion of them was due to the demands made upon him, both by his own army and by the army of officials that descended on him from Spain.

Cortés wrote five letters to the Emperor Charles. They were a strange blend of military dispatches, plunder accountancy and political pleading. The second and third, which cover the Conquest from the time the Spaniards left the coast until the fall of Mexico, were published in Seville in 1522 and 1523, in each case about two years after they were written. The fourth, dealing with events immediately after the destruction of Mexico and dated October 15, 1524, was published in Toledo and Saragossa in 1525. For three centuries the first and fifth letters were missing. The eighteenth-century Scottish historian, Dr Robertson, finally sleuthed them out in the Imperial Library in Vienna, a not unreasonable place to find them since Charles was ruler of the Habsburg empire (the only feather head-dress attributable to ancient Mexico is in the Völkerkunde museum in Vienna). The first letter, however, is not the one Cortés wrote from Vera Cruz, which has never been found, but the very similar one sent to the Emperor by the Council of the newly-formed settlement. Thus, the whole history of events in New Spain, from the beginning of 1519 until 1527, is on record, and, in the main, written by the man chiefly involved.

The second letter (the first of the four that are by Cortés himself) opens: *Very Great and Powerful and Very Catholic Prince, Most Invincible Emperor, Our Lord* – and ends: *From Your Sacred Majesty's very humble servant and vassal, who kisses the royal hands and feet of Your Highness – Hernán Cortés*. All his letters are punctuated with the fulsome adjectives expected by the omnipotent feudal rulers of the period – *Caesarean Majesty, Sacred Majesty, I kiss your feet a thousand times* – and this, together with the necessity of justifying actions taken without legal sanctions of the crown, gives the Letters a certain coldness, almost an artificiality. Nevertheless, they are a day-to-day record of the Conquest written at the time and on the spot. We have become accustomed now to generals' dispatches and diaries, but few such meticulous records exist of campaigns more than four centuries ago, and certainly not by generals as physically involved in the fighting as Cortés. I have, therefore, regarded this as the prime source of facts, dates and numbers of men involved. On the nature and description of the fighting and in matters of detail, the letters are less explicit - they are, after all, war dispatches and politically orientated.

The *Historia de las Indias* by Francisco López de Gómara, together with the second part, entitled the *Historia de la Conquista de Mexico*, was published in Saragossa in 1552. A year later it was suppressed. Gómara met Cortés in the disastrous Algerian expedition of 1541, when Cortés was wrecked and lost his five priceless 'emeralds'. He became his secretary and personal chaplain and, since he could refer to Cortés for details and amplification, his work must be regarded as a sort of extension of the Letters. In 1541 Cortés, though Marqués del Valle, was no longer the absolute ruler of New Spain. The ecclesiastics and bureaucrats had taken over, his health was beginning to suffer, his fame to tarnish. By the time the book was published he was dead, worn out by the hardships he had suffered in winning an empire for an ungrateful monarch. Gómara was the first writer to publish an account of the Mexican Conquest in a separate volume. Inevitably, its value as a source is marred by its obvious bias. Everything is attributed to his master – Cortés is everywhere on the battlefield, a master of strategy, and when things go wrong he is never to blame. Not having been there, Gómara's writing often lacks clarity, and his facts, particularly in the numbers of men involved, are sometimes at variance with the figures given by Cortés at the time of his dispatches. If, as has been suggested, Cortés virtually dictated the history to his secretary as a sort of justification at secondhand of his claims for the recognition of his services by the crown, then one can only assume that he possessed no copy of his dispatches and that his memory was occasionally at fault. The suggestion cannot be taken very seriously, since Gómara's style is very different from that of Cortés. Nevertheless, he had constant access over a period of six years to the one man who had the whole picture of the Conquest in his mind, and, therefore, Prescott's assessment of his work as one of the two pillars upon which the story of the Conquest mainly rests, must be accepted.

The other pillar is the *Historia verdadera de la Conquista de la Nueva España* by Bernal Díaz del Castillo. This is without question one of the most remarkable documents to come out of any war.

> I, Bernal Díaz del Castillo, citizen and town councillor of the most loyal city of Santiago de Guatemala, one of the first discoverers and conquerors of New Spain and its provinces, and of the Cape of Honduras and Higueras, native of the most noble and famous city of Medina del Campo, and son of its former town councillor Francisco Díaz del Castillo, known as the Courteous – and his legal wife María Diez Rejón - may their souls rest in glory! – tell you the story of myself and my comrades: all true conquerors, who served His Majesty in the discovery, conquest, pacification, and settlement of the provinces of New Spain; one of the finest regions of the New World yet discovered, this expedition being undertaken by our own efforts, and without His Majesty's knowledge.

He was seventy when he wrote that opening to his long and fantastically detailed account of discovery, adventure and hardship, and six years later he made his fair copy of it. He was born in 1492, the same year that Columbus discovered America, and he went to the New World as an ordinary soldier of fortune in 1514 when he was twenty-two years old. He was in Darién, then in Cuba. He served with Córdoba, Grijalva, finally with Cortés. What is so astonishing is his memory for detail. His is an uncomplicated, unpolitical mind, and the things he saw were so strange, the hardships he suffered so great, that they appear to have become indelibly imprinted on that simple mind. He had already written sixteen chapters when his attention was drawn to Gómara's work. It riled him that this man, who had never been near the events he described, should have ignored the men who fought so long and so bravely, with so little reward, and given all the credit for the conquest to Cortés. The result is unfortunate in that Bernal Díaz, in his determination to correct the balance, sometimes appears biased in reverse – Cortés never takes a decision that is not first recommended to him by his men, every rumour of misappropriation of loot, every accusation against the leader is given undue prominence, and Bernal Díaz himself appears as more important than he really was. He is too un-practised a writer, however, for the truth not to be read between the lines, and since he was there – the only eye-witness, other than Cortés himself, to write at length of the Conquest – he does not attempt to detract from his leader's bravery in battle. And though it is probable that he glosses over some of the crueller excesses of his companions, nobody reading his book can think of him as other than an honest writer. His True History is a complement of Gómara's political history, the two together giving as complete a picture as one can ever expect to obtain of a campaign of that period. His detail is so remarkable, the background to it so strange, that his work will always remain a classic.

So, too, will the work of William Hickling Prescott. No note on the bibliography of the Conquests would be complete without a reference to this brilliant American historian, who ruined the sight of his one remaining eye in original research of the material for his two masterpieces of descriptive writing, *The Conquest of Mexico* and *The Conquest of Peru*. He continued working right up to his death in 1859, and though much source material has been unearthed since, this and the digs of archaeologists have tended to confirm rather than to detract from Prescott's writings of more than a century ago.

In the actual discovery and conquest of the Inca empire, centred on what is now Peru, every student is faced with the difficulty that Pizarro wrote no dispatches to his Emperor. Unlike Cortés, he was illiterate. Nor was there in the ranks of his adventurers any equivalent of Bernal Díaz del Castillo, though as early as 1534 an account of the capture and death of Atahualpa, written by an unnamed soldier, was published in Seville under the title – *La Conquista del Peru*. Nevertheless, there are again two main pillars available: Pedro de Cieza de León and Garcilaso de la Vega. The life of each of these writers is a fascinating story in itself.

Cieza de León was born at Llerena, an almost Arab town in Southern Spain, in 1520. At the age of fourteen, travelling with his father, who was a merchant, he saw Atahualpa's ransom treasure unloaded at Seville. A year later, in 1535, he sailed for Cartagena. He was sent straight into battle against the Indians. By the age of twenty he was writing as well as fighting. By 1547 he was in the north of Peru. He fought through the civil wars of the conquistadors, riding with Belalcázar. Having covered Colombia, he went on to cover the whole of Peru in a period when the history of the Conquest was still being hammered out and the whole structure of the Inca empire and civilization was still fresh in the minds of the Indians and largely visible to the eye of this Spanish soldier-reporter. In 1548 he was appointed the official Indian chronicler. By 1550, when he returned to Spain, the whole great work was complete – eight histories, approximately 8,000 foolscap sheets. In the fifteen years he had been in South America he had marched and ridden thousands upon thousands of leagues, fighting, suffering, writing – one of the most dedicated reporters ever to put pen to paper. It was from the manuscripts of this man that most of the later historians drew their material, not bothering to acknowledge the source – this is particularly true of the manuscripts not published before his death in 1554; these included his 'official' account of the discovery and conquest and also of the civil wars.

The second pillar of Inca history is the equally classic *Commentarios Reales* of Garcilaso de la Vega. He is often referred to as 'el Inca', for his mother, Princess Isabel Chimpu Occlo, was of the blood royal. His father, Captain Garcilaso de la Vega, was an *hidalgo* and a conquistador; he was governor of Cuzco from 1533 until his death in 1559. Garcilaso was born in 1539 and he left for Spain shortly after his father's death. It is the twenty years of his youth that provided the material for his books, for he never went back to Peru. The impact of those early years is demonstrated by the wealth of detail about his mother's people that he could reproduce in the Commentaries, published forty-eight years after he left Peru. This work was regarded as the literal truth about Peru for almost two centuries. But he was a highly imaginative writer, and biased, so that later his reputation as an authority became suspect. 'However, the consequence of Garcilaso's prejudices, the omissions, exaggerations, and confusions, did not alter the fact that in his philosophy and in his very conception of history he remains astonishingly original and ahead of his time.' This is a comment from Alain Gheerbrant's introduction to his French edition. Garcilaso is now lauded in Peru as the original writer of a glorious past. As Gheerbrant reminds us, he died in 1616, in the same year as Shakespeare and Cervantes – he is not only irreplaceable as a source of information about the Inca people and their customs, but in style and in story-telling ability he is one of the great writers of the period.

Acknowledgments for Illustrations

The producers wish to express their thanks to the trustees and staffs of the libraries and museums, and to the individuals, who have allowed objects from their collections to be reproduced in this book, and to the photographers who have supplied illustrations, as listed below.

The most important sources for illustrations are designated by key words in the Acknowledgments as follows:

DURAN. Engravings in Fray Diego Duran, *Historia de las Indias de Nueva España: Atlas*, 1880. Although not published until the nineteenth century, these engravings are apparently based upon drawings made for Father Diego Duran by a Mexican artist between about 1560 and 1580. The illustrations are reproduced from a copy of the book in the British Museum.

LIENZO DE TLAXCALA. A Mexican illustrated document, compiled between 1550 and 1564 by Tlaxcalan artists, representing the Conquest from the Tlaxcalan point of view. The original has been lost but a careful copy was reproduced in *Antiguedades Mexicanas*, published by the Junta Colombina de Mexico in 1892. The illustrations are reproduced from a copy of this book in the British Museum.

CODEX MENDOZA. Document compiled for the Spanish viceroy between about 1536 and 1550. The Spanish manuscript annotations were set down by a Spanish priest from the interpretations of the picture-writing by Mexicans. An annotated facsimile was published in 1938. The original is in the Bodleian Library, Oxford, (MS. Arch. Selden A.I), by whose courtesy the illustrations are reproduced.

MIGUEL GONZALEZ (1). A series of twenty-four small paintings on mother-of-pearl, 97 x 53 cms, representing incidents from the Conquest of Mexico, signed Miguel González and dated 1698. They are now in the Museo de America, Madrid.

MIGUEL GONZALEZ (2). A series of six large paintings on mother-of-pearl, each containing half a dozen or more incidents, similar in subject matter and treatment to MIGUEL GONZALEZ (1) and provisionally attributed to the same artist. They are now in the Museo de America, Madrid, by whose courtesy both these series are reproduced.

BRITISH EMBASSY, MEXICO CITY. A series of eight oil paintings representing incidents from the Conquest of Mexico, attributed to an anonymous seventeenth-century Spanish artist. They are the property of Miss M. L. A. Strickland, by courtesy of whom they are reproduced, and are on loan to the Department of the Environment and are hung in the British Embassy, Mexico City.

HARL. MS 4034. A volume of charts, combined with views from seaward, of the Pacific coast of Central and South America. It was compiled by a seventeenth-century Spanish navigator who completed it in 1669. The volume was captured by an English buccaneer, Bartholomew Sharpe, in 1680; it was then brought to England, an English translation was added to the Spanish text, and an English manuscript text, with copies of the charts, was produced by William Hack in 1684 (Sloane MS 44). Both volumes are now in the Department of Manuscripts, British Museum, by whose courtesy this manuscript is reproduced.

POMA DE AYALA. A Peruvian codex entitled *Nueva Corónica y Buen Gobierno*, compiled by Felipe Huaman Poma de Ayala and completed in 1613. The original is in the Royal Library, Copenhagen, and a facsimile was published in 1936. The illustrations are reproduced from this edition by courtesy of the publishers, the Institute of Ethnology, Paris.

COLOUR PLATES

Page 1 Sword G35; sixteenth-century helmet D31. Armeria Real, Madrid. Photograph authorized by the Patrimonio Nacional.

2 A Portolano drawn by Diego Homen, probably executed for Philip II during the

Page 126 LIENZO DE TLAXCALA.
129 Antonio de Solis (see p. 45).
135 *Top* LIENZO DE TLAXCALA. *Bottom* BRITISH EMBASSY, MEXICO CITY. Photo British Crown copyright.
137 Praeclara Ferdinadi, *Cortesii de Nova Maris Narratio*, 1524. British Museum.
139 Ignacio Marquina, *Arquitectura Prehispanica*. Photo Museo Nacional de Antropología, Mexico City.
152 Codex Baranda. Reproduced in *Antiguedades Mexicanas*, 1892. British Museum.
159 LIENZO DE TLAXCALA.
160 Archivo de las Indias, Seville. Photo Mas.
162 DURAN.
165 LIENZO DE TLAXCALA.
166-7 BRITISH EMBASSY, MEXICO CITY. Photo Ministry of Public Building and Works.
172 LIENZO DE TLAXCALA.
173 LIENZO DE TLAXCALA.
174 LIENZO DE TLAXCALA.
175 LIENZO DE TLAXCALA.
177 BRITISH EMBASSY, MEXICO CITY. Photo Ministry of Public Building and Works.
178 LIENZO DE TLAXCALA.
179 *Left* LIENZO DE TLAXCALA. *Right* DURAN.
182 *Top* Antonio de Solis (see p. 45). *Bottom* LIENZO DE TLAXCALA.
185 LIENZO DE TLAXCALA.
191 LIENZO DE TLAXCALA.
192 *Top* BRITISH EMBASSY, MEXICO CITY. Photo Ministry of Public Building and Works. *Bottom* LIENZO DE TLAXCALA.
196 Archivo de las Indias, Seville. Photo Mas.
209 HARL. MS 4034. Photo British Museum.
210 Jorge Juan and Antonio de Ulloa, *Relacion Historica del Viage a la America Meridional*, 1748. British Museum.
213 Maritiem Museum 'Prins Hendrik', Rotterdam. Photo Prins Hendrik Museum.
216 *Top* HARL. MS 4034. Photo British Museum. *Bottom* Alexander de Humboldt, *Vues des Cordilléres*, 1816. British Museum.
219 HARL. MS 4034. Photo British Museum.
220 HARL. MS 4034. Photo British Museum.
227 POMA DE AYALA.
228 HARL. MS 4034. Photo British Museum.
232 POMA DE AYALA.

Page 236 Photo Stephen Harrison.
238 Photo Hammond Innes.
243 Museo de Ejercito, Madrid.
246 Photo Stephen Harrison.
249 Photo Hammond Innes.
256 *Top* Brooklyn Museum, New York. Photo Ferdinand Anton. *Bottom* Musée de l'Homme, Paris. Photo F. L. Kenett.
257 *Left* Linden-Museum, Stuttgart. *Right* University Museum of Archaeology and Ethnology, Cambridge University. Photos Ferdinand Anton.
258 POMA DE AYALA.
259 Alexander de Humboldt (see p. 216).
260 POMA DE AYALA.
261 Photo Stephen Harrison.
266 POMA DE AYALA.
269 Hũaraz, Peru. Photo Ferdinand Anton.
271 Photo Stephen Harrison.
278 *Left* Photo Stephen Harrison. *Right* POMA DE AYALA.
288 POMA DE AYALA.
293 POMA DE AYALA.
296 de Ulloa (see p. 210).
297 *Left* Dumbarton Oaks, Washington. Photo Nickolas Murray. *Right* American Museum of Natural History, New York. Photo American Museum of Natural History.
300 POMA DE AYALA.
307 Photo Stephen Harrison.
310 Photo Stephen Harrison.

The names of photographers or institutions holding the copyright of photographs reproduced in this book are given under the individual acknowledgments. Commissioned photographs have been taken specially for this book by the following photographers:

Manso, Madrid. Pages 1, 19, 20, 53, 54, 131, 132, 169, 170, 187, 188, 205, 223, 243, 251, 254.

Copytek, Mexico City. Pages 142-3.

John Freeman, London. Pages 45, 46 *right*, 56, 57, 74 *top*, 79, 83, 84, 85, 102 *bottom*, 125 *top*, 126, 129, 135 *top*, 137, 152, 159, 162, 165, 172, 173, 174, 175, 178, 179, 182, 185, 192 *bottom*, 210, 216 *bottom*, 227, 232, 258, 259, 260, 266, 278 *right*, 288, 293, 296, 300.

Acknowledgments for Quotations

Quotations in the text have been taken from the following copyright works, and acknowledgment is made to the publishers who have granted their permission:

Ignacio Bernal, *Mexico before Cortés,* translated by Willis Barnstone. Doubleday & Co.

Hernando Cortés, *The Five Letters,* translated by J. Bayard Morris. Routledge & Kegan Paul, and W. W. Norton & Company.

Francisco López de Gómara, *Cortés – the Life of the Conqueror,* translated by Lesley Byrd Simpson. University of California Press.

Bernal Díaz, *The Conquest of New Spain,* translated by J. M. Cohen. Penguin Books Ltd.

Miguel Leon-Portilla, edited by, *The Broken Spears.* Beacon Press.

Clement R. Markham, *Reports on the Discovery of Peru.* Burt Franklin.

Pedro de Cieza de León, *The Incas,* edited by Victor von Hagen and translated by Harriet de Onis. University of Oklahoma Press.

Garcilaso de la Vega, *Royal Commentaries of the Incas,* edited by Alain Gheerbrant and translated by Maria Jolas. Grossman Publishers Inc.

Patricia de Fuentes, *The Conquistadors.* Grossman Publishers Inc.

Index

Explanatory Notes

1. '*bis*', '*ter*', '*quat*' or '*quin*' after a page reference means that the name or topic is mentioned two, three, four or five times *in separate paragraphs* on the page indicated; '*passim*' means 'here and there' (scattered references); '*q.v.*' means '*quod vide*' (which see).

2. For pronunciation of Aztec and Mexican names, see page 321.

Index of Maps